ROOSEVELT AND THE MUNICH CRISIS

PRINCETON STUDIES IN

INTERNATIONAL HISTORY AND POLITICS

Series Editors
Jack L. Snyder and Richard H. Ullman

———————————

Contents

ROOSEVELT AND THE MUNICH CRISIS

A STUDY OF POLITICAL
DECISION-MAKING

Barbara Rearden Farnham

PRINCETON UNIVERSITY PRESS   PRINCETON, NEW JERSEY

Library of Congress Cataloging-in-Publication Data

Farnham, Barbara.
Roosevelt and the Munich crisis : a study of political
decision-making / Barbara Rearden Farnham.
p.   cm. — (Princeton studies in international history and politics)
Includes bibliographical references and index.
ISBN 0-691-02611-4 (cloth : alk. paper)
1. United States—Foreign relations—Germany—Case studies.
2. United States—Foreign relations—1933–1945—Decision
making—Case studies.   3. Germany—Foreign relations—United
States—Case studies.   4. Munich Four-Power Agreement (1938).
5. Roosevelt, Franklin D. (Franklin Delano), 1882–1945.
I. Title.   II. Series.
E183.8.G3F37   1997
940.53'2273—dc20   96-27218

To William T. R. Fox and Robert Jervis

Preface

FOR HISTORIANS, explaining Franklin Delano Roosevelt's foreign policy in the years before World War II has long represented a major challenge. An equally vexing problem for students of international politics has been to understand the impact of domestic politics on foreign policy. Believing that progress in unravelling one of these puzzles might help in deciphering the other, I have brought them together. As a consequence, this book offers both a theory of how the domestic political context affects foreign-policy decisions and a fresh interpretation of Roosevelt's policies following the Munich crisis, which is based largely on the insights that theory provides.

Between 1936 and 1938, in the face of uncertainty about the possibility of socializing the fascist dictators to the norms of the international system, Roosevelt searched for ways to influence the deteriorating international situation. His behavior during this period has often been characterized as drifting. In fact, he was experimenting with a number of different options in an effort to discover one that might work. In 1938, when Hitler's behavior during the Munich crisis showed him to be incorrigibly aggressive, Roosevelt, his uncertainty dispelled, settled on the policy of aiding the European democracies, a course to which he adhered despite substantial opposition from congress and members of his own administration. This option attracted him principally because it allowed him to deal with a serious problem he had perceived in the aftermath of the Munich crisis: the conflict between the need to stop Hitler and the domestic imperative to avoid any risk of American involvement in a war.

Establishing these connections shed a good deal of light on Roosevelt's behavior, but it did not explain it. In search of additional insight, I turned to decision-making theory. Unfortunately, existing theoretical approaches to value conflict offered little help, largely because they ignored the influence of political factors on decision-making. This led me to seek a fresh perspective, which I have called a political approach to decision-making. This approach focuses on the impact that an awareness of the imperatives of the political context can have on decision-making processes and, through them, policy outcomes. In particular, this approach suggests that in dealing with a clash of central values such as Roosevelt faced, decision-makers who are aware of the demands of the political context are likely to be reluctant to make trade-offs, seeking instead a solution that gives some measure of satisfaction to all the values implicated in the decision.

The political approach to decision-making thus attempts to show both why domestic factors are important from the decision-maker's point of view and how they are likely to affect foreign-policy decisions. Viewing Roosevelt's behavior in this light has allowed me to uncover patterns, link events, and find meaning in behavior that others have characterized as random or drifting. Rather than paralysis in response to the fear of domestic repercussions, we see purposeful behavior directed at balancing international imperatives against domestic acceptability. To be sure, Roosevelt's policies can still be criticized, but at least they begin to make sense.

To the extent that this new approach is successful, it underlines the value of bringing the perspectives of a number of disciplines to bear on a common problem. Recognizing, however, that all readers are not equally interested in history, political science, and psychology, the most important chapter here for those concerned with decision-making theory is chapter 2, which lays out the political approach to decision-making, and the three appendices, which describe the traditional approaches to decision-making and provide a more detailed discussion of the political approach. Those whose primary interest is the development of Roosevelt's foreign policy may find that chapter 1 provides enough theoretical background to allow them to follow my analysis of his behavior and prefer to go directly to the four historical chapters.

In carrying out this work, I was aided by financial support from several sources. At the dissertation stage, I received a President's Fellowship from Columbia University, a 1905 Fellowship from Mount Holyoke College, and two Ford Foundation Fellowships, given through the Research Institute on International Change at Columbia. More recently, time spent as a fellow at the Olin Institute at Harvard University and the Institute of War and Peace Studies at Columbia allowed me to prepare the book for publication. I thank all of these sources for their generosity.

For support of a different sort, I owe Robert Jervis and the late William T. R. Fox more than I can properly express—Bill Fox for starting me on the project and for encouraging me during the years when no apparent progress was being made. Without that support, it is very doubtful that I would have continued, and I am only sorry that he did not see the completion of a project that owes so much to him. I also owe an enormous debt to Bob Jervis, first for agreeing to take on a student who did not fit the usual profile, and thereafter for giving generously of both his critical intelligence and knowledge of the field, which are abundant, and his time, which is not. This book is dedicated to them both.

I also wish to thank a number of people who commented on all or part of the manuscript, especially Tom Berger, Richard Betts, David Epstein, Alexander George, Fred I. Greenstein, Waldo Heinrichs, Samuel P. Huntington, Robert Jervis, Yuen Foong Khong, Deborah Larson, Ruth C. Lawson, Jack Levy, Rose McDermott, Eldar Shafir, Jack Snyder, and several Olin fellows, particularly Gil Merom and Gideon Rose. A number of friends and colleagues at Columbia also helped and encouraged me in a variety of ways, especially Stephen Bennett, Cheryl Koopman, Ene Sirvet, and Anna Hohri. The assistance of the knowledgable staffs at the National Archives, the Library of Congress, Yale University Library, and in particular the Roosevelt Library at Hyde Park, N.Y., was also invaluable.

Finally, I would like to thank my family for their support, encouragement, and especially their patience—my husband, Nicholas, without whose ability to unravel the mysteries of the information revolution this study would never have been put on paper, and my sons, Thomas and Brian, who literally grew up with it.

Abbreviations Used in the Footnotes

DBFB   _Documents on British Foreign Policy, 1919–1939._ Rohan
Butler and Sir E. L. Woodward, ed. 3d series. Vols. 1–7.
London: His Majesty's Stationery Office, 1951.

FDRL   Franklin D. Roosevelt Library, Hyde Park, N.Y.

FRUS   United States Department of State. _Foreign Relations of the
United States: Diplomatic Papers._ Washington, D.C.: U.S.
Government Printing Office.

LC   Library of Congress, Washington, D.C.

MSS   Manuscripts

NARS   National Archives, Washington, D.C.

PL   Roosevelt, Elliot, ed. _F.D.R: His Personal Letters._ Vol. 3.
New York: Duell, Sloan and Pearce, 1950.

PPA   Roosevelt, Franklin D. _Public Papers and Addresses._ Vols.
5–8. New York: Macmillan, 1938, 1941.

PPF   President's personal file, Franklin D. Roosevelt papers

PSF   President's secretary's file, Franklin D. Roosevelt papers

RG   Record Group, National Archives, Washington, D.C.

ROOSEVELT AND THE MUNICH CRISIS

CHAPTER I

Roosevelt, the Munich Crisis, and Political Decision-Making

THE WORLD of the late 1930s was a threatening place for anyone committed to democracy. Weakened by global depression, demoralized by antidemocratic ideologies arising from both the left and the right, and facing increasingly insistent demands from an expanding cohort of revisionist dictators, many European democratic leaders had a sense of impending disaster: war seemed inevitable—unless something intervened to prevent it.

This volatile mix produced a host of painful foreign-policy dilemmas for the world's democracies, not least the United States, which had come to Europe's rescue less than twenty years before. Now the major question mark was America's role in the unfolding drama. What could she do? What ought she to do? Finding answers to these questions was the overriding foreign-policy challenge of Franklin Delano Roosevelt's presidency, one that he was forced to address in a domestic climate dominated by the isolationism which had produced a public that was at best skeptical about the results of America's previous foray into world affairs, at worst openly hostile to it.

Roosevelt's response to this dilemma has often been criticized. Indeed, because his prewar policies remain controversial to this day, there is a real sense in which the questions of the thirties have yet to be answered. Why did the President wait so long to begin a substantial rearmament effort? Why did he not confront isolationist sentiment and educate the American people to the realities of the international situation?

I believe that Roosevelt's response to the downward spiral of events preceding the outbreak of war in September 1939 can only be understood by confronting a number of long-standing historical and theoretical puzzles. The historical problem is to discover, in the face of continuing disagreement, what Roosevelt's policies actually were; the theoretical challenge is to explain why he chose them.

The two sets of puzzles are intimately connected. On the one hand, we cannot evaluate the conflicting interpretations of Roosevelt's policies without examining the decision-making processes that produced them—understanding the structure of his thinking is essential to explaining its outcome. On the other hand, trying to unravel the puzzle of Roosevelt's post-Munich policies raises a number of questions about how best to analyze foreign-policy decisions.

The benefits of reexamining Roosevelt's prewar foreign policy are, like the issues it raises, both historical and theoretical. Learning how and why he made his policy choices is crucial to understanding America's progress from isolation to active engagement in World War II, and may even shed light on the form that war ultimately took.[1] If some of the confusion surrounding Roosevelt's earlier moves can be dispelled, the rationale behind his subsequent behavior may become clearer as well. Moreover, the Munich period highlights two critical foreign-policy themes, one universal, the other quintessentially American. The first centers on the tension between the values of peace and security and appears in Roosevelt's struggle to reconcile his need to deal with the new threat from Germany with the long-standing domestic imperative to avoid war at all costs. The second appears in the conflict between the temptation to withdraw into a fortress America as the way of resolving that dilemma and the need to play an active role in world affairs.

Because these themes persist even today,[2] examining the development of Roosevelt's policies may offer considerable insight into both contemporary foreign-policy dilemmas and more general theoretical issues relating to the formulation of foreign-policy. For one thing, Roosevelt's response to this clash of deeply held values raises the question of how political decision-makers deal with value conflict, a subject that goes to the heart of political choice.[3] For another, tracing Roosevelt's struggle to craft a security policy in the face of strong domestic opposition to international involvement forces us to confront one of the most vexing issues in the contemporary study of international politics: how to develop a systematic account of the role of domestic factors in the formulation of foreign policy.

---

[1] See Theodore Abel, "The Element of Decision in the Pattern of War," *American Sociological Review* 6 (1941): 853–59.

[2] Frequently expressed, for example, in the fear that the cold war's end will tempt the United States to return to its traditional isolationist posture. Cf. the reaction to Patrick Buchanan's candidacy in the 1992 presidential primaries: Leslie Gelb, "Sleeper Issue in 1992," *New York Times*, March 16, 1992. Some also saw President Reagan's Strategic Defense Initiative as an example of this isolationist temptation. See Robert Reich, "The Fortress-America Myth," ibid., March 3, 1987.

[3] "Both individuals and collectivities must, inescapably, face choices among values from time to time. At the very least, even the most harmonious systems of values require selectivity in the balancing of different claims to time, energy, and other resources. Not all desiderata can be equally met at any one time." Robin Williams, Jr., "The Concept of Values," *International Encyclopedia of the Social Sciences*, ed. David Sills, (New York: Macmillan and Free Press, 1968), 287.

THE MUNICH CRISIS AND THE EVOLUTION OF ROOSEVELT'S FOREIGN POLICY

Franklin Roosevelt's foreign policy in the late 1930s was the subject of heated controversy from the outset. After an initial engagement between early revisionists such as Charles Beard, who claimed that Roosevelt's policies were deliberately designed to lead the United States into the European war, and "orthodox historians" such as Basil Rauch, who defended these policies as measures necessary to deal with a very real security threat but also shaped partly by the need to cope with isolationist opposition,[4] the debate seesawed between the two sides, with less extreme analysts occupying the middle ground.[5] Even today, there is little agreement about what Roosevelt actually wished to do before Pearl Harbor, let alone why he wished to do it. Moreover, controversy about when he decided America would have to play a considerably more active role in Europe persists as well.

Historians such as Robert Divine and Arnold Offner believe that for much of this period Roosevelt shared the isolationist point of view, while others portray him as a frustrated interventionist chafing at his domestic constraints. Within the latter camp, revisionists criticize him for pushing too hard against those constraints, while orthodox historians lament his caution. A third group, including historians such as Edward Bennett and political scientists such as James MacGregor Burns, sees Roosevelt as drifting, either because he lacked a policy altogether, or because he was a political opportunist, pushed by domestic politics first in one direction and then another.[6]

[4] Robert Divine, "Diplomatic Historians and World War II," *Causes and Consequences of World War II*, ed. Robert A. Divine (Chicago: Quadrangle Books, 1969), 4. The term "orthodox historian" was coined by Divine. He offers a thorough account of this debate. See also Wayne Cole's earlier treatment, "American Entry into World War II: A Historiographical Appraisal," *Mississippi Valley Historical Review* 42 (1957): 595–617, as well as Charles A. Beard, *American Foreign Policy in the Making, 1932–1940* (New Haven: Yale University Press, 1946), *President Roosevelt and the Coming of the War, 1941* (New Haven: Yale University Press, 1948); and Basil Rauch, *Roosevelt: From Munich to Pearl Harbor* (New York: Creative Age Press, 1950). A recent entry on the revisionist side is Frederick W. Marks III, *Wind Over Sand: The Diplomacy of Franklin D. Roosevelt* (Athens, Ga.: University of Georgia Press, 1988).

[5] Robert Dallek, for example, portrays Roosevelt as proceeding cautiously after Munich and not finally deciding that the United States should enter the war until August 1941. Robert Dallek, *Franklin D. Roosevelt and American Foreign Policy, 1932–1945* (New York: Oxford University Press, 1979), chap. 8 and pp. 267, 285. See also Waldo Heinrichs, *Threshold of War: Franklin D. Roosevelt and American Entry into World War II* (New York: Oxford University Press, 1988), 9–10.

[6] Robert Divine, *Roosevelt and World War II* (Baltimore: Johns Hopkins University Press, 1969), 7; Arnold A. Offner, "Misperception and Reality: Roosevelt, Hitler, and the

Since these conflicting interpretations cannot all be valid, addressing the historical puzzle requires a fresh look at the available evidence. Somewhat unexpectedly, such a review leads directly to the conclusion that the Munich crisis was a decisive turning point in Roosevelt's prewar foreign policy. In its wake, both his assessment of the threat and the measures he was willing to take to meet it underwent a qualitative change. His experience of Munich dispelled his uncertainty about Hitler's intentions, leading him to conclude that the führer was implacably aggressive and that a German-dominated Europe would pose a clear security threat to the United States. This, in turn, ended Roosevelt's ambivalence about what course to take and he settled on aid to the European democracies as the means of preventing Hitler from controlling Europe, a policy to which he steadfastly adhered despite determined challenges from Congress and his own administration.

The Munich crisis thus marks a critical juncture in American foreign policy during which the basic policy lines that the country would follow until Pearl Harbor were laid down. Despite the many dramatic changes in the international situation during the more than three years between Munich and America's entry into World War II, Roosevelt's strategy of aiding the democracies—developed in the immediate aftermath of the crisis—was never effectively challenged.

EXPLAINING ROOSEVELT'S FOREIGN POLICY

Why did Roosevelt choose the course of aiding the democracies rather than a more isolationist policy—or a more interventionist one? Most historians cite the exigencies of domestic politics.[7] For example, notwithstanding their obvious differences, all the historical interpretations just reviewed suggest that Roosevelt was prevented from responding effec-

---

Search for a New Order in Europe," *Diplomatic History* 15 (1991): 613; Edward M. Bennett, *Franklin D. Roosevelt and the Search for Security: American-Soviet Relations, 1933–1939* (Wilmington, Del.: Scholarly Resources, 1985), 192; James MacGregor Burns, *Roosevelt: The Lion and the Fox* (New York: Harcourt, Brace, 1956), 262.

[7] Explanations at the domestic-politics level of analysis hold that foreign policy is best accounted for by a state's social and economic structure or internal politics, and foreign-policy making is usually seen as a highly political process in which the outcomes are a by-product of a domestic political struggle. Robert Jervis, *Perception and Misperception in International Politics* (Princeton: Princeton University Press, 1976), 21–24. On the levels of analysis, see ibid., chap. 1; J. David Singer, "The Level of Analysis Problem in International Relations," *World Politics* 14 (Oct. 1961): 77–92; Kenneth Waltz, *Theory of International Politics* (Reading, Mass.: Addison-Wesley, 1979); Arnold Wolfers, "The Actors in International Politics," in Arnold Wolfers, ed., *Discord and Collaboration*, (Baltimore: Johns Hopkins University Press, 1962), 3–24.

tively to the demands of the international situation by domestic political pressures.

Despite its popularity, however, this explanation is unsatisfying. If domestic politics had been the controlling factor, Roosevelt's policies should have conformed to the isolationist attitudes that dominated the United States throughout the 1930s. Thus, he would have responded to the darkening international situation with a policy of increasing withdrawal combined with a unilateralist approach to those contacts that were absolutely necessary. Instead, though deeply concerned with preserving peace, Roosevelt actively sought involvement in international affairs. Fully aware of his domestic constraints, from at least 1936 on he consistently pushed against them, trying to influence the European situation whenever possible. After Munich, he moved steadily to prevent the outbreak of war in Europe and to insure the success of the democracies should war nevertheless occur. Certainly cautious, often less than candid, Roosevelt was willing to act in the international arena when he thought it necessary. Thus, while domestic forces may be able to account for his circumspection, they cannot explain his readiness to move the United States as far along the path of involvement as he actually did.

An alternative explanation for this behavior points to the structure of the international system.[8] After all, Roosevelt did eventually recognize and attempt to deal with the German threat to American security, and his post-Munich policy of aiding the democracies can be interpreted as a balancing strategy. Turning again to the evidence, however, it becomes clear that a structural-realist explanation is as unsatisfactory as a domestic political one. Most troubling is that Roosevelt, having made a realist diagnosis of the international situation, failed to follow up as the theory predicts. Recognizing the importance of balancing Hitler, he failed to take the steps that would have allowed him to do so effectively.[9] The gap of nearly two years between his perception of the German threat to American security after Munich and his initiation of the Charlottesville Program and substantial aid to the democracies in the late spring and summer of 1940 is thus embarrassing for an explanation based on the imperatives of the international system.

Since neither domestic nor international forces were sufficiently power-

---

[8] A theory operating at the level of the international system predicts that states facing a security threat from an expansionist power will balance, attempting to increase their power either through coalition-building or by augmenting their own capabilities. Waltz, *Theory of International Politics*, 103–4, 117–18, 121–22.

[9] Stephan Pelz has outlined both the realists' diagnosis, which Roosevelt did adopt, and their policy conclusions, which he did not. "Changing International Systems, the World Balance of Power, and the United States, 1776–1976," *Diplomatic History* 15 (Winter 1991): 65–66, 71.

ful to constrain Roosevelt's choices in the aftermath of the Munich crisis decisively, our remaining alternative is a decision-making explanation.[10] Based on the notion that outcomes are strongly affected by decision-making processes and/or a leader's personality, these theories acknowledge both domestic politics and the international environment as constraints, but ones that do not alone account for the outcomes. Rather, decision-making explanations recognize that "environmental variables cannot directly produce public policy, . . . political choice must in the nature of the case intervene between them, and . . . historically this intervention has been very large indeed."[11]

In the Munich case, a decision-making perspective does, in fact, yield a number of important insights into Roosevelt's policies. It clarifies his intentions by showing that he perceived his problem in the aftermath of the Munich crisis as not merely a threat to security, but a value-conflict dilemma between the German menace and the domestic demand not to risk American involvement. Moreover, it establishes that unlike either isolationists or internationalists, both of whom dealt with these conflicting values by acknowledging the primacy of one of them and trading off, Roosevelt tried to transcend that value conflict with the policy of aiding the European democracies.

Clearly this interpretation runs counter to much of the standard historical analysis. Although there is a fairly broad consensus that the Munich crisis led to some change in Roosevelt's attitude toward the European situation,[12] there is less agreement that it triggered a consequential policy

[10] "When the situation is not so compelling as to produce uniform behavior in all people one must look to the differences among individuals for at least part of the explanation." Robert Jervis, "Political Decision-Making: Recent Contributions," *Political Psychology* 2 (Summer 1980): 96. The Munich case meets two other conditions for explanation at the decision-making level of analysis: the situation was not routine and the relevant decisions were made at the top of the decision-making structure, where the participants are relatively free from organizational constraints. Ole Holsti, "Foreign Policy Formation Viewed Cognitively," in *The Structure of Decision*, ed. Robert Axelrod (Princeton: Princeton University Press, 1976), 29–31.

[11] Gabriel A. Almond and Stephen J. Genco, "Clouds, Clocks, and Politics," *World Politics* 29 (1977): 498.

[12] See for example, Robert A. Divine, *The Reluctant Belligerent* (New York: John Wiley and Sons, 1965), 55, and *Roosevelt and World War II*, 23; Waldo H. Heinrichs, Jr., "The Role of the Navy," in *Pearl Harbor as History*, ed. Dorothy Borg and Shumpei Okamoto (New York: Columbia University Press, 1973), 216; and David Reynolds, *The Creation of the Anglo-American Alliance, 1937–1941* (Chapel Hill, N.C.: University of North Carolina Press, 1982), 40–41. For contemporary opinion along the same lines, see Joseph Alsop and Robert Kintner, *American White Paper* (New York: Simon and Schuster, 1940), 6; Samuel Rosenman, *Working with Roosevelt* (New York: Harper and Brothers, 1952), 181; and Philip E. Jacob, "Influence of World Events on U.S. 'Neutrality' Opinion," *Public Opinion Quarterly* 4 (1940): 48. Exceptions to this consensus are Arnold Offner, Norman Graebner, and William Bennett: Offner, "Misperception and Reality," 613–14 (see also

decision. Even Waldo Heinrichs, while acknowledging that the Munich crisis motivated Roosevelt to aid the democracies, argues that isolationist sentiment kept the United States a "helpless onlooker" until the disappearance in May 1940 of the "free security" she had "enjoyed . . . since the Napoleonic Wars" led to a dramatic increase in American arms production.[13]

Careful scrutiny of the decision process shows, however, that Roosevelt had begun to anticipate the disappearance of America's "free security" in the immediate aftermath of the Munich crisis, devising the policy of aiding Great Britain and France in order to deal with precisely that eventuality, while at the same time honoring the domestic imperative to avoid American involvement in war. Arms production was expanded after May 1940, not because either the German threat or the policy of aiding the democracies had just dawned on Roosevelt, but because the blitzkrieg, by raising the specter of allied defeat, put that policy in jeopardy.

Viewing the puzzle of Roosevelt's prewar policies through the lens of his decision-making thus offers a fresh perspective on the historical evidence that substantially improves our understanding of those policies. David Reynolds has argued that "the ambiguities of F.D.R.'s foreign policy grew as much out of his own character and attitudes as they did out of his celebrated deference to the dictates of public opinion."[14] A decision-making analysis expands on this insight by explaining the processes through which these characteristics came to be expressed, allowing them to shape policy. Such an explanation not only enriches our understanding of Roosevelt's policies but, if the analysis is based on a well-conceived theory of decision-making, moves beyond the domain of personal idiosyncrasy into the realm of theoretical generalization.[15]

Traditionally, political scientists have based their explanations of foreign-policy decision-making on theories borrowed from other disciplines, most frequently the rational-actor model from economics and cognitive

---

606, 619); Norman A. Graebner, *America as a World Power* (Wilmington, Del.: Scholarly Resources, 1984), 54–55; Bennett, *Search for Security*, 127, 137, 192–93.

[13] Heinrichs, *Threshold*, 9–10. The term "free security" was coined by C. Vann Woodward. Personal communication from Heinrichs to the author. See also Robert A. Divine, *The Illusion of Neutrality*, (Chicago: The University of Chicago Press, 1962), 230–31; and Richard M. Leighton, "The American Arsenal Policy in World War II: A Retrospective View," in *Some Pathways in Twentieth-Century History*, ed. Daniel R. Beaver (Detroit: Wayne State University Press, 1969), 223.

[14] Reynolds, *Creation*, 26–27.

[15] Alexander L. George, "Case Studies and Theory Development: The Method of Structured Focussed Comparison," *Diplomacy: New Approaches*, ed. Paul Gordon Lauren (New York: Free Press, 1979), 43–49.

and motivational models from psychology.[16] Recently, however, many have begun to feel that by overlooking the influence of context, these traditional models often miss the essential character of political decision-making, especially in the case of a clash of deeply held values such as Roosevelt faced.[17] Richard Neustadt, for one, points out that normative theories of decision-making cannot account for the notorious reluctance of political decision-makers to make sharp value trade-offs, even to obtain higher expected value, while psychological theories explain this failure as error or bias, leaving us to conclude that much of the observed behavior of political decision-makers is inexplicable or foolish.[18] Moreover, because there have been few attempts to discover the rationale behind such behavior, not only do our explanations of political decision-making fall short, but our theories are often less useful to policymakers than we would like them to be.[19]

Thus, we need a new theoretical perspective concerned specifically with political decision-making and focused on value conflict. Such an approach would build on the insight that, in a political context, when a decision problem entails significant tension between two or more consequential values, there are enormous incentives to reconcile them and the

[16] The rational model and its two competitors from psychology offer "integrated views of the decision process," combining the various subprocesses of a decision "to arrive at an overall realistic view of how people deal with ill-defined decision problems." Robert P. Abelson and Ariel Levi, "Decision Making and Decision Theory," in *Handbook of Social Psychology*, ed. Gardner Lindzey and Elliot Aronson (New York: Random House, 1985), 1:277, 279–80.

[17] Philip E. Tetlock, "Accountability: The Neglected Social Content of Judgment and Choice," *Research in Organizational Behavior* 7 (1985): 295–332; Richard E. Neustadt, "Presidents, Politics, and Analysis," Brewster C. Denney Lecture Series, Institute of Public Management, Graduate School of Public Affairs, University of Washington, May 13, 1986, 3–35. See also Robert P. Abelson, Donald R. Kinder, Mark T. Peters, and Susan T. Fiske, "Affective and Semantic Components in Political Person Perception," *Journal of Personality and Social Psychology* 42 (1982): 620. For a discussion of these criticisms and of the need to develop a specifically political approach to decision making, see Barbara Farnham, "Political Cognition and Decision-making," *Political Psychology* 11 (March 1990): 83–89, and "Value Conflict and Political Decision-Making: Roosevelt and the Munich Crisis, 1938" (Ph.D. diss., Columbia University, 1991), 140–42, 148–50. Some who study mass politics have also begun to express an interest in looking at the impact of context on decision making, See Bryan D. Jones, *Reconceiving Decision-making in Democratic Politics: Attention, Choice, and Public Policy* (Chicago: University of Chicago Press, 1994; and Robert Huckfeldt and John Sprague, *Citizens, Politics, and Social Communication: Information and Influence in an Election Campaign* (Cambridge: Cambridge University Press, 1995).

[18] Neustadt, "Presidents, Politics, and Analysis," 3–4.

[19] Ibid. As Robert Jervis has noted, "political scientists do not have a good theory of political decision-making" at the individual level of analysis. "Political Decision-Making," 86. See also Alexander George, *Bridging the Gap: Theory and Practice in Foreign Policy* (Washington, D.C.: United States Institute of Peace, 1993), 7–11.

effort to deal with such pressures frequently accounts for policy choices, including foreign-policy choices, considerably better than the alternative explanations.

Developing a distinctively political approach to decision-making requires identifying the features of the political context that affect decision-making behavior. For this, I consulted the "first wave" theorists of political decision-making: Roger Hilsman, Samuel Huntington, Richard Neustadt, and Warner Schilling, who examined the requirements of effective action in the political context and attempted to define the decision-maker's uniquely political problems and the strategies commonly used to cope with them.[20] In addition, I used the work of both contemporary policy analysts and other political scientists who examine decision-making, in particular Alexander George and Paul Diesing.[21]

The second step in developing a political approach to decision-making is to analyze how decision-makers incorporate an awareness of the imperatives of the political context into their policy deliberations. The goal here is to link the psychological and contextual determinants of decision-making[22] by mapping insights from political science about the nature of the political context onto psychological theories of decision-making behavior.[23]

In the course of this attempt to derive an ideal type of political decision-making from the practice of decision-makers, I found that the central feature of the political context is a pervasive concern with accept-

[20] Robert J. Art, "Bureaucratic Politics and American Foreign Policy: A Critique," *Policy Sciences* 4 (1973): 468–69. A fuller treatment of Art's discussion of the first and second wave of the analysts of political decision-making and an extension of it to a third wave of analysts, such as Alexander George and Robert Jervis, who draw on psychological theories of decision-making, may be found in Farnham, "Political Cognition," 85–89, and "Value Conflict," 150–57. Roger Hilsman himself has also noted Art's discussion of this group and offered his own "expanded political process model" building on its work. Roger Hilsman, *The Politics of Policymaking in Defense and Foreign Affairs* (Englewood Cliffs, N.J.: Prentice-Hall, 1987), vii-viii.

[21] Alexander George, *Presidential Decisionmaking in Foreign Policy: The Effective Use of Information and Advice* (Boulder, Colo.: Westview Press, 1980), 26–34; Paul Diesing, *Reason in Society* (Urbana, Ill.: University of Illinois Press, 1962), 9.

[22] As Herbert Simon states the challenge, "we must both construct a theory of the system's processes and describe the environments to which it is adapting." Herbert A. Simon, "Invariants of Human Behavior," *Annual Review of Psychology* 41 (1990): 6–7.

[23] "The problem . . . is to show how a process in one theory can be described as quite a different process in the other theory." Glen H. Snyder and Paul Diesing, *Conflict Among Nations* (Princeton: Princeton University Press, 1977), 355. On the challenge of applying the insights of political scientists into the nature of the political context to decision-making, see Peter J. May, "Politics and Policy Analysis," *Political Science Quarterly* 101 (1986): 120–21, and Paul A. Anderson, "Justifications and Precedents as Constraints in Foreign Policy Decision-Making," *American Journal of Political Science* 25 (1982), 757–58.

ability. Simply put, effective action in the political context requires a "sufficient consensus,"[24] and that frequently depends on acceptability. The political decision-maker's greatest challenge is thus to find a policy around which a consensus can be formed that also deals satisfactorily with the substantive issues. This leads to a basically strategic approach to decision-making marked by the constant interplay of evaluations of the substantive merits of a proposal and assessments of its acceptability.[25]

CONNECTING THE PUZZLES: THE MUNICH CASE
AS A PLAUSIBILITY PROBE

The hypothesis that adding a political dimension to decision-making will help us to understand and explain foreign-policy outcomes must, of course, be evaluated in the light of actual events. One way of doing this is to show that the predicted behavior can actually be found in the real world. Roosevelt's response to the Munich crisis offers an appropriate vehicle for exploring the plausibility of such an approach—and not merely because a case that has not received a satisfactory explanation after more than fifty years of continuous attention is a challenge to any theory.[26] Rather, since this episode has several characteristics favoring a political approach, failure to discover it here would seriously damage its claims.[27]

For one thing, Roosevelt's reputation as one of America's most politically sensitive and accomplished presidents leads us to expect such an

[24] That is, a decision must be acceptable to some minimum number of relevant groups and individuals. George, *Presidential Decision-Making*, 1, 3. See also Diesing, *Reason in Society*, 214; Roger Hilsman, *To Move a Nation* (Garden City, N.Y.: Doubleday, 1967), 547; and below, chap. 2.

[25] While Tetlock also employs the concept of acceptability, his use differs from mine. See below.

[26] On the role of single case studies in theory development, see George, "Case Studies," 43–68; Alexander L. George, "Case Studies and Theory Development," paper presented to the second annual Symposium on Information Processing in Organizations, Carnegie-Mellon University, Pittsburgh, October 15–16, 1982; George, "The Causal Nexus between Cognitive Beliefs and Decision-Making Behavior: The 'Operational Code' Belief System," in *Psychological Models in International Politics*, ed. Lawrence S. Falkowski (Boulder, Colo.: Westview, 1979), 95–124; Harry Eckstein, "Case Study and Theory in Political Science," in *Handbook of Political Science* 7, ed. Fred I. Greenstein and Nelson W. Polsby (Reading, Mass.: Addison-Wesley, 1975), 113–23; Janice G. Stein and Raymond Tanter, *Rational Decision-Making* (Columbus, Ohio: Ohio State University Press, 1980), 83–85; and Stephen D. Krasner, "Toward Understanding in International Relations," *International Studies Quarterly* 29 (1985): 140–41. On the nature of plausibility probes, see Eckstein, "Case Study," 109; George, "Case Studies" (1982), 34, and "Case Studies" (1979), 58; and Farnham, "Value Conflict," 26–32.

[27] Eckstein, "Case Study," 111–12.

approach. Almost without exception, those observing him have attested to his political astuteness and ability;[28] even contemporaries who found fault with much else acknowledged Roosevelt's political acumen. Raymond Moley, for one, testified that despite a reputation for promoting administrative confusion, "There was no such muddling in the mind of Roosevelt the politician."[29] Thus, if ever there was a decision-maker who might be expected to approach decisions politically, it is this one.

Moreover, because the Munich case features an unambiguous conflict between two central values, it offers precisely the sort of situation in which a political approach to decision-making should be found. Given Roosevelt's political sensitivity and skill we would expect to see policies aimed not only at preserving both values, but also at giving up as little of each as possible. Failure to find such policies (or finding instead antithetical policies, such as those based on sharp value trade-offs) would be embarrassing to the theory.[30]

The effort to explain Roosevelt's policies begins with a discussion of the political approach to decision-making. This approach shares at least three characteristics with theories traditionally used to analyze political decision-making (analytical, intuitive, and motivational):[31] a dominant

[28] According to Neustadt, for example, "No President in this century has had a sharper sense of personal power, a sense of what it is and where it comes from; none has had more hunger for it, few have had more use for it, and only one or two could match his faith in his own competence to use it." Richard E. Neustadt, *Presidential Power* (New York: John Wiley and Sons, rev. ed., 1980), 118–19. Arthur Schlesinger, Jr., as well, has observed that Roosevelt's "power sprang from his preternatural sensitivity to the emerging social moods and needs of his time—this allied with astute realism and unlimited resourcefulness about means and a generous, buoyant, at times almost ingenuous, idealism about ends." *San Francisco Chronicle*, April 13, 1970.

[29] Raymond Moley, "History's Bone of Contention," *Franklin D. Roosevelt: A Profile*, ed. William Leuchtenberg (New York: Hill and Wang, 1967), 157.

[30] This is not to say that Munich constitutes a crucial case for the political approach to decision-making such that the absence of those policies would conclusively disconfirm that theory. It does mean, however, that given the existence of conditions that seem highly favorable to the use of a political approach, failure to find them would suggest that it "could hardly be expected to hold widely" elsewhere. For a discussion of the requirements of a crucial case, see Eckstein, "Case Study," 113–23.

[31] For a discussion of these approaches to decision-making, see appendix A. The word "intuitive" is used here to designate nonanalytic cognitive processes, restoring the term "cognitive" to its orginial meaning, which includes both analytical and intuitive processes. This usage is enjoying increasing currency within the field of psychology. Jay Meddin, "Attitudes, Values and Related Concepts: A System of Classification," *Social Science Quarterly* 55 (1975): 893. See also D. R. Price-Williams, "Cognition," in *A Dictionary of the Social Sciences*, ed. Julius Gould and William Kolb (New York: Free Press, 1964); Stein and Tanter, *Rational Decision-Making*, p. 26 n. 5; and John W. Payne, James R. Bettman, and Eric J. Johnson, "Behavioral Decision Research: A Constructive Processing Perspective," *Annual Review of Psychology* 48 (1992): 112.

concern that drives the entire decision process, a set of typical decision-making procedures, and the distinctive outcomes these produce. Moreover, all four theories offer competing accounts of how decision-makers deal with a clash of values such as Roosevelt faced in the aftermath of the Munich crisis.

Analytical decision-makers, driven by a concern with utility, seek the "best" solution, or one which is at least "good enough" according to some explicit standard of value. They are expected to use such decision-making processes as comprehensive analysis and optimizing decision rules to produce an outcome with the greatest utility in terms of the relevant values—that is, one that is optimal. Such decision-makers handle value conflict by comparing all known alternatives to a fixed standard of value and trading off, sacrificing some values in order to serve others.[32]

Intuitive decision-makers, on the other hand, are driven by the desire for simplicity and/or consistency. They employ such processes as judgmental heuristics and intuitive decision strategies, and their choice is likely to be the intuitively obvious solution, one that is consistent with past decisions or salient for some other reason. Value trade-offs are often avoided because they have been overlooked or are too difficult to perform, and the decision is presented as serving all important values equally well.[33]

The motivational approach, by contrast, is dominated by a need to preserve emotional well-being. Emphasizing the influence of "desires and drives to minimize psychological discomfort,"[34] it sees decision-making as inherently stressful, calling up a variety of negative emotions such as fear, anxiety, and guilt, and leading to characteristic behaviors such as avoidance, denial, bolstering, and crude satisficing.[35] Its outcome is likely

[32] In other words, they use a compensatory decision strategy. Zur Shapira, "Making Trade-offs Between Job Attributes," *Organizational Behavior and Human Performance* 28 (1981): 333.

[33] Jervis, *Perception*, 128–42; Philip E. Tetlock and Charles McGuire, Jr., "Cognitive Perspectives on Foreign Policy," unpublished version of a chapter in *Political Behavior Annual*, ed. S. Long; and Stein and Tanter, *Rational Decision-Making*, 45, 34–36. See also Roger N. Shepard, "On Subjectively Optimum Selection Among Multi-attribute Alternatives," in *Human Judgments and Optimality*, ed. Maynard W. Shelly II and Glenn L. Bryan (New York: John Wiley and Sons, 1964), 257.

[34] Robert Jervis, "Foreign Policy Motivation: A General Theory and a Case Study, by Richard Cottam," *Political Science Quarterly* 93 (1978): 328.

[35] See, for example, Irving Janis and Leon Mann, *Decision-Making* (New York: Free Press, 1977); Irving L. Janis, "Decisional Conflicts: A Theoretical Analysis," *Journal of Conflict Resolution* 3 (March 1959): 6–27, and *Crucial Decisions* (New York: Free Press, 1989); George, *Presidential Decisionmaking*, 25–28, and "Adaptation to Stress in Political Decision Making: The Individual, Small Group, and Organizational Contexts," in *Coping and Adaptation*, ed. George V. Coelho, Daniel A. Hamburg, and John E. Adams (New York: Basic Books, 1974), 176–245; Ole R. Holsti and Alexander George, "Effects of Stress on the Performance of Foreign Policy-Makers," *Political Science Annual*, ed. Cor-

to be the decision that produces the least amount of stress. Serving the decision-maker's emotional needs, it is marked by the avoidance of painful choice, and frequently involves denial that the chosen alternative entails the sacrifice of any important values—not because the need for this is difficult to see or calculate, but because it is too painful to acknowledge.

Finally, political decision-makers, driven by the need for acceptability, characteristically deal with competing objectives by trying to reconcile them.[36] This impulse arises from an awareness that many values and interests are deeply held and not easily given up. Thus, if conflict is to be moderated, such sacrifices must be minimized—even if the resulting policy is less than optimal. Where this logic operates, a theory that takes decision-making processes into account can often tell us more about policy outcomes than one that merely analyzes them in terms of optimality. The end product of a process in which acceptability is a pervasive concern, in which diverse interests are habitually woven together rather than traded off and in which an effort has been made to accommodate as many such interests as possible, is likely to look rather different than the product of straightforward value maximization.

After outlining the main characteristics of this political approach to decision-making, I examine Roosevelt's decision-making in some detail, beginning with the years 1936–1938 when he tried to assess the challenge posed by the dictators and sought a way to deflect them from an increasingly warlike path, continuing with the crisis itself, and concluding with its aftermath as he began to focus on the value conflict that would dominate his thinking until Pearl Harbor. Demonstrating Roosevelt's understanding of the clash between the desire to stay out of war and the need to prevent a German victory and showing how he responded with the policy of aiding the democracies is the focus of the historical inquiry. Explaining it is the task of the theoretical enterprise, and the political approach to decision-making offers a perspective that allows me to do this in a way that would otherwise have been impossible. It also clarifies Roosevelt's attitude toward rearmament and the timing of his attempt to gain neutrality revision.

Establishing the plausibility of a political approach, however, requires not only showing that Roosevelt's policies are compatible with its predictions but also that it provides a better account than alternative theories. Thus, at each stage of the historical inquiry, I develop a theoretical expla-

nelius Cotter (Indianapolis: Bobbs-Merrill, 1975), 6:255–319; Ole Holsti, "Crisis, Stress and Decision-Making," *International Social Science Journal* 23 (1971): 53–67; Samuel A. Kirkpatrick, "Psychological Views of Decision-Making," in Cotter, *Political Science Annual*, 6:76–79; and Richard Ned Lebow, *Between Peace and War* (Baltimore: Johns Hopkins University Press, 1981), 107–16.

[36] Neustadt, "Presidents, Politics, and Analysis," 4.

nation of his behavior, pitting the predictions of the political approach against those of the three other decision-making theories.[37]

Finally, after analyzing Roosevelt's decision-making in terms of the predictions of the four approaches, I revisit the question of whether his choices might be better explained in terms of forces operating at other levels of analysis. The domestic-politics explanation offers a particularly serious challenge to a political approach to decision-making because it too tries to account for policy outcomes in terms of the effect of the political context. Its consistent success would thus suggest that the political approach amounts to little more than a translation into the language of decision-making of a theory actually operating at another level of analysis. If, however, that approach can be shown to provide a distinct, and more plausible, explanation of Roosevelt's response to the Munich crisis, the area decision-making explanations can illuminate is widened appreciably. Moreover, by successfully describing how the political context affects a decision-maker's effort to balance international and domestic constraints, such an approach contributes substantially to our understanding of the impact of domestic politics on foreign policy. In particular, analyzing the clash between domestic and international pressures as a value conflict that is often resolved through the agency of a political decision-maker should provide considerable insight into how domestic political forces are transformed into foreign policy.

[37] That is, a close examination of alternative explanations is combined with process tracing to establish a necessary connection between cause and effect by trying to identify the actual decision-making processes Roosevelt employed. George, "Case Studies" (1982), 14–15, 19–31, 35, 41, "Causal Nexus," 105, and "Case Studies" (1979), 57–58. See also Philip L. Beardsley, *Redefining Rigor: Ideology and Statistics in Political Inquiry* (Beverly Hills: Sage, 1980), 60; Arthur Stinchombe, *Constructing Social Theories* (New York: Harcourt, Brace, and World, 1968), 20–25, 68; and Stein and Tanter, *Rational Decision-Making*, 85.

Part One

THEORY

CHAPTER II

The Political Approach to Decision-Making

THE POLITICAL CONTEXT, like any other context, affects decision-making behavior by encouraging the development of distinctive ways of thinking about decision problems and procedures for dealing with them.[1] Such contextual guidelines originate in traditional practices within a field and in formal and informal constraints arising from the field's characteristic organization.[2] One example of such a customary practice is the use of precedent to decide cases in the legal field; another is medicine's characteristic decision rule, "When in doubt, diagnose illness."[3]

In each context, conventions about what to consider and procedures for deciding come to be favored because they promote effective action.[4]

[1] Tetlock defines context as a natural decision environment whose "fundamental or invariant features" encourage the development of typical behavioral strategies. According to Herbert Simon, "since . . . [cognitive] performance depends heavily on socially structured and socially acquired knowledge, [cognitive psychology] must pay constant attention to the social environment of cognition. Many of the invariants we see in behavior are social invariants. . . . Social variables must be introduced to set the boundaries of our generalizations." Tetlock, "Accountability," 306; Simon, "Invariants," 16. Hermann has described the impact of context on political leadership in similar terms. Margaret G. Hermann, "Ingredients of Leadership," *Political Psychology*, ed. Margaret G. Hermann (San Francisco: Jossey-Bass, 1986), 173. See also W. Lance Bennett, "Perception and Cognition: An Information Processing Framework for Politics," *Handbook of Political Behavior* ed. S. L. Long (New York: Plenum, 1981), 1:172–73.

[2] James A. Robinson, "Decision-Making: Political Aspects," in Sills, ed., *International Encyclopedia*, 59. On contextual "rules," see also Morton H. Halperin, *Bureaucratic Politics and Foreign Policy* (Washington, D.C.: Brookings Institution, 1974), 110. For a discussion of the nature of context and how it can shape decision-making behavior, see Farnham, "Value Conflict," 140–50.

[3] Stein and Tanter, *Rational Decision-Making*, 26.

[4] In political science, Harold Lasswell's analysis of the policy sciences is based on a similar understanding of the role of context, as is the work of a number of contemporary policy analysts. In sociology, the concept of role or social context is used frequently to classify decisions because roles can significantly influence the processes by which decisions are made. In political theory, Diesing's analysis of the varieties of rationality has established the usefulness of this definition of context by showing that there is a distinct type of rationality peculiar to each context that embodies different principles of decision-making and produces its own unique kind of good. Harold D. Lasswell, *A Pre-View of Policy Sciences* (New York: American Elsevier, 1971), 14–15, 18; Arnold J. Meltsner, "Political Feasibility and Policy Analysis," *Public Administration Review* 32 (1972): 864; Robert A. Heineman

Take, for example, the problem of choosing the site for a bridge.[5] Engineers, concerned with technical efficiency, will analyze the width and depth of the river at alternative locations, while economists concentrate on cost and the efficient distribution of goods. Political decision-makers, though not blind to such considerations, will tend to focus on the impact of the bridge site on a variety of key groups, a preoccupation influenced in no small measure by their relative power. Such distinctive concerns not only lead decision-makers to approach the same question differently, but also encourage them to reason differently and to employ diverse decision strategies, which frequently results in different policy recommendations.[6]

Those who are sensitive to context learn that attending to its imperatives is as necessary to their ability to act effectively as efficiency in terms of substantive issues.[7] As a 1988 controversy over research priorities between Congress and the National Institutes of Health shows, failure to do so can have unfortunate consequences. Officials of the Institutes argued that it was most efficient to allocate available funds to research areas "ripe for exploitation" and insisted that the decision was the province of scientific administrators and experts. Members of Congress, on the other hand, found this approach "elitist," contending that allocation decisions were "essentially political" and should be made only by Congress.[8] Forcing the administrators to back down, they drove home the point that when the context of a decision is political, the most efficient solution in terms of the substantive issues may nonetheless fail to achieve effective action.

---

et al., *The World of the Policy Analyst: Rationality, Values, and Politics* (Chatham, N.J.: Chatham House, 1990), 1; Orville G. Brim, Jr., et al., *Personality and Decision Processes* (Stanford Calif.: Stanford University Press, 1962), 14, 17, 18; and Diesing, *Reason in Society*, 2, 4, 9. I am indebted to the late William T. R. Fox for bringing Lasswell's work on contextuality to my attention.

[5] Roger Hilsman also uses a decision about locating a bridge to illustrate the distinction between political and technical decision-making. *To Move a Nation*, 554.

[6] Analysts as well as practitioners are affected by context. Thus, James Voss has found that "people who have different professional backgrounds and information approach the same problem-solving situation" differently. "When asked to write an essay on agricultural reform in the USSR, subjects who are experts in agronomy address themselves to entirely different variables and strategies than subjects who are experts on Russian political affairs." Cited in Simon, "Invariants," 16.

[7] Diesing uses the distinction between efficiency and effectiveness to differentiate between technical and political rationality. *Reason in Society*, 3. Alexander George also distinguishes between efficiency and effectiveness. "Limits of Rationality in Designing Public Policy and Developing Policy-relevant Theory: A Discussion Paper," Dartmouth College, n.d., 4–5.

[8] *New York Times*, July 8, 1988.

THE POLITICAL PROCESS AND THE CONDITIONS
OF EFFECTIVE ACTION

The possibilities for effective action in the political context are shaped by a political process in which the twin themes of conflict and cooperation are inextricably intertwined. This juxtaposition of clashing interests and values and the need to reconcile them is the fundamental feature of the political context, influencing behavior of all kinds, including decision-making behavior.

A political process is distinguished from other ways of making group decisions by three characteristics: disagreement about ends and means, "competing clusters of people . . . identified with . . . alternative goals and policies," and the fact that these groups possess varying degrees of political power.[9] This suggests that effective action in the political context normally requires a "sufficient consensus" in support of proposed policies, which makes acceptability as well as utility the mark of a successful policy.[10]

Even when dealing with an international problem, a political decision-maker must consider acceptability, which often comes as a shock to those used to a more analytical approach. For example, in moving from the State Department to the White House, press officer Edward Djerejian "expressed surprise at 'the interaction of domestic politics and foreign policy. . . . At the State Department you make the best judgments on the foreign policy interests of the U.S. Here you have to be abundantly aware, and put in the equation, domestic political considerations. That's new for me.'"[11] Some, of course, never come to understand this— witness the separation of political and policy concerns practiced by President Bush and his secretary of state, James Baker.[12] If the need to recon-

---

[9] Hilsman, *To Move a Nation*, 552–55; See also Roger Hilsman, "The Foreign Policy Consensus: An Interim Report," *Journal of Conflict Resolution* 3 (1959): 365–66. Subsequently, Hilsman added a fourth characteristic, Schilling's notion of a "strain toward agreement," or the "effort to build a consensus, a push for accommodation, for compromise, for some sort of agreement on the policy decision." *Politics of Policymaking*, 69, 75–77.

[10] "The test of policy is not that it will most effectively accomplish an agreed-upon value but that a wider number of people decide to endorse it." Hilsman, *To Move a Nation*, 547, and "Foreign Policy Consensus," 364. In his discussion of the legislative character of strategic policy-making, Huntington points out that this view of the policy process also applies to military policy. In fact, he stresses the need to bargain and the requirement of not merely consensus but unanimity. Samuel P. Huntington, *The Common Defense: Strategic Programs in National Politics* (New York: Columbia University Press, 1961), 126, 146–48, 152, 155.

[11] *New York Times*, Oct. 16, 1985.

[12] According to Michael Mandelbaum, "For these guys, there is no relationship between politics and policy. . . . In the Bush-Baker world view, you do ugly, distasteful things to get

cile substance and support is recognized, however, decision-making processes may be strongly affected, particularly in dealing with a serious conflict of values.

The Role of Power

In the political context, acceptability is inextricably connected to power.[13] Even in a democratic society, pressure for consensus derives not only from democratic principles and constitutional rules, but also from the fact that various groups and individuals possess a degree of power.[14] Similarly, even in the most authoritarian governments, insofar as any individual or group commands a measure of power, effective action will require some attention to acceptability.[15]

Note, however, that a concern with acceptability amounts to more than a simple calculus of relative power, because the more a decision is the product of some kind of genuine acceptance, the more effective it will

---

elected. . . . And then when you get into office, you do what you think is right. The idea that you should have to explain yourself . . . is grubby." *New York Times*, March 29, 1992.

[13] As Neustadt expresses it, "the essence of a President's persuasive task . . . is to induce [people] to believe that what he wants of them is what their own appraisal of their own responsibilities requires them to do in their own interest," which "amounts to more than charm or reasoned argument. . . . For the men he would induce to do what he wants done on their own responsibility will need or fear some acts by him on his responsibility." Neustadt, *Presidential Power* (1980), 35, 27. Emphasis removed.

[14] The central role of power distinguishes the political context from other social contexts. In Lasswell and Kaplan's terms, "conduct is political in the degree that it is determined by considerations of power." For this reason, Tetlock's definition of the political context in terms of accountability is unsatisfactory, especially his assumption that a desire for approval is the motivating force behind political decision-making behavior and the basis for a concern with acceptability. As Machiavelli pointed out, the kind of acceptance that moves people to do a decision-maker's political bidding does not always bring social approval. Lasswell and Kaplan, *Power and Society*, 144–46; (see also 72, 85, 240); Tetlock, "Accountability," 308–9; Niccolo Machiavelli, "The Prince" in *The Portable Machiavelli*, ed. Peter Bandanella and Mark Musa (New York: Penguin Books, 1979); chap. 17. See also Neustadt's discussion of presidential reputation in *Presidential Power* (1980), 48; and James L. Payne et al., *Motivations of Politicians* (Chicago: Nelson-Hall, 1984), 1, 3, 78ff. For a critique of Tetlock's concept of the political context and his "politician research program," see Farnham, "Political Cognition," 90–92, and "Value Conflict," 142–46.

[15] "To remain in high office in both democracies and dictatorships, a man must either satisfy the values of the groups with power or pit the power of one group against the power of another, and usually he must do a bit of both. The number of groups that have power is undoubtedly smaller in a dictatorship . . . but they do exist." Roger Hilsman, *Strategic Intelligence and National Decisions* (Glencoe, Ill.: Free Press, 1956), 147–48.

usually be. As the history of agricultural collectivization in the Soviet Union demonstrates, even in totalitarian states the effectiveness of a policy may depend on its being at least minimally acceptable to those at whom it is directed.[16]

Thus, in terms of the importance of acceptability, all political societies can be located on a continuum that ranges from a condition of near anarchy in which almost everyone has a veto to the most extreme form of tyranny in which almost no one does. The degree to which those approaching a decision politically are constrained by acceptability depends on where their society falls on this continuum.

Acceptability and Political Decision-Making

Every policy proposal must be judged not only on its merits but also in terms of its implications for the politics of governing (can it pass the Congress? will state and local governments accept it?), the politics of nomination and the politics of election. . . . In a very real sense, you face no greater challenge in functioning as the domestic president than to blend policy and politics properly.[17]

What is the relationship between a political process in which acceptability is often a condition of effective action and the intellectual process of decision-making? Hilsman's analysis implies that the essential role of the decision-maker is to formulate the kinds of policies around which a consensus can be built.[18] Again, the critical importance of this task derives directly from the nature of a political process in which even a "fairly clear-cut decision" may "become the signal for enormous efforts by dif-

---

[16] As Carl Kaysen points out, "even authoritarian and repressive governments in modern societies need the consent, however tacit and grudging, of the mass of the governed." "Is War Obsolete?" *International Security* 14 (Spring 1990), 57. For an example, see the evidence that Khrushchev was "influenced by Soviet public opinion" during the Cuban missile crisis in Richard N. Lebow and Janice G. Stein, *We All Lost the Cold War* (Princeton: Princeton University Press, 1994), 144.

[17] Memorandum to President Reagan at the start of his first term. Cited in May, "Politics and Policy Analysis," 114.

[18] Hilsman, *Politics of Policymaking*, 78. See also "Foreign Policy Consensus," 372; George, "Domestic Constraints on Regime change in U.S. Foreign Policy," *Change in the International System*, ed. Ole R. Holsti, Randolph Siverson, and Alexander L. George (Boulder, Colo.: Westview Press, 1980), 234–35; and Henry A. Kissinger, "Reflections on Power and Diplomacy," *Dimensions of Power and Diplomacy*, ed. E.A.J. Johnson (Baltimore: Johns Hopkins University Press, 1964), 24.

ferent groups within the government itself to reverse it."[19] Decision-makers can reduce this risk if their deliberations produce an acceptable policy. Indeed, their skill (or lack of it) in performing this subjective adjustment of competing values can have a critical impact on the level of conflict within a given political system—hence George's observation that the decision-maker's intellectual processes can provide an *alternative* to conflict in the political arena as a means of developing policy.[20]

There is ample evidence that political decision-makers are sensitive to this need for accomodation.[21] Faced with a potential conflict, their aim is generally to defuse it, possibly because they realize they are likely to get more by dealing strategically with anticipated conflict through a well-constructed decision than by leaving the outcome to be determined by the clash of political forces. The amount of effort decision-makers must devote to political combat following a decision is, in fact, likely to be inversely proportional to their pre-decisional success in developing such policies.[22]

This relationship is nicely illustrated by Roosevelt's bitter court-packing fight, which was the consequence of a rare departure from his customary practice of "education and persuasion, rather than . . . arbitrary action or dictation." In this instance, Roosevelt "just sprang his plan, in effect saying, 'I've just won an overwhelming mandate, and this is the way I've chosen to put it into effect.' He consulted almost no one, least of all the Congress, and he spurned compromise. This was a most uncharacteristic design for defeat."[23] The norms and conventions of the political context assist decision-makers to avoid a similar fate by helping them to formulate policies that are designed for success.

The need to reach agreement in the political context leads to a dynamic and fundamentally strategic approach to decision-making involving a

[19] Hilsman, "Foreign Policy Consensus," 362.

[20] "The top executive is expected . . . to reconcile competing values and interests by going through an 'internal debate.' The hope is that a subjective ordering and aggregation of the competing values by the executive will enable him to offer a satisfactory solution to what would otherwise be left to be settled entirely via conflict and bargaining among the actors within the policymaking system." George, *Presidential Decisionmaking*, 28.

[21] See, for example, Hilsman, *To Move a Nation*, 553–54.

[22] This focus on intellectual activity is not intended to minimize the conflictual aspects of politics, but to highlight the predecisional anticipation of conflict and the attempt to deal with it by shaping a decision that will reduce it as much as possible. Of course, political activity to influence people's choices is also widespread, and political decision-making and political action are rarely completely separate in practice.

[23] Samuel Rosenman, cited in John Emmet Hughes, ed., *The Living Presidency* (New York: Coward McCann, 1972), 359–60.

constant interplay of evaluations of substantive merit and assessments of acceptability.[24] Moreover, political decision-makers are likely to incorporate a strategy for getting agreement into the decision itself. Indeed, they rarely choose an option without first considering how to implement it. Unlike analytic decision-makers, they do not treat decisions as though they were "self-executing."[25]

This pervasive concern with acceptability does not, however, mean that political decision-makers are always passive in the face of the acceptability constraint. Because acceptability and utility are each necessary but not sufficient conditions of political rationality, political decision-makers try to reconcile them by balancing the various values and interests involved in a decision.[26] Many politicians have an intuitive understanding of this need to balance acceptability and substance, as former New York City Mayor Edward Koch inadvertently revealed following his 1985 primary election victory:

> Mr. Koch acknowledged—despite his frequent claim that he is guided by the merits of an act, not popular opinion—that he has sometimes given in to political expediency. He pledged to do less of that. "I'm not going to tell you that everything I've done was the most pristine—I've wanted to get re-elected. . . . But I am telling you now I'm going to run the third term as if it

[24] As George describes it, the decision-maker

does not take a passive stance toward the environment on which he is dependent for the multiple payoffs he seeks, rather, while deferring his decision, he takes soundings, prepares the ground, interacts with other political actors whose interests are involved or who can be helpful to him, and manipulates and orchestrates the political process as part of his search for a decision that will secure for him as much as possible of the multiple stakes he seeks.

"Adaptation to Stress," 185.

[25] Personal communication from Carl Kaysen.

[26] As even a "realist" like Hans Morgenthau argued, the statesman "must strike a prudent balance between adapting himself to [popular passions] and marshaling them in the support of his policies." Neustadt captures the complexity of the kind of calculation this involves:

It may be, in a given situation, that counsels both of power and of policy point in the same direction. . . . Even so, a consciousness of power stakes apart from policy affords a President protection toward the future. . . . In other situations it may be that an event or policy leaves no room for maneuver, regardless of the risk in personal terms. . . . *A sensitivity to power's stakes and sources is no cure-all.* Oversensitivity to any one aspect at any time might wreck the very things a President most wanted and leave him beneath the ruins.

Neustadt, *Presidential Power* (1980), 110. Hans J. Morgenthau, "The Future of Diplomacy," *International Politics*, 2d ed., ed. Robert J. Art and Robert Jervis (Glenview, Ill.: Scott, Foresman, 1985), 109.

were the last term. So whatever I do, I'm going to take the most pristine and do-able solution."[27]

The word "pristine," presumably a reference to the mayor's intention to judge issues on their merits, represents one side of the equation of political rationality. Even in the act of forswearing expediency, however, Koch found himself unable to omit "do-ability," which is the other side of the equation.[28]

Decision-makers may also deal with the acceptability constraint by attempting to push against its boundaries, using a number of traditional strategies that have developed in the political context. These strategies, such as calculated procrastination and sequencing, are at the heart of a political approach to decision-making, being directed primarily at avoiding the sacrifice of value, which reduces acceptability and threatens consensus—in other words, at avoiding sharp value trade-offs.[29] In addition, the political context suggests ways of altering the acceptability constraint itself by extending the domain of acceptability, for example by attempting to educate the public about the need for a given policy.[30] This is as much a part of a strategic approach to decision-making as manipulating policies to increase their acceptability.

DEVELOPING ACCEPTABLE POLICIES

The political context offers a range of guidelines to mark the limits of acceptability and develop policies that fall within them.[31] Most importantly, acceptability serves as a prior concern that must be addressed before the other attributes of an alternative can be seriously considered, and as an unavoidable constraint that fundamentally shapes the decision-making process. It thus drives the political decision-maker's characteristic approach to value conflict, leading to a quest for transcendent solutions and an effort to weave together competing interests rather than

[27] *New York Times*, Sept. 11, 1985.

[28] Neustadt cites Roosevelt's success in achieving a proper balance between political and substantive goals in the service of effective action: "He wanted power for its own sake; he also wanted what it could achieve. The challenge and the fun of power lay not just in having, but in doing. His private satisfactions were enriched by public purposes and these grew more compelling as more power came his way." *Presidential Power* (1980), 119.

[29] See below and appendix C.

[30] See below.

[31] The strategies for achieving such decisions are "quite clearly different from the procedures used in reaching economic or legal decisions" because they are not concerned solely with attaining the "best" decision in terms of the substance of the issue, but one which is capable of commanding sufficient support. Diesing, *Reason in Society*, 203.

trade them off. Because value conflicts reduce acceptability, there is considerable motivation to identify and diffuse them.[32]

Recognizing Value Conflict

Decision-makers who are aware of the demands of the political context are likely to consider acceptability throughout the entire course of the decision process.[33] Part of the task of problem diagnosis, for example, is determining whether there is a political as well as a policy problem.[34] Thus, in foreign policy, their concern with acceptability leads such decision-makers to evaluate domestic sentiment as well as the international situation. Moreover, because they need to learn about whatever might reduce consensus, they are usually open to new information about both the

[32] Value conflicts arise in situations marked by value complexity ("the presence of multiple, competing values and interests that are imbedded in a single issue") and complicated by uncertainty. They are usually triggered by a need for action. (See George, *Presidential Decisionmaking*, 26; Milton Rokeach, "Some Unresolved Issues in Theories of Beliefs, Attitudes, and Values," *Nebraska Symposium on Motivation, 1979: Beliefs, Attitudes and Values*, ed. Monte M. Page (Lincoln, Neb.: University of Nebraska Press, 1980), 295–96. This can either bring values not previously thought incompatible into conflict or, as in Roosevelt's case, disclose a conflict between values that often do compete. The controversy over the decision to build a major access road to the Carter presidential library on the outskirts of Atlanta is an example of the first type. Until the issue of the road connected them, one could scarcely have imagined that the goal of making presidential papers accessible to the public and the desire to preserve the character of suburban communities would turn out to be competitors (*New York Times*, Oct. 3, 1986). On the second type, see William A. Scott, "Rationality and Non-rationality of International Attitudes," *Journal of Conflict Resolution* 2 (1958): 11.

[33] Diesing, *Reason in Society*, 229, and Meltsner, "Political Feasibility," 865. Many believe that the best way to analyze decision-making is to break the process down into a series of stages. Brim et al., *Personality and Decision Processes*, 9–10. See also John S. Carroll, "Analyzing Decision Behavior: The Magician's Audience," in *Cognitive Processes in Choice and Decision Behavior*, ed. Thomas S. Wallsten (Hillsdale, N.J.: Lawrence Erlbaum Associates, 1980). I use Stein and Tanter's five-stage model, in which the decision-maker determines the nature of the problem (diagnosis), acquires information to reduce uncertainty (search), updates "estimates in response to new information" (revision), identifies and orders relevant values, comparing them to the alternatives (evaluation), and applies a characteristic decision rule to the surviving alternatives (choice). *Rational Decision-Making*, 23–26, 64–65. While evaluation and choice are logically distinct, they may not always be separable in practice. Furthermore, as Abelson and Levi point out, "Decision processing is frequently iterative and cyclical," which means that cognitive processes characterizing one stage may often appear in others as well. Abelson and Levi, "Decision Making," 277, 235; Amos Tversky, "Elimination by Aspects," *Psychological Review* 79 (1972): 281–99. See also John W. Payne, "Contingent Decision Behavior," *Psychological Bulletin* 92 (1982): 388–90; Hillel J. Einhorn and Robin M. Hogarth, "Behavioral Decision Theory: Processes of Judgement and Choice," *Annual Review of Psychology* 32 (1981): 73.

[34] Diesing, *Reason in Society*, 228–29.

problem and the prospects of success of various alternatives. As a consequence, search and revision are likely to be thorough, with particular attention given to information about acceptability.

The clear implication of the acceptability constraint is that political decision-makers need to identify serious value conflicts. Although they may not be fond of value trade-offs, they will want information about their possible necessity in order to ameliorate their effects and protect against their consequences—even if this involves considerable cognitive effort.[35] Thus, the political context offers a number of incentives for decision-makers to be aware of both their own values and those of various groups and interests in the society.[36]

That accountability is often a feature of the political context, for example, may be an inducement for decision-makers to examine and structure their own values.[37] Thus, political candidates are often expected to express and defend their values.[38] Moreover, the notion that political decision-makers have structured value systems is supported by much of the work on belief systems. George's concept of the operational code, for example, seems to have much in common with Rokeach's notion of value systems, and he too emphasizes the systematic character of cognitive organization.[39]

To formulate acceptable policies, political decision-makers also need

---

[35] For example, Fred Greenstein has referred to Roosevelt's "constant intelligence gathering," "The Virtuosic Leadership of Franklin Delano Roosevelt," unpubl. ms., 16. See also Burns, *Lion*, 284–85.

[36] Hilsman, *Strategic Intelligence*, 146–48.

[37] Tetlock, "Accountability."

[38] However superficial campaign discussions of values may be, decision-makers' real understanding of values, like their views underlying various policy positions expressed during campaigns, may be more complex than their campaign rhetoric reveals. See Philip E. Tetlock, "Pre- to Postelection Shifts in Presidential Rhetoric: Impression or Cognitive Adjustment?" *Journal of Personality and Social Psychology* 41 (1981): 207–12. A recent study supports the notion of a hierarchy of values and attitudes about foreign policy affecting policy choices. Jon Hurwitz, Mark Peffley, and Mitchell Seligson, "Foreign Policy Belief Systems in Comparative Perspective: The United States and Costa Rica," *International Studies Quarterly* 37 (1993): 245–70. See also Ole Holsti's discussion of public opinion and foreign policy citing a growing body of evidence that "attitudes about foreign affairs are in fact structured in at least moderately coherent ways." "Public Opinion and Foreign Policy: Challenges to the Almond-Lippman Consensus," *International Studies Quarterly* 36 (1992): 448.

[39] George, "Causal Nexus," 97–101; Milton Rokeach, *The Nature of Human Values* (New York: Free Press, 1973). See also Philip Tetlock, "Cognitive Style and Political Belief Systems in the British House of Commons," *Journal of Personality and Social Psychology* 46 (1984): 365; Donald D. Searing, "Measuring Politicians' Values: Administration and Assessment of a Ranking Technique in the British House of Commons," *American Political Science Review* 72 (March 1978): 65–79; Ole R. Holsti, "Cognitive Dynamics and Images of the Enemy," *Journal of International Affairs* 21 (1967): 18–19; and Tetlock and McGuire, "Cognitive Perspectives," 13–17.

to understand the values of others so they can identify value conflicts among those whose support is needed for effective action. Fortunately, the nature of the political process ensures that diverse values are brought to their attention by a myriad of groups and interests constantly pressing their claims.[40] Moreover, because even individual decision-makers normally operate in group settings, value conflicts can surface during argumentation.[41]

Thus, since the behavior of political decision-makers is characterized by the energy they put into identifying value conflicts, there is a good possibility that they will recognize them. Opportunities for bias exist because values with little political support may be slighted, but decision-makers who want to act effectively generally need information about as many of the values involved as possible.

Resolving Value Conflict

How do political decision-makers find policies that can resolve value conflicts? The political context suggests a number of hypotheses about what processes they use as they move along the "search-design continuum."[42] Among the most prominent of these are an initial screening for acceptability, a search for transcendent solutions, and the use of traditional political strategies to improve acceptability.

Since acceptability is a prior concern and an unavoidable constraint, evaluation in the political approach to decision-making normally begins with a screening of the alternatives for acceptability, and a policy judged incapable of being brought to some minimal level of acceptability is un-

[40] Hilsman, *Strategic Intelligence*, 146–47, 149. Hilsman is not completely consistent on this issue, however. See "Foreign Policy Consensus," 363.

[41] Robert Axelrod, "Argumentation in Foreign Policy Settings," *Journal of Conflict Resolution* 21 (1977): 728. See also Michael D. Cohen and Robert Axelrod, "Coping with Complexity: The Adaptive Value of Changing Utility," *American Economic Review* 74 (1984): 30–42; and James G. March, "Bounded Rationality, Ambiguity, and the Engineering of Choice," *Bell Journal of Economic Management Science* 9 (1978): 587–608. Milburn and Billings have noted that values in the political context appear to change during the course of a decision. Thomas Milburn and Robert S. Billings, "Decision-Making Perspectives from Psychology: Dealing with Risk and Uncertainty," *American Behavioral Scientist* 20 (Sept.–Oct. 1976): 114. This tendency also seems to operate during diplomatic negotiations. See Fred Charles Ikle, *How Nations Negotiate* (New York: Harper and Row, 1964), 22–23, 59.

[42] The phrase is Abelson and Levi's, "Decision Making," 272. "Search is evoked to find ready-made solutions; design is used to develop custom-made solutions or to modify ready-made ones. This distinction is fundamental—the difference between what psychologists call convergent and divergent thinking. It is one thing to find a needle in a haystack, quite another to write a fugue." Henry Mintzberg, Duru Raisinghani, and Andre Theoret, "The Structure of Unstructured Decisions," *Administrative Science Quarterly* 21 (1976): 255.

likely to be evaluated further. Lyndon Johnson, for example, is reported to have seriously considered no alternative he had not already judged achievable in political terms.[43]

In line with the notion that people will conserve cognitive resources if conditions permit, political decision-makers will probably first consider readily available alternatives.[44] These may be found in analogies to similar situations in the past, traditional practices, political scripts, or, perhaps most salient of all, the current policy.[45]

During the initial screening, the decision-maker matches the alternatives against the acceptability constraint, performing what amounts to a calculus of political feasibility. Ideas about this process appear throughout the writings of the first-wave theorists and have been operationalized by contemporary policy analysts such as Peter May.[46] Thus, political decision-makers must assess the probability that a proposed policy will be "do-able,"[47] devise political strategies for gaining its acceptance,[48] and weigh it in terms of political prices, opportunity costs, and consequences.[49] The latter is a particularly prominent feature in the political

[43] Communication to the author from Adam Yarmolinsky, principal deputy assistant secretary of defense for international security affairs in the Johnson Administration. On this general point, see also Diesing: "any suggested course of action must be evaluated first by its effects on the political structure. . . . It sometimes happens that political and nonpolitical problems can be solved together, but if this is not possible, the political problem must receive primary attention." *Reason in Society*, 228; see also 229–32.

[44] See Amos Tversky and Daniel Kahneman, "Availability: A Heuristic for Judging Frequency and Probability," *Cognitive Psychology* 5 (1973): 207–32, and below; Abelson and Levy, "Decision Making," 273.

[45] On scripts and how decision-makers learn from history, see appendix A, and Tetlock, "Accountability," 313. On the salience of current policies, see Charles E. Lindblom, "The Science of 'Muddling Through,'" *Public Administration Review* 19 (1959): 74–88.

[46] May, "Politics and Policy Analysis," 111–13.

[47] Ibid., 111. That is, it must prove "manageable to the men who must administer it, acceptable to those who must support it, tolerable to those who must put up with it" Neustadt, *Presidential Power* (1980), 135. In his discussion of "backward mapping," Neustadt advocates a strategy that is very similar to applying an acceptability constraint: "Presidents might try . . . looking into policy for clues to power problems they might otherwise miss. The aspect of a policy at which to look is its requirement for implementing action, in a word its 'do-ability.'" *Presidential Power* (1990), 214–15.

[48] May, "Politics and Policy Analysis," 112. See also Hilsman, *Politics of Policymaking*, 78.

[49] "Even if enacted (and certainly if not enacted)," a policy proposal entails "opportunity costs of not giving attention to other, perhaps more profitable, issues. . . . [It] may be feasible in the sense that it has sufficient probability of enactment, but the political costs or consequences may be sufficiently large to argue against the proposal." May, "Politics and Policy Analysis," 113. See also Grandomenico Majone, "On the Notion of Political Feasibility," *European Journal of Political Research* 3 (1975): 265; and Eugene Bardach, *The Skill Factor in Politics* (Berkeley and Los Angeles: University of California Press, 1972), 263.

context, where no decision is ever made in isolation but is linked to a host of other decisions, present and future (and to past decisions as well, since those may serve as precedents that constrain the decision-maker).[50] Thus, political decision-makers habitually work with extended time horizons.[51]

Beyond these general considerations, it is difficult to describe a decision-maker's calculus of acceptability apart from actual situations.[52] Because the need to be concerned with acceptability varies from society to society, the content of any particular acceptability calculus will vary as well. Moreover, the degree of acceptability needed is partly contingent on the type of decision,[53] and the range of factors to consider often depends on the decision-maker's place in the policy hierarchy. Because of the nature of their responsibilities, for example, presidents must consider acceptability from a variety of international and domestic perspectives, whereas those lower down the scale need be concerned only with some of them.[54]

While subjective judgment clearly plays a prominent role in determining acceptability,[55] however, such assessments are usually shaped by the need for effective action on the decision at hand and the need to preserve and foster a capacity for effective action in the political context as a whole.[56] Within the framework of these overarching concerns, a whole range of norms and conventions have evolved that identify both the individuals and groups whose support is needed for effective action and the qualities that contribute to acceptability. Assisting the political decision-

[50] Lasswell and Kaplan's definition of a politician makes this concern explicit: "The term has reference . . . not merely to the holding or striving for political office, but to the tendency to consider always the effect on influence or power position of projected lines of conduct." Lasswell and Kaplan, *Power and Society*, 146 (see also 74–75); and May, "Politics and Policy Analysis," 113.

[51] The negative impact of President Bush's early fight to nominate Senator John Tower as secretary of defense on his subsequent relationship with Congress shows the unfortunate consequences of failing to balance a desire to act in the present against the desire to be effective in the future. *New York Times*, Aug. 9, 1992.

[52] Majone, "On the Notion of Political Feasibility," 264; and George, "Domestic Constraints," 236.

[53] See George, *Presidential Decisionmaking*, 1; Hilsman, *To Move a Nation*, 553, 561. The amount and kind of acceptability needed to get effective action on a new weapons system, for example, is bound to differ from that needed to launch a social program. Similarly, there may be differences between the kind of acceptability required by domestic and foreign policies.

[54] See Neustadt, *Presidential Power* (1980), 135. Halperin also notes this phenomenon, *Bureaucratic Politics*, 81.

[55] For a discussion of the different kinds of judgment brought to bear in foreign policy decision-making, see George, *Bridging the Gap*, 22–28.

[56] Diesing, *Reason in Society*, 171.

maker to fill in the empty boxes of the acceptability calculus, they set forth the traditional interpretation of the acceptability constraint and provide guidance in applying it.[57]

Our analysis also suggests that the acceptability constraint often includes each of the values implicated in the decision. Indeed, because they may be needed in the future, ignoring the values of even those whose support is not crucial to a decision may be unwise.[58] Clearly, this widens the scope of evaluation considerably, and the *degree* of acceptability political decision-makers commonly seek may make it more demanding still. Striving at minimum to satisfy Diesing's injunction that a decision "must be at least tolerable to the loser,"[59] they may try to achieve a good deal more since creating the broadest possible consensus often serves not only their present requirements but future needs as well. Thus, decision-makers may extend their screening for acceptability beyond the search for political problems in order to identify political opportunities, widening the scope of the decision to serve additional interests. As Dror notes, "in many political situations, much broader coalitions than needed to 'win' are required—to demonstrate support, strengthen cohesion, and build up power for the future."[60]

The close tie between consensus and effective action may also explain why we see fewer attempts to get around the acceptability constraint than we would expect from a decision-maker devoted solely to optimizing. Political decision-makers habitually treat acceptability not as an exogenous constraint to be overcome in the interests of value maximization but as a given that is an integral part of the decision problem and respected as such. Thus, they do not generally try to loosen the acceptability constraint until one or another substantive value has become extremely pressing.[61] As Neustadt describes it,

> Preferences these people do not voice, concessions they defer. Instead they stand eyeball to eyeball, waiting for the others to blink first. And frequently they are prepared to go another round, await another session. . . , because

[57] A discussion of the acceptability calculus may be found in appendix B. On contextual rules in general, see Halperin, *Bureaucratic Politics*, 110.

[58] See Hilsman, "Foreign Policy Consensus," 371; and Majone, "On the Notion of Political Feasibility," 261.

[59] Diesing, *Reason in Society*, 210.

[60] Yehezkel Dror, *Ventures in Policy Sciences* (New York: American Elsevier, 1971), 87 n. 6. Meltsner has also noted the tendency for more and more people to be drawn into a decision. "Political Feasibility," 861. See also Hilsman, "Foreign Policy Consensus," 371, and above, n. 10.

[61] Neustadt, "Presidents, Politics, and Analysis," 4. Jervis suggests that this aspect of the acceptability constraint may be the most difficult for rational-choice theory. Personal communication to the author.

time seems to them a free good, or anyway freer than choices their constituents or country might decry.

The screening process itself is noncompensatory: alternatives that fail to reach a minimal level of acceptability are generally eliminated because a serious deficiency on the political dimension cannot be offset by high scores on other dimensions. Since a policy that lacks a sufficient consensus is unlikely to succeed, it is inherently unattractive in a political context, even though this may well result in diminished utility in terms of substantive values. When it comes to acceptability, in other words, the decision-maker's preferences are close to being lexicographic.[62]

The hypothesis that political decision-makers are likely to begin an evaluation with a noncompensatory screening of the alternatives is supported by experimental evidence as well as the practice of actual decision-makers. Alex Mintz and Nehemia Geva, for example, found not only that decision-makers consider domestic political factors when making foreign-policy decisions, but that they consider them first. With respect to the behavior of actual decision-makers, anecdotal evidence of an initial screening for acceptability is abundant. May, for example, cites the statement of a White House assistant in the Kennedy administration that "The first question was always, Will it fly on the Hill?"[63]

Of course, screening for acceptability could suffer from the same flaws as any elimination strategy because an alternative with the greatest overall utility could be dropped at the outset.[64] For a political decision-maker, however, this may not be a very serious drawback. For one thing, in situations where the decision-maker's utility structure includes one

[62] For a decision-maker who has lexicographic preferences, one dimension is "incomparably more important" than the others, and there can be no value trade-offs. Elster notes that "lexicographic orderings are perhaps more frequent in political life than in economic life." Jon Elster, *Ulysses and the Sirens* (New York: Cambridge University Press, 1984), 124–27. See also John W. Payne, "Task Complexity and Contingent Processing in Decision Making: An Information Search and Protocol Analysis," *Organizational Behavior and Human Performance* 16 (1976): 366–87; Ernest R. Alexander, "Design of Alternatives in Organizational Contexts," *Administrative Science Quarterly* 24 (1979): 382–404; Ola Svenson and Henry Montgomery, "On Decision Rules and Information Processing Strategies for Choices Among Multiattribute Alternatives," *Scandinavian Journal of Psychology* 33 (1976): 283–91; Abelson and Levi, "Decision Making," 260; Peter C. Ordeshook, *Game Theory and Political Theory* (New York: Cambridge University Press, 1986), 17–18. On compensatory and noncompensatory strategies, see below.

[63] Alex Mintz, "The Decision to Attack Iraq: A Non-compensatory Theory of Decision-making," *Journal of Conflict Resolution* 37 (1993): 595–618; Nehemia Geva and Alex Mintz, "The Experimental Analyses of Conflict Processes Project: Preliminary Findings," *International Studies Notes* 18 (Spring 1993): 15–29. May, "Politics and Policy Analysis," 111. See also Lyndon Johnson's practice, above.

[64] On the suboptimality of screening strategies, see Abelson and Levi, "Decision Making," 268.

value whose dominance is such that no combination of the other values could compensate for its loss, a "noncompensatory strategy might be *as likely* to be optimal as a compensatory one."[65] For another, owing to the ongoing nature of politics, decision-makers often have the option of re-trieving previously considered alternatives.[66] This is related to the incre-mental character of much political decision-making. If a decision ad-dresses only part of a problem, that problem is likely to recur, and with it a number of alternatives initially judged infeasible.[67]

While a concern for acceptability is not necessarily biased, at times it can be.[68] Reconciling substance and support may be particularly difficult in foreign policy when a value enjoys a degree of support from key do-mestic groups that is disproportionate to its substantive importance. In such circumstances, decision-makers may be tempted to end an evalua-tion as soon as they have identified an alternative with a fairly high de-gree of acceptability.[69] Judging alternatives on the basis of acceptability alone, they refuse to make unavoidable trade-offs between values with equalivalent political support, advancing instead policies that seem to satisfy more interests than they really do. Furthermore, a preoccupation with acceptability can lead to conservatism in the form of failure to offer needed policy initiatives[70] or reluctance to alter currently acceptable poli-cies despite a pressing need for change, a tendency compounded by the difficulty of "renegotiating a majority coalition."[71]

[65] Noreen M. Klein, "Utility and Decision Strategies, a Second Look at the Decision Maker," *Organizational Behavior and Human Performance* 31 (1983): 6–7.

[66] The general ability to retain alternatives for future consideration is shown by Ruth M. Corbin, "Decisions That Might Not Get Made," in Wallsten, *Cognitive Processes*, 58.

[67] Lindblom, "Science," 74–88.

[68] Thus, Dror advises that "care must be taken to avoid a mistake widespread in practice and sometimes supported by theory, that feasibility becomes a dominant criterion of a preferable alternative." For Diesing, on the other hand, political rationality can never con-flict with other kinds of rationality because the proper functioning of the decision-making structure is a prerequisite for achieving any value at all. Dror, *Ventures,* 83–84. Diesing, *Reason in Society,* 170, 203–4, 228, 231–32.

See George, *Presidential Decisionmaking,* 42. For example, politically biased decision-makers might employ Tetlock's acceptability heuristic, simply adopting "positions likely to gain the favor of those to whom they feel accountable." "Accountability," 310–11.

[70] Israeli Prime Minister Shimon Peres may have been biased in this way. According to the New York *Times,* "In those areas where Mr. Peres . . . had a national consensus already behind him . . . his managerial skills enabled him to score some impressive achievements. But where he did not have a built-in consensus already . . . , he tended to compromise or hesitate and failed to shape any new reality." *New York Times,* Oct. 13, 1986.

[71] Snyder and Diesing, *Conflict Among Nations,* 351. See also George, "Domestic Con-straints," 248. I do not base the distinction between rational and biased political decision-makers on whether or not the outcomes are rational, which would be circular. Rather it is based on the processes they use—in particular how they weight acceptability and utility.

Political bias can also be driven by the personal interests of the decision-maker, a form of value extension in which excessive concern with acceptability is fueled by a preoccupation with personal power.[72] Again this bias manifests itself in a reluctance to make necessary choices[73] or an unwillingness to take needed policy initiatives.[74] Unlike decision-makers subject to motivated bias, however, politically biased decision-makers are not defensive; nor do they avoid thinking about the problem.[75] Rather, they deliberately sacrifice other values to get acceptability, and do not conceal their behavior from themselves. Indeed, they are quite likely to justify their actions in terms of political expediency as "just the way politics is."[76]

By contrast, unbiased decision-makers continue to evaluate on other grounds the alternatives that have satisfied the acceptability constraint, trying to balance utility against acceptability. Given the critical importance of acceptability, moreover, political decision-makers are likely to try to discover which of the acceptable alternatives is best on that dimension as well. Thus, the search for acceptable policies can go beyond the initial screening, influencing evaluation in a number of characteristic ways.

---

[72] Of course, biased behavior can be influenced by both political and personal motives. See Neustadt's discussion of the motivation behind Lyndon Johnson's deceptiveness about the potential costs of the Vietnam War. Neustadt, *Presidential Power* (1990), 210–12. For value extension, see appendix A.

[73] Jacques Delors, the French president of the European Community Commission, was "notably apathetic on GATT questions to avoid being blamed by French farmers for what they are sure to regard as a bad deal. This would damage Mr. Delors thinly disguised French presidential ambitions." *New York Times*, Nov. 11, 1992.

[74] Thus, a supporter of President Bush noted with some puzzlement that in the months after the Persian Gulf War, Bush "was king of the mountain. . . . He could have achieved almost anything. He was so popular that if he had gone to Capitol Hill and battled for it, Congress would not have dared defy him. But he didn't do anything at all." Ibid., Nov. 4, 1992. A reporter explained this inaction in terms of political bias: "From the beginning of his Administration, it was clear that [Mr. Bush] had no ideas or programs he wanted to enact, that his greatest pleasure came from simply being President. After his first hundred days in office, it was clear that he was practicing the politics of minimalism." Ibid., Nov. 5, 1992.

[75] On motivated bias, see appendix A.

[76] Political bias is frequently confused with both motivated and intuitive bias. For example, behavior attributed to psychological stress may often be more accurately explained in terms of political survival. Janis and Mann's analysis of the San Francisco School District's desegregation planning, or lack of planning, in 1970–1971 as defensive avoidance is a case in point. The procrastination and buck-passing of the Board of Education and the top executives in the school system that Janis and Mann attribute to psychological stress can be explained as satisfactorily, and more parsimoniously, in terms of political necessity. Buck-passing was enshrined as a political strategy long before it was ever analyzed as a psychological one. *Decision-Making*, 109–19. This example was suggested by Robert Jervis.

The ultimate goal of political decision-makers is to find a transcendent alternative, one which aims at preserving all the values involved, sacrificing none.[77] Such an alternative maximizes acceptability, serving all the values whether they are judged in terms of their intrinsic worth or the importance of the interests behind them.[78] Translated into the vocabulary of decision-making, the quest for such an alternative involves a search for dominant solutions, or those which are best on all dimensions.[79] Even if a decision-maker must eventually settle for compromise, which many believe to be the hallmark of political decision-making, that is not what he or she seeks initially. Thus, according to former congressman Mickey Edwards, political decision-makers never begin with compromise. Rather, they are inclined to push for every last bit of what they want until they can get no more. Not until they finally "hit that brick wall," do they entertain the idea of compromise.[80]

One way of finding a solution with "multiple payoffs" is to use one of the more demanding noncompensatory strategies such as a sophisticated form of satisficing in which decision-makers assess available alternatives against a fairly high standard of value until they arrive at a "favorite."[81]

[77] George calls this the strategy of "seeking multiple payoffs," as "the individual tries to invent a single policy or option that will yield some satisfaction for all or most of the salient stakes and motivations involved." "Adaptation to Stress," 184–85. For an interesting example of how this motivation works out in practice, see DeRivera's discussion of Truman's 1950 budget decision. Joseph DeRivera, *The Psychological Dimension of Foreign Policy* (Columbus, Ohio: Charles E. Merrill, 1968), 112–13.

[78] Transcendence is sometimes spoken of as a purely psychological mechanism for maintaining inconsistency, while reducing its impact. Herbert C. Kelman and Reuben Baron, "Determinants of Modes of Resolving Inconsistency," in *Theories of Cognitive Consistency*, ed. Robert P. Abelson et al. (Chicago: Rand McNally, 1968), 673–76. See also Robert P. Abelson, "Modes of Resolution of Belief Dilemmas," *Journal of Conflict Resolution* 3 (1959): 343–52. This use differs from both Carnevale and Isen's concept of integrative solutions (see n. 80) and the political strategy discussed here. A genuinely transcendent solution to a value conflict must actually solve the problem. A purely psychological solution is a form of value-conflict avoidance. George, *Presidential Decisionmaking*, 32–34; Tetlock, "Value Pluralism," 820.

[79] Fischhoff suggests that a propensity to search for dominant solutions may occur in decision-making of all types. However, it is particularly likely to characterize political decision-making because the latter is concerned with serving all the values at stake in a decision. See appendix A.

[80] Personal communication. Neustadt makes a similar point in "Presidents, Politics, and Analysis," 20–21. In psychology, transcendent, or "integrative," solutions are specifically contrasted with compromise in which "concessions are made to a middle ground on some obvious dimension. . . . [A] compromise is a solution that only partly satisfies the two parties' interests. . . . The integrative solution gives each more of what she/he wants." Peter J. D. Carnevale and Alice M. Isen, "The Influence of Positive Affect and Visual Access on the Discovery of Integrative Solutions in Bilateral Negotiation," *Organizational Behavior and Human Decision Processes* 37 (1986): 2.

[81] See appendix A. The duration of this process seems likely to depend on time con-

Another is experimenting, which is a characteristic method of evaluating alternatives in a political context, particularly in the face of uncertainty.[82] This is especially true for acceptability: it is often difficult to know what will be acceptable without in some sense trying it out, particularly if a policy's acceptability is in doubt because of uncertainty about its workability.[83]

While the quest for transcendent solutions may lead to quite cognitively demanding strategies,[84] political decision-makers may not be willing to use compensatory strategies even when assessing alternatives they believe to be minimally acceptable.[85] Although they may be forced to trade off if two or more key groups have irreconcilable goals, they will make such sacrifices reluctantly, and usually only after first trying to accommodate all the interests involved.[86] Trading off may at times be necessary, but it is never the first thing political decision-makers are inclined to do[87]—not merely because trade-offs are difficult to justify publicly, but because they may hamper the achievement of effective action.

There is, however, at least one exception. While political decision-makers have a profound respect for terminal values, or ends, they tend to

---

straints, the costs of continued search, and the importance of the issue. George, *Presidential Decisionmaking*, 1–3. For a discussion of sophisticated satisficing see appendix A. See also C. Whan Park, "A Conflict Resolution Choice Model," *Journal of Consumer Research 5* (1978): 124; Payne, "Task Complexity," 367; and Steven M. Shugan, "The Cost of Thinking," *Journal of Consumer Research* 7 (Sept. 1980): 100.

[82] As Voss explains it, "in the political domain, a solution may be proposed and adopted, but it usually is by no means clear that the solution will work. Solutions in the political arena are in fact often more like hypotheses that need to be tested then [*sic*] they are 'real' or 'correct' solutions." James F. Voss, "Finding Another Policy: Problem Representation and Problem Solution," paper presented at the annual meeting of the International Society of Political Psychology, Washington, D.C., July 10, 1990, 10.

[83] See Hilsman, *To Move a Nation*, 548.

[84] As George observes, "Some political leaders are unusually inventive and ingenious. . . . If we examine their behavior more closely, we find that they are committed to an 'optimizing' rather than a 'satisficing' approach to decision making. . . . They like to extract every ounce of value and credit from every decision and action they take, and to minimize all of its possible costs and risks." "Adaptation to Stress," 184.

[85] This accords with Neustadt's observation that political decision-makers will avoid making value trade-offs as long as they can, preferring instead "to resist trade-offs, to dispute them or deny them, to press incompatible objectives until the last moment—if not past it—for concessions from opponents on all sides." "Presidents, Politics, and Analysis," 3–4.

[86] George, *Presidential Decisionmaking*, 1. George sees decision-makers as facing trade-offs not only between quality and acceptability but also between both of these and the factor of time and other policy resources. Ibid., 1–3; *Bridging the Gap*, 22–24.

[87] See, for example, Neustadt's account of the appeal to Congress of the 1985 Gramm-Rudman Act in terms of its promise to ease the pain of necessary trade-offs. Neustadt, "Presidents, Politics, and Analysis," 15.

be pragmatic about instrumental values, or means,[88] possibly because the need for acceptability encourages a willingness to entertain a wide range of approaches.[89] Thus, although they are reluctant to sacrifice ends, flexibility about how to attain them encourages trade-offs involving means.[90]

If no satisfactory alternative has emerged from the search process, political decision-makers can tinker with one to make it so or design a new one.[91] Since their goal is serving a number of values, "blending," or combining elements of several alternatives is likely to be a prominent feature of the design process.[92] In particular, decision-makers may blend the survivors of the initial screening for acceptability in order to incorporate as much of each value as possible.[93]

In preference to designing a new policy, a political decision-maker can try to enhance acceptability by modifying an existing option.[94] The procedures for doing so are largely incorporated into five traditional political strategies: transcendence, calculated procrastination, compromise, se-

[88] Rokeach argues that value systems have two separate, though functionally related, components: terminal values relating to ends and instrumental values relating to means. Rokeach, *Nature*, 7, 12. See also Rokeach, "Some Unresolved Issues," and "Attitudes: The Nature of Attitudes," in Sills, ed., *International Encyclopedia*, 449–58.

[89] According to Freidel, Roosevelt's desire to build the New Deal on as broad a base as possible was an important factor behind his initial receptivity to new ideas, and Cole has remarked of Roosevelt, that he "did not lock into rigid formulas or styles of thinking. He explored a wide range of possibilities without necessarily endorsing or rejecting them." Unfortunately, this disposition can also lead to accusations of inconsistency, even deviousness, as it frequently did in Roosevelt's case. See below, chap. 3, Frank Freidel, *Franklin D. Roosevelt* (Boston: Little Brown, 1956), 3:63–64; Wayne H. Cole, *Roosevelt and the Isolationists, 1932–45* (Lincoln, Neb.: University of Nebraska Press, 1983), 246.

[90] Bardach puts the "capacity to perceive and invent functional substitutes" high on his list of the qualities of the "skillful politician, . . . who is committed only to his ends, not his means." *Skill Factor*, 262.

[91] Experimental evidence shows that decision-makers use both design and manipulation. Mintzberg et al., "Structure of Unstructured Decisions," 255–56; Alexander, "Design," 384; Abelson and Levi, "Decision Making," 273; Allen Newell and Herbert A. Simon, *Human Problem Solving* (Englewood Cliffs, N.J.: Prentice-Hall, 1972).

[92] See appendix A. President Eisenhower's combination of the very diverse recommendations of three task forces on U.S. policy toward Eastern Europe offers an example of blending. By mixing elements of each, Eisenhower replaced the sharply defined alternatives and clear-cut trade-offs of the task force reports with a formulation which served both his substantive concerns and his political needs. According to General Goodpaster, one of the participants, the task forces were not at all happy to see their product thus "mongrelized." "'Project Solarium': a Collective Oral History," transcript of the John Foster Dulles Centennial Conference, Princeton University, Feb. 27, 1988, 13–14.

[93] Abelson and Levi, "Decision Making," 273.

[94] May, "Politics and Policy Analysis," 111–12. See also Hilsman on the techniques of accommodation, "Foreign Policy Consensus," 365–66.

quencing, and minimal decisions.[95] These strategies increase acceptability in at least two ways: by bringing unacceptable decisions into an acceptable range and by broadening the consensus supporting an already acceptable policy through the inclusion of other interests. Each of these strategies can be rational or biased. Rational strategies are marked by recognition and resolution of value conflicts, as well as considerable attention to the substantive concerns at stake in the decision. Biased strategies tend to mask value conflicts and either avoid or resolve spuriously those that are recognized, sacrificing substance to acceptability. This results in spurious transcendence, delay in the face of an urgent need to decide, "disjointed incrementalism," biased compromise, or deciding without choosing.[96]

Biased or not, these strategies are an integral part of the decision-making process. Reflecting the notion that the alternatives are not fixed but malleable, they are used to manipulate the decision in order to make it more acceptable, as opposed to manipulating people with standard political tactics, such as logrolling, to get them to accept the decision. Thus, the decision-maker figures out the limits of acceptability, then tinkers with a preferred alternative until it fits within them. In reality of course, both of these processes are apt to be going on at the same time. Nevertheless, they are logically distinct. Indeed, one reason for using such strategies is to avoid the expenditure of political capital that more overt political tactics entail.

Loosening the Acceptability Constraint: Time-Buying and Education

Taken together, the classical political strategies reflect a reliance on time-buying to sidestep the kind of value trade-offs that reduce acceptability. In the face of value conflict, decision-makers influenced by the nature of the political context often bide their time and rely on the logic of events. If there is nothing to be done at the moment, they are content to wait for things to change in a more favorable direction.[97] They are not anxious to

---

[95] A fuller discussion of these strategies can be found in appendix C.

[96] See appendix C.

[97] New York City Mayor Edward Koch used this strategy in developing a policy toward the homeless. The New York *Times* wrote: "Mayor Koch has again demonstrated his acute sense of popular opinion and political timing. The Mayor has positioned himself at the fore of growing public sentiment to do something. . . . Now, the Mayor said, he is pressing the plan more strongly because the public mood has changed. 'Common sense has taken over the city,' he said. 'The public is in our corner. What I think is what most people think.'" *New York Times*, Dec. 8, 1987. This statement shows the strategy of calculated procrastination as well as the attitude toward timing that underlies it.

foreclose choice prematurely because better, more acceptable, solutions may emerge—solutions that will alienate fewer people.

This resistance to acting until the time is right has long been remarked.[98] Neustadt gives its rationale in explaining the behavior of Ronald Reagan, "a President consistently refusing, time after time, year after year, the trade-offs his own analysts press on him." What Neustadt sees in this behavior is

> an implicit mode of thought about priorities and timing. Beneath these lie commensurate values and notions of risk. To wit: If you have three incompatible objectives—say, tax cuts, defense hikes, and balanced budgets—and you really want them all, *don't* trade them off, hang on. . . . In an uncertain world, some *unexpected* good might come of hanging onto everything you can. . . . Time enough to trade off if and as [advisers'] warnings start to be substantiated without offsetting advantage. But wait upon events; events might break in a more favorable way.[99]

Related to this strategy is a reluctance to plan too far ahead. Thus Roosevelt has been described as showing "more confidence in the logic of events than in close planning in advance."[100] Similarly, Winston Churchill told the House of Commons on returning from Yalta in 1945, "It is a mistake to look too far ahead. . . . Only one link in the chain of destiny can be handled at a time."[101] Such a disposition does not necessarily indicate a lack of long-range goals, but rather a desire to be flexible about when and how to attain them.[102]

Buying time may afford an opportunity to increase people's receptivity to measures decision-makers want to adopt.[103] Not only do political

---

[98] Machiavelli, for one, advised that "the man who adapts his course of action to the nature of the times will succeed and, likewise, . . . the man who sets his course of action out of tune with the times will come to grief." Machiavelli, "The Prince," and "The Discourses on Livy," in *Portable Machiavelli*, ed. Bandanella and Musa, 160, 344–45.

[99] Neustadt, "Presidents, Politics, and Analysis," 20–21. Franklin Roosevelt once told his wife that she would "never be a good politician" because she was "too impatient." It was necessary to wait until people were ready to support changes, otherwise they would revolt. Cited in Freidel, *Franklin D. Roosevelt*, 4:500.

[100] Cited in Kent Roberts Greenfield, *American Strategy in World War II: A Reconsideration* (Baltimore: Johns Hopkins University Press, 1963), 77.

[101] Cited in Kenneth S. Davis, *FDR* (New York: Random House, 1971), 1:411n.

[102] For such goals, evaluation may be stretched out over a considerable period of time. George's account of the development of Roosevelt's Grand Design for the postwar international order offers a particularly good example of how this works. "Domestic Constraints," 245ff.

[103] In criticizing President Bush for inadequate support of Russian democracy, Richard Nixon argued that "the mark of great political leadership is not simply to support what is popular, but to make what is unpopular popular." *New York Times*, March 10, 1992.

decision-makers view the alternatives as manipulable, they also see people's preferences as malleable. Thus, although highly sensitive to the constraints, they sometimes try to alter them, deciding on a policy first and then creating support for it.[104] Over the long term, political decision-makers can use the time gained with the traditional political strategies not only to avoid unacceptable trade-offs but also, as Roosevelt did in years before America's entry into World War II, to increase consensus by actually changing what people find acceptable—in other words, by engaging in what many believe is one of the most important functions of political leadership: teaching.[105]

Many political leaders recognize that one of their primary responsibilities is to educate.[106] While they may sometimes be willing (or forced) to confront tough issues for which support is lacking, they rarely do so without a concomitant effort to show the public why a painful trade-off may be necessary and thus make it more acceptable, so that even if such a trade-off cannot be avoided, at least a bruising political battle can be. As Neustadt explains it: "If the voters understand what they must bear and why, they may accept it with a better grace and beat less *on* [the president]."[107] So fundamental is the understanding in the political context of the need to use the time gained with the classical political strategies to educate that the absence of such an effort is probably a good indication of bias. The rational political decision-maker takes advantage of the time gained by delay, sequencing, minimal decisions,

---

[104] Dror argues that "any political feasibility estimate, however carefully derived and however correct at its time, must . . . be regarded as provisional, sometimes to be taken up as a challenge rather than accepted as an absolute constraint." *Ventures*, 92.

[105] Edward Bennett contrasts Roosevelt's attitude toward the need to educate the public to the dangers of the international situation before World War II with that of his secretary of state, Cordell Hull: "The secretary was aware of the possibility, and even the probability, of a developing world war and its accompanying threat to American security, but he balked at any move to prepare for it publicly because public opinion terrified him." *Search for Security*, 104.

[106] Arthur Schlesinger, Jr., for example, describes New York governor Al Smith as one who "knew that reform would not endure except on the basis of popular understanding. His programs succeeded in the end because he saw politics as an educational process." *The Age of Roosevelt* (Boston: Houghton Mifflin, 1957), 1:98. See also Frances Perkins's account of Roosevelt's advice on gaining Senate approval of the International Labor Organization treaty, *The Roosevelt I Knew* (New York: Viking Press, 1946), 340–41. By contrast, Bush administration speech writer Peggy Noonan faulted the president for his failure to understand his obligation to take on the role of educator: "He stopped seeing the connection between words and action. He did not communicate. . . . But the public part of the Presidency, the persuading-in-the-pulpit part, is central to leadership." *New York Times*, Dec. 15, 1992.

[107] Neustadt, *Presidents, Politics, and Analysis*, 24–25.

and compromise to enlarge the domain of acceptability, while biased decision-makers, having used these strategies to attain some minimum level of agreement, let the substantive issue slide.

Apart from a long-term education campaign to extend the range of acceptability, decision-makers may also need to create short-term support. This is likely to occur when the issue is important and time pressure considerable.[108] Such attempts to sell policies to the voters should be distinguished from a genuine educational effort:[109] selling involves manipulating preferences in the short run, while education strives for a long-term change in values.[110]

The extensive literature on the processes and prospects of selling decisions lacking in support suggests that while political leaders have some latitude, they are limited in a number of ways.[111] However much decision-makers may wish to extend the domain of acceptability, it is not always possible to loosen the constraints—witness Roosevelt's answer to criticism that he had not moved ahead with legislation his progressive supporters desired:

> I think the impression was that Lincoln was a sad man . . . because he could not do all he wanted to do at one time, and I think you will find examples where Lincoln had to compromise to gain a little something. . . . If you ever

[108] The controversy over the American commitment to send troops to Bosnia may be an example of such an issue. According to the New York *Times*, the chairman of the Joint Chiefs of Staff, General John M. Shalikashvili, "reaffirmed Washington's commitment, . . . but acknowledged that the Administration lacks public support to do so," warning that it "still had 'an awful lot of explaining to do.' . . . 'I don't think the American public today is sold on that. . . . But if the American public understands what the alternative is, and what the cost is of not helping to bring this war to the end, I think they'll support it.'" In discussing the number of troops that might be needed, however, the general took pains to distinguish his own role as a military decision-maker from the president's as a political one: "'I am responsible for recommending the number that I think will do the job, not the one that is politically salable.'" March 10, 1994.

[109] Stanley A. Renshon, "Character, Judgment, and Political Leadership," in *The Clinton Presidency*, ed. Stanley A. Renshon (Boulder, Colo.: Westview Press, 1995), 80–81.

[110] The behavior of the French government in 1992 over the issue of trade policy in the face of bitter opposition by French farmers is an example of the former. The New York *Times* reported that, "France appears to have begun a public relations effort that could amount to a preparation for an eventual concession. . . . If a GATT accord can be shown to be no more harmful to farmers than what has already been undertaken in the reform, then it may be politically salable." Nov. 11, 1992.

[111] Thus Rieselbach concludes that "the president . . . can help to shape the broad limits which constrain his policy choices. Within these limits, he has a good deal of latitude. . . . But even here, he cannot go his own way." Leroy N. Rieselbach, *The Roots of Isolationism* (New York: Bobbs-Merrill, 1966), 184, 193.

sit here, you will learn that you cannot, just by shouting from the housetops, get what you want all the time.[112]

Thus, awareness of the need for acceptability tends to promote acceptance of limited aims. While this quality is the hallmark of incrementalism, all the traditional political strategies reflect the recognition that it is not usually possible to have it all—or at least not all at once. Because a decision must be acceptable, sweeping changes are feasible only under conditions that are relatively rare.

Roosevelt expressed this sense of limits in a fireside chat in 1938. While claiming that his job was to try to understand everyone's deepest problems and needs, he offered a qualification about what could be accomplished: "I always try to remember that reconciling differences cannot satisfy everyone completely. Because I do not expect too much, I am not disappointed."[113] Jimmy Carter, on the other hand, was often disappointed precisely because he expected to get everything. Not only did he thus put satisfaction beyond his reach, but also, by assessing outcomes according to a standard of perfection that turned success into failure, damaged his reputation and thereby his effectiveness.[114]

CHOICE AND OUTCOMES

Deriving from its unavoidable concern with acceptability, the decision rule of a political approach to decision-making enjoins the decision-maker to "enhance acceptability." Thus, a political decision-maker is likely to choose the alternative that satisfies the greatest number of values. It will be at least minimally acceptable and at most genuinely transcendent, and value conflicts will have been recognized and resolved.[115] If the process has been unbiased, the decision will strike a bal-

---

[112] Cited in Joseph P. Lash, *Roosevelt and Churchill, 1939–1941: The Partnership That Saved the West* (New York: W. W. Norton, 1976), 124. This statement also shows the political decision-maker's less than enthusiastic attitude toward compromise.

[113] "Fireside Chat on Economic Conditions," *PPA* (1938), 7:247–48.

[114] William B. Quandt, *Camp David: Peacemaking and Politics* (Washington, D.C.: Brookings Institution, 1986), 336–38.

[115] Following George, I label the outcomes of decisions characterized by value conflict "resolution," "acceptance," and "avoidance." However, while he uses resolution and avoidance for psychological as well as genuine solutions to value conflict, here those terms refer only to the way decision-makers actually treat the conflict. This allows me to put all the rational solutions under the heading of either resolution or acceptance and to define all the irrational forms (even "psychologically comforting" ones) as avoidance. George, *Presidential Decisionmaking*, 28–29.

ance between acceptability and substantive concerns. If it has been biased, acceptability will have been overweighted at the expense of utility. In foreign policy, this approach produces outcomes that are the result of neither international nor domestic pressures alone, but of the decision-maker's subjective adjustment of the claims of both realms.

Because of the pervasive concern with acceptability, however, even in its rational form the outcome of a political approach to decision-making is likely to differ from the product of a pure optimizing strategy in several ways. It may exhibit fewer sharp trade-offs between important values, since political decision-makers will often search past alternatives involving such trade-offs to find one with greater acceptability. Moreover, political decision-makers may choose an acceptable alternative even if it has a lower expected value in terms of substantive values than one that was bypassed.

Also reflecting the desire to increase acceptability, the outcome of a political approach to decision-making may include additional values and interests not initially implicated in the decision.[116] Thus, one may find foreign-policy decisions in which domestic interests have been included for little reason other than to increase support.[117] Moreover, decisions may be stretched out in order to make them more acceptable, as in sequencing. Finally, one may expect to see policies reflecting a certain amount of risk-taking to increase acceptability. For example, a political decision-maker might choose a policy that was less certain of success on the international dimension but satisfied political constraints over one that was more likely to work internationally but less acceptable domestically. Such choices may be encouraged by the tendency to discount long-range consequences more heavily than those likely to be felt in the short run, since gains and losses in domestic politics may be more immediate than those in the international arena.[118]

Our analysis establishes, then, that the political approach to decision-making shares the defining qualities of the traditional approaches discussed earlier. Acceptability is an unavoidable concern affecting every stage of decision-making, leading to a number of characteristic decision-making processes and resulting in a distinctive outcome. In order to es-

---

[116] Hilsman explains how this is done: "Getting a wide variety of people who hold different values to sit down and decide on how to rank those values would be next to impossible; but getting people to agree on a particular policy that serves a mix of values is done all the time. One group accepts a policy because it serves one value, and another group accepts the policy because it also serves another, quite different value." Hilsman, "Foreign Policy Consensus," 363–64.

[117] David Epstein has suggested the term "bundling" for this practice.

[118] Robert Jervis, "Domino Beliefs and Strategic Behavior," in *Dominoes and Bandwagons*, ed. Robert Jervis and Jack Snyder (New York: Oxford University Press, 1991), 4.

tablish its plausibility, however, the political approach must at minimum compete successfully with these other approaches in explaining an actual case. Roosevelt's decision-making at the time of the Munich crisis offers such a case.

Part Two

ROOSEVELT AND THE MUNICH CRISIS

THE YEAR Franklin Delano Roosevelt assumed the presidency, 1933, was also the year Adolf Hitler came to power in Germany. Consequently, despite his desire to concentrate on pressing domestic problems, Roosevelt was forced to devote increasing attention to European developments. The following chapters trace the evolution of his thinking as he struggled to interpret the behavior of the dictators and shape American policy toward them from 1936 to 1938, and during the Munich crisis and its aftermath.

The period from 1936 to 1938, which A.J.P. Taylor has called the "watershed between two wars," marks a critical stage in Roosevelt's transition from a domestic to an international focus and is essential for understanding his subsequent decision-making.[1] Revealing his initial uncertainty about how to evaluate and deal with the international situation, these years throw Roosevelt's postcrisis resolve into high relief and establish Munich as a turning point in his prewar foreign policy. Moreover, because Roosevelt later returned to many of the ideas he developed then, they also show us the antecedents of his post-Munich policies.

Equally important is the crisis itself, which was a genuine learning experience, providing the information that enabled Roosevelt to form a settled judgment about Hitler's challenge to the United States, in sharp contrast to his previous uncertainty. The full impact of the crisis, however, began to be felt only in its aftermath as Roosevelt assimilated its lessons and concluded that Germany would ultimately threaten American security. Set against his perception of the domestic climate of opinion, this diagnosis exposed a serious value conflict between the foreign-policy imperative of protecting American security and the domestic

---

[1] "Post-war ended when Germany reoccupied the Rhineland on 7 March 1936; pre-war began when she annexed Austria on 13 March 1938. From that moment, change and upheaval went on almost without interruption until the representatives of the Powers, victorious in the second World War, met at Potsdam in July 1945." A.J.P. Taylor, *Origins of the Second World War* (New York: Atheneum, 1962), 131. For a comprehensive review of the foreign policies and military strategies of the European powers during this period, see Williamson Murray, *The Change in the European Balance of Power, 1938–1939* (Princeton: Princeton University Press, 1984), chaps. 1–4.

demand to avoid war that Roosevelt chose to resolve aiding the European democracies.

A comparison of Roosevelt's behavior during these years with the predictions of the four decision-making approaches (analytical, intuitive, motivational, and political) shows that his approach was essentially political, reflecting a desire to act, flexibility about means, and above all a pervasive concern with acceptability. Roosevelt thus experimented in the face of uncertainty from 1936 to 1938, diagnosed a security threat largely on the basis of Hitler's disdain for the processes of accommodation that signal limited aims and the desire to settle disputes peacefully, and chose the policy of aiding the democracies, even though it apparently did not maximize utility as well as another, such as rearmament, might have done.

Our analysis also shows that this behavior cannot be explained by pointing to forces outside Roosevelt's control. Contrary to much of the common wisdom, his decisions were not driven solely by the imperatives of domestic politics, nor were they exclusively the product of a "Realist" appraisal of the dangers of the international situation. Rather, throughout, they reflected a political decision-maker's effort to achieve effective action by balancing competing domestic and international values.

CHAPTER III

The "Watershed" between Two Wars: 1936–1938

MOST ANALYSTS agree that Roosevelt worried about the international situation and wished to have a positive influence on it well before Munich. When it comes to explaining his policies, however, this consensus breaks down, with some contending that he understood the proper course but failed to act for fear of the domestic political repercussions,[1] and others arguing that he was merely drifting.[2] A review of the historical evidence calls both assumptions into question.

To be sure, concern for his domestic program led Roosevelt to exercise caution in the international sphere, but before the Munich crisis the gap between what he felt he could do politically and what he wished to do was never very large. Uncertainty about what would work and doubts about British policy were at least as important in his hesitation as domestic political considerations.[3] Nor can his behavior be labeled drifting. Rather, his uncertainty led to the experimenting that was the main source of the apparent contradictions in his policies.

At the beginning of his administration, Roosevelt formulated two foreign-policy goals: "How to slow down the world drift to war" and how to avoid American involvement if war occurred nevertheless. The difficulty was that these objectives, though consistent in principle, led to policies that were seemingly incompatible: while "international coopera-

---

[1] See Burns, *Lion*, 262, and Francis L. Loewenheim, "An Illusion That Shaped History: New Light on the History and Historiography of American Peace Efforts Before Munich," in Beaver, *Some Pathways*, 214–19. Some historians go further and suggest that in this period Roosevelt was at heart an isolationist See Divine, *Roosevelt and World War II*, 7–10; and William L. Langer and Everett S. Gleason, *The Challenge to Isolation, 1937–1940* (New York: Harper and Brothers, 1952), 16. The weight of the evidence, however, especially since the publication of the Nixon volumes, suggests otherwise. See *Franklin D. Roosevelt and Foreign Affairs*, vols. 1–3, ed. Edgar B. Nixon (Cambridge, Mass.: The Belknap Press of Harvard University Press, 1969); Arthur Schlesinger, Jr., "Franklin D. Roosevelt and Foreign Affairs," *The New York Times Book Review*, July 6, 1969; and Dallek, *Franklin D. Roosevelt*, 28–29, 68–69, 114, 136.

[2] See Bennett, *Search for Security*, 192.

[3] For a similar view, see Heinrichs, *Threshold*, 7–8. See also John Lewis Gaddis, *Russia, the Soviet Union, and the United States: An Interpretive History* (New York: John Wiley and Sons, 1978), 137.

tion . . . offered means of stopping war . . . , neutrality offered means of staying out of it."[4]

By 1936, spurred by the deteriorating international situation, Roosevelt had largely settled on the first path. Fresh uncertainties produced new puzzles, however, in particular how to assess the character and potential for cooperation of the dictator states. Would their demands for the adjustment of current international arrangements ultimately prove reasonable? Could they be persuaded to pursue them peacefully? Would it, in other words, be possible to bring them into the international community? Lacking answers to these questions, Roosevelt had difficulty deciding whether the drift toward war could best be slowed by engaging the dictators in schemes for disarmament and economic cooperation or by promoting sanctions to deter them from aggression.

Interestingly enough, uncertainty led Roosevelt not to inaction, as might have been expected, but to experimentation, and between 1936 and 1938 his ambivalence about German intentions was reflected in his pursuit of sometimes contradictory schemes to influence international developments. Just as his hopes were embodied in his peace moves, his doubts were expressed in a flirtation with isolating the aggressors through some kind of collective action. Even the German takeover of Austria did not lead him to a firm conclusion about the international situation. Throughout 1938, Roosevelt's reservations about appeasement were accompanied by the hope that a peaceful way of dealing with the dictators might yet be found. Indeed, though by the spring of 1938 he had come to believe that Germany had the ability to harm the United States, not until the Munich crisis ended his uncertainty about Hitler's intentions could he finally settle on a policy.[5]

SETTING THE SCENE: ROOSEVELT'S APPROACH TO INTERNATIONAL POLITICS, 1933–1935

Rather than pursuing the literal isolation of the United States, isolationists advocated distancing America as much as possible from the conflicts of others, a view that commanded a level of support far beyond the num-

---

[4] Schlesinger, "Franklin D. Roosevelt." On Roosevelt's internationalism, see also William Leuchtenberg, *Franklin Roosevelt and the New Deal* (New York: Harper and Row, 1963), 210–11; Dallek, *Franklin D. Roosevelt*, 78; Cole, *Roosevelt*, 6–7; and Selig Adler, *The Uncertain Giant* (London: Collier Books, 1965), 232, 242. Secretary of State Hull also described these goals as America's twin objectives. "Address Delivered by the Secretary of State at Ann Arbor, Michigan, June 17, 1935," United States Department of State, *Peace and War: United States Foreign Policy, 1931–1941* (Washington, D.C.: U.S. Government Printing Office, 1943), 258–65. See also Schlesinger, *Age of Roosevelt*, 1:192.

[5] Gaddis, *Russia*, 137.

ber of their nominal adherents.[6] Indeed, on the need to stay out of war the isolationists were joined by the president of the United States himself. The critical difference between Roosevelt and the isolationists was about how to achieve that objective.

Isolationists put their faith in unilateralism, the notion that "political commitments tying American policy to the policies of other nations were unnecessary and dangerous."[7] Most also favored appeasement in Europe as a way of avoiding war,[8] believing that European conflicts merely reflected a traditional sort of jockeying for power and lacked moral substance, and that the United States could do no more to solve European problems in the 1930s than it could have after World War I.[9] American involvement being useless as a practical matter, and morally irrelevant as well, appeasement seemed an appropriate way for Europeans to work out their differences.

As to American security, most isolationists believed in the impregnability of the Western Hemisphere, differing only on whether adequate defense required any additional effort. Some were complacent about the protection afforded by geography and unconcerned about modern technology's potential to breach the barrier of distance. Others felt that natural advantages should be supplemented with sizable defense expenditures. In either case, the question of defense spending posed something of a dilemma because, while building up the armed forces looked like "a step toward war," even isolationists who believed that America was protected by geography were aware of "the desirable deterrent effects of a powerful military establishment." Thus, they were not always opposed to strengthening the military, and Congressional isolationists even found it possible to vote almost simultaneously for both defense and neutrality.[10] Moreover, although isolationists agreed among themselves that

---

[6] American isolationism in the 1930s was directed primarily at political rather than economic or social issues, and consequently much of the business of foreign relations remained beyond its scope. Manfred Jonas, *Isolationism in America* (Ithaca, N.Y.: Cornell University Press, 1966), 4. See also Cole, *Roosevelt*, 6–7. Arthur M. Schlesinger, Jr., "Franklin D. Roosevelt's Internationalism," in *FDR and His Contemporaries*, ed. Cornelius A. Van Minnen and John F. Sears (New York: St. Martin's Press, 1992), 8. Other treatments of isolationism in America can be found in Selig Adler, *The Isolationist Impulse: Its Twentieth-Century Reaction* (New York: Abelard-Schuman, 1961); Divine, *Reluctant Belligerent*; and Betty Glad, *Key Pittman: The Tragedy of a Senate Insider* (New York: Columbia University Press, 1986).

[7] Jonas, *Isolationism*, 5–6, 15–16, 23. See also Cole, *Roosevelt*, 7. Isolationists did, however, differ about specific policies, on the basis of which Jonas identifies five different types of isolationists. *Isolationism*, 32–69. On diversity within the isolationist camp in other respects, see ibid., 17–22; Cole, *Roosevelt*, 6, 8, 128–29; and Divine, *Reluctant Belligerent*, 7–8.

[8] Jonas, *Isolationism*, 109.

[9] Ibid., 111, 120–21.

[10] Ibid, 121–33; Cole, *Roosevelt*, 7.

America should remain neutral in the event of war, they differed substantially about what that meant.[11] This did not prevent them from supporting the Neutrality Act of 1935, however, because their mutual suspicion of Roosevelt's intentions united them in desiring to limit executive discretion in foreign policy.[12]

But what in fact were those intentions? During the early years of his presidency, Roosevelt frequently voiced the conviction that America must remain at peace, and initially he believed that this meant distancing it from European political problems.[13] Thus, after the collapse of the Geneva Disarmament Conference, he concluded that such problems had "temporarily ruled out success in the disarmament talks and that attempts to involve the United States in European political conversations should be consistently turned aside,"[14] somewhat redundantly declaring "I think we should stay out of relations relating to European peace."[15]

This statement by no means reflected the whole of Roosevelt's thinking about America's proper role in world affairs, however. In particular, he was very much alive to the potential danger posed by the European dicta-

[11] "Belligerent isolationists," such as Senators Hiram Johnson and William E. Borah and theoreticians John Bassett Moore and E. M. Borchard stressed the importance of defending traditional neutral rights in the areas of trade and travel. "Timid isolationists," like Senators Gerald P. Nye, Bennett Champ Clark, and Arthur H. Vandenberg, were willing to give up these traditional rights in order to avoid incidents that might provoke American public opinion and perhaps draw the nation into conflict. The movement to legislate neutrality found its greatest support within this latter group. Glad, *Key Pittman*, 272; John C. Donovan, "Congressional Isolationists and the Roosevelt Foreign Policy," in Divine, *Causes and Consequences*, 72. The terms originate with Jonas, *Isolationism*, 34–35.

[12] Divine, *Reluctant Belligerent*, 21; Glad, *Key Pittman*, 236–37; Donovan, "Congressional Isolationists," 73. As Cole has observed, "By the latter part of the 1930s . . . Nye and many other isolationists began to view the president as a force for war quite as dangerous as munitions makers and international bankers." *Roosevelt*, 142. For a highly political expression of this point of view see Joe Martin, *My First Fifty Years in Politics* (New York: McGraw-Hill, 1960), 90. For background on the Nye Committee, see Wayne S. Cole, *Senator Gerald P. Nye and American Foreign Policy* (Minneapolis: University of Minnesota Press, 1962). On the origins of the Neutrality Acts, see Glad, *Key Pittman* 231–37, and Divine, *Reluctant Belligerent*, 18–22.

[13] Cole, *Roosevelt*, 5. This account of Roosevelt's foreign-policy attitudes begins with the first year of his presidency. To summarize the period before that, his defense of the League of Nations as a vice-presidential candidate was tempered in the 1920s and early 1930s by his recognition of strong antiwar sentiment in America. This trend culminated in his disavowal of the League of Nations in the 1932 election campaign in the hope of capturing the support of William Randolph Hearst. For a discussion of Roosevelt's foreign-policy beliefs prior to 1933, see Dallek, *Franklin D. Roosevelt*, 9–18; Divine, *Roosevelt and World War II*, 49–53, and Freidel, *Franklin D. Roosevelt* 4:102–6, 122–23, 365, 390.

[14] Dallek, *Franklin D. Roosevelt*, 69. On Roosevelt's policies toward the Geneva Disarmament Conference, see ibid., 66–71.

[15] Quoted in Roland N. Stromberg, *Collective Security and American Foreign Policy: From the League of Nations to NATO* (New York: Frederick A. Praeger, 1963), 90.

tors, especially Hitler, telling French Ambassador Paul Claudel in March 1933: "Hitler is a madman and his counselors, some of whom I personally know, are even madder than he is," and writing to Ramsay MacDonald in August, "I am concerned by events in Germany for I feel that an insane rush to further armaments in Continental Europe is infinitely more dangerous than any number of squabbles over gold or stabilization of tariffs."[16]

Roosevelt wanted to do something about this dangerous trend but, unlike the isolationists, he believed that the best way to avoid participating in the next war was to work actively to prevent it. Moreover, he disagreed about the virtues of unilateralism, favoring cooperation wherever it would advance the cause of peace, not only in Europe, but also in Latin America. Thus he abandoned the isolationist policy of unilateral defense of the hemisphere and sought to accomplish his goal at least partly through the policy of the Good Neighbor.[17] These differences with the isolationists are captured by Roosevelt's remarks to Colonel House about the Nye Committee in September 1935. The problem, he wrote, with

> some of the Congressmen and Senators who are suggesting wild-eyed measures to keep us out of war . . . is that they belong to the very large and perhaps increasing school of thought which holds that we can and should withdraw wholly within ourselves and cut off all but the most perfunctory relationships with other nations. They imagine that if the civilization of Europe is about to destroy itself through internal strife, it might just as well go ahead and do it and that the United States can stand idly by.[18]

The president did not agree.

[16] Davis, FDR, 3:125. Roosevelt to MacDonald, Aug. 30, 1933, FRUS, 1933, 1:210. Also quoted in part in Schlesinger, "Franklin D. Roosevelt." See also William E. Kinsella, Leadership in Isolation: F.D.R. and the Origins of the Second World War (Boston: G. K. Hall, 1978), 33; and Arnold A. Offner, American Appeasement: United States Foreign Policy and Germany, 1933–1938 (New York: W. W. Norton, 1969), 166–67, 172–73. Roosevelt's attitude toward Mussolini was initially much less pessimistic. Kinsella, Leadership, 52; Dallek, Franklin D. Roosevelt, 91. Other examples of Roosevelt's feelings of unease about European developments can be found in PL: Roosevelt to House, Apr. 10, 1935, 3:472–73; Roosevelt to Dodd, Apr. 16, 1935, 3:475; Aug. 14, 1935, 3:501; Dec. 2, 1935, 3:530–31.

[17] Tracy Kittredge, "United States Defense Policies and Global Strategy," unpubl. ms., Modern Military History Branch, National Archives, Record Group 218, chap. 6; Dallek, Franklin D. Roosevelt, 38–39, 87.

[18] Roosevelt to House, Sept. 17, 1935, PL 3:506–7. Former Secretary of State Henry L. Stimson's opinion that from the beginning "Mr. Roosevelt's basic view of foreign affairs [was] the same as his own" also suggests the degree to which Roosevelt's attitudes differed from those of the isolationists. Henry L. Stimson and McGeorge Bundy, On Active Service in Peace and War (New York: Harper and Brothers, 1948), 297–98.

Although Roosevelt's beliefs about what the United States could and should do internationally differed significantly from those of the isolationists, for reasons of both domestic and foreign policy his activity before 1936 was rather limited. The critical importance of some domestic objectives meant not only that he frequently found it necessary to balance international against domestic goals, but also that the latter sometimes took precedence, as shown by his willingness to abandon the London Economic Conference in 1933. On these occasions, emphasizing domestic needs was Roosevelt's own preference. He gave them priority not because he was forced to do so by one or another political-interest group, but because he himself found them more pressing than international problems.[19] At other times, political interests dominated because Roosevelt wanted to avoid alienating those whose support he needed to carry out his domestic program.[20] However, in both his successful effort to obtain recognition of the Soviet Union and his unsuccessful attempt to gain American adherence to the World Court, he showed his willingness to buck domestic opposition on foreign-policy issues where he judged effective action possible.[21]

In addition to domestic pressures, Roosevelt felt limited in his ability to act by the international environment. Though painfully aware of the dangerous drift of events, he was at a loss as to how to improve the situation, writing to Ambassador to Germany Thomas Dodd in April 1935 that he felt "very helpless to render any particular service to immediate or permanent peace at this time."[22] Not only was the proper course of action

---

[19] Robert H. Ferrell, *American Diplomacy*, (New York: W. W. Norton, 1975), 541. As late as the spring of 1935, Roosevelt, while repeating to Senator Tom Connally "his deep desire to further the international policy of Wilson to bring nations together and end the threat of wars," argued that "the time isn't ripe yet. . . . We can't go out with a broomstick to exercise moral leadership among the nations of the world. We have to get our own economic house in order before we can do anything in the foreign field." Tom Connally, *My Name is Tom Connally* (New York: Thomas Y. Crowell, 1954), 218. This statement differs from the typical isolationist view that solving domestic problems was an *alternative* to activity in world affairs.

[20] Ferrell, *American Diplomacy*, 548. In this connection Cole cites Roosevelt's stand in 1933 and 1934 on the Johnson Act, which dealt with the issue of loans to states that had defaulted on war debts. *Roosevelt*, 92–93.

[21] Bennett, *Search for Security*, and Dallek, *Franklin D. Roosevelt*, 78–81, describe the effort to recognize the Soviet Union. Cole, *Roosevelt*, 120–25, discusses the World Court fight.

[22] *PL*, 3:475. Roosevelt was feeling no less uncertain as the year drew to a close, writing Lincoln MacVeagh, "Things move so fast that no one can tell what will be the story a month from now. Meanwhile, as you know, we are really keeping our skirts pretty clear of any involvement." "Roosevelt to Lincoln MacVeagh, Minister to Greece, Athens," Nov. 2, 1935, *PL*, 3:52. See also "Roosevelt to John Cudahy, Ambassador to Poland, Warsaw," Oct. 28, 1935, ibid., 37.

unclear, but Roosevelt also found it difficult to see how, given British and French tendencies toward appeasement, he could act effectively even if he had known what to do. Thus, he wrote to Colonel House in April 1935 that he had thought about several "methods by which the weight of America could be thrown into the scale of peace and of stopping the armament race," but had rejected each because he feared that "any suggestion on our part would meet with the same kind of chilly, half-contemptuous reception on the other side as an appeal would have met in July or August, 1914."[23]

The tension between Roosevelt's worries about the international situation and his awareness of the obstacles to effective action shaped his attitudes toward specific policies. From 1933 to 1935, he seemed, like Hull, to believe that pursuing the traditionally acceptable goals of free trade and disarmament offered the United States the best chance to participate in world affairs and possibly move them in a peaceful direction.[24] Although he first saw disarmament in terms of "a multilateral pact of non-aggression" and universal self-restraint,[25] he increasingly sought to involve the United States in the peace efforts of others.[26] In fact, by March 1935 Roosevelt was advocating the blockade as a sanction for disarmament that he could safely support.[27] Moreover, he quickly pro-

[23] Ibid., 3:472. See also James R. Leutze, *Bargaining for Supremacy: Anglo-American Naval Collaboration, 1937–1941* (Chapel Hill, N.C.: University of North Carolina Press, 1977), 5; Kinsella, *Leadership*, 59; and Cole, *Roosevelt*, 332. For Roosevelt's reservations about the British in particular, see his letter to the Ambassador to Britain, Robert Bingham, in 1935. Quoted in Gloria J. Barron, *Leadership in Crisis: FDR and the Path to Intervention* (Port Washington, N.Y.: Kennikat Press, 1973), 43. See also Reynolds, *Creation*, 24–25.

[24] Thus, despite the apparently unilateralist complexion of his withdrawal of support from the London Economic Conference in 1933, in 1934 Roosevelt stood behind Hull's effort to gain legislation promoting tariff reciprocity as a means of reducing tariff barriers worldwide. Ferrell, *American Diplomacy*, 543. For Roosevelt's views on economic nationalism and internationalism leading up to and including the London Economic Conference, see Schlesinger, *Age of Roosevelt*, 2: chaps. 11–13.

[25] Stromberg, *Collective Security*, 90.

[26] Thus, in 1933, Roosevelt had Norman Davis present a plan to the Geneva Disarmament Conference whereby the United States would consult with others in the event of a threat to peace and, upon a determination of aggression, "refrain from any action tending to defeat a collective effort to punish a state the United States and other nations saw as an aggressor," including supplying the aggressor with arms. Dallek, *Franklin D. Roosevelt*, 43–47; Divine, *Illusion*, 48, 50–51; Davis, *FDR*, 3:127. After the Disarmament Conference ended in disappointment in October 1933, although he rejected "attempts to involve the United States in European political conversations," Roosevelt continued to promote various disarmament schemes. Dallek, *Franklin D. Roosevelt*, 69; Schlesinger, "Franklin D. Roosevelt."

[27] As Roosevelt explained the idea to Secretary of the Treasury Henry Morgenthau, "England, France, Italy, Belgium, Holland, Poland and possibly Russia should get together

gressed to the idea of using it as part of "some form of joint military and naval action against Germany," writing in April 1935 to Colonel House:

> if France, Italy, England and the "Little Entente" decide on positive action they would be far wiser not to invade Germany but rather to establish a complete blockade of Germany. . . . If we found it was an effective blockade, . . . recognition of the blockade by us would obviously follow. This, after all, is not a boycott nor an economic sanction, but in effect it is the same thing. A boycott or sanction could not be recognized by us without Congressional action but a blockade would fall under the Executive's power after establishment of the fact.[28]

While nothing came of this idea in 1935, owing both to the failure of the European powers to take it up and growing support for neutrality in the United States,[29] the blockade notion featured many elements that were particularly congenial to Roosevelt (the idea of containing an enemy with naval forces alone, avoiding ground warfare, bypassing Congress, and the possibility of domestic acceptability among them) and he returned to it regularly in the coming years, even advocating it as a strategy for the Allies after the outbreak of World War II in September 1939.[30] In 1935, however, his disarmament schemes having all fared badly, he saw little choice but to turn to neutrality.[31]

Although Roosevelt was not opposed to neutrality legislation per se, he very much wanted executive discretion in applying it.[32] Thus, when Con-

---

and agree on a ten-year disarmament program. . . . These countries would sign this pact themselves and would then approach Germany and ask her to sign. If she refused, these countries would then establish a two-way blockade around Germany, not permitting anything at all to enter or leave Germany. . . . *We would send an Admiral abroad who would assist in seeing that our ships did not run through this blockade.*" Cited in Dallek, *Franklin D. Roosevelt*, 102–3, emphasis added. See also Kinsella, *Leadership*, 43. Even earlier, in October 1934, Roosevelt had privately proposed an "international boycott of all trade with Germany, comparing it to a "boycott without war." Richard A. Harrison, "The United States and Great Britain: Presidential Diplomacy and Alternatives to Appeasement in the 1930s," *Appeasement in Europe*, ed. David F. Schmitz and Richard D. Challener (Westport, Conn.: Greenwood Press, 1990), 119.

[28] Roosevelt to House, Apr. 10, 1935, *PL*, 3:472–73. See also Leuchtenberg, *Franklin D. Roosevelt*, 210–11.

[29] Dallek, *Franklin D. Roosevelt*, 103, and Kinsella, *Leadership*, 43.

[30] Reynolds, *Creation*, 64–65. Note that in 1935 Roosevelt suggested only that the United States respect such a blockade. He was not at that time suggesting active American participation.

[31] Schlesinger, "Franklin D. Roosevelt."

[32] Roosevelt's somewhat complicated feelings about the Neutrality Act of 1935 were revealed in a letter to Ambassador Dodd in December: "If you had been here I do not think that you would have felt the Senate Bill last August was an unmitigated disaster. The crux of the matter lies in the deep question of allowing some discretion to the Chief Executive. . . . I hope that next January I can get an even stronger law, leaving, however, some

gressional sentiment veered toward a strict and impartial embargo on the sale of arms to all participants in the event of war, he tried to block it. Failing that, he accepted the proposed legislation, albeit with reservations.[33] If his ambivalence about the neutrality legislation suggested some inclination to soft-pedal his advocacy of American involvement in world affairs, however, the hiatus was only temporary. During the coming year, as the international situation continued to deteriorate, Roosevelt felt increasingly called upon to act.[34]

1936: "PREWAR" BEGINS

1936 marked a critical juncture in the interwar period. Among the year's troubling events were the Italo-Ethiopian war—which continued until the Ethiopians' defeat in the spring—German remilitarization of the Rhineland in March, and the eruption of the Spanish Civil War in the summer. Such disturbances forced Roosevelt to turn his attention increasingly toward international politics, a shift that was reinforced by growing opposition to his domestic policies.[35] Thus, 1936 became a transitional period, during which he combined determination to act to slow the drift to war with a willingness to try a variety of means of doing so.

Roosevelt began the year with a public warning about the warlike trend of international relations and continued to voice his uneasiness on numerous occasions.[36] In January, he wrote Norman Davis that he wor-

---

authority to the President." Roosevelt to Dodd, Dec. 2, 1935, PL, 3:530–31. A good discussion of the neutrality issue and Roosevelt's attitude toward it in 1934 and 1935 may be found in Davis, FDR, 3:552–62.

[33] In addition to his desire not to jeopardize his domestic legislative program with a bruising fight over neutrality legislation, Roosevelt's understanding of the way it would operate in the Italo-Ethiopian conflict made him more willing to accept it. His sympathies lay with the Ethiopians and he realized "that discretionary control over neutrality in an Italo-Ethiopian conflict was of little practical consequence." Dallek, Franklin D. Roosevelt, 106. See also Cole, Roosevelt, 117, 182; and Offner, American Appeasement, 126–27. Davis deals with the domestic political issues that were aroused by this question, FDR, 3:588–92.

[34] Even at the end of 1935, Roosevelt remained concerned about the course of world affairs. Referring at a press conference in November 1935 to a report from Bernard Baruch on conditions in Europe, he said, "It is not encouraging. Nothing that comes over is particularly encouraging. That is why I am spending such an awful lot of time on the foreign situation. It is a good deal more worry to me than the domestic situation." Nixon, Franklin D. Roosevelt, 3:54–55.

[35] Cole, Roosevelt, 10–11.

[36] "Annual Message to the Congress. January 3, 1936," Franklin D. Roosevelt, PPA, 5:8–9. Hull dates his own turning point in recognizing the dangerous drift of world affairs to mid-1935. Cordell Hull, The Memoirs of Cordell Hull (New York: Macmillan, 1948), 1:392. See also Dallek, Franklin D. Roosevelt, 117.

ried about world affairs more than domestic problems, including the election, and a month later he observed to Jesse Straus: "One cannot help feeling that the whole European panorama is fundamentally blacker than at any time in your life or mine. . . . The armaments race means bankruptcy or war—there is no possible out from that statement."[37]

These feelings of apprehension were joined to both a sense of being called upon to act and uncertainty about what to do.[38] Initially, Roosevelt seemed able to imagine only the most traditional measures. In his State of the Union address, for example, the course he envisioned for the United States in the event of world conflict was a combination of neutrality, "adequate defense," and example and encouragement to "persuade other Nations to return to the ways of peace and good-will."[39] Before long, however, he was considering changing the neutrality legislation and using economic measures to affect the European situation.

Partly because Roosevelt desired to influence the direction of the Italo-Ethiopian war, he hoped to use the arms embargo's impending expiration to gain greater flexibility in cooperating with other countries against an aggressor.[40] Unfortunately, his efforts to increase presidential discretion provoked serious isolationist opposition and, deciding not to risk a fight, he supported instead a fourteen-month extension of the existing law, revised to include a prohibition on loans.[41]

[37] Roosevelt to Norman Davis, Jan. 14, 1936, PL, 3:545; Roosevelt to Jesse Straus, Jan. 14, 1936, ibid., 556. See also Roosevelt to Dodd, Jan. 6, 1936, and March 16, 1935, ibid., 543, 571; Offner, American Appeasement, 135; and Kinsella, Leadership, 75. Ambassador Bullitt also expressed anxiety about the possibility of war, writing to Roosevelt on March 4, 1936, "As I said to you in Washington, we are . . . back where we were before 1914 when the familiar and true remark was, 'Peace is at the mercy of an incident.'" For the President: Personal and Secret Correspondence, ed. Orville H. Bullitt (Boston: Houghton Mifflin, 1972), 149. For more of the disturbing messages from Roosevelt's envoys and his own expressions of concern, see Bennett, Roosevelt and the Search for Security, 77–78.

[38] As he observed to Ambassador Dodd, "everything seems to have broken loose again in your part of the world. . . . If in the days to come the absolutely unpredictable events should by chance get to the point where a gesture, an offer or a formal statement by me would, in your judgment, make for peace, be sure to send me immediate word." Roosevelt to Dodd, March 16, 1936, PL, 3:547. See also Roosevelt to Cudahy, Jan. 21, 1936, ibid., 571; Loewenheim, "Illusion," 210; and Rexford Tugwell, In Search of Roosevelt (Cambridge, Mass.: Harvard University Press, 1972), 258.

[39] "Annual Message to the Congress." Jan. 3, 1936, PPA 5:12. Roosevelt wrote to Becker of the D.A.R. in a similar vein on April 20, 1936, PL, 3:575. Hull, too, saw no way for the United States to deal with the problems of this period other than arming for "adequate defense." Cole, Roosevelt, 79.

[40] Glad, Key Pittman, 238. See also Dallek, Franklin D. Roosevelt, 117–21.

[41] Ibid., 120. Kanawada draws a convincing picture of the role of Italian-American pressure in an election year in defeating the neutrality legislation. Its success, however, in preventing the inclusion of such measures in the Neutrality Act of 1936 seems to be due more to its impact on Congress than its effect on Roosevelt. Leo V. Kanawada, Franklin D.

Roosevelt's attempts to use economic weapons to influence the course of international affairs fared somewhat better, foreshadowing the policy of "measures short of war" to which he would later attach some importance. In early 1936, it took the form of countervailing duties on German goods and efforts to help the French with their monetary policy, and Roosevelt's persistence in pursuing such measures in the face of actual and potential opposition during an election campaign suggests the seriousness with which he took them.[42]

Roosevelt's increasing attention in mid-1936 to the impending election has led some to interpret his statements and activities as evidence of submission to isolationist sentiment. In particular, his August speech at Chautauqua, New York, which was in part intended to convince Senator Nye to support his reelection campaign, is cited as evidence of a politically motivated attempt to curry favor with the isolationists.[43] But while stating his concern about the dangers of the international situation and pledging unremitting effort to keep war from the United States, Roosevelt also used the Chatauqua speech to warn of the difficulties of remaining aloof from international problems and to express skepticism about the efficacy of the neutrality laws.[44] Consequently, internationalists as well as isolationists were able to applaud the speech and, despite Roosevelt's concern with reelection, there is little evidence that the campaign caused him to yield anything of substance to the latter.[45]

Roosevelt's Diplomacy and American Catholics, Italians, and Jews (Ann Arbor: University of Michigan Press, 1982), 80–81. See also Dallek, *Franklin D. Roosevelt*, 119; Divine, *Illusion*, 158–61; and Davis, *FDR*, 2:593–95. On American business's defiance toward the administration's attempt to institute a "moral embargo" on trading in essential war materials with Italy, see Offner, *American Appeasement*, 127–28.

[42] For Roosevelt's eagerness to act against Germany with countervailing duties despite a division of opinion in the Treasury Department and opposition from the State Department, and his willingness to strengthen the French government by supporting the devaluation of its currency despite some concern that this might have a negative effect on his reelection campaign, see *From the Morgenthau Diaries: Years of Crisis, 1928–1938*, ed. John Morton Blum (Boston: Houghton Mifflin, 1959) 1:151, 156; and Dallek, *Franklin D. Roosevelt*, 125–26.

[43] Cole, *Nye*, 136–37. Nye did not give Roosevelt his endorsement. See also Cole, *Roosevelt*, 200–202.

[44] "We are not isolationists except in so far as we seek to isolate ourselves completely from war. Yet we must remember that so long as war exists on earth there will be some danger that even the Nation which most ardently desires peace may be drawn into war. . . . No matter how well we are supported by neutrality legislation, we must remember that no laws can be provided to cover every contingency." Roosevelt, "'I Have Seen War . . . I Hate War'—Address at Chautauqua, N.Y. August 14, 1936," *PPA* 5:285–92.

[45] Cole, *Roosevelt*, 202. This conclusion is supported by the fact that he was at this time also toying with the idea of another peace initiative, even allowing Arthur Krock to publish a story to that effect in the middle of the campaign. Dallek, *Franklin D. Roosevelt*, 129–30.

When Roosevelt returned to activity on the international scene at the end of 1936, his focus was Latin America, where he had for some time been concerned about the growing German threat to security.[46] He thus had high hopes for the Inter-American Conference in December 1936 and traveled to Buenos Aires to address it.[47] In his speech, Roosevelt launched an appeal for collective action that apparently had two goals: allowing nonbelligerents to have an impact on the course of events during a war while protecting them from involvement (collective neutrality), and developing mechanisms for collective action toward conflict outside the hemisphere (collective nonbelligerency).[48] As well as limiting conflict, these measures were intended to have a deterrent effect.[49]

In the end, the conference adopted a declaration emphasizing the possibility of collective action by the American states in conflicts outside the hemisphere. Moreover, "the general idea that the neutral countries of the Americas might, under certain circumstances, adopt a common neutrality policy was inserted in other agreements which were approved by the conference."[50] Henceforth, whenever Roosevelt contemplated deterring or punishing aggressor states, the alternatives of embargo and an organization of neutrals were readily available, and he returned to them often.

Pleased with the outcome of the conference, Roosevelt ended his Latin American trip with a renewed sense of mission. On his return to Wash-

[46] Hull has noted that by the time of the Inter-American Conference in December 1936, "Axis penetration had made rapid, alarming headway." According to the reports he received, the Nazis were organizing the considerable number of Germans living in Latin America, establishing contact with the military there, and seeking to undermine United States trade relations with Latin American countries. *Memoirs*, 1:496. For evidence that Roosevelt and Hull's concern was not without foundation, see Alton Frye, *Nazi Germany and the American Hemisphere, 1933–1941* (New Haven: Yale University Press, 1967); Saul Friedlander, *Prelude to Downfall: Hitler and the United States, 1939–1941* (New York: Alfred A. Knopf, 1967); and Gerhard L. Weinberg, *The Foreign Policy of Hitler's Germany: Starting the War, 1937–1939* (Chicago: University of Chicago Press, 1980).

[47] Harold Ickes, *The Secret Diary of Harold Ickes* (New York: Simon and Schuster, 1954), 2:7. See also Dorothy Borg, "Notes on Roosevelt's Quarantine Speech," *Political Science Quarterly* 72 (1957): 406–9.

[48] Roosevelt, "Address before the Inter-American Conference," *PPA* 5:606–7; Dorothy Borg, *The United States and the Far East Crisis of 1933–39* (Cambridge, Mass.: Harvard University Press, 1964), 373. Collective neutrality was advanced by Secretary Hull in a draft convention that proposed to commit "neutral American countries, in case of war between two or more American republics, to apply laws comparable to the neutrality legislation existing in the United States." Collective nonbelligerency, on the other hand, involved the "creation by the American states of a moral front which would adopt measures, such as the severance of diplomatic relations, [or the refusal to trade in war materials] that were noncoercive but not neutral." Borg, "Notes," 407.

[49] Borg, *United States*, 371.

[50] Ibid., 372.

ington in December, he told Ickes that in all the countries he had visited, people looked to him as the defender of democracy, and his behavior during the following year shows that he took that mandate seriously.[51] Indeed, as the international scene continued to darken, Roosevelt retrieved the ideas of blockade and collective neutrality and wove them together in his famous proposal for a quarantine of aggressor nations.

1937: THE TWO THREADS

Renewed calls for action, together with a deteriorating international situation and growing problems with his domestic program, encouraged Roosevelt to hasten the transition from domestic to international affairs and to intensify his search for ways to be effective in the international sphere.[52] Because of the numerous uncertainties facing him, however, he was unable to settle on a definitive plan and the year before the Anschluss continued to be a time of experimentation. Much as Roosevelt desired new solutions to international problems, he could not yet bring himself to abandon the old. Instead, he alternated between them, at times even pursuing two different lines of policy simultaneously.

At the beginning of 1937, Roosevelt expressed considerable frustration about not only the seeming impossibility of developing an effective peace policy but also his inability to understand the international situation. As he complained to Ambassador Phillips on February 6, "What confusion it all is. Every week changes the picture."[53] In a July press conference, he vented his frustration over demands that he do something to improve matters:

> All over Europe almost everybody . . . feels that . . . they are up against a stone wall and that there is nobody in Europe that can solve it. . . . Therefore, it is a perfectly logical thing for them to look around for somebody outside of Europe to come forward with a hat and a rabbit in it and they think I got a hat with a rabbit in it. Well, that is about all there is to it. I haven't got a hat and I haven't got a rabbit in it.[54]

[51] Ickes, *Diary*, 2:15.

[52] Exemplifying the calls for actions is Ambassador Bullitt's postelection letter noting that: "There . . . is a universal belief that Europe is drifting toward war and that no man on the continent has imagination enough to devise any method of reconciliation. Every minister of a small European state who has yet called on me has expressed the hope that you might intervene, saying that if you did not, his country would certainly be destroyed by the inevitable conflict." Bullitt, *For the President*, 179.

[53] William Phillips, *Ventures in Diplomacy* (Boston: Beacon Press, 1952), 203.

[54] Press conference, July 13, 1937, Donald B. Schewe, *Franklin D. Roosevelt and Foreign Affairs, January 1937–August 1939* (New York: Garland Publishing, 1979), 2: no.

Roosevelt's puzzlement about how to act effectively was directly connected to his uncertainty about how to analyze the situation: he could not settle on a course of action because he was still unable to diagnose the problem. Although he heartily disliked the dictators, especially Hitler,[55] and was skeptical about the virtues of appeasement, the idea of bringing Hitler and Mussolini to cooperate in the interest of preserving peace continued to attract him.[56] On July 29, he wrote cordially to Mussolini, expressing the hope that they might work together for disarmament and the reduction of trade barriers.[57] As late as January 1938, in fact, Roosevelt seemed uncertain about whether even Hitler himself was altogether determined to disregard international norms. For example, when Vice President Garner cited Goebbels's statement that Germany would pay no attention to treaties and asked what point there was in signing treaties with such a country, "The President suggested to Hull that he send for

---

375. (This is a ten-volume facsimile edition of documents from the Roosevelt Library relating to Roosevelt and foreign affairs. It is a continuation of the Nixon volumes.) In August, Roosevelt wrote again to Phillips that "just about everything international is on a day to day basis," ibid., 3: no. 436.

[55] On Roosevelt's feelings about Hitler at this time, see Ickes account of a Cabinet discussion on March 5, 1937, of New York City Mayor Fiorello LaGuardia's remarks that the upcoming World's Fair should have a chamber of horrors, and one of the central figures should be a "brown-shirted fanatic who is trying to embroil the world in war." The German press was furious and Secretary Hull had to apologize. Ickes observed that "It was plain that [Roosevelt] would like to see a gold medal pinned on LaGuardia's lapel for what he had said about Hitler." *Diary* 2:89–90. For Roosevelt's later expression of similar views, see Ickes's account of a Cabinet meeting on August 7, 1937, ibid., 187. Additional evidence of Roosevelt's suspicions in early 1937 may be found in a letter to Ambassador Phillips on February 6, 1937. Phillips, *Ventures*, 203. See also Joseph E. Davies, *Mission to Moscow* (New York: Simon and Schuster, 1941), 255–56.

[56] Roosevelt's attitude toward appeasement may be seen in his January 15, 1937, criticism of a draft memorandum advocating political appeasement in Europe as a way of reducing the dangers in Europe and the Far East: "This written by junior underling in State Department about Jan. 15, 1937 is half baked and certainly *not* our current policy." Schewe, 1: no. 20. He also told a Cabinet meeting in February that Great Britain could have thwarted the attack on Ethiopia if she had taken a strong stand against Italy. Ickes, *Diary*, 2:84.

[57] "I am confident, my dear Duce, that you share with me the fear that the trend of the present international situation is ominous to peace . . . [and] the desire to turn the course of the world toward stabilizing peace. I have often wished that I might talk with you frankly and in person because from such a meeting great good might come." Schewe, 2: no. 407. Loewenheim uses this letter to support his view that "Roosevelt seems long to have had a remarkable trust in Mussolini's peaceful intentions in international politics." "Illusion," 210–11. This attitude persisted even after Munich when Roosevelt decided that Hitler could not be counted on to adhere to international norms, but clearly put Mussolini into a different category. See below, and Donald F. Drummond, *The Passing of American Neutrality, 1937–1941* (Ann Arbor: University of Michigan Press, 1955), 75.

the German Ambassador and ask him whether this was the official position of his country."[58]

This ambivalence about the dictators' attitudes toward peace led Roosevelt in 1937 and early 1938 to pursue two contradictory lines of policy. On the one hand, he promoted schemes requiring their cooperation. On the other, he experimented with the notion of isolating them in order to limit the impact of, or even deter, their aggressiveness.

For Roosevelt, the first half of 1937 was a period of "watchful waiting" rather than bold policy initiatives.[59] Unable to see his way clearly, but feeling the need to act, he returned to earlier schemes. In February, at Morgenthau's suggestion, he resurrected the idea of sponsoring a disarmament conference, including the notion of an economic boycott against any state failing to comply with the will of the majority. However, he quickly became discouraged about involving other countries[60] and turned again to addressing the economic and social causes of war, this time with Canadian Prime Minister Mackenzie King.[61]

For a time, Roosevelt continued to think along these lines, but soon concluded that economic arrangements in the absense of disarmament were futile.[62] He wrote Ambassador Phillips on May 17 that the more he

---

[58] Ickes, *Diary*, 2:291. At least in 1937, Roosevelt's cautious optimism about involving the dictators in a cooperative effort of some kind was not totally unrealistic. Citing widespread expectations that he would intervene in the cause of peace, Borg notes that

> The net result of all this talk of a program to resolve the existing crisis was that, by the spring of 1937, there were repercussions even in the European dictatorships. Mussolini, in a highly publicized interview, virtually invited the President to take the initiative in bringing the statesmen of the world together to settle some of the outstanding causes of tension. Hitler was rumored to have said that he would attend a conference for the improvement of the international situation if Mr. Roosevelt convened it.

Borg, "Notes," 409.

[59] The phrase is Roosevelt's, appearing in a letter of February 6, 1937, to Ambassador Phillips. Phillips, *Ventures*, 203. In the same vein, Roosevelt wrote to Ambassador Cudahy on January 15, 1937, that he did not contemplate "any move of any kind" in Europe under present conditions. Schewe, 1: no. 23.

[60] See Blum, *Morgenthau Diaries* 1:458–59, for the talks between Morgenthau and Roosevelt on February 9 and 16, and Dallek, *Franklin D. Roosevelt*, 138, for the talk on February 26.

[61] As King's notes make clear, Roosevelt was still seeking ways to allow nations to act collectively in the interests of peace without using the threat of military force. Thus, he and King agreed that "Collective security should not be identified with reliance upon force. Collective security of nations lies in the sense of social justice being secured through investigation and exposure of social wrongs." "Mackenzie King to F.D.R., March 6, 1937," *PL*, 3:664, 666, 668. See also Borg, *United States*, 373.

[62] For example, on March 19 he asked Norman Davis to get the reaction of European leaders to these ideas and to seek a basis for a cooperative effort "to arrest the rapid deterio-

studied the situation, the more he was "convinced that an economic approach to peace is a pretty weak reed for Europe to lean on. . . . Anything, of course, that postpones war is that much to the good. The progress of the disease is slowed up but the disease remains—and will probably prove fatal in the next few years."[63] He did, however, retain his faith in disarmament. Even after Prime Minister Chamberlain's dismissive reply to his March inquiry about mutual cooperation in that area,[64] Roosevelt continued to hope for both an international agreement leading to peace and a meeting with Chamberlain, asking Norman Davis in May to conduct another series of discussions with European leaders. Chamberlain, however, had come to believe that any settlement would have to be based on political appeasement and, while agreeing in principle to the desirability of a meeting with Roosevelt, failed to respond to subsequent overtures from Davis and Roosevelt until October, at which time he declared that the international situation still made it impossible to expedite such a meeting.[65]

By the summer of 1937 Roosevelt's attempts to promote collective action to preserve peace in Europe had come to naught. Moreover, the international situation had become increasingly worrisome. Not only had the Spanish Civil War taken an extremely violent turn, with Germany and Italy's roles becoming even more blatant, but on July 7 fighting again broke out between the Chinese and Japanese.[66]

The threat to peace posed by the increased activity of the dictators, combined with the failure of diplomatic initiatives to promote the kind of joint action that might have coopted them, suggested Roosevelt's next move. Still desiring to promote peace, he changed his modus operandi from diplomacy to a campaign to educate the public to the realities of the

---

ration of the international situation." Davis reported on April 13 that he encountered only "skepticism about comprehensive world talks." Borg, *United States*, 374. Roosevelt was also interested at this time in getting feedback on a scheme to neutralize the Pacific area. Dallek, *Franklin D. Roosevelt*, 139.

[63] Note the imagery of illness and disease that appears in Roosevelt's thinking throughout early 1937 and culminates in the Quarantine Speech in October. Phillips, *Ventures*, 204–5. See also Roosevelt's statement to the cabinet on April 24. Ickes, *Diary*, 2:124.

[64] Schewe, 2: no. 275a. Chamberlain's letter is dated March 20 and was received by Morgenthau, who made the initial inquiry, on March 26. Ibid., no. 275. See also Blum, *Morgenthau Diaries* 1:458, 463–67, and Dallek, *Franklin D. Roosevelt*, 139.

[65] Borg, "Notes," 409–11, and *United States*, 375–77.

[66] For Roosevelt's reactions to these events, see Dallek, *Franklin D. Roosevelt*, 140–47. In June, Roosevelt and Hull had considered applying the Neutrality Act to Germany and Italy for their actions in Spain, but abandoned the idea in deference to the British view that this would make it more difficult to confine the conflict to Spain.

international situation and replaced the goal of collective action to coopt potential aggressors with that of promoting collective measures that, in the spirit of Buenos Aires, sought to isolate them. Thus, in a meeting with Clark Eichelberger on July 8, Roosevelt suggested "the possibility of evolving a comprehensive international program" providing for "far-reaching economic measures, drastic disarmament, and a renovation of the existing peace machinery." Nonbelligerents would enforce their will on aggressors by denying them "the economic benefits of the more nearly just international society," principally by refusing to engage in trade.[67] Telling Eichelberger that he desired to make a "dramatic statement," Roosevelt proposed to disseminate these ideas in a public forum, and when Hull and Davis suggested in September that he make a speech to counteract a growing isolationist trend, he quickly agreed.[68]

In his Quarantine Speech in Chicago on October 5, 1937, Roosevelt warned that if "the present reign of terror and international lawlessness" continued, America could not hope to remain untouched. Declaring that the "overwhelming majority" of nations who wanted to live in peace must join forces against practices that "are creating a state of international anarchy and instability from which there is no escape through mere isolation or neutrality," he launched his famous image to suggest the direction of such an effort:

> When an epidemic of physical disease starts to spread, the community approves and joins in a quarantine of the patients in order to protect the health of the community against the spread of the disease. . . . The will for peace on the part of peace-loving nations must express itself to the end that nations that may be tempted to violate their agreements and the rights of others will desist from such a cause. There must be positive endeavors to preserve peace.[69]

[67] Borg, "Notes," 422 n. 34. See also Borg, *United States*, 379; and Dallek, *Franklin D. Roosevelt*, 148. On September 14, Roosevelt disclosed a similar plan to Ickes that involved "writing a letter himself to all the nations of the world, except possibly the 'three bandit nations,' as he denominated Germany, Italy, and Japan, in which he would suggest that . . . if any nation should invade the rights or threaten the liberties of the other nations, the peace-loving nations would isolate it. What he has in mind is to cut off all trade with any such nation and thus deny it raw materials." Ickes, *Diary*, 2:213. See also Borg, *United States*, 379, and "Notes," 419; Dallek, *Franklin D. Roosevelt*, 148. Borg wrongly gives the date of this conversation between Ickes and Roosevelt as September 19, which is the date of Ickes's entry into the diary. As the text makes clear, the actual discussion took place after a cabinet meeting five days earlier.

[68] Dallek, *Franklin D. Roosevelt*, 148; Borg, *United States*, 379, and "Notes," 413; Hull, *Memoirs*, 1:544.

[69] "Address Delivered by President Roosevelt at Chicago, October 5, 1937," *Peace and*

Over the years, there has been considerable controversy about both the meaning of the Quarantine Speech and Roosevelt's assessment of the reaction to it. While historians initially tended to see it as an important departure from previous policy that Roosevelt was forced to abandon by a hostile public, more recently Dorothy Borg has successfully argued that Roosevelt had been searching for a program to reduce the danger of war before the speech and continued to do so thereafter.[70] This interpretation is supported by our review of Roosevelt's policy initiatives in early 1937 and further substantiated by the process of drafting the speech, Roosevelt's own attempts to explain his meaning, and the absence of any real proof that a negative public response forced him to back away from the speech's ideas.[71] This suggests that he viewed the speech as a kind of strategic probe with at least three objectives.

First, he meant it as the sort of warning to the dictators that had been discussed at Buenos Aires. Frustrated in his efforts to promote world peace with a disarmament scheme that would include the dictators, he was now experimenting with the idea of deterring aggression by threatening collective action against them. Secondly, Roosevelt wanted to shape world public opinion, leading it, as he told Eichelberger, "on the upward path." Third, he wished to educate domestic opinion, possibly with the goal of moving it toward acceptance of the sort of collective

---

War, 383–87. After hearing the Quarantine Speech, Secretary Ickes recalled proudly that it was he who had given the president, in their September 14 meeting, this imagery. Ickes, *Diary*, 2:222. Welles on the other hand claims that Roosevelt used the word "quarantine" in July when describing his idea for a long-range naval blockade against Japan in cooperation with the British. Welles, *Seven Decisions That Shaped the World* (New York: Harper and Brothers, 1951), 8, 71–72. See also John McVickar Haight, Jr., "Franklin D. Roosevelt and a Naval Quarantine of Japan," *Pacific Historical Review* 40 (1971): 203–4.

[70] Langer and Gleason, *Challenge*, 18–19; Divine, *Illusion*, 212–13; Borg, "Notes," 405; and see Haight, "Naval Quarantine," 205. On the basis of the available evidence, Dallek also accepts Borg's interpretation, *Franklin D. Roosevelt*, 148–49. Divine later came to agree with Borg that the Quarantine Speech reflected a groping for a policy. He still maintained, however, that it represented a major shift in Roosevelt's thinking. *Roosevelt and World War II*, 17–18. For similar interpretations, see Grace G. Tully, *FDR, My Boss* (New York: Charles Scribner's Sons, 1949), 231–33, and Thomas H. Greer, *What Roosevelt Thought* (East Lansing, Mich.: Michigan State University Press, 1958). For a brief review of both sides of the controversy on the meaning of the Quarantine Speech, see John Wiltz, *From Isolation to War, 1931–1941* (New York: Thomas Y. Crowell, 1968), 62–63.

[71] Obviously, if Roosevelt did not intend a radical departure from previous policy to begin with, his later attempts to elucidate his meaning can hardly be characterized as backing down. Borg, "Notes," 424. Moreover, it seems that neither the public's reaction to the Quarantine Speech nor Roosevelt's assessment of it were as negative as they have often been portrayed. For a more detailed analysis of Roosevelt's intentions in the Quarantine Speech based on the drafting process and his own explanations, see Farnham, "Value Conflict," chap. 3 and appendix.

action he had recently been contemplating. According to Eichelberger's understanding of this strategy, once the world had adopted the principles of consultation among nonbelligerents embodied in the Buenos Aires agreements, "the American people would be willing to accept the idea of denying trade to the aggressor."[72]

Moreover, as Roosevelt's actions in the aftermath of the speech show, whatever criticism his quarantine idea provoked, he still thought it timely. He not only continued to be optimistic about educating the American public to accept it,[73] but in planning for the Nine Power Conference in Brussels later that year he also experimented with the notion of actually using it against the Japanese.[74]

While Roosevelt was trying at Brussels to work out a way of coercing one of the dictator states to end an aggression, he was also considering a plan to draw all of them into a cooperative effort to preserve peace. Two days after the Quarantine Speech, Sumner Welles presented him with a proposal to exhort the governments of the world to agree to "the essential principles of international conduct," methods of disarmament, ways of promoting economic security and stability, and respect for "humanitarian considerations" in the event of war.[75]

[72] Ickes, *Diary*, 2:213; Borg, "Notes," 422 n. 34. See also Haight, "Naval Quarantine," 205. Roosevelt also alluded to this education theme on September 20, telling Morgenthau that he was dropping the idea he had broached on September 16 of offering to act as a "clearing house of peace": "I now think that it is a matter of longtime education, and I am not going to do anything which would require a definite response or action on the part of anybody.'" Dallek, *Franklin D. Roosevelt*, 147.

[73] See Roosevelt to Peabody, Oct. 16, 1937, *PL*, 3:716–17; and John McVickar Haight, Jr., "Roosevelt and the Aftermath of his Quarantine Speech," *Review of Politics* 24 (1962): 233–36.

[74] The day after the Quarantine Speech, the League of Nations Assembly condemned Japan for initiating hostilities in China and called for a conference of the Nine Power Treaty signatories. Roosevelt's preparations for this conference and his direction of United States' policy during it reveal a good deal about the kind of action he thought proper to implement the ideas expressed in the Quarantine Speech. This episode is discussed in detail in Farnham, "Value Conflict," chap. 3 and appendix, where it is argued that, contrary to Borg's interpretation, Roosevelt took the conference seriously as an opportunity to act on his new scheme for dealing with the aggressor states. However, because his conditions for American participation (relating primarily to his need to package collective action so that it would be acceptable politically) were not met, nothing came of his efforts. Borg, *United States*, 384, 538–39. (See also 405–7, 537), and Dallek, *Franklin D. Roosevelt*, 149–52. The two best accounts of the development of American policy and the politics of the conference have been provided by Haight, whose interpretation, as Borg has acknowledged, "differs radically" from her own. "Roosevelt and the Aftermath," 252–59, and John McVickar Haight, Jr., "France and the Aftermath of Roosevelt's 'Quarantine' Speech," *World Politics* 14 (1962): 282–306.

[75] Sumner Welles, *The Time for Decision* (New York: Harper and Brothers, 1944), 64–

Some have interpreted Roosevelt's enthusiasm for Welles' scheme as a retreat from the Quarantine Speech. In the light of his activities during the Brussels Conference and the subsequent *Panay* incident, however, it is clear that he regarded the Welles Peace Plan not as an alternative to stronger measures but as another means to the same end.[76] Moreover, as Langer and Gleason have suggested, Roosevelt's attraction to it may have been stimulated by an October 11 memorandum by Assistant Secretary of State George Messersmith that identified Germany as the chief threat to peace, warned that "the United States are the ultimate object of attack" of the dictator states, and asserted the need to employ all possible means to avert war.[77] In the end, however, faced with the determined opposition of Secretary Hull, Roosevelt temporarily ceased to pursue Welles's idea.[78]

In the months immediately before the Anschluss, Roosevelt's approach to the problem of how to best influence world politics remained experimental. Although by mid-November he had been forced to abandon both the notion of collective action against the dictators embodied in his plans for the Brussels Conference and a peace initiative including them represented by the Welles Plan, the hiatus in his activity was only temporary. In December and January, responding to continued deterioration in the international situation, Roosevelt picked up the two threads and from this point forward pursued both lines of policy almost simultaneously, apparently viewing them as complementary, rather than alternative, strategies.

At the close of the Brussels Conference, Roosevelt had told Stimson that he still desired to support the Chinese "if the occasion presents itself to shape events."[79] Thus, when the Japanese sank the American gunboat *Panay* on December 12, 1937, he returned at once to his quarantine idea,

---

66, and *Seven Decisions*, 21–24; Borg, *United States*, 377. Welles's memo regarding the implementation of his plan can be found in Schewe, 3: no. 542.

[76] Borg views the Welles Peace Plan as an alternative to the quarantine idea. On the other hand, Welles himself, at least retrospectively, saw it as assisting the efforts at collective action being made at the Brussels Conference. Langer and Gleason also adopt this explanation. Borg, *United States*, 412–13; Welles, *Time*, 65; Langer and Gleason, *Challenge*, 19–20.

[77] Ibid., 21–22. See also Offner, *American Appeasement*, 192–93. The text of the Messersmith memo is in *FRUS, 1937*, 1:140–45. On Messersmith's career, see Kenneth Moss, "George Messersmith and Nazi Germany," in *U.S. Diplomats in Europe, 1919–1941*, ed. Kenneth Paul Jones (Santa Barbara, Calif.: ABC-Clio, 1981), 113–26.

[78] Welles, *Time*, 66. On the entire episode of the Welles plan see also Langer and Gleason, *Challenge*, 22–23; Offner, *American Appeasement*, 190–93; and Hull, *Memoirs* 1:546–48.

[79] PPF, Box 2–20, folder 20: Stimson, Henry L., 1934–1944.

calling British Ambassador Lindsay to the White House on December 16 to discuss a naval quarantine of Japan.[80] His plan, which strongly resembled the one he had outlined to Welles in July, was to use the British and American navies to isolate Japan economically.[81] Moving from diplomatic and economic measures that were "non-coercive but not neutral," to military measures that involved "hostilities" but not "war," this conception of quarantine went far beyond collective action based on the Buenos Aires principles that Roosevelt had been willing to contemplate at the Nine Power Conference.

These steps attracted Roosevelt for several reasons. First of all, as he pointed out to British Ambassador Lindsay, they were within the power of the executive. There would be no need to involve an uncooperative Congress.[82] Secondly, he believed that a naval blockade of Japan would not incur the risk of war, although why he thought so is not entirely clear.[83] Possibly he still believed that the Japanese would back down in

[80] On December 14 Roosevelt, sounding quite bellicose, explored with Secretary Morgenthau even stronger economic measures, such as freezing Japanese funds. He referred again to this idea in a cabinet meeting on December 17 and allowed Morgenthau to explore it with the British. However, they were unenthusiastic and the matter ended there. Blum, *Morgenthau Diaries* 1:486–92. See also Haight, "Naval Quarantine," 209–10.

[81] Ibid. See also Leutze, *Bargaining*, 19–21. Roosevelt's scheme also recalls Admiral Yarnell's plan for a war of "naval strangulation" in the Pacific, which Roosevelt had not only commended but specifically related to his own quarantine idea. "Roosevelt to Admiral William D. Leahy, Chief of Naval Operations, November 10, 1937," Schewe, 3, no. 607. Yarnell's memo of October 25 and Leahy's letter of November 8 transmitting it to Roosevelt are, respectively, no.s 599a and 599.

[82] According to Ickes, in a cabinet meeting on December 17, 1937, Roosevelt "called attention to certain powers granted him by the Congress in 1933 which he had forgotten that he had. A statute was passed in that year giving the President very wide powers—in effect the right to impose economic sanctions 'in order to prevent war.' The President believes that these powers are so broad that he could embargo cotton, oil, etc., so far as Japan is concerned." Ickes, *Diary*, 2:274. See also Morgenthau's account of this meeting. Blum, *Morgenthau Diaries*, 1:489. Roosevelt's newfound understanding of his powers was the result of a memorandum prepared in the Treasury Department by Herman Oliphant. Ibid., 486–87. See also Reynolds, *Creation*, 31.

[83] In answer to Lindsay's suggestion that it would constitute a causus belli, Roosevelt "said no. . . . There was 'new doctrine and technique' regarding war, and the United States had waged undeclared war before. Lindsay offered what he described as 'horrified criticisms' but felt that they made little impact on the president, who seemed 'wedded to this scheme for preventing war (but not "hostilities").'" Leutze, *Bargaining*, 19. The following day, Roosevelt expanded on these ideas to his cabinet. Alluding to his putative discretionary powers to institute economic sanctions, he declared, "We want these powers to be used to prevent war." Moreover, in reply to the bellicose fulminations of the secretary of the navy, "the President remarked that he wanted the same result that Swanson did but that he didn't want to have to go to war to get it." Blum, *Morgenthau Diaries*, 1:487–89; Ickes, *Diary*, 2:274–77. See also Haight, "Naval Quarantine," 211–12; and Dallek, *Franklin D. Roosevelt*, 154.

the face of a strong stand by the democracies.[84] He may also have associated his naval blockade with new methods of conducting international relations invented by the dictators. Noting their success in getting their way without having to declare war, Roosevelt seemed to suggest that, bad as they were in other respects, they might be worth emulating in this. For example, at a December 17 cabinet meeting he declared that economic sanctions could be genuinely effective, but added, "We don't call them economic sanctions; we call them quarantines. We want to develop a technique which will not lead to war. We want to be as smart as Japan and as Italy. We want to do it in a modern way."[85]

Roosevelt's willingness to use stronger measures than he had previously thought prudent also seems to have reflected a conviction that the public would support them because they would not be readily associated with traditional forms of military force.[86] Thus he told Ambassador Lindsay at their December 16 meeting that "public opinion was moving favorably" since the *Panay* incident, and expressed the belief at a press conference on December 21 that both the press and public supported his handling of it.[87] Moreover, although there is some evidence he may have thought he could keep the entire quarantine operation secret, he was not overly concerned with doing so.[88]

Clearly then, Roosevelt's response to the *Panay* incident refutes the argument that concern with public opinion caused him to drop his

[84] This is the impression that Secretary Ickes took away from a cabinet meeting on December 23. *Diary*, 2:277. In July, Roosevelt had told Welles that his blockade idea would not result in war because "Japan was so heavily committed in China that her economy was stretched to the breaking point." Thus, she would have to back down in the face of these economic measures. Welles, *Seven Decisions*, 8, 71–72.

[85] Blum, *Morgenthau Diaries*, 1:489. Roosevelt also suggested to French Senator Baron Amaury de La Grange on January 16, 1938, that "Since the Germans, the Italians and the Japanese have invented a new method which consists of carrying on military operations without declaring war, why not do likewise?"—especially since avoiding a declaration of war meant that the neutrality laws would not apply. Haight, "Naval Quarantine," 222–23, and "Roosevelt as Friend of France," in Divine, *Causes and Consequences*, 89. See also Reynolds, *Creation*, 31. For a later expression of this view, see Roosevelt's remarks to Morgenthau in April 1939 about his plans for a neutrality patrol, below, chap. 6.

[86] Roosevelt demonstrated a similar attitude toward this type of warfare during the Munich crisis. See his September 19, 1938, conversation with Ambassador Lindsay, below.

[87] Haight, "Naval Quarantine," 211; Schewe, 4: no. 699.

[88] According to Leutze's account of Lindsay's report of their meeting, "It was Roosevelt's opinion that this blockade could be established covertly and would be denied as official policy if questioned." *Bargaining*, 19. However, his suggestion to Captain Royal E. Ingersoll on December 23 that in such a blockade naval vessels could be supplemented with private yachts argues against a concern with secrecy. Moreover, according to Leutze, Roosevelt told Ingersoll that the "important thing was to interrupt Japanese trade, and [he] did not much care how it was done." Ibid., 23.

quarantine idea. Rather, as Ickes noted after the December 23 cabinet meeting, "the President is still pursuing the thought of an economic blockade against Japan. . . . [He] sees in this incident an opportunity for the democratic governments to reassert themselves in world affairs."[89] This attitude can also be seen in his subsequent actions, which included the planning and implementation of naval-staff talks with the British,[90] naval moves in the Far East,[91] and an effort to build American naval strength.[92] All of these measures are important antecedents of the policies Roosevelt adopted when he finally decided that the dictators could not be socialized. In working out his blockade scheme, he was in fact beginning to lay the foundation for future Anglo-American cooperation and rearmament.[93]

Even as Roosevelt was trying to implement a naval quarantine against

[89] Dallek's conclusion that Roosevelt's concern with acceptability caused him to try to "find a new anti-war technique" and to retreat from his blockade idea is therefore in error. Moreover, that Roosevelt did not immediately move to institute the blockade cannot be taken as evidence that he had abandoned the idea. As his remarks to Lindsay make clear, the quarantine was never intended as a direct response to the *Panay* incident, but rather to the "next outrage" by the Japanese. Dallek, *Franklin D. Roosevelt*, 154–55. Ickes, *Diary*, 2:277.

[90] On the planning, execution, and results of the Ingersoll mission see Leutze, *Bargaining*, 20–27; Haight, "Naval Quarantine," 210–19; Heinrichs, "The Role of the Navy," 197–223; Kittredge, "United States," chap. 5; Mark S. Watson, *Chief of Staff* (Washington, D.C.: Department of the Army, 1950), 93. It should be noted that by this time, Roosevelt had already initiated staff talks with Canada. C. P. Stacey, *Arms, Men and Governments: The War Policies of Canada, 1939–1945* (Ottawa: Ministry of National Defense, 1970), 96–97; James Eayrs, *In Defense of Canada: Appeasement and Rearmament* (Toronto: University of Toronto Press, 1965), 179–83. Correspondence between Welles and Roosevelt on this subject from January 10–14, 1938 can be found in PSF, Departmental, State Department: Welles 1937–1938, Box 95, Roosevelt Library. Schewe also contains memos and correspondence on the subject from Roosevelt, Welles, and Armour, see 4: no.s 690, 706, 749, 749a, 760.

[91] Haight, "Naval Quarantine," 219, 215; Ickes, *Diary*, 2:279; Leutze, *Bargaining*, 25. See also Dallek, *Franklin D. Roosevelt*, 156; and Cole, *Roosevelt*, 253–62.

[92] See "Roosevelt to Admiral William D. Leahy, Chief of Naval Operations, November 10, 1937," Schewe, 3: no. 607. According to one contemporary account, the opportunity the *Panay* incident afforded "to add drama to an already dramatic situation" caused the Administration to shelve its plan to gain public support for arms expansion by tying it to industrial recovery and concentrate instead on justifying it in terms of the international situation. Simon Bourgin, "Public Relations of Naval Expansion," *Public Opinion Quarterly* 3 (1939): 113–15. While Roosevelt's accomplishments in rearmament exceeded past efforts, they by no means signaled a major reorientation of American defense policy. As Watson points out, Roosevelt's own later claim that his January 28 defense message to Congress was the "beginning of a vast program of rearmament" was greatly exaggerated. Watson, *Chief of Staff*, 126 n.2.

[93] See Reynolds, *Creation*, 31.

one of the dictator states, however, he was also picking up the other policy thread of involving those states in a peace initiative. Thus, on January 11, 1938, he resurrected the Welles Peace Plan, communicating to Chamberlain his desire for "an international conference on arms reduction, international law, and some form of economic agreement."[94] Although some see this move as a change in emphasis from the Far East to Europe, not only had Roosevelt not given up his plans for naval action in the Pacific, but he probably viewed the two as complementary.[95] Certainly, the simultaneous pursuit of policies based on differing assessments of the dictators' disposition toward international cooperation was entirely consistent with the pattern of experimentation Roosevelt had shown throughout 1937.

In any case, on January 13, without consulting Foreign Secretary Eden, Chamberlain vetoed Roosevelt's suggestion for a conference. As Haight explains it, Chamberlain linked Roosevelt's conference idea with his naval quarantine of Japan, and by rejecting it "effectively sabotaged a Far Eastern blockade and removed a fundamental challenge to his current personal efforts to appease Mussolini."[96] If such was Chamberlain's purpose, he was eminently successful. Roosevelt, though expressing reservations about the prime minister's course, acknowledged on January 17 that he "had no alternative but to postpone his plan," a postponement that proved to be permanent.[97] Thus, Roosevelt's desire to influence the direction of international politics was frustrated once again owing, as in the case of his plans to quarantine the dictators, not so much to an absence of domestic support, which was never really tested, as to the inability of the British and Americans to find a basis for cooperation.[98]

[94] Leutze, *Bargaining*, 26. Discussions of this episode can be found in Haight, "Naval Quarantine," 219–25; Anthony Eden, *Facing the Dictators* (Boston: Houghton Mifflin, 1962), 622–25; *The Diaries of Alexander Cadogan, 1938–1945*, ed. David Dilks (London: Cassell, 1971), 35–36, 56; Welles, *Time*, 66. The record of the early 1938 talks with Great Britain on the proposal for international action to promote world peace is in *FRUS, 1938*, 1:115–30. Roosevelt's interpretation of his peace initiative can be found in the draft of a speech he wrote on February 15, 1938. Schewe, 4: no. 837.

[95] Ambassador Lindsay, for one, thought that "a major purpose of the [proposed] conference was to align American opinion behind Roosevelt's foreign policy" of supporting the democratic governments. Haight, "Naval Quarantine," 220.

[96] Leutze, *Bargaining*, 26; Haight, "Naval Quarantine," 221–22. For a sympathetic analysis of the British perspective on Roosevelt's proposals, see Loewenheim, "Illusion," 188–200, 205–6. For the opposite view, see Harrison, "United States."

[97] Although Eden later prevailed upon Chamberlain to respond more positively to Roosevelt's initiative, his own resignation on February 20 effectively ended all hope of British cooperation with either of the President's schemes. Langer and Gleason, *Challenge*, 27–28; Dallek, *Franklin D. Roosevelt*, 157; Haight, "Roosevelt and a Naval Quarantine," 225.

[98] Haight, "Naval Quarantine," 225. See also Leutze, *Bargaining*, 28; Arnold A. Offner,

1938: FROM THE ANSCHLUSS TO MUNICH

The failure of both Roosevelt's schemes for promoting world peace did nothing to alleviate his fear that the world was sliding toward a disastrous war, and he worried that appeasement would prove ineffective in preventing it.[99] He was not absolutely certain about this, however, and at no time, either before or after the German takeover of Austria, was he prepared to oppose that policy openly, let alone offer the kind of commitment that might have made a different course more appealing to the British. The months preceding the Munich crisis were thus a time of much anxiety but little action. On the one hand, Roosevelt continued to receive troubling reports about the dictators. On the other, he was confronted with British optimism about working out a settlement with them. Absent hard information either way, he temporized, revealing increasing concern about the dictators in private, while giving half-hearted support to British efforts in public. Indeed, his behavior shows less direction than at any time during the watershed period before Munich. Largely in deference to the British experiment with appeasement, Roosevelt had ceased his own experimenting.

That he was far from confident about the success of appeasement, however, is shown by his response in January to the French desire to purchase one thousand American army planes. He supported this effort and, according to the French emissary Baron La Grange, showed a thorough awareness of the German threat and the need for a concerted effort by the democracies to meet it. Moreover, while he cautioned that the arms embargo "would not permit France in time of war to replenish its supplies 'with complete freedom'" and urged La Grange to be discreet in his inspection of the aircraft industry so as not to alert the press or Congress, La Grange concluded that "France could expect a broad inter-

---

America and the Origins of World War II (New York: W. W. Norton, 1969), 123; Weinberg, *Foreign Policy of Hitler's Germany*, 106–11; and Harrison, "United States."

[99] Roosevelt was particularly concerned about British appeasement of Italy, believing that the de jure recognition of Mussolini's conquest of Ethiopia would have an adverse effect on American public opinion, which he thought had begun to shift in the right direction. Haight, "Naval Quarantine," 222; Langer and Gleason, *Challenge*, 26–28; and Harrison, "United States," 106. See also his letter to Arthur Murray on February 10, in which he observed that events in Germany had demonstrated Murray's "rightness making unkind remarks about some people who see in Nazi-ism ideals of peace and good will," and in Ickes's account of Roosevelt's support, over the objection of the State Department, of the Secretary's desire to make an antifascist speech. *PL*, 1938, 4:757; Ickes, *Diary*, 2:322–23.

pretation of the embargo. The Senator personally thought this might mean 'surreptitious delivery via Canada.'"[100]

Roosevelt's worries about appeasement were undoubtedly reinforced by two communications he received in February. Certainly, any presidential concern about military aviation aroused by La Grange's visit was only aggravated by Charles Lindbergh's memorandum on German air power, which was received on February 9. Two conclusions stood out dramatically in Lindbergh's detailed account based on his recent tour of German plane-production facilities: "German aviation development is without parallel [and] . . . it is doubtful that any country in Europe will be able to catch up with them in the next few years."[101] On the heels of this alarming report of German capabilities, Roosevelt received a trenchant analysis of their intentions from Assistant Secretary of State Messersmith. Strongly antiappeasement in tone, Messersmith's second memorandum was even more pessimistic than his first about the future course of events in Europe and their impact on the United States. Predicting Germany's impending absorption of Austria, he declared that

> if France and England had spoken in any definite way . . . the present catastrophe would have been avoided, for Hitler is not yet ready to go to war. England and France have not spoken above a whisper and I do not see how Benes can hold on in Czechoslovakia for more than four or five months. . . . I think we must definitely face the fact that if the movement continues, which it shows every promise of doing, there is no small country in Southeastern or in Northern Europe which can have any further illusions as to its security.

Messersmith went on to describe in no uncertain terms the consequences of this development for the United States:

> if Germany gets economic or political control, or both, of Southeastern Europe she will be in a position to put England and France into a secondary

---

[100] Haight, "Naval Quarantine," 225–26; John McVickar Haight, *American Aid to France, 1938–1940* (New York: Atheneum, 1970), 7–8, and "Roosevelt as Friend of France," 89. Roosevelt was not totally unprepared for the French overture, having received a letter from Ambassador Bullitt on November 23, 1937, telling him that according to the French military attaché Germany had between five and six thousand battle-ready planes while the French had less than two thousand. Unfortunately, as La Grange soon discovered, America's effort to produce combat planes was even less advanced. Bullitt, *For the President*, 234; Haight, "Roosevelt as Friend of France," 89–90.

[101] Roosevelt sent copies of this memorandum to Chief of Naval Operations Leahy and Army Chief of Staff Craig, who both replied that it accorded with information they had received from other sources. PSF, Departmental, Box 78, Folder Navy, 1938 Jan.–Feb. See also Wayne S. Cole, *Charles A. Lindbergh and the Battle Against American Intervention in World War II* (New York: Harcourt Brace Jovanovich, 1970), 37 n. 16. Kennedy's letter to Roosevelt transmitting this report and the report itself are in Schewe, 4, no.s 824, 824a.

place in Europe and practically immobilize them. . . . We in this country would stand practically alone, and that our troubles would come a little later does not give me any comfort.[102]

Perhaps it was the combined effect of these gloomy missives that led Roosevelt to express a heightened sense of the possibility of war and, in a meeting at the end of February with Ambassador Bullitt and a French emissary, Jean Monnet, to declare his willingness to revise or circumvent the neutrality laws in order to supply American arms to the democracies in the event of war.[103] Dramatic as Roosevelt's assurances to Monnet were, however, it would be wrong to interpret them as proof of a decisive alteration in his thinking about the likely course of events in Europe, let alone a change in American policy.[104] Despite his reservations about appeasement, he was still undecided about whether it might work.[105] Thus, in the same three days in March he both agreed with his ambassador to Ireland about its dangers and told his ambassador to Spain that "it was impossible to guess whether Chamberlain would succeed 'in establishing reasonable assurance of peace for two or three years' through 'concessions' or whether he would fail and be overthrown for giving too much and receiving too little."[106]

[102] "Memorandum by the Assistant Secretary of State (Messersmith) to the Secretary of State, February 18, 1938," *FRUS*, 1938, 1:17–24.

[103] The French sought reassurances from Roosevelt that La Grange had not misinterpreted his intentions regarding their request for planes. These Roosevelt gave, responding that he was already trying to repeal the arms embargo and expected to be successful. Moreover, if war did come he would rush neutrality revision through. However, "If worse came to worst and he failed in this final effort, . . . he would have the planes pushed across the border into Canada. He told Bullitt to search for areas where planes could land on the American side, and he sketched a map indicating likely places." Haight, "Roosevelt as Friend of France," 90. Roosevelt's interest in aiding the democracies in this manner is also shown by his willingness in March, over the objections of the Army, to allow a French pilot to fly a P-36 fighter plane. Ibid., 91; and Haight, *American Aid*, 10–12.

[104] Haight, "Roosevelt as Friend of France," 90.

[105] Only days after the meeting with Bullitt and Monnet, he told Kennedy, "Joe, I still have not lost heart. If Chamberlain succeeds in pacifying the dictators, the time may soon come when my plan [for proposing "a world economic and political structure based on 'fundamental rules' of international conduct"] can be put into effect. . . . We shall have to mark time until we see whether or not Chamberlain accomplishes anything." Interview between Roosevelt and Kennedy, Feb. 24, 1938, Joseph Kennedy's unpublished diplomatic memoir, chap. 1, cited in Michael R. Beschloss, *Kennedy and Roosevelt* (New York: W. W. Norton, 1980), 162.

[106] In reply to Ambassador Cudahy's criticism of British appeasement as "encouraging the dangerous adventures of both Mussolini and Hitler." Roosevelt wrote: "As someone remarked to me—'If a Chief of Police makes a deal with the leading gangsters and the deal results in no more hold-ups, that Chief of Police will be called a great man—but if the gangsters do not live up to their word the Chief of Police will go to jail. Some people are, I think, taking very long chances—don't you?" "Cudahy to Roosevelt," Mar. 1, 1938,

The fulfillment on March 12 of Messersmith's prediction about Austria brought little change. Official American reaction was subdued and Roosevelt continued in the pattern he had followed since January: privately expressing concern and making a few relatively insignificant gestures, but failing to act in any serious way.[107] At a press conference on March 15, his response to the question, "Do events in Europe of last week make any difference in our defense situation?" was "None at all—as recommended by me." As Messersmith explained to Wiley, the American Chargé in Austria, "You can take it that there will be no change in our policy no matter what may take place elsewhere. The President and the Secretary are determined that we shall hold on to the line that we have taken. There will be no swerving from it in any detail."[108]

Perhaps the Anschluss failed to provoke a significant alteration in American policy because it did not seem to forecast an increase in the German threat to American security. A number of Americans like Senator Borah thought that Germany's takeover of Austria was in some sense "natural." Even Roosevelt seemed to view it as having a certain inevitability, telling Morgenthau matter-of-factly on March 16 that he had believed for three months that Hitler and Mussolini had made a deal giving Germany a free hand in Central Europe and Italy carte blanche in the Mediterranean.[109]

Schewe, 5: no. 874; "Roosevelt to Cudahy," Mar. 9, 1938, ibid., no. 904. Roosevelt's March 7 letter to Claude Bowers, ambassador to Spain, is quoted in Dallek, *Franklin D. Roosevelt*, 157–58. Roosevelt's ambivalence toward the British effort at appeasement before the Anschluss was reflected in American policy. As Under Secretary Welles explained to the British Ambassador on March 8, the United States was "adopting an attitude of contemplation." It wished the British well, but would undertake neither to support nor to discourage their efforts at appeasement. "Memorandum of Conversation Between Sumner Welles, Under Secretary of State and Ronald C. Lindsay, British Ambassador to the United States, March 8, 1938," Schewe, 5: no. 899a. See also Langer and Gleason, *Challenge*, 28–30.

[107] Dallek, *Franklin D. Roosevelt*, 158.

[108] "Press Conference in the White House, March 15, 1938," Schewe, 5: no. 919; assistant Secretary of State Messersmith to Chargé in Austria Wiley, March 16, 1938, *FRUS*, 1938, 1:451–52. The American diplomatic record of the Austrian crisis can be found in ibid., 384–482. See also "Address by the Secretary of State, delivered at Washington, March 17, 1938," *Peace and War*, 407–19. Hull and Roosevelt did, however, prevent Ambassador Kennedy from stating categorically in a speech on March 18 that the United States would not give assistance in the event of a major war. Moreover, Roosevelt expressed his unease at European developments in small ways—directing that an American ship show the flag at a Dominican port at the same time that a German ship was there, and allowing Ickes, over the objection of the State Department, to discuss fascism critically in a speech. Cole, *Roosevelt*, 277–78. PL, 5:767; see also Schewe, 5: no.s 924, 929. Ickes, *Diary*, 2:348.

[109] Cole, *Roosevelt*, 278; Blum, *Morgenthau Diaries*, 1:501. In fact, Roosevelt had expressed to Ickes on December 17, 1937, a view that was similar to Borah's. Ickes, *Diary*, 2:275. Not everyone failed to see the implications of the Anschluss. Apart from Mes-

In the months between the Austrian and Czech crises, Roosevelt continued to combine concern about the course of international affairs with the hope that a peaceful way of dealing with the demands of the dictators might yet be found. Though increasingly worried about the prospects for war in general and threats to the Western Hemisphere in particular, he publicly supported the fruits of a major effort at appeasement, even giving his approval to Britain's recognition of the Italian conquest of Ethiopia.[110] As his remarks in two press conferences show, however, Roosevelt was far from sanguine about the course of world affairs. On April 20 and 21 he took the opportunity to criticize the neutrality law, observing that it was "so rigid that, acting on it in accordance with its rigidity, may mean a complete lack of neutrality." As examples he cited its likely effect on the Spanish Civil War and the conflict in China.[111]

These press conferences also show a shift in Roosevelt's rationale for hemisphere defense. While in February he had seemed concerned primarily about ideological penetration, telling Ickes of plans to counter German propaganda in Latin America,[112] on April 20 he was speculating about a Spanish Civil War type of situation on America's southern border:

Suppose certain foreign governments, European governments, were to do in Mexico what they did in Spain. Suppose they would organize a revolution, a Fascist revolution in Mexico. Mexico is awfully close to us, and suppose they were to send planes and officers and guns and were to equip the revolutionists and get control of the whole of Mexico and thereupon run the Mexican Government, run the Mexican Army and build it up with hundreds of planes. Do you think that the United States could stand idly by and have this European menace right on our own borders? Of course not.

Roosevelt went on to emphasize that America's ocean barriers would not protect her from this kind of threat and that, therefore, a navy large

---

sersmith's earlier analysis, Ambassador Cudahy pointed out to Roosevelt on April 6 that "The basic thing about Austria is that now there is no balance on the continent," and on April 11 Ambassador Bowers castigated Chamberlain's conduct as "the most dishonorable and treacherous, antidemocratic and deceptive in the history of England for a century." Schewe, 5: no.s 993, 1006.

[110] Dallek, *Franklin D. Roosevelt*, 158. Ickes, *Diary*, 2:377. See also Drummond, *Passing of American Neutrality*, 75–76.

[111] "Press Conference in the White House, April 20, 1938, 2:20 P.M.," "Press Conference in the White House, April 21, 1938, 9:00 P.M.," Schewe, 5: no.s 1031, 1034. In the first press conference Roosevelt specifically declared his remarks off the record. The second press conference was off the record in any case. During the course of it, however, Roosevelt stated both his desire to get his views on the neutrality law across to the public and his reservations about the appropriateness of that particular forum for doing so.

[112] Ickes, *Diary*, 2:317. The entry is for February 11, 1938. For concerns about German economic penetration at this time, see Frye, *Nazi Germany*, 65–79.

enough to enforce the Monroe Doctrine and check the development of such a situation at the outset was needed. Stressing the proximity of several Latin American countries, such as Venezuela and Brazil, to the United States and Europe, he underlined the potential vulnerability of even the American heartland to air attack with a story about the Japanese bombing of the interior of China (which he graphically labeled the "Iowa of China"). He also acknowledged the difficulty of having to confront hostile states on both the Atlantic and the Pacific oceans and outlined a strategy to deal with them, telling the press "you have to be a bit shifty on your feet. You have to lick one of them first and then bring them around and then lick the other. That is about the only chance."[113]

Nevertheless, Roosevelt continued to be ambivalent about what could be expected from the dictators. In March 1938, Secretary Ickes declined to sign a previously agreed upon contract to sell helium to Germany, standing his ground in the face of Hull's desire for the sale to go through for diplomatic reasons and Roosevelt's professed belief that the United States had a moral obligation to sell. Roosevelt's effort as late as May 1938 to persuade the recalcitrant Secretary shows clearly that even the Anschluss was not enough to cause him to rule out completely the possibility of fair dealing from Hitler. "The President said that . . . we would not ship the helium unless we had a guarantee from Hitler that it would not be used for military purposes," to which Ickes responded: "Who would take Hitler's word?"[114] The question went unanswered, but it is clear that, at least on this issue, Roosevelt was prepared to do so. Evidently he did not subscribe to Messersmith's view that German treatment of Austria had proved conclusively that Hitler could not be trusted to keep agreements.[115]

ANALYSIS

Tracing the development of Roosevelt's policies during these watershed years from 1936 to 1938 casts considerable doubt on the domestic-politics explanation favored by so many. Indeed, it shows that his hesi-

[113] "Press Conference in the White House, April 20, 1938," Schewe, 5: no. 1031. Roosevelt's earlier interest in military aid for Latin American countries is seen in Ickes's account of his authorization of arms and training aid over the objections of Secretary Swanson on February 27 and April 2, 1937. Ickes, *Diary*, 2:86, 111.

[114] Ickes, *Diary*, 2:344, 391–93. Ickes gleefully chronicled the helium incident in its entirety. See also 2:324–25, 346–47, 368–69, 372–73, 375–77, 385, 396–99, 406, 414, 419–20, 427–28, 575. See also Michael Reagan, "The Helium Controversy," in *American Civil-Military Decisions*, ed. Harold Stein (Birmingham, Ala.: University of Alabama Press, 1963).

[115] "Memorandum by the Assistant Secretary of State (Messersmith) to the Secretary of State, February 18, 1938," *FRUS*, 1938, 1:17–24.

tancy, indecision, and apparent contradictions owed far more to uncertainty than to fear of domestic repercussions. In particular, the view that Roosevelt fully understood the need to stop the dictators but was immobilized by the isolationists is simply not supported by the evidence. Worried about the implications of a major war, he felt strongly that one was likely to occur if international politics continued on its present course, but at no point during the period from 1936 to 1938 did he contemplate dealing with the impending threat by withdrawing into isolation. Rather, he tried repeatedly to alter that course, often following two lines of policy based on contrary assessments of the possibility of socializing the dictators. It is this behavior that needs to be explained.

The Will to Act

The intensity of Roosevelt's desire to affect the course of international affairs is striking. Undeterred by frustration or uncertainty, he seldom lapsed into inactivity, and then not for long. So strong was his impulse to act that having failed to gain revision of the neutrality legislation in early 1936, he had come up with the idea of collective neutrality before the year was out. Obliged to be neutral, Roosevelt would find a way for neutrals to act.

Traditional approaches to decision-making cannot explain this powerful impulse to act. The analytical approach is silent about what motivates action and the motivational approach generally expects psychological withdrawal in the face of conditions such as Roosevelt faced.[116] But even though Roosevelt feared that war might well occur if things were left to themselves and was uncertain about how to change them, he exhibited no particular stress on that account. Even with important values at stake, his response to uncertainty was neither panic nor withdrawal; nor is there the slightest hint of defensive avoidance. Rather, he sought out the responsibility of making decisions, attempting to act even when not compelled to do so by immediate events.

Not generally expecting action in the face of uncertainty, the intuitive approach to decision-making would also fail to predict Roosevelt's practice of launching initiatives even when unsure of their possible consequences.[117] While the intuitive tendency to resolve uncertainty subjectively with "categorical inferences" might explain, if not the strong desire to act in the face of uncertainty, at least how a decision-maker might find it psychologically possible to do so, Roosevelt showed no disposition to reduce uncertainty with cognitive devices such as judgmental heuris-

[116] See appendix A.
[117] Ibid.

tics.[118] Rather, he tested the alternatives by trying them out and dropped those he found wanting.

While none of the traditional approaches deals satisfactorily with Roosevelt's striking will to act, the political approach to decision-making does not find it surprising for a decision-maker to launch policies that have not been thoroughly evaluated in preference to remaining passive. Based on the notion that political decision-makers are moved by a desire for effective action, the political approach expects them to make vigorous efforts to act and to find such efforts stimulating rather than stressful.

Experimenting in the Face of Uncertainty

While some have praised Roosevelt's tendency to experiment and others have deprecated it, it has never been analyzed in theoretical terms.[119] Looking at it in the light of the predictions of the four decision-making approaches allows us to do so. Again, the motivational and analytical approaches are least helpful. Under the circumstances Roosevelt faced, the motivational approach does not expect a decision-maker to act at all, let alone to experiment with evident enthusiasm. Nor does his behavior accord with the predictions of the analytical approach.[120] Instead of carefully weighing the advantages and disadvantages of alternative policies and making trade-offs, Roosevelt experimented. Moreover, his experiments do not appear to have involved direct comparisons of alternative policies. Nor did he evaluate them sequentially, as in satisficing. Rather, his usual practice was to field simultaneously somewhat contradictory policies that he apparently regarded not as competitors, but as equally reasonable possibilities that could be assessed only by trying them out. Thus he entertained the idea of an international conference that would include the dictators at the very time he was planning a naval blockade against at least one of them. Indeed, Roosevelt habitually launched alternatives that had not even been fully evaluated individually. Moreover, there is no indication that he attempted to deal with uncer-

[118] Ibid.

[119] Welles, for example, in detailing Roosevelt's efforts to find a way to act against the Japanese, praises his "exceptionally fertile mind . . . which usually refused to concede that any problem was insoluble. He was unwilling to agree that in the realm of statesmanship there could be such a thing as a dead-end street. . . . To me the ingenuity with which he so often devised the most effective solution in a given circumstance was a constant source of amazement." *Seven Decisions*, 77–78. Borg, on the other hand, describes these same efforts as "pursuing a variety of nebulous schemes for warding off catastrophe." "Notes," 405. On the experimental character of Roosevelt's decision-making, see also Cole, *Roosevelt*, 246, and Borg, *United States*, 377–78, 384–86, 537.

[120] See appendix A.

tainty by calculating outcome probabilities. Rather, he put policies forward and then waited to see how they did. Such behavior is all the more puzzling for the analytical model because Roosevelt had no pressing need to act in this fashion, not being forced by a crisis situation, for instance, to make decisions with incomplete information and insufficient time.

Experimenting with alternatives based on contrary premises also generally violates the intuitive approach's expectation of a need for consistency. However, such a response to uncertainty might be explained by the intuitive notion of uncommitted thinking according to which

> the high-level policy maker, beset with uncertainty and sitting at the intersection of a number of information channels, will tend at different times to adopt *different* belief patterns for the same decision problem. Since his own experience does not commit him to a particular belief pattern, he will adopt several competing patterns, not at once, but in sequence.[121]

Nevertheless, while Roosevelt's decision-making between 1936 and 1938 seems superficially to fit the pattern, this explanation has serious problems. There is little evidence that Roosevelt wavered among the views of his advisers according to which was most forceful. Not only did his own experience make him less vulnerable to the opinions of experts, but also his uncertainty was shared by a number of his advisers. Moreover, his vacillation was caused as much by unfavorable developments in the external environment, such as Chamberlain's rejection of his conference idea in the spring of 1938, as by any disagreement among his advisers.[122]

In contrast to the intuitive approach, the political approach to decision-making specifically predicts a disposition to experiment in the face of uncertainty.[123] In fact, trying out different alternatives (as opposed to reflecting on them as an analytical decision-maker would or employing one of the psychological coping mechanisms) follows as naturally from the drive to act of political decision-makers as it does from their pragmatic attitude toward means.[124] For Roosevelt, who believed

[121] John D. Steinbruner, *Cybernetic Theory of Decision* (Princeton: Princeton University Press, 1974), 128–30; Halperin, *Bureaucratic Politics*, 24.

[122] The sole example of Roosevelt switching between policies because of his advisers (alternating in the fall and winter of 1937–1938 between the views of Welles and Hull over the desirability of holding an international conference) was due to a political, rather than a cognitive, problem. Roosevelt liked the idea behind the Welles Peace Plan and never really adopted Hull's belief that it would not work. He withdrew it initially not because he had changed his mind about it, but because it was unacceptable to his secretary of state, bowing to Hull's political weight rather than to the force of his arguments.

[123] See above, chap. 2.

[124] Roosevelt expressed this attitude publicly at the beginning of his experimenting. "There are counselors these days who say: 'Do nothing'; other counselors who say: 'Do

that, left to itself, international politics was headed for disaster, experimentation provided a way out of the dilemma posed by his uncertainty on the one hand and his desire to prevent war on the other. By experimenting, he was forced neither to remain passive in the face of impending catastrophe nor to commit himself fully to solutions of dubious efficacy. Rather, he could keep his options open, politically and strategically, while he searched for a policy that would work both domestically and internationally.

Equally important, by allowing Roosevelt to acquire information, experimenting reduced uncertainty itself. Unsure of the dictators' intentions, Roosevelt could float a policy initiative and observe their reactions. Launching a scheme like the Welles Peace Plan was a way to test their willingness to cooperate with the international community. Moreover, experimenting could help him evaluate policy alternatives by testing their feasibility, internationally as well as domestically.[125] In meetings with La Grange and Monnet in January and Bullitt in February 1938, for example, Roosevelt showed a characteristic willingness to improvise policy ideas in response to new developments and present them to others without apparently having put them through a systematic assessment process, possibly in the belief that this would help him gauge reactions about how they would be received.[126]

Secondly, Roosevelt experimented in order to elicit suggestions for improving his policies. As Borg notes, in searching for a way to allow neu-

---

everything.' Common sense dictates an avoidance of both extremes. I say to you: 'Do something,' and when you have done something, if it works, do it some more; and if it does not work, then do something else." Address to the Young Democratic Club of Baltimore, April 13, 1936. Quoted in Geoffrey C. Ward, ed., *Closest Companion* (New York: Houghton Mifflin, 1995), 80.

[125] Roosevelt used a number of techniques to get feedback about both substance and acceptability. To test the reactions of foreign leaders he usually resorted to diplomatic feelers, sometimes through channels, as with his inquiries to the British about the Welles Peace Plan, sometimes not, as in his use of Secretary Morgenthau to float the idea of British-American staff talks after the *Panay* incident. To test domestic reaction, Roosevelt either broached the subject himself, as in the Quarantine Speech, or had someone like Ickes do it for him. Abe Fortas recalled

watching FDR quite deliberately use Harold Ickes . . . by encouraging him to make a speech outlining a position that was considerably in front of where the nation stood at the time. The speech given, Roosevelt would sit back—his antennae waving in the air and his cigarette holder pointing toward heaven—and wait for the playback from the country. Or to change the figure of speech: he would see if an Ickes could open a hole in the defensive line of public opinion. If so, Roosevelt would take the ball and run through it. If not, he would toss his head and deplore Ickes' rashness.

Abe Fortas, "The Presidency as I Have Seen It," in Hughes, *Living Presidency*, 332.

[126] Both Roosevelt's blockade idea and the Welles Peace Plan both failed this test, foundering on their inability to elicit support from the British. Haight, "Naval Quarantine," 225.

trals to influence the international situation without becoming involved if war should break out, he "tended to follow a practice of giving expression to some half-formulated concept in the hope that others would be stimulated to improve upon it until it reached the point of furnishing a possible basis for action."[127] Indeed, Roosevelt's own testimony suggests that he saw the Quarantine Speech as precisely this kind of experiment. As he explained to reporters, he was "actively searching" for a way to promote peace, but he could not yet say what the method would be. His speech indicated an "attitude, and it does not outline a program; but it says we are looking for a program."[128]

The Quarantine Speech may also be an example of Roosevelt's use of experimental evaluation to test for domestic acceptability. Experimenting provides a way to conduct the screening for acceptability that the political approach to decision-making predicts as the first stage of evaluation.[129] To the extent that it may not be sensible for busy policymakers to expend energy spelling out the details of a proposed policy before learning whether it is at least minimally acceptable, moreover, experimenting promotes efficiency. Thus, Borg's complaint about the absence of detail in Roosevelt's proposals misses the point.[130] He launched initiatives such as the Quarantine Speech to get things moving and, in particular, to get information about acceptability. There was no urgency about working out the details before he had satisfied himself on this point.

Nevertheless, Roosevelt's experience between 1936 and 1938 suggests that despite its advantages, experimenting has drawbacks. For one thing, it may result in an incomplete evaluation of the alternatives. Trying out options successively means that they are unlikely to be compared directly, preventing a thorough understanding of their relative advantages and disadvantages. Moreover, experimenting with a number of different, and possibly contradictory, policies may cause confusion, even anger.

[127] Borg, *United States*, 378. See also "Notes," 406.

[128] "The Four Hundredth Press Conference, October 6, 1937," *PPA* 6:414–25; Borg, *United States*, 383.

[129] Roosevelt's propensity for conducting this sort of experiment was noted approvingly by one of his closest advisers:

No President should commit himself completely to a specific course of action . . . until he has some idea of the support he may expect and the opposition he may encounter. Roosevelt frequently guarded himself against premature or improvident action by encouraging members of his administration to advance controversial proposals, sometimes rival or even conflicting proposals, to test public reaction before he would take a definite position.

Benjamin V. Cohen, "The Presidency as I See it," in Hughes, *Living Presidency*, 322. On the political need to keep options open see Schlesinger, *Age of Roosevelt*, 1:420, 423–24, 452–55.

[130] Borg, *United States*, 378.

Thus, some historians believe that Roosevelt's behavior in 1937 was at least partly responsible for the British feeling that it would be undesirable to join him in the cooperative ventures he proposed.[131] Whether these fears actually drove British policy, as well as whether Roosevelt could have done anything to alleviate them given his genuine uncertainty about the appropriate course of action, is unclear, and much of his uncertainty was due to his own concern about *British* unreliability. Nonetheless, the possibility that experimenting can lead to misunderstanding should not be overlooked.

In the end, the usefulness of an experimental evaluation depends on the decision-maker's awareness that fielding an idea is not the same as evaluating it completely. If the original purpose of seeking information and ideas is kept firmly in mind, however, experimenting can perform a number of useful functions that distinguish it clearly from the wavering of the uncommitted thinker.[132] In this connection it is instructive to compare Roosevelt's behavior in the years before Munich to President Carter's in 1979 during the Iran hostage crisis. The contrast between the purposeful maneuvering of a political decision-maker and the vacillation of one who is really drifting is readily apparent.[133]

On occasion, of course, Roosevelt himself drifted,[134] but for the most

[131] Chamberlain, and other British statesmen as well, still

doubted Roosevelt's willingness or ability to act. . . . The president's proposals did bear the stamp of impetuous improvisation. These qualities not unnaturally concerned the British, who reasoned that careful preparations to meet consequences should precede strong moves. . . . Roosevelt reinforced the impression of influential members of the Chamberlain government that he was erratic, vacillating, and undependable.

Leutze, *Bargaining*, 28. See also Loewenheim, "Illusion," 192–95 and Harrison, "United States," which documents the British misperception of Roosevelt's approaches to them throughout the period from 1933 to 1938.

[132] Roosevelt's remarks to the press about the intent of the Quarantine Speech, as well as his practice of fielding rather extreme proposals in private conversations with foreign envoys that he later allowed the State Department to qualify considerably, seem to indicate his awareness of this. See Acting Secretary of State Welles's attempts to clarify Roosevelt's remarks to Jules Henry during the Nine Power Conference about possible American actions in the Far East in response to a Japanese attack on British or French possessions. "The Acting Secretary of State to the Ambassador in France (Bullitt)," *FRUS*, 1937, 4:170–71.

[133] Betty Glad, *Jimmy Carter* (New York: W. W. Norton, 1986), 459–60. Deborah W. Larson provides another example of real drift in her description of President Truman's behavior toward the Soviet Union in 1946, *Origins of Containment* (Princeton: Princeton University Press, 1985), chap. 6.

[134] See Schlesinger's description of his handling of the Tammany Hall scandals during his first term as governor, *Age of Roosevelt* 1:393–95. Steinbruner uses Roosevelt's treatment of economic policy in the winter of 1934–1935 as an example of uncommitted thinking. *Cybernetic*, 128, 131.

part throughout his career his decision-making was characterized by true experimenting. Moreover, few have more clearly understood the essential connection between the political decision-maker's drive to act and a commitment to experimenting in the face of uncertainty. Thus, calling for "bold, persistent experimentation," he observed that "It is common sense to take a method and try it: If it fails, admit it frankly and try another. But above all, try something."[135]

Acceptability

During the pre-Munich period, Roosevelt showed a marked disinclination to transgress the limits of acceptability. This, of course, is the hallmark of a political approach to decision-making and only the analytical approach offers an alternative explanation. Analytic decision-makers can either treat acceptability as a value at stake in the decision, trading it off against the others in order to maximize utility, or they can treat it as a constraint that establishes a feasible set of alternatives within which optimizing can then take place.[136]

Clearly, Roosevelt did not do the former. For him, acceptability was a prior concern: alternatives were evaluated on that dimension early and those that were deficient were seldom pursued unless the defect could be rectified. Moreover, he apparently did not integrate acceptability with other values and trade off to achieve the greatest utility, but rejected or altered alternatives lacking in acceptability regardless of how well they served other values. But although Roosevelt used acceptability as a screening device, he did not treat the remaining alternatives as a feasible set. Indeed, he habitually retrieved discarded alternatives and tried them again. Rather than optimizing, he experimented, even when that involved launching contradictory policies simultaneously.

While Roosevelt's way of approaching acceptability problems does not bear out the predictions of the analytical approach to decision-making, it does conform to those of the political approach. In particular, he usually declined to insist on his policies if they failed to meet an acceptability criterion. At times he balanced his goals in the decision at hand against his objectives in other areas and, if he judged the latter more important,

135 Cited in Geoffrey C. Ward, *Before the Trumpet, Young Franklin Roosevelt: 1882–1905* (New York: Harper and Row, 1986), 6. Most striking of course is the essentially experimental character of the New Deal. Roosevelt's willingness to experiment can be seen even earlier, for example, in his organization of the Temporary Emergency Relief Agency when he was governor of New York. Schlesinger, *Age of Roosevelt*, 2: chap. 16; Freidel, *Roosevelt*, 3:223, 4:64.

136 Elster, *Ulysses*, 113, and Jon Elster, "Introduction," *Rational Choice*, ed. Jon Elster (New York: New York University Press, 1986), 4.

backed away from the decision—at least temporarily—frequently sacrificing an international objective to achieve a domestic one. For example, at the Nine Power Conference when a groundswell of support for action against Japan failed to materialize, he refused to jeopardize needed domestic economic reforms for the sake of a move that at best had uncertain international support.[137] At other times, if the acceptability constraint could not be satisfied, Roosevelt avoided the issue, for example by moving the decision to another arena. Thus, being more pessimistic about support for his policies in Congress than in the public at large, he concentrated his energies on steps like the Welles Peace Plan and a quarantine of the Japanese that did not necessarily require congressional cooperation.[138]

Roosevelt also dealt with a lack of acceptability by attempting to increase it. One way of doing this was by manipulating an alternative to improve its acceptability, as his instructions to Davis before the Nine Power Conference show. Aware that collective action against Japan had to be acceptable to the American public, he insisted on the creation of a record of accommodation by the democracies that would serve to "mobilize public opinion and moral force" in the event the Japanese refused to cooperate. He also demanded that any action be agreed upon unanimously in order to command the moral authority that could only be lent by the agreement of all peace-loving nations.[139] On similar grounds, Roosevelt objected to the word "sanctions." At the Nine Power Conference and again during the *Panay* incident, his insistence on finding new

[137] This behavior may also be seen in his earlier attempt to alter the neutrality legislation.

[138] Roosevelt's remark to Luther Gulick in the summer of 1937 that Woodrow Wilson's only mistake was failing "to do the things that were required to bring the Congress along" can be interpreted in this light. When Roosevelt believed he could not bring Congress along, he avoided going to it. When he could not help going to Congress, as in the case of Lend Lease in 1940, he made every effort to make the legislation acceptable to it. As Sam Rosenman recalled, when Roosevelt allowed the Lend Lease debate to drag on for three months, many "urged him to do something to cut it short. But he always replied that this would be a departure from the American tradition and that he *preferred* a full and exhaustive debate, so that its conclusion with the passage of the law by Congress could be seen as a democratic sign of real national unity. In those months, I marveled at his patience." Luther Gulick, *Administrative Reflections from World War II* (Birmingham, Ala.: University of Alabama Press, 1948), 42. Rosenman, "The Presidency," 361.

[139] Davis Memo, October 20, 1937, Norman H. Davis Papers, Box 4, Brussels Conference/Nine Power Conference Folder, Library of Congress; and Farnham, "Value Conflict," chap. 3 and appendix. Roosevelt also demonstrated his awareness of the need to shape an alternative to make it more acceptable to public opinion in his talk with La Grange in January 1938, telling him that one of the virtues of his blockade plan was that, even if it eventuated in war, the dictators would have to be the ones to make the formal declaration. Haight, "Naval Quarantine," 223, 225–26.

terms like "quarantine" seems to have been based on the notion that his policies would be acceptable to the public if they were not associated with traditional forms of military force.[140]

Acceptability can also be increased by using one of the traditional political strategies, and Roosevelt used procrastination deliberately, and very skillfully, during the helium controversy to defuse a situation in which any decision would have been unacceptable to one of two powerful Cabinet members. As Ickes himself described Roosevelt's strategy, "His thought is to drag the thing along."[141] What is particularly striking about this episode is that, for Roosevelt, the whole helium controversy was about politics from start to finish. At no time did he show any real interest in the substantive issue of whether Germany received the helium or not. What he did care about was finding a solution acceptable to Ickes and Hull in order to prevent the disruption of his political organization.[142]

A decision-maker can also deal with the acceptability constraint by trying to loosen it. The traditional political strategies are intimately connected to time-buying and education, and Roosevelt employed both during this period. The relationship between his generally activist temperament and his attitude toward the passage of time is especially interesting. As suggested by his reaction to the failure of the Nine Power Conference and his response to the *Panay* incident, his desire for effective action was accompanied by considerable patience in the face of setbacks. When for any reason he was unable to move, be it lack of British cooperation or absence of domestic support, he did not display great annoyance or frustration. Rather, he seemed to sense that however desirable action might be, nothing could be accomplished until the time was right.

This equanimity may also have been due to a sense that the passage of time could bring certain advantages. Future events might not only clarify the situation and improve Roosevelt's understanding of what would

[140] Such thinking may also have been behind his refusal to agree to Ambassador Lindsay's proposal at the time of the *Panay* incident that the United States join the British in a massive naval demonstration in the Far East. Ibid., 210; Leutze, *Bargaining*, 20.

[141] Roosevelt successfully avoided dealing with the dispute between Hull and Ickes from March to May 1938. Although he did try to pressure Ickes into signing the contract with Germany in May, the Secretary's intransigence again caused him to drop the matter; in the end the issue disappeared without Roosevelt having seriously alienated either Hull or Ickes. In the aftermath of the Munich crisis, Hull, no longer as eager to conciliate Germany, failed to pursue the matter further, and Ickes felt completely vindicated by the German attack on Poland in September 1939. See Ickes, *Diary*, 2:344, 373, 376–77, 385, 391–94, 396–98. See also Ickes's remarks on the President's delaying tactics on April 21 and July 3, 2:377, 418; and Reagan, "The Helium Controversy," 53–54.

[142] Note that this accords with Diesing's notion of political rationality in which the health of the political organization takes priority over all substantive concerns. *Reason in Society*, 170, 228, 231–32.

work, but also make it easier to enact the appropriate policies by educating the public to the need for positive action. For example, despite his
failure to create support for a move against Japan at the Nine Power
Conference, his activities may have had a positive effect in educating
public opinion in America and abroad about the Japanese threat, as he
himself was well aware. Thus, he instructed Davis to prolong the conference as long as possible, even if he failed in his principal aims, in order to
"strengthen the moral climate against the war-making states and to educate public opinion."[143]

Roosevelt's attitude toward the Quarantine Speech is another example
of his use of education to loosen the acceptability constraint. As Haight
points out, his remarks to Endicott Peabody about his struggle against a
long-standing "public psychology which comes close to saying 'Peace at
any price, . . . were not just offhand remarks . . . but reflected one of
Roosevelt's basic goals, education of the public to the need of preventing
war."[144] This goal was also reflected in his observation to French Chargé
Jules Henry on November 6 that he had been fighting the idea that "a
policy of neutrality at all costs gave security" and that "his Chicago
speech had played a part in this campaign."[145] Henry came away with
the impression that the President was determined to persist in his effort to
educate public opinion and, by February 1938, Roosevelt believed he
was succeeding, writing to Arthur Murray that he was "in the midst of a
long process of education—and the process seems to be working slowly
but surely."[146]

[143] Cole, *Roosevelt*, 251. For additional evidence that Roosevelt came to believe that
long-term education would be a more appropriate method for dealing with the problem at
this time, see Farnham, "Value Conflict," 945.

[144] Haight, "Roosevelt and the Aftermath," 235. See also Roosevelt's remarks to
Eichelberger, above.

[145] Haight, "France and the Aftermath," 299–300. Divine concurs in this analysis—see
Roosevelt and World War II, 18–19. Bennett thinks getting the public's attention was the
"sum and essence" of the Quarantine Speech. *Search for Security*, 101. Welles interprets
Roosevelt's emphasis on the educational aspects of the Quarantine Speech somewhat differently. Believing that the speech really did refer to Roosevelt's July blockade idea, Welles
argues that he settled for an educational purpose only when prevented by public outcry and
lack of support from adopting the stronger measures he desired. *Seven Decisions*, 13.

[146] Viscount Elibank, "Franklin Roosevelt, Friend of Britain," *Contemporary Review*
187 (1955): 363. (Arthur Murray later became Viscount Elibank.) Roosevelt also continued to think that he could educate an even wider audience, believing that he "could persuade . . . '90 percent of the population of the world' to quarantine the aggressor," and that
his Quarantine Speech had already gone a long way toward doing just that. For example,
on October 22, he wrote to Cardinal Mundelein that "the Chicago Speech has had a definite effect in at least the will to peace in many parts of the world." Haight, "Roosevelt and
the Aftermath," 233. Roosevelt to Mundelein, Oct. 22, 1937, *PL*, 3:720–22. See also
Roosevelt to Clarke, Oct. 22, 1937, ibid., 3:722–23; Roosevelt to Biddle, Oct., 27, 1937,
ibid., 3:725; and Ickes, *Diary*, 2:232.

Information Processing in the Political Approach to Decision-Making

Just as a political approach to decision-making explains much of Roosevelt's behavior in these watershed years, that behavior illustrates several ways the political context affects information processing that are difficult for psychological models based on laboratory experiments to capture. Roosevelt's use of experimenting as both a diagnostic tool and a method of evaluation has already been cited. Moreover, his decision-making demonstrates that in a political context, some alternatives do surface repeatedly and are thus assessed more than once, a phenomenon intensified by the practice of experimentation. It also shows that even though an alternative has been evaluated previously, it may be redefined when the opportunity to act arises. Faced with the possibility of putting a policy into effect, a political decision-maker will explore its implications more thoroughly, attempting to discover what would be needed to implement that option, and trying to tailor it to the circumstances in which it might operate. Thus, for example, the blockade scheme appears to have undergone some modification at Roosevelt's hands each time he considered it.

What also emerges from analyzing Roosevelt's evaluations in this period is that no matter how closely an alternative is considered, it may still not be compared with the other options. Rather, a previously considered alternative may be subject to "blending."[147] In developing the blockade idea, for example, Roosevelt seems to have incorporated his 1935 notion of respecting a rather traditional naval blockade into the more activist conception of collective neutrality that surfaced at Buenos Aires in 1936. Further modification in the summer of 1937 ultimately producd the scheme of isolating the aggressor states he presented in the Quarantine Speech and later refined during the planning for the Brussels Conference.[148]

CONCLUSION

In the three years before Munich, Roosevelt's uncertainty about how to assess the foreign-policy problem facing him, together with his strong disposition to act and his understanding of the profound domestic reluc-

---

[147] See appendix A.

[148] A related, but less normative, possibility is "confirmation processing" of a favored alternative (appendix A). However, although Roosevelt does not seem to have compared his blockade policy to other alternatives, there is no indication of this practice. The fact that he was simultaneously pursuing the quite different notion of an international conference that would include the dictators argues against the idea that he had a favored alternative at all. Indeed, it may be presumed that a decision-maker who is busily experimenting with a number of different alternatives by definition lacks one that is preferred on all dimensions.

tance to contemplate any steps that might risk American involvement in war, led him to experiment, alternately picking up and dropping two threads of policy based on quite different notions of the prospects of socializing the dictators to the norms of the international system. In identifying this behavior as a natural outgrowth of a political decision-maker's response to the demands of the political context, the political approach to decision-making is able to explain what many have attributed to weakness, cynicism, or drift and indecision. In turn, Roosevelt's behavior supports its prediction that, under uncertainty, the will to act and the need to consider acceptability combine to encourage experimenting to gather information that might help define the situation and to test the feasibility of various alternatives.

Unfortunately, in Roosevelt's case, experimenting did not yield sufficient information to dispel his uncertainty. His April 20, 1938, press conference shows that analyses like Lindbergh's and Messersmith's, together with recent events, had made an impression on him. His heightened concern about the impact of the neutrality laws and a possible military threat via Latin America suggests that he had reached the conclusion that the dictator states in fact had the ability to threaten American security. Moreover, his advocacy of a large Navy and fresh criticism of the neutrality laws imply that he had begun to think in terms of balancing the dictators' strength by augmenting American capabilities and aiding other states. Nevertheless, Roosevelt's awareness of the dictators' capacity to jeopardize American security did not move him to formulate a policy to meet that threat because he still had not made a firm diagnosis about their intentions. For the President, unlike Messersmith, the Anschluss did not provide definitive evidence of Hitler's implacable will to expand. His doubts about appeasement notwithstanding, he had not yet concluded that working with the dictators was completely out of the question. Despite fresh worries, as Hitler prepared his next move, Roosevelt's ambivalence and uncertainty persisted.

CHAPTER IV

The Munich Crisis

ANXIOUS TO HEAD OFF the dangerous drift in international affairs, but plagued by uncertainty about the intentions of the major European players, from 1936 to 1938 Roosevelt alternated between two somewhat contradictory lines of policy. How the Munich crisis affected this pattern has long been a matter of controversy, raising at least two important issues of historical interpretation. The first concerns Roosevelt's intentions during the crisis itself: did he support British and French efforts to appease Hitler? The second concerns Munich's influence on his thinking about American security. Was the crisis in some sense a turning point in the development of Roosevelt's foreign policy?

In addressing the first question, some historians argue that Roosevelt was basically sympathetic to appeasement before and during the crisis, as well as for some time thereafter.[1] For them, the answer to the second question is obvious: the crisis had little impact. Even some who believe that Roosevelt was skeptical about appeasement, however, hold that he remained detached during the crisis and substantially unchanged after it.[2] I take issue with this view. Far from supporting appeasement, Roosevelt disapproved of it and sought throughout the crisis to strengthen the will of the democracies. Moreover, the experience of Munich had a profound impact on him, affecting not only his activities during the crisis, but also his subsequent diagnosis and policies.

In order to provide a baseline against which the effect of the crisis can be measured, I begin by showing the limited nature of Roosevelt's willingness to involve himself in the European conflict before Munich. Up to the very eve of the crisis, despite his awareness of a sharply deteriorating situation and a desire to help, his uncertainty about what he could do, coupled with reservations about the motives of Britain and France, kept him from acting forcefully. Once the crisis began in earnest, his decision-making unfolded in two distinct stages, with the Godesberg meeting between Hitler and Chamberlain serving as the line of demarcation. The first, which was characterized by Roosevelt's marked disinclination to intervene, extended from September 13 to September 22, coming to a climax with his conversation with British Ambassador Lindsay on Sep-

---

[1] E.g., Offner, *American Appeasement*, 269–70, and "Misperception," 613.
[2] See Burns, *Lion*, 385.

tember 19. The second, which began on September 23 as the initial reports of Hitler's Godesberg ultimatum reached Washington, continued until the signing of the Munich Agreement on September 30. From an American perspective, its high point was Roosevelt's change of heart about the desirability of intervening in the crisis, culminating in his appeals of September 25 and 27.

This dramatic reversal of preferences from inaction to intervention is the most puzzling aspect of Roosevelt's decision-making during the Munich crisis. Because we have been able to develop a fairly detailed picture of his behavior during the crisis, however, it is possible to compare alternative explanations of his decision-making processes, producing several theoretically interesting results. For one, prospect theory, Tversky and Kahneman's theory of judgment and choice under risk, offers the most satisfactory explanation of Roosevelt's abrupt departure from his previous policy toward the crisis. For another, because the Munich crisis shared many of the conditions under which Janis and Mann's decisional-conflict model is said to apply, the failure of his behavior to conform to its predictions raises questions about its usefulness.[3] Finally, Roosevelt's decision-making during the crisis is marked by a number of the themes that characterized it in the three preceding years: a desire to act, a concern with acceptability, and an awareness of the need to balance international and domestic concerns. Even during a crisis, Roosevelt continued to act as a political decision-maker.

SPRING AND SUMMER 1938

Ostensibly arising out of the unsatisfied demands of three and one half million Germans living in the Sudeten region of Czechoslovakia, the Munich crisis began to brew shortly after the German takeover of Austria. In the spring of 1938, encouraged by Hitler, the leader of the Sudeten Germans, Konrad Heinlein, demanded complete autonomy. The Czech government refused and France and Britain were drawn into the controversy. France was obligated to defend Czechoslovakia from unprovoked attack under the terms of the 1925 Treaty of Mutual Assistance; Britain, though committed by the Treaty of Locarno to assist France against such aggression, had no specific obligation to defend Czechoslovakia. However, as Telford Taylor points out, "under Britain's traditional balance-of-power strategy in Europe, the defeat of France by

[3] See appendix A.

Germany could not be tolerated," making France's commitment to Czechoslovakia a source of considerable anxiety.[4]

What made the Czech crisis critical was that, lacking a common border with Czechoslovakia, France and Britain had no way to assist her short of general war.[5] It is thus not altogether surprising that they reacted to the demands of the Sudeten Germans by "urging maximum possible concessions and informing Berlin of their eagerness for a settlement." The Czechs, however, were initially determined to stand firm and, in response to the failure of negotiations with Heinlein and reports of German troop concentrations on their borders, partially mobilized on on May 20, 1938. The British, French, and Russians backed this move and the so-called May Crisis subsided.[6] The sporadic efforts of the British and French to settle the crisis continued until September when it became clear that autonomy for the Sudeten Germans would no longer suffice. Annexation of the Sudetenland was the only outcome Hitler would now tolerate.[7]

Contemplating the worsening climate in Central Europe in the spring and summer of 1938, Roosevelt was worried about the possibility of war but uncertain about the intentions of the major players, owing to contradictory reports from abroad, the conflicting views of members of his administration, and his own suspicions about the resolve of the British and French and their motives in trying to involve the United States. This mixture of uncertainty and concern was reflected in Roosevelt's determination not to be drawn in. While sympathetic to the democracies and frustrated by his inability to find a way to support them, he declined to join openly in their attempts to deal with the German threat, despite the persistent efforts of some members of his administration.

From the outset, Roosevelt received a steady stream of alarming reports from his ambassadors in Europe, especially Bullitt and Kennedy. In a personal letter to Roosevelt on May 20, for example, Bullitt stated his belief that the United States should act to prevent a cataclysmic war.[8] To

[4] The Soviet Union, too, had a defensive alliance with Czechoslovakia, but enforcement by either party was contingent upon prior action by France. Telford Taylor, *Munich* (New York: Doubleday, 1979), 2–3.

[5] Taylor, *Origins of the Second World War*, 151. See also Stromberg, *Collective Security*, 122.

[6] Dallek, *Franklin D. Roosevelt*, 162.

[7] Divine, *Reluctant Belligerent*, 53; Taylor, *Munich*, 6–7.

[8] "I feel it would be an unspeakable tragedy if France, to support Czechoslovakia, should attack the 'Siegfried Line.' . . . If you believe as I believe, that it is not in the interest of the United States or civilization as a whole to have the continent of Europe devastated, I think we should attempt to find some way which will let the French out of their moral commitment." Bullitt, *For the President*, 261–62. See also Taylor, *Munich*, 518–19, and

this end, he proposed that if the Germans marched across the Czech frontier, the President should call a four-power conference (Great Britain, France, Germany, and Italy) to work out a peaceful settlement, making a personal appeal to the parties and sending an American representative to sit with the conferees. Since such a meeting would probably produce a recommendation for a plebiscite in Czechoslovakia, a Czech refusal to carry out it out would provide the French "with an escape from their desperate moral dilemma" and avert a European war. Roosevelt should not worry about the charge of "selling out a small nation." Accepting such opprobrium was a small enough price to pay to avoid general war.[9]

Bullitt's alarm was based largely on fears about German air power and Roosevelt, too, was getting new reports, reinforcing earlier ones, about the disparity between Hitler's air forces and those of the democracies. Initially, however, he was neither greatly affected by the pessimism of his advisers nor disposed to act precipitously.[10] As he observed to Ambassador Cudahy on June 13, "Things are very definitely in a dangerous balance and all we can do is hope for the best." The United States government would continue to maintain an "attitude of contemplation."[11]

As the summer wore on, Roosevelt did begin to cast about for ways to influence the European situation, but not in the direction of appeasement as Bullitt had suggested. Rather, he tried to stiffen the democracies' resistance to Hitler's demands by offering them at least verbal support. While these steps signal some change from his previous inactivity, they also show the limited character of what he was willing to do.

In August, Roosevelt attempted to deter Hitler from pursuing his aggressive designs in Czechoslovakia by creating, in Berle's words, "a certain amount of doubt abroad as to what our intentions may be. This, it is thought, may have a moderating effect."[12] Thus, in a speech in Kingston,

---

John McVickar Haight, Jr., "France, the United States, and the Munich Crisis," *Journal of Modern History* 32 (1960): 341–42.

[9] Bullitt, *For the President*, 262–63; Taylor, *Munich*, 4–5; and Dallek, *Franklin D. Roosevelt*, 162. For other communications of a similar character from Bullitt during this period, see *FRUS*, 1938, May 17, 21, 24, June 6, 1938, 1:505, 508–9, 519, 524–25, and Schewe 6: no.s 1156, 1159. The general tenor of Bullitt's correspondence at this time is conveyed by Secretary Ickes, who visited him in early June: "He is most pessimistic and since my return I find that he has been writing to the President in tones as hopeless as those in which he spoke to us." Ickes, *Diary*, 2:410.

[10] As Ickes reported after lunching at the White House on June 26, "The President had seen Joe Kennedy and had been hearing from Bill Bullitt about the European situation. I think the President regards their attitude as being a bit pessimistic." Ickes, *Diary*, 2:415. See also Beschloss, *Kennedy and Roosevelt*, 174; Ickes, *Diary*, 2:420.

[11] "Roosevelt, Hyde Park, to John Cudahy, Minister to the Irish Free State, June 28, 1938," Schewe, 6: no. 1175; Langer and Gleason, *Challenge*, 32.

[12] "Adolf A. Berle, Jr., Assistant Secretary of State, to Roosevelt, August 15, 1938," Schewe, 6: no. 1225.

Ontario, on August 18, Roosevelt emphasized the inevitability of American concern about events in Europe and pledged that the United States would "not stand idly by" if Canada were threatened, declaring, "We in the Americas are no longer a far away continent, to which the eddies of controversies beyond the seas could bring no interest or no harm."[13] Roosevelt described these sentiments to Lord Tweedsmuir on August 31, 1938, as "so obvious that I cannot quite understand why some American President did not say it half a century ago," noting that "the occasion seemed to fit in with the Hitler situation and had, I hope, some small effect in Berlin." Since Roosevelt's pronouncement in Kingston was concerned primarily with the defense of the Western Hemisphere, however, it is not altogether surprising that Hitler remained undeterred in Central Europe and that alarming reports continued to arrive in Washington.[14]

By the end of August, predictions of a September war abounded and Roosevelt, frustrated by British inaction, observed to Ambassador Claude Bowers on August 31, "I do wish our British friends would see the situation as it seems to be—but, as you know, they are doing everything to stall off controversy until at least 1940."[15] Roosevelt, on the other hand, continued to search for ways to deter Hitler, asking Morgenthau on August 30 to come up with a plan to set up a special fund for French and British gold. The following day, the secretary presented him with three alternatives and raised the possibility of using the threat of countervailing duties to deter Germany.

Roosevelt was pleased with these plans and ultimately approved them.[16] As Morgenthau had feared, however, Secretary Hull was uneasy, observing that "there was such a thing as doing too much at this time. . . . We are apt to get the American people up on their toes over the European

---

[13] "Speech by Roosevelt, Queens University, Kingston, Ontario, Canada, August 18, 1938," ibid., no. 1234. See also Hull, *Memoirs*, 1:586–88; Stetson Conn and Byron Fairchild, *The Framework of Hemisphere Defense* (Washington, D.C.: Office of the Chief of Military History, Department of the Army, 1960), 4; and Haight, "France, the United States, and the Munich Crisis," 343.

[14] "FDR to Tweedsmuir, August 31, 1938," PPF, 3381–3421, no. 3396. Dallek, *Franklin D. Roosevelt*, 163; Offner, *American Appeasement*, 256. The flavor of the reports received at this time may be sampled in Charge in United Kingdom to Hull, Aug. 18, 1938, and Messersmith to Hull, Aug. 20, 1938, *FRUS*, 1938, 1:66–67. On August 19 Bernard Baruch also telephoned Roosevelt from Scotland to tell him that "the democracies had nothing with which to stop Hitler." Bernard Baruch, *The Public Years* (New York: Holt, Rinehart, and Winston, 1960), 273.

[15] "Roosevelt to Claude G. Bowers, Ambassador to Spain, St. Jean de Luz, France, August 31, 1938," Schewe, 6: no. 1257. For communications about the imminence of war, see ibid., no.s 1258–60.

[16] "Morgenthau Diary," Aug. 31, 1938, FDRL, 137:227–31. Accounts of this meeting can also be found in Blum, *Morgenthau Diaries* 1:515–16, and Dallek, *Franklin D. Roosevelt*, 163.

situation." Roosevelt persisted nonetheless, returning to the theme of deterring Germany and suggesting that the German representative be told that if Germany attacked Czechoslovakia the United States might apply countervailing duties. "In rehearsing how he would put it to the German charge, he at one time said, 'It's a hundred-to-one shot that I will do this if you go into Czechoslovakia' and another time he said, 'I hope you won't force my hand.'"

Although Hull remained unconvinced and Roosevelt took no action on Morgenthau's plans, the critical factor was not the secretary of state's reservations but disturbing news from Britain.[17] While the president had been seeking ways to support the Allies in whatever resolve they were able to muster and to deter Hitler from pressing the Czechs even harder, his ambassador to Britain was busily pursuing the opposite course. Hating the idea of war and harboring by no means entirely negative feelings toward Germany, Ambassador Kennedy assumed "the role of conciliator between his own country and Germany."[18] Practicing his own brand of diplomacy, Kennedy held a number of unusually cordial talks with the German ambassador to Great Britain, Herbert von Dirksen. In July, for example, he went so far as to tell von Dirksen that Roosevelt "would be prepared to support Germany's demands vis-à-vis England or to do anything that might lead to pacification," sentiments that Roosevelt would surely have had difficulty recognizing as his own.[19]

Kennedy also described Roosevelt's views quite differently, though no less inaccurately, to Prime Minister Chamberlain, telling him on August 30, "that if France went in and [Britain] had to go in too, the United States would follow before long." Worse yet, Kennedy stated his conviction that Roosevelt had "decided 'to go in with Chamberlain; whatever course Chamberlain desires to adopt he would think right.'"[20]

By the time Roosevelt, Morgenthau, and Hull reconvened on the morning of September 1, word of Kennedy's maneuvering had reached them. Furthermore, press reports of an interview between Kennedy and Halifax led them to suspect that the British were trying to manipulate the United States into taking responsibility for their decision about fighting: "Hull pointed out that . . . Britain was talking one way to the French and

[17] "Morgenthau Diary," Aug. 31, 1938, 137:229–30.

[18] Taylor, *Munich*, 767.

[19] Ibid., 767–69. See also William W. Kaufmann, "Two American Ambassadors: Bullitt and Kennedy," in *The Diplomats, 1919–1939*, ed. Gordon A. Craig and Felix Gilbert, (New York: Atheneum, 1963), 2:659.

[20] "Halifax to Lindsay, September 29, 1938," *Documents on British Foreign Policy, 1919–1939*, Third Series, ed. Rohan Butler and Sir E. L. Woodward (London: His Majesty's Stationery Office, 1951), 3:213. See also Taylor, *Munich*, 769; Kaufmann, "Two American Ambassadors," 661; and Richard Whalen, *The Founding Father* (New York: New American Library, 1964), 236.

another way to the Germans and a third way to Kennedy." Roosevelt expressed irritation with both the British and Ambassador Kennedy, declaring that

> Chamberlain was "slippery"; you could not trust him under any circumstances and that Chamberlain was playing the usual game of the British— peace at any price—and would try to place the blame on the United States for fighting or not fighting, and his inquiry to Kennedy was designed to place the blame on us, . . . Chamberlain was interested in peace at any price if he could get away with it and save his face.

Kennedy was criticized roundly for proposing to give a speech that, as Roosevelt put it, amounted to saying, "I can't for the life of me understand why anybody would want to go to war to save the Czechs." Roosevelt, marveling that the British had been able "to take into camp a redheaded Irishman," observed: "The young man needs his wrist slapped rather hard."[21]

Under these circumstances, Roosevelt, Hull, and Morgenthau agreed that it was best to take no further action. Although, as Roosevelt had observed earlier, "we can take these plans and put them in our middle drawer and . . . get at them in a moment's notice," for the present his scheme to deter Hitler with economic measures foundered on his suspicions about British motives.[22] Even so, he did not completely suppress the impulse to support the democracies. Over Hull's objections, he allowed Bullitt, in a speech at Pointe de Graves on September 4, to paraphrase an earlier declaration, saying, "We hope and pray that we may remain at peace with every nation in this world. But as I suggested on the twenty-second of February, 1937, if war should break out again in Europe, no human being could undertake to prophesy whether or not the United States would become involved in such a war."[23]

Authorizing this statement marked the outer limit of Roosevelt's willingness before Munich to intervene in the European situation,[24] and he

---

[21] "Morgenthau Diary," Sept. 1, 1938, 138:33–35. Hull and Roosevelt forced Kennedy to remove the offending paragraph from his speech and reminded him that all that the United States wished to say on the subject was contained in their own recent speeches. Hull to Kennedy, Sept. 1, 1938, *FRUS*, 1938, 1:586; and "Roosevelt to Hull, September 1, 1938," PSF, Cordell Hull, 1938 folder. See also Berle, *Navigating*, 182–84; Cole, *Roosevelt*, 67–68; Blum, *Morgenthau Diaries*, 1: 517–18; Dallek, *Franklin D. Roosevelt*, 163–64; Taylor, *Munich*, 770–71; Beschloss, *Kennedy and Roosevelt*, 174–75; and Whalen, *Founding Father*, 230–32, 237. Despite this reprimand, Kennedy continued his unauthorized maneuvering throughout September.

[22] "Morgenthau Diary," Sept. 1, 1938, 138:33–35.

[23] Haight, "France, the United States, and the Munich Crisis," 345.

[24] Hull told Bullitt that the President agreed with him that they both "had gone as far as our people would well understand." Ibid.

rebuffed all further efforts to enlist the United States openly on the side of Britain and France, particularly those of French Foreign Minister Bonnet.[25] However sympathetic he may have been toward the democracies, he was not disposed to join with them in any overt way to deal with the German threat to Czechoslovakia.

While this reluctance was in part related to Roosevelt's suspicions about the British and French, it may also have been a reaction to the confusion he perceived on every side. Venting his frustration with the quality of the reports he was getting during this period, he complained to reporters,

> there are so many stories that come through that are just rumors that you cannot tell. . . . You see . . . [reporters] cannot get news. . . . There is no way in which they can get the dope, the plain facts. The same thing happens to us. While our State Department dispatches are not as wild as the newspaper stories, they are darned near, and that is saying a lot.[26]

With some envoys expecting war momentarily, others predicting that there would be no fighting over Czechoslovakia, and still others (especially Bullitt and Kennedy) expressing each of these views alternately, Roosevelt had something to complain about.[27]

The confusing array of opinion appearing in the diplomatic traffic was mirrored by disagreement within the Administration on all aspects of the European situation save staying out of war. Administration views about the challenge Hitler's activities posed for the United States ran the gamut from fears of a cataclysmic war ending in the destruction of European civilization to "realist" assurances that what was occurring was merely a normal adjustment of the European system to changes in the balance of

[25] Not only did Bonnet's suggestions that Roosevelt act as an arbitrator in the Czech crisis (September 8) and urge Hitler not to use force (September 12) fall on deaf ears, Roosevelt also rejected in no uncertain terms his effort to depict the United States as a kind of "comrade in arms." Asked at a press conference on September 9 to comment on the growing impression abroad "that the United States is allied morally with the democracies of Europe in a sort of 'Stop Hitler' movement," he insisted that such an interpretation was "100% wrong," and instructed the press with some asperity not to "put words into people's mouths that they have not said." "Press conference, Hyde Park, September 9, 1938, 5:30 P.M.," Schewe, 7: no. 1273. See also Taylor, *Munich*, 525–26; Blum, *Morgenthau Diaries* 1:518; Langer and Gleason, *Challenge*, 32–33; and Haight, "France, the United States, and the Munich Crisis," 345–48.

[26] "Press Conference, Hyde Park, September 6, 1938, 8:45 A.M.," Schewe, 7: no. 1270.

[27] See, for example, "Bullitt to FDR, May 20, 1938," above; "Kennedy to Hull, August 31, 1938," *FRUS*, 1938, 1:565–66; "William C. Bullitt, Ambassador to France, to Roosevelt, August 31, 1938," Schewe, 6: no. 1260; "Roosevelt to Cordell Hull, Secretary of State, August 31, 1938," ibid., no. 1259; "William Phillips, Ambassador to Italy, to Roosevelt, September 1, 1938," ibid., no. 1263; "Bullitt to Hull, September 12, 1938," *FRUS*, 1938, 1:589; and "Kennedy to Hull September 9 and 10, 1938," ibid., 584–85.

power. The middle ground was occupied by those like Ickes, Morgenthau, and Roosevelt himself, who believed that a potentially dangerous situation for the United States might be in the making, but stopped short of apocalyptic predictions of doom.[28]

These divergent views found expression in equally diverse policy prescriptions. Assistant Secretary of State Berle denied that "the virtual absorption of some, if not all, of Czechoslovakia" by Germany was cause for alarm, and recommended doing nothing.[29] Secretary Hull, by no means as sanguine about the future and certainly no friend of appeasement, also favored inaction on the theory that since the United States could do little to improve the situation, it was best to rest with the few efforts already made. The policy prescriptions of those like Kennedy and Bullitt, who were interested in avoiding war at all costs, fluctuated between advising that Roosevelt attempt to make peace and urging that the United States simply keep its distance from the whole unfortunate situation.[30]

Such quasi-isolationist recommendations contrasted sharply with Ickes's and Morgenthau's policy prescriptions. As early as May 1938, Ickes pointed out the differences between his and Bullitt's views of the proper course for the United States:

> Bullitt . . . is strongly for the United States keeping out of European embroilments. . . . I assured him that I was in favor of the United States keeping out of any war but I suspect that I see the situation somewhat differently. . . . If the democratic theory of government is fighting for its life, we will have to fight for it sooner or later, and if we put it off too long, watching other democratic governments succumb to fascism, we will be forced to fight in the most disadvantageous circumstances.[31]

[28] Blum, *Morgenthau Diaries*, 1:452, 457; and Ickes, *Diary*, May 1, 1938, 2:381–82. "Memo from Adolf Berle to the President, September 1, 1938," PSF, State Department, Berle Folder, Box 93. Also in Schewe, 7: no. 1262. Abraham Ben Zvi has classified the attitudes of the members of the Roosevelt Administration toward Japan prior to Pearl Harbor along similar lines. His classification however, is not useful for the Munich period. Not only are several different actors involved, but also even some of the same actors fall into somewhat different categories in the two periods. See Abraham Ben-Zvi, *Illusion of Deterrence: the Roosevelt Presidency and the Origins of the Pacific War* (Boulder, Colo.: Westview Press, 1987).

[29] Hitler's moves east would merely result in a "reconstituted great Germany, plus the old Austro-Hungarian region. . . . Were the actor anyone other than Hitler . . . we should regard this as merely reconstituting the old system, undoing the obviously unsound work of Versailles and generally following the line of historical logic." It was thus wrong to assume that such a development would "recreate a power which will invariably attack western Europe." Memo from Adolph Berle to the President, Sept. 1, 1938, PSF, State Department, Berle Folder, Box 93.

[30] Kaufmann, "Two American Ambassadors," 662–64.

[31] Ickes, *Diary*, May 1, 1938, 2:381–82.

Morgenthau, too, saw the need to be involved in the coming struggle, delivering a strongly antitotalitarian speech in June in which he declared that, "The retention of the decencies and amenities of civilized life involves, nay demands, a struggle in which we all . . . must participate."[32]

Faced with these divisions among his advisers and the confusing crosscurrents of opinion they represented, and plagued by suspicions about British and French motives, Roosevelt, while quite possibly agreeing with Morgenthau's and Ickes's analyses, acted as Hull recommended and did nothing further, despite his awareness of a sharply deteriorating situation. Thus, he entered the period of the Munich crisis anxious about the possibility of war, but as uncertain as ever about what the United States could, or should, do about it.

THE CRISIS, SEPTEMBER 1938

The Munich crisis unfolded in the latter part of September 1938 as Great Britain and France sought to cope with German pressure on Czechoslovakia while avoiding war and preserving at least the appearance of honoring their commitments.[33] The proximate cause of the crisis was Hitler's escalation of his demands on Czechoslovakia from autonomy for the Sudeten Germans, to which the Czechs had already agreed, to outright cession of the Sudetenland to Germany. Rather than give in to German pressure, Czechoslovakia turned to France and Britain for help. As a consequence of this appeal, Chamberlain offered to conduct direct negotiations with Hitler.

On September 15, Chamberlain met the Führer at Berchtesgaden and heard his demands. Chamberlain then undertook to persuade the French, and pressure the Czechs, into agreeing to them. Having succeeded in both aims, Chamberlain met Hitler on September 22 at Godesberg only to discover that he was now also demanding the cession of territory in which Germans were a minority and insisting that all transfers be carried out by October 1. In reaction to this development, "British and French public opinion stiffened, and by September 25 it seemed likely that Chamberlain and Edouard Daladier, the French Premier, would fight rather than surrender completely to Hitler."[34] At this point, Roosevelt chose to intervene, first with an appeal to all states involved not to break off negotiations, and then with a message to Hitler alone proposing that

---

[32] Henry Morgenthau, *The Road Ahead* (Philadelphia, 1938), 8–9.

[33] Brief descriptions of the events of the Munich crisis may be found in Taylor, *Munich*, 7–11; Offner, *American Appeasement*, 259–68; Divine, *Reluctant Belligerent*, 51–55; and Divine, *Roosevelt and World War II*, 20–21. Gerhard L. Weinberg, "Munich after Fifty Years," *Foreign Affairs* 67 (Fall 1988): 165–78, provides a review of more recent historical interpretations.

[34] Divine, *Roosevelt and World War II*, 20.

the talks be expanded into a conference that would include all interested parties. After a further intervention by Mussolini, Hitler issued invitations to Great Britain, France, and Italy to meet at Munich on September 29 and 30.[35] This conference

> marked the climax of appeasement. In return for Hitler's promise not to seek an additional foot of territory in Europe, Britain and France agreed that Germany should occupy the Sudeten area in four stages between October 1 and October 7, leaving the final disposition of a 5th zone to an international commission. The Czechs agreed to the terms on the morning of September 30, and thus became the sacrificial victims of the worldwide demand for peace at any price.

At this point, the democracies having found a way to give Hitler all he desired without putting him to the trouble of fighting for it, the crisis ended.[36]

Roosevelt's Response

STAGE I: SEPTEMBER 13–22, 1938

The onset of the Munich crisis brought no dramatic change in Roosevelt's thinking. While his assessment of the likelihood of war varied according to the news from Europe, his determination to avoid intervening did not. Thus, in the days before and during the Berchtesgaden meeting (September 13 through September 16), Roosevelt's diagnosis of the situation and his policy preferences mirrored his pre-crisis attitudes.[37] Despite his initial uncertainty about the outcome of the impending Berchtesgaden meeting,[38] within a day he was telling Ickes that there would be no general war in Europe because the democracies would quickly abandon Czechoslovakia:

[35] Taylor, *Munich*, 9–10.

[36] Divine, *Reluctant Belligerent*, 54. In the same vein, see Hull, *Memoirs*, 1:595–96.

[37] Roosevelt kept himself well informed about the progress of the crisis. In an interview on December 23, 1939, replying to a question that dealt specifically with the post-Munich period, he said, "I got the cables once a day after Munich, and read them in the late afternoon, evening and the next morning. The intricate ones on the dollar and the pound I ignored, but I read all the rest." Joseph and Stewart Alsop Papers, Box 96, folder 1, Manuscript Division, Library of Congress, Washington, D.C. See also notes on an interview that took place after the start of the war in Europe in September 1939. "Original Notes," "R," Alsop Interview, undated, Box 96, folder 5. The Alsop papers contain a series of interviews with Roosevelt and members of his administration in preparation for *American White Paper*, which shed considerable light on their thinking and, as far as I can determine, have not been cited previously. See also Alsop and Kintner, *American White Paper*, 3; and Langer and Gleason, *Challenge*, 19 n. 11.

[38] "Roosevelt, En Route to Washington, to William Phillips, Ambassador to Italy, September 15, 1938," Schewe, 7: no. 1277. Also in *PL*, 2:810–11.

The President thinks that Chamberlain is for peace at any price. . . .
Czechoslovakia apparently has resisted pressure from England and France
to agree to a plebiscite. Lacking a plebiscite, Hitler will move in. . . . Because it will not have submitted to the demands of France and England,
Czechoslovakia will be left by these supposed allies to paddle its own canoe.
This will mean a swift and brutal war . . . [which] will leave Czechoslovakia
dismembered and prostrate. . . . [Then] England and France . . . will 'wash
the blood from their Judas Iscariot hands.'[39]

While Roosevelt did not expect war, he did think that this scenario
would have serious consequences, pointing out to Ickes that "this betrayal of an international obligation" would mark "a further important
advance by Germany toward a predominant international position."[40]
Moreover, although his assessment of the democracies was harsh, Roosevelt had not the slightest sympathy for Hitler, telling Ambassador Phillips
that, unlike the situation in 1914, "today . . . ninety per cent of our
people are definitely anti-German and anti-Italian in sentiment," a "natural sympathy" he would "strongly encourage."[41] Nevertheless, his dis-
gust with both appeasement and fascism made it difficult for him to arrive at a settled judgment about any aspect of the situation and, given the
pusillanimity of the states most concerned, he concluded that there was
no meaningful action for him to take. Thus, on September 13, he agreed
with Hull that it would be best to do nothing at all. As Moffat reported in
his diary, this decision was reaffirmed on September 16.[42]

Despite his reluctance to act at this time, the onset of the crisis did lead
Roosevelt to think about the possibility of action in the future. Thus he
told Phillips: "You are right in saying that we are an unemotional people
over here in the sense that we do not easily lose our heads, but if we get

[39] Ickes, *Diary*, 2:468. Roosevelt discussed these matters with Ickes privately, at a cabinet meeting on September 16, and again with Ickes alone on September 17. Ickes's account
summarizes the views the president expressed on these three occasions, so it is possible that
the remarks just cited were made on the seventeenth instead of the sixteenth. However,
because most of the reports of the meeting at Berchtesgaden Roosevelt received on the
seventeenth were already stressing the increasing likelihood of general warfare, it seems
plausible that he made them on the sixteenth.

[40] Ickes, *Diary*, 2:468. Another indication of the seriousness with which Roosevelt
viewed the situation was his withdrawal on September 15 "in view of the European crisis"
of his previous acceptance of Assistant Secretary of State Adolf Berle's resignation. Berle
Papers, State Department correspondence, 1938–1945, FDRL. Also in Schewe, 7: no.
1276.

[41] "Roosevelt to Phillips, Sept. 15, 1938," ibid., no. 1277.

[42] Alsop and Kintner, *American White Paper*, 7–8; *The Moffat Papers: Selections from
the Diplomatic Papers of Jay Pierrepont Moffat, 1919–1943*, ed. Nancy H. Hooker (Cambridge, Mass.: Harvard University Press, 1956), 202–3, 205. See also memorandum of a
conversation between Hull and the French Ambassador, *FRUS*, 1938, 1:598–99.

the idea that the future of our form of government is threatened by a coalition of European dictators, we might wade in with everything we have to give."[43]

Nevertheless, for the present Roosevelt confined himself to a minimal demonstration of support for the democracies by sending the light cruiser *Nashville* to England in readiness to transport British gold reserves to New York.[44] Should war break out, the gold could be used to purchase munitions in the United States.

When word from Berchtesgaden finally arrived, it was not encouraging. On the morning of September 17, Kennedy reported Chamberlain's finding that Hitler "was perfectly willing to take on a world war" over the principle of self-determination for the Sudeten Germans, leading Roosevelt to consider a European war somewhat more probable.[45] Later that day he disclosed to Ickes his theories about the proper strategy for conducting the impending conflict. Observing that conditions in Europe made it unlikely that a traditional land war could be successful, Roosevelt said that after reassuring Germany about her territorial integrity, he would move to close her borders, rely on the British fleet to bottle up the German fleet, and pressure the surrounding small countries into joining the alliance against her. According to Ickes, Roosevelt

> would make the war principally one of the air. He believes that with England, France, and Russia all pounding away at Germany from the air, Germany would find it difficult to protect itself even with its present preponderance in the air. It is his opinion that the morale of the German people would crack under aerial attacks much sooner than that of the French or the English. He says that this kind of war would cost less money, would mean comparatively few casualties, and would be more likely to succeed than a traditional war by land and sea.

Roosevelt also remarked that there was already a movement afoot to "establish in Canada factories for manufacturing and assembling airplanes and other munitions for war."[46]

Alarming reports about the meeting at Berchtesgaden continued to arrive throughout September 17 and 18. In a telegram received on the evening of the seventeenth, Kennedy elaborated on his report of Chamberlain's impressions of Hitler: "He is cruel, overbearing, has a hard look and thoroughly convinced Chamberlain that he would be completely ruthless

---

[43] "Roosevelt to Phillips, Sept. 15, 1938."

[44] "Morgenthau Diary," 141:69. On September 19, Roosevelt also indicated his willingness to publicize the gold shipments. Ibid., 115. See also Kittredge, "United States," 28.

[45] Kennedy to Hull, Sept. 17, 1938, *FRUS*, 1938, 1:607–8, received at 10 a.m.

[46] Ickes, *Diary*, 2:469–70. Ickes indicates clearly that this part of his talk with Roosevelt took place on the seventeenth.

in any of his aims and methods." On the issue of self-determination, Hitler said he would "chance a world war if necessary." Emphasizing his lack of confidence in the French and his opinion of their "appalling" air situation, Chamberlain also informed Kennedy that he had told Hitler that Czechoslovakia was "merely an incident" and had indicated his desire to move on to other far more important world problems. "Hitler said he was too occupied and worried about the Czechoslovak problem to think about anything else."[47]

Despite a number of such dismaying reports, Roosevelt remained disinclined to intervene in the crisis. In a conversation on either September 18 or 19 with the secretary-general of a French labor union, Leon Jouhaux, he

> pointed out that he did not feel the situation warranted any initiative from him. Such an initiative, if not accepted, might make the situation even worse than it was. Mr. Jouhaux then asked the President if he could not summon a conference. The President had replied that the same considerations would militate against this, but that if England and France should summon a conference and invite the United States, he was prepared to accept.

Jouhaux came away from this meeting thoroughly puzzled as to Roosevelt's intentions, especially with regard to nature and the timing of such a conference.[48]

September 19 saw the climax of the first phase of Roosevelt's response to the Munich crisis. As he continued to assimilate the news from Berchtesgaden, he further adjusted his expectations about the likelihood of war

[47] Kennedy to Hull, Sept. 17, 1938, *FRUS*, 1938, 1:609–12, received at 8:30 p.m. On September 18, Kennedy's observations were supported by Ambassador Wilson, who cabled British Ambassador Henderson's view that if the democracies refused to adopt the principle of self-determination, or adopted it with many conditions, there would be "no use in talking to Hitler again. Indeed, the latter will march and a general European war will be the result." Citing the "grave risk" that Czech President Benes might refuse to accept the principle of self-determination, Henderson urged that "immediate pressure" be put on him. American Minister to Czechoslovakia Carr, on the other hand, conveyed the belief of the Czech minister for foreign affairs that if France and Britain showed a united front and real firmness, a German attack could be averted. However, the Czech minister also expressed the view that the danger was "real and imminent." Wilson to Hull, Sept. 18, 1938, ibid., 612–14, received at 2:50 p.m.; Carr to Hull, Sept. 18, 1938, ibid., 614–15, received at 6:43 p.m.

[48] "Memorandum by J. Pierrepont Moffat, Chief, Division of European Affairs, Department of State, September 20, 1938," Schewe, 7: no. 1289a. Also in *FRUS*, 1938, 1:625–26, and Hooker, *Moffat Papers*, 206–7. Moffat's memorandum was transmitted by Hull to Roosevelt on September 20. There is some confusion about the date of this meeting. Haight gives it as September 19, but his source unclear. "France, the United States, and the Munich Crisis," 351. The Moffat memo of September 20 says that the president saw Jouhaux "a day or two ago."

without, however, altering his policy on the crisis itself. By the morning of the nineteenth, Roosevelt expected it to end in war, telling Secretary Morgenthau that the Czechs would fight and repeating the strategy for prosecuting the war he had outlined to Ickes on September 17.[49] Morgenthau thought that Roosevelt was "ready to go pretty far in demonstrating United States sympathy for such a move," and was himself very much in agreement, declaring, "if we don't stop Hitler now he is going right on down through the Black Sea—then what? . . . The fate of Europe for the next one hundred years is settled."

Convinced that a defensive war based on a blockade offered the democracies their best chance of vanquishing the Germans, Morgenthau and Roosevelt discussed the most effective way to get this idea across. Owing to his reservations about Kennedy and Bullitt's ability to convey his meaning, the President decided to do the job himself, making an appointment with the British ambassador for that evening.[50]

Throughout the day, troubling reports continued to arrive at the White House. At 1:30 p.m., for example, a telegram was received from Bullitt stating that "General European war appears to be closer this morning than at any previous time." Hitler was determined to incorporate the Sudetenland with or without war, and war would be absolutely disastrous given German and Italian air superiority over Britain and France. The United States government should in no way encourage France to go to war. Nothing could be "more dishonorable than to urge another nation to go to war if one is determined not to go to war on the side of that nation, and I believe that the people of the United States are determined not to go to war against Germany." At about the same time, Kennedy cabled the substance of the joint British-French proposal to Benes to cede all territories that were 50 percent German. This news was later confirmed by Bullitt, who added that if the Czechs refused, neither the British nor the French would support them. A subsequent cable from Kennedy asserted his opinion that "England does not propose to fight on the Czechoslovak issue." Finally, Ambassador Wilson telegraphed that "in these anxious days of waiting the Italian attitude assumes a growing importance." Wilson also pointed out that while Mussolini did not desire war, his place would be with Hitler should war come.[51]

---

[49] "He says that he has thought out this idea to get word to France that if she gets into this fight that she is not to attack but stay behind the Maginot Line and that the countries surrounding Germany if they decide to go to war should make it a defensive one and then both on land and sea to shut off Germany's supplies." "Morgenthau Diary," 141:115. Also in Blum, *Morgenthau Diaries*, 1:519–20.

[50] Ibid.

[51] Bullitt to Hull, Sept. 19, 1938, *FRUS*, 1938, 1:615–18; Kennedy to Hull, Sept. 19, 1938, ibid., 618–19, received at 1:15 p.m.; Bullitt to Hull, Sept. 19, 1938, ibid., 620–21,

However Roosevelt assessed these communications, he remained committed to the meeting with Ambassador Lindsay.[52] Roosevelt opened the discussion by declaring that, while he would like to be of some immediate assistance, having "no illusions as to the effect of his previous public statements," he was reluctant to make any pronouncements about the present situation: "Today he would not dare to express approval of the recommendations put to the Czechoslovak Government. He would [also] be afraid to express disapproval of German aggression lest it might encourage Czechoslovakia to vain resistance. He thus felt unable to do anything." Canvassing various alternative outcomes to the crisis, Roosevelt reverted briefly to the conference idea he had discussed with Jouhaux. As Lindsay pointed out, however, "This part of his idea was not strongly emphasized."

What Roosevelt really wished to discuss was his strategy for conducting the war he believed the Western powers would soon be forced to fight. This was "the very secret part of his communication," about which "it must not be known to anyone that he has even breathed a suggestion. If it transpired he would almost be impeached and the suggestion would be hopelessly prejudiced."[53] Expressing his belief that the Czechs would fight and that "the Western Powers would find themselves at war with Germany and probably Italy," Roosevelt declared that "they should carry on the war "purely by blockade and in a defensive manner." Any states that did not cooperate would be threatened with having their overseas supplies rationed. (Lindsay thought that this plan may have been "what was in the President's mind when he talked about quarantine in his Chicago speech.")

When Lindsay remarked that Roosevelt's idea

> was reminiscent of sanctions [the president] said that any suggestion of sanctions must be most carefully avoided. Blockade must be based on loftiest humanitarian grounds and on the desire to wage hostilities with minimum of suffering and the least possible loss of life and property, and yet

---

received at 3:53 p.m.; Kennedy to Hull, Sept. 19, 1938, ibid., 621–22, received at 5:45 p.m.; Wilson to Hull, Sept. 19, 1938, ibid., received at 5:13 p.m.

[52] According to Lindsay's account, Roosevelt called him personally in the afternoon and asked him to come to the White House that evening. He particularly stressed his desire that no one should learn of this interview, including, Lindsay gathered, the State Department. "Sir R. Lindsay (Washington) to Viscount Halifax (Received September 20, 10:40 a.m.)," *DBFP*, Series 3, 7:627–29. See also Taylor, *Munich*, 846–48; Lash, *Roosevelt and Churchill*, 25–28; Offner, *American Appeasement*, 261; Cole, *Roosevelt*, 300.

[53] Although this paragraph in Lindsay's report immediately precedes the one dealing with the conference idea, given the scant importance Roosevelt attached to the latter it appears to refer primarily to his ideas about the war and the role the United States might play in it.

to bring enemy to his knees. In this connexion he mentioned bombing from the air. He said only defence to this was to retaliate in the same way; but bombing from the air was not the method of hostilities which caused really great losses of life.

Roosevelt's reason for wanting the blockade presented in this way soon became clear: it would win popular approval in the United States and make it easier for him to assist the allies.[54]

Roosevelt was still not willing to evade the provisions of the neutrality laws by "turning a blind eye" to the export of arms to the Allies, though he insisted that munition parts could be exported to Canada and set up there. What he clearly desired was to avoid bringing those laws into play in the first place so that he could continue to aid the democracies. He urged that the democracies should avoid "declaring war on Germany at all. Let them call it defensive measures or anything plausible. . . . He even indicated that . . . if Germany declared war on us and we refrained from doing so he might yet be able to find that we were not at war, and that the prohibition of export of arms need not be applied to us."

Finally, having observed earlier that even if Czech capitulation avoided war in the current crisis, other German demands elsewhere in Europe were bound to follow, Roosevelt predicted that the present German aggression would awaken similar tendencies around the world. Possibly it was this perception that led him to communicate to Lindsay the feeling several times during the course of their meeting that

> somehow or other in indefinable circumstances the United States might again find themselves involved in an European war. In that case he regarded it as almost inconceivable that it would be possible for him to send any American troops across the Atlantic even if his prestige were as high as it had been just after the 1936 elections. But it was just possible that if Germany were able to invade Great Britain with a considerable force, such a wave of emotion might arise, that an American army might be sent overseas.[55]

Clearly, the news from Berchtesgaden did move Roosevelt to take some sort of action, but what is most striking is the type of action he

---

[54]
Though he himself could not possibly take any initiative in the matter he pointed out that it is entirely within the constitutional prerogative of a President on his own authority, to declare that a blockade was of an effective character. He could thus help blockading Powers and would be willing to do so, in the absence of unfavourable circumstances. Under the Neutrality Act he was empowered to forbid United States vessels to enter a danger zone except at their own risk.

A similar logic seems to have been behind Roosevelt's advocacy of a blockade during the *Panay* incident. See above.

[55] Note the similar thought expressed in Roosevelt's letter to Phillips on September 15.

chose. His heightened expectation of war led him neither to try to avert it, nor to alter his policy of nonintervention in the crisis. Instead he responded to the deteriorating situation in Europe by attempting to bolster the courage of the democracies in the present and guide their strategy in any future struggle.[56] Thus, his purpose in seeing the British ambassador seems to have been to derail the appeasement policy, principally by instilling confidence in eventual American support should a firm line result in war. However dramatic his conversation with Lindsay on the evening of September 19 may appear, then, it reflected not a departure from the policies he had followed up to that time, but their culmination. Even after Berchtesgaden had greatly increased his estimate of the probability of war, he remained reluctant to intervene openly in the crisis.

After Roosevelt's conversation with Lindsay, there followed several days of waiting. This period, which began with Czech acquiescence to British and French demands and ended with Chamberlain's arrival at Godesberg, saw no change in either Roosevelt's diagnosis of the situation or his policies. It did, however, afford him an opportunity to observe the unedifying spectacle of the democracies pressuring the Czechs, as well as time to reflect on the importance of air power in influencing the course of the crisis.[57]

In the end, as Bullitt cabled on the morning of September 21, the Czechs, having received no support for their position, "accepted flatly and unconditionally the British-French proposal." Since Roosevelt's expectation of war was based on the belief that the Czechs would fight, this development reduced his estimate of its likelihood. The forthcoming meeting of Chamberlain and Hitler at Godesberg would merely be a matter of arranging the details of implementing what had already been agreed.[58] Unfortunately, Hitler was not to be so accommodating.

STAGE II: SEPTEMBER 23–29, 1938

The war scare in Europe has occupied all minds during the last few days practically to the exclusion of everything else. With troops rushing to their respective borders in France, Germany, Czechoslovakia, Hungary, and Poland; with France preparing to evacuate Paris and boxing up the treasures of

[56] Dallek shares this interpretation. *Franklin D. Roosevelt*, 164–65.

[57] Bullitt to Hull, Sept. 20, 1938, *FRUS*, 1938, 1:627, received at 11:25 a.m.; Memorandum of Conversation, by the Chief of the Division of European Affairs (Moffat), Sept. 20, 1938, ibid., 626–27; "William C. Bullitt, Ambassador to France, to Roosevelt, September 20, 1938," Schewe, 7: no. 1288.

[58] Bullit to Hull, Sept. 21, 1938, *FRUS*, 1938, 1:630–31, received at 8:35 a.m. According to Dallek, the president was surprised at the Czech decision but felt that there was now "agreement in principle" between the German and Czech governments. *Franklin D. Roosevelt*, 165.

the Louvre and the priceless glass of Chartres Cathedral for transport to areas where they might be safe from German shells and bombs; with England concentrating its fleet at strategic points in the Baltic and the Mediterranean, with Mussolini rattling his saber; it seemed that war was only a matter of hours.[59]

For Roosevelt, as for other Americans, the Munich crisis truly began on September 23. Primarily as a consequence of the talks between Hitler and Chamberlain at Godesberg on September 22 and 23—in which the Führer unexpectedly laid down new and "humiliating" requirements regarding the mechanics of relinquishing the Sudetenland to Germany that were completely unacceptable to the other parties—expectations of general war in Europe increased dramatically.[60]

Ickes has described Roosevelt's initial reaction to the news from Godesberg in his account of a cabinet meeting on the afternoon of September 23, in which the European situation was "canvassed very fully," beginning with Hull's briefing on the possible consequences of the latest developments. Expressing his belief that there were "undoubtedly" defensive alliances between Italy, Germany, and Japan, Hull declared that Japan would support Germany and Italy in their bid to dominate Europe while itself trying to gain complete control over Asia. Consequently, as Ickes understood it,

> France may soon find itself to be a helpless country lying between an enlarged and strengthened Germany and Italy. England might even be reduced to the status of a third- or fourth-rate power with many of her colonies gone. If this should happen, there might follow attempts on the part of Germany, Italy, and Japan to penetrate South America. This would mean that the United States would have to go to the defense of South America, in which event we would be called upon to defend both the Atlantic and the Pacific seaboards from powerful enemies.

Roosevelt, in line with his previously expressed views, was considerably less pessimistic about the democracies' chances, repeating that they should fight a strictly defensive war and declaring that Britain and France would control both the Atlantic Ocean and the Mediterranean and thus bottle up the Germans and the Italians. For the first time, however, he expressed concern about German preponderance in the air, labeling it "the worst thing about the situation." Roosevelt also mentioned a plan for the British to buy and assemble munitions in Canada using nonmilitary material purchased in the United States, and declared that "in carrying out our neutrality laws we would resolve all doubts in favor of the

[59] Ickes, *Diary*, Sept. 30, 1938, 2:476–77.
[60] Dallek, *Franklin D. Roosevelt*, 165.

democratic countries." The meeting closed with the President reading from an analysis of the situation just handed to him that suggested that war was imminent.[61]

While the news of Hitler's unreasonable demands at Godesberg produced an immediate upward revision in Roosevelt's estimate of the likelihood of war, it did not lead him to change his policy.[62] Still having no thought of intervening to prevent that war, he continued to focus on how the democracies should fight it. According to Ickes, as late as the afternoon of September 23, there was "no doubt of the President's desire to avoid any embroilment in European quarrels."[63] That he had decided to intervene in the crisis at least by the afternoon of September 25 is thus puzzling.

Throughout September 24, bad news poured into the White House. Despite the six-day respite Hitler had generously granted the Czechs, the situation remained menacing.[64] The Czechs, while disclaiming aggressive intent, informed the State Department that they had mobilized the previous evening. The French as well called up an additional five hundred thousand men early on the morning of the twenty-fourth, raising the total under arms to one million.[65] Roosevelt wrote his cousin Margaret Suckley, "Things are worse. . . . It looks like war in a week."[66]

All reports received at the White House emphasized Hitler's intransigence, leaving no doubt that the responsibility for war would rest with

[61] Ickes, *Diary*, 2:473–74. Ickes's speculation that the message was from Ambassador Bullitt was correct. See "Memorandum to Roosevelt, September 23, 1938," Schewe, 7: no. 1294. For a detailed account of the Godesberg meeting itself, see Taylor, *Munich*, 806–19.

[62] Although Bullitt's message had suggested that the president should now act directly with respect to the crisis and referred obliquely to his previous conference idea, Roosevelt appears to have made no mention of this in presenting the alternatives to the cabinet.

[63] Ickes, *Diary*, 2:473–74. That immediate action was not at the forefront of Roosevelt's thinking on September 23 is shown also by his negative reply to Nicholas Murray Butler's suggestion that he make an appeal to the parties and by Hull's evasive, but essentially discouraging, reply to the inquiries of the French Ambassador about Roosevelt's remarks to Jouhaux on the possibility of attending an international conference. "Roosevelt to Nicholas Murray Butler, President, Columbia University, September 23, 1938," Schewe, 7: no. 1295; Hull Memo, Sept. 23, 1938, *FRUS*, 1938, 1:638–39.

[64] Roosevelt had the news of this respite by the afternoon of September 23, but not before the Cabinet meeting where he nevertheless still continued to manifest a disinclined to intervene. Moreover, since the clock continued to run and all the news from Europe was bad, it is doubtful that Hitler's gesture greatly reduced the pressure. "Memorandum by Henry M. Kannee, Assistant to Marvin H. McIntyre, September 23, 1938," and "Memorandum to Roosevelt, September 23, 1938," Schewe, 7: no.s 1293, 1294. Schewe reverses the order of these two memoranda, but it is clear that no. 1294 was received in time to be read to the Cabinet at 2 p.m., whereas no. 1293 bears the time 4:50 p.m.

[65] Czechoslovak Legation to the Department of State, Sept. 24, 1938, *FRUS*, 1938, 1:645–46; Haight, "France, the United States, and the Munich Crisis," 352.

[66] Ward, *Closest Companion*, 125. See also Ickes, *Diary*, 2:473.

him alone.[67] Kennedy, for example, cabled that Hitler's answers to the British were "preposterous."[68] Carr, as well, telegraphed that Hitler's letter to Chamberlain was "entirely uncompromising," and observed that "a survey of the record leaves no room for doubt that if a war occurs Germany must bear the responsibility for deliberately bringing it about." Meanwhile, Bullitt, certain that the American people would desire "some effort by our Government . . . even though the effort may prove to be a failure," renewed his plea that Roosevelt appeal to the parties to confer at the Hague, send a representative to such a conference, and issue a "strong warning against armies crossing frontiers."[69]

Despite such entreaties, Roosevelt took no action of any kind on September 24. He was, however, apparently beginning to think that some kind of intervention might be desirable. (Berle observed that by the morning of the 25th, he was "playing with the idea.")[70] Certainly, by then all indicators pointed to war as throughout the day Roosevelt continued to receive reports about the draconian terms Hitler sought to impose and their complete unacceptability to the other parties. There was, for example, a "flood" of telegrams from Bullitt detailing Hitler's demands and emphasizing their extraordinary harshness. According to Bullitt, the German note to Chamberlain was "totally unacceptable."[71]

[67] As Alsop and Kintner describe the scene in the State Department, "Late afternoon cables, rushed paragraph by paragraph from the decoding room . . . indicated that negotiations were collapsing. Hitler was ready to precipitate war by seizing his objectives by force." *American White Paper,* 9.

[68] "Hitler not only wants what everybody was willing to give him but it looks as if he wants a great deal more. . . . Cadogan feels that . . . they have taken every possible opportunity to demonstrate they believed there was some sanity in Hitler and to save the world from the horrible results of war. . . . Hitler's answers prove there is no sanity left in the man." Kennedy to Hull, Sept. 24, 1938, *FRUS,* 1938, 1:642–43, received at 10 a.m.

[69] Carr to Hull, Sept. 24, 1938, ibid., 643–44, received at 4:40 p.m. Bullitt to Hull, Sept. 24, 1938, ibid., 641–42. See also Hull, *Memoirs,* 1:590.

[70] By the morning of the twenty-fifth, the impulse to act had penetrated even to the State Department. The Berle diary reveals a dramatic change in attitude in the State Department, showing that while on September 21 Berle, Hull, Moffat, and Dunn had canvassed the situation and "all agreed that there was nothing for us to do except steer clear and keep quiet" (a decision they reaffirmed on the twenty-second), by the morning of the twenty-fifth, the same group, with the addition of Welles, Norman Davis, and Stanley Hornbeck, had decided to draft a presidential appeal to the parties. (The date of the second meeting is given erroneously by the editor of the Berle diary as Sunday, September 23. Sunday was the twenty-fifth, and all other evidence points to the meeting having been held on that date.) Berle, *Navigating,* 186. See also Hooker, *Moffat Papers,* 211–12; Hull, *Memoirs,* 1:590–91; Alsop and Kintner, *American White Paper,* 9.

[71] Haight, "France, the United States, and the Munich Crisis," 352; Bullitt to Hull, Sept. 25, 1938, *FRUS,* 1938, 1:648–49, received at 11:35 a.m. See also Bullitt to Hull, Sept. 25, 1938, ibid., 646–48, received at 9:15 a.m., and 650–52, received at 12:25 p.m. Bullitt's reports were supplemented by a cable from Carr transmitting the Czech president's plea to

As these alarming reports poured in, planning for an American response continued in the State Department. Earlier Berle and Moffat had volunteered to produce a draft presidential statement and, after considering and ruling out Bullitt's conference plan, settled on a message that would be, as Berle desired, "not merely an appeal but a definite suggestion that we would use our good offices in a draft leading to the revision of the Versailles Treaty." Hull, though disapproving of the idea of treaty revision as "too dangerous," took the draft statement to the president at six o'clock.[72]

There is no doubt that by this point Roosevelt wanted to act. Henceforth, he was completely focused on the imminence of war and the need to end the crisis before it could occur. As Morgenthau observed to his staff early the following morning, "the President [is] very anxious to get in and stop this war in Europe."[73] Thus, the drafting of the appeal went forward. Bullitt wanted it to include an offer by the president to arbitrate. Hull disliked the idea and, along with Norman Davis, also opposed the less extreme step of a tender of good offices. (In fact, Hull was against any appeal whatsoever.)[74] In the end, Roosevelt acceded to these objections, and any hint of mediation was removed from the message. According to Moffat, this was done both because of the fear of "untoward domestic effects," and because the president believed that the notion of good offices was implicit.[75]

Roosevelt finished revising the draft by midnight, and it was sent to Hitler, Benes, Chamberlain, and Daladier at 1 a.m. on September 26. In it, he pointed out that the "fabric of peace . . . is in immediate danger,"

---

prevent "the assassination of the state" by urging the British and French not to desert Czechoslovakia. Moreover, Hugh Wilson, the American ambassador to Germany, telegraphed later in the day to convey the opinion of the British ambassador to Germany that unless the British and French managed to pressure the Czechs into accepting the German troops, there would almost certainly be war. Carr to Hull, Sept. 25, 1938, ibid., 649–50, received at 10:20 a.m.; Wilson to Hull, Sept. 25, 1938, ibid., 654–56. received 7 p.m. See also Hull, *Memoirs*, 1:590–91.

[72] Berle, *Navigating*, 186; Hooker, *Moffat Papers*, 211–12; Offner, *American Appeasement*, 262–63 (this account is based on the original Moffat diary); Haight, "France, the United States, and the Munich Crisis," 353; Alsop and Kintner, *American White Paper*, 9.

[73] "Morgenthau Diary," 142:342 Hull told Moffat on the night of the twenty-fifth that Roosevelt had gotten such bad telephone reports from both Bullitt and Kennedy that he could no longer keep silent. Hooker, *Moffat Papers*, 212–13. In his memoirs Hull asserts that Roosevelt decided to intervene, not because he thought he would be successful, but because he wanted to do *something* and sending a message would at least do no harm. However, the evidence suggests that Roosevelt, while fearing that he risked failure, hoped for more. Hull, *Memoirs*, 1:591–92.

[74] Ibid.; Hooker, *Moffat Papers*, 212–13; Berle, *Navigating*, 186–87.

[75] Ibid., 187; Hull, *Memoirs*, 1:592; Hooker, *Moffat Papers*, 212–13; Offner, *American Appeasement*, 263.

and stressed that, while the United States eschewed "political entangle-ments," it could not escape the consequences of general war. He, there-fore, reminded the parties of their obligation to settle their differences peacefully, and called on them not to break off negotiations.[76]

September 26 was another anxious day. According to Hull, they "waited almost breathlessly for the replies," especially Hitler's.[77] While no word from the Führer was immediately forthcoming, Roose-velt received ample evidence of the democracies' continued resolve, as well as numerous expressions of their gratitude for his message and as-surances about its positive influence, which he found particularly gratifying.[78]

Unfortunately, when Hitler's reply to the president's message finally arrived, it was not nearly so pleasing. In a speech heard in the United States on the afternoon of September 26, he was anything but concilia-tory, declaring "that if the Czechs did not give the Sudeten Germans immediate freedom, 'we will go and fetch this freedom for ourselves.'" As Ickes intrepreted this response, Hitler "had made his demands and he would not abandon them by one jot or tittle. War seemed to be inevita-ble, with every tick of the clock bringing it closer."[79] Moreover, his for-mal reply to Roosevelt's message offered as little solace as his speech. Disclaiming all responsibility should further developments lead to war, he recited at length German grievances against the Czechs and ended with the ominous declaration that "The possibilities of arriving at a just settlement by agreement are . . . exhausted with the proposals of the Ger-man memorandum. It does not rest with the German Government, but with the Czechoslovakian Government alone, to decide whether it wants peace or war." As Roosevelt reported to his cabinet the following day, the tone of Hitler's reply was "truculent and unyielding."[80]

[76] Alsop and Kintner, *American White Paper*, 10; Offner, *American Appeasement*, 263; Roosevelt to Hitler, Sept. 26, 1938, *FRUS*, 1938, 1:657–58.

[77] Hull, *Memoirs*, 1:592.

[78] *FRUS*, 1938, 1:661–73. For accounts of allied determination and expressions of ap-preciation, see Kennedy to Hull, Sept. 26, 1938, ibid., 659, received at 8:30 a.m.; Bullitt to Hull, Sept. 26, 1938, ibid., 668, received at 2 p.m. Welles told Kennedy on the telephone that the President "was enormously pleased and deeply gratified with a message which Chamberlain sent in reply" to his statement, Memorandum of a phone conversation be-tween Welles and Kennedy, Sept. 26, 1938, 1:30 p.m., ibid., 660–61.

[79] Offner, *American Appeasement*, 263–64; Ickes, *Diary*, 2:477. For an account of Hitler's intransigence during this period see Taylor, *Munich*, 870–75.

[80] Hitler to Roosevelt, Sept. 26, 1938, *FRUS*, 1938, 1:669–72, received 9:14 p.m. This message was not received in written form in the White House until September 27. ("Adolf Hitler, Chancellor of Germany, to Roosevelt, September 27, 1938," Schewe, 7: no. 1302.) However, Assistant Secretary of State George Messersmith phoned the substance of it to Roosevelt on the evening of the twenty-sixth. Berle, *Navigating*, 187. Ickes, *Diary*, 2:478.

On the morning of the twenty-seventh, a group of State Department officials met to consider a response to the latest developments.[81] Berle and Welles were deputized to draft a second message to Hitler, which they did, opting for the path of "boldness" by including in it a call for a conference at the Hague. Just before lunch, Hull and Welles took this draft statement to the president, by which time still more evidence of Hitler's unwillingness to cooperate had arrived.[82] Both Kennedy and Bullitt cabled that his reception of Chamberlain's latest notes was "completely and definitely unsatisfactory." In Bullitt's words, his reply "was the most violent outburst possible; . . . nothing could have been more unhelpful." By way of contrast, this demonstration of Hitler's intransigence was accompanied by continued expressions of gratitude for Roosevelt's message from France and Britain.[83]

The news of Hitler's obduracy and aggressive posturing had two implications for Roosevelt's assessment of the crisis. First of all, it underlined the Führer's sole responsibility for the continued slide toward war. Secondly, it increased expectations that war would actually occur—unless something happened to prevent it.[84] Apparently the confluence of these perceptions shaped Roosevelt's decision on the morning of September 27 to take further action. At his meeting with Welles and Hull, two of the proposals discussed earlier in the State Department (a request to other governments to support the American appeal to continue negotiations and a personal appeal to Mussolini) were approved without reservation.[85] The notion of a conference, however, did not fair nearly as well because Hull, "depressed" by the possible dangers of so bold a step, op-

[81] Present at this meeting were Berle, Hull, Welles, Messersmith, State Department Counselor Judge R. Walton Moore, Dunn, Moffat, and Legal Adviser Green H. Hackworth. Berle, *Navigating*, 187. See also Alsop and Kintner, *American White Paper*, 10; and Hooker, *Moffat Papers*, 215–16.

[82] Berle, *Navigating*, 187.

[83] Kennedy to Hull, Sept. 27, 1938, *FRUS*, 1938, 1:673, received at 7:05 a.m.; Bullitt to Hull, Sept. 27, 1938, ibid., 673–74, received at 9:15 a.m., and 674–75, received at 11:10 a.m. A cable from Carr also underlined the unreasonableness of Hitler's demands from the point of view of Czech military security. Carr to Hull, Sept. 27, 1938, ibid., 679, received at 1:20 p.m.

[84] Supporting the first point is Welles's statement to Bullitt that any action by the President would be directed solely at Hitler. Memorandum of Telephone Conversation between Bullitt and Welles, Sept. 27, 1938, *FRUS*, 1938, 1:675–76, 2:40 p.m. The second point is corroborated by Welles's later statement that on September 27, " 'Information of unquestioned authenticity' had come through that at 2:00 p.m. on the next day, September 28, Hitler would march his armies into Czechoslovakia unless the Godesberg terms were met." Haight, "France, the United States, and the Munich Crisis," 355. This account was confirmed by Roosevelt himself when he told Arthur Murray on October 14, 1938, that he had received news on the twenty-seventh that Hitler would take action on the next day. Arthur Murray, *At Close Quarters* (London: John Murray, 1946), 95.

[85] These were sent that afternoon. Hull to Officers in Charge of American Diplomatic Missions, Sept. 27, 1938, *FRUS*, 1938, 1:677–78 (n. 86; "Marginal note on the original telegram: 'OK, FDR.' "); Hull to Phillips, Sept. 27, 1938, ibid., 677.

posed it. Ultimately, Welles was instructed to ask Bullitt and Kennedy to obtain Daladier's and Chamberlain's views on the desirability of such a plan. If they approved, the message addressed to Hitler might suggest a conference at a neutral European capital, although the promise of American participation would be omitted.[86]

While Welles made these calls and worked with Berle on redrafting the message to Hitler, Roosevelt met with his cabinet. He had arranged for them to listen to Chamberlain's speech at 2 p.m., and, as he told Arthur Murray two weeks later, it was a very moving experience:

> When it was finished I looked round the table and there were tears in the eyes of at least four Members of the Cabinet, and I felt that way myself. I had listened to Hitler on the Monday, and so had most of my Cabinet. The contrast between the two just bit into us—the shouting and violence of Hitler, and the roars, through their teeth, of his audience of 'Krieg, krieg,' and then, the quiet, beautiful statement of Chamberlain's.[87]

For the rest of the meeting, "the European situation was the almost exclusive subject of discussion." Informing the cabinet that he had received an unsatisfactory reply to his first message to Hitler, Roosevelt suggested the possibility of sending a second. He then led a discussion of this idea which, despite the emotion generated by Chamberlain's speech, amounted to a fairly dispassionate appraisal of the alternatives. According to Ickes, sentiment in the cabinet favored aiding the allies "in every way possible" while keeping the United States clear of any involvement in war. The president also reiterated his belief that in the event of war the democracies would be the victors.[88]

[86] Berle, *Navigating*, 187; Alsop and Kintner, *American White Paper*, 10. Memorandum of a Telephone Conversation between Bullitt and Welles, Sept. 27, 1938, *FRUS*, 1938, 1:675–76, 2:40 p.m.; Memorandum of a Telephone Conversation between Kennedy and Welles, Sept. 27, 1938, ibid., 678–79, 3:00 p.m.

[87] Murray, *Close Quarters*, 95. According to Murray, these are Roosevelt's own words as noted by Murray at the time. Ickes also gives an account of this emotional episode (*Diary*, 2:477), and Berle noticed later in the day that the President had been "much impressed" with Chamberlain's speech (*Navigating*, 189). On September 26, Roosevelt wrote Margaret Suckley about Hitler's speech: "His shrieks, his histrionics and the effect on the huge audience—They did not applaud—they made noises like animals." Ward, *Closest Companion*, 125.

[88] Ickes, *Diary*, 2:481. This is disputed by Kinsella on the basis of Roosevelt's statement to Josephus Daniels (Jan. 16, 1939) that he himself would have had to act as Chamberlain had because of Allied weakness in air power relative to Germany. However, this comment reflects his retrospective assessment of the situation. (For one thing, as Daniels's account shows plainly, the information on which Roosevelt based this view was received after the crisis.) Moreover, as his remarks to the Cabinet make clear, although he was concerned by that point about the preponderance of Germany and Italy in the air, he was also still fairly confident that the democracies could win a war with Germany. Kinsella, *Leadership*, 124; Carroll Kilpatrick, *Roosevelt and Daniels: A Friendship in Politics* (Chapel Hill, N.C. University of North Carolina Press), 181–83.

Sometime during the course of the afternoon, Roosevelt decided to send his second message to Hitler as soon as possible. As he told Murray, "I had intended to send a message to Hitler on the Wednesday morning. But on the top of Chamberlain's radio speech came news from our people in Berlin that Hitler was to take action at two o'clock on Wednesday afternoon. So I got down at once about five o'clock to the draft of my message, and Hull came across again from the State Department. By about nine o'clock we had hammered out the message, and Hitler had it with his breakfast."[89]

Following this conversation with Kennedy, Welles took Roosevelt the latest draft of the message to Hitler. After dinner the president worked on it with Welles, Hull, and Berle in a two-hour session. "The President worked at his littered desk, smoking incessantly and shooting questions at the other three. They sat nervously near him, Berle fidgeting, Hull swearing softly under his breath, and Welles for once almost out of countenance." A moment of considerable tension occurred when "a report came in that the Germans might march in the night, forcing a war to no purpose. For a moment the President showed real anger." However, as the report was not confirmed and time of the essence, the work continued. By nine the draft was well enough in hand to allow the secretary of state to go home to bed, and at 9:30 it was signed by the president.[90]

Roosevelt's second message to Hitler was sent at 10:18 p.m. Recalling his earlier emphasis on the importance of pacific settlement and the complete lack of justification for threats of force, which could result in general warfare, he pointed out that these considerations were even more germane since agreement in principle had already been reached between Germany and Czechoslovakia. He therefore urged continuation of the negotiations, raising the possibility of expanding them to include "all the nations directly interested in the present controversy" and holding them at a neutral spot in Europe. While reiterating that the United States had

[89] Murray, *Close Quarters*, 95. Apparently Roosevelt had decided not to wait to hear from Chamberlain and Daladier. By the time Kennedy called at 5:45 p.m. to relay Chamberlain's opinion, Welles was able to state that the President "will send his message tonight without fail." Memorandum of a Telephone Conversation between Kennedy and Welles, Sept. 27, 1938, *FRUS*, 1938, 1:679–80. This decision could have been reinforced by the letter from Lindbergh to Admiral Land that Roosevelt saw on the twenty-seventh. Painting a "depressing picture," Lindbergh predicted war in 1939, and declared that, because of German superiority over the British and the French, it was "'absolutely necessary to avoid a war next year if there is any possibility of doing so.'" Cole, *Roosevelt*, 285 n. 28.

[90] Alsop and Kintner, *American White Paper*, 10–11. See also Berle, *Navigating*, 188; and Murray, *Close Quarters*, 95. With respect to Roosevelt's contribution, Berle remarked somewhat peevishly that "It is difficult to appraise any one part in the transaction. I note that Steve Early is indicating publicly that all drafting was done by President Roosevelt, who virtually assumed control of the State Department. Of course, the actual documents show the precise contrary; though the President certainly wanted action." Berle, *Navigating*, 188–89.

"no political involvements in Europe," Roosevelt nevertheless declared that, "The conscience and the impelling desire of the people of my country demand that the voice of their government be raised again and yet again to avert and to avoid war."[91]

With respect to Roosevelt's purpose in sending this message, according to Ickes on September twenty-seventh the entire cabinet expected war and everyone, the president included, viewed the message more as an attempt to build a record than a serious effort to influence Hitler. While it is undoubtedly true that Roosevelt saw "the importance of clarifying the issue so that if war started there could be no doubt . . . as to who was responsible for starting it," it is also clear that he very much hoped his message would help to prevent that war.[92] His own testimony that the combination of Chamberlain's speech and the report that Hitler would take action the following afternoon caused him to send the message immediately suggests that he expected it to have an influence. This interpretation is supported by both the account of the drafting process and Roosevelt's determined attempts to learn the impact of his message.[93]

There is some controversy about exactly how Roosevelt expected his message to avert war. It has been argued both that he intended it to support the cause of collective action and that he was attempting to reinforce efforts to avoid war at almost any price. Haight contends, for example, that "given the background of the conference plan since Bullitt's suggestion of May 20, it is obvious that collective action to maintain the

[91] Roosevelt to Hitler, Sept. 27, 1938, *FRUS*, 1938, 1:684–85. Although Haight suggests that Roosevelt held off sending this message until he had learned from Bullitt of Daladier's firmness, he does not offer any evidence for this. A cable was received from Bullitt at 9:46 stating that the French president approved the idea of both Roosevelt's appeal and a conference, and vowed that France would fight before allowing Hitler " 'to make his wish law in Europe.' " However, as Offner points out, by this time, the appeal had not only already been drafted but signed. Moreover, all available accounts of that evening suggest that Roosevelt was anxious to get his message off as soon as possible and was prepared to do so even without hearing from Bullitt. While he may have known of Daladier's stand before he sent his message, it is unlikely to have been the decisive consideration in his decision to dispatch that message. Ibid., 686–89; Haight, "France, the United States, and the Munich Crisis," 355; Offner, *American Appeasement*, 266–67. This argument is supported by Roosevelt's and Welles's statements to Murray and Kennedy cited above.

[92] Ickes, *Diary*, 2:477–78.

[93] Hull also gives the impression that the appeal was meant seriouly, and Berle conveys his sense that the general belief that war was practically inevitable was combined with the hope that it could nevertheless somehow be averted. Hull, *Memoirs*, 1:593; and Berle, *Navigating*, 188. See also Offner, *American Appeasement*, 264 n. 77. Ickes himself gives evidence that the President seriously intended his actions during the Munich crisis to prevent war: "In one of our private conferences the President told me that he had wanted to avoid the mistake that Wilson had made in 1914. He felt that if Wilson had expressed himself vigorously then, war might have been averted." *Diary*, 2:481. The entry is for September 30. For the President's attempts to assess the efficacy of his appeal, see below.

peace formed the basis for Roosevelt's call." The cautious phrasing of the message was due only to his concern about isolationist reaction and the reservations of Hull and his other advisers.[94] Offner, on the other hand, suggests that Roosevelt, fully aware that Chamberlain would not fight if he could possibly get out of it and "would go nearly any length" to give Hitler what he demanded, wanted negotiations to continue solely for the purpose of avoiding war.[95]

Haight's claim that Roosevelt made his appeal in support of collective action seems exaggerated, not only because his evidence (that Roosevelt waited to send the message until news of Daladier's firmness had reached him) is dubious, but also because it is based on a misreading of Bullitt's conference idea. On the other hand, Offner also exaggerates in claiming that Roosevelt's message was intended to support peace at any price. In the first phase of the crisis, Roosevelt gave every indication of wanting the democracies to resist Hitler's demands.[96] In the second phase, while less concerned with the general political situation and more focused on ending the crisis without war (because he no longer saw any basis for it, the Czechs having agreed to Germany's terms), he thought Hitler's new demands thoroughly unreasonable, and there is little to suggest that he either expected or desired the democracies to bow any further to German pressure.[97]

After the Godesberg meeting, then, Roosevelt had considerable evidence that a line had been drawn beyond which the Allies were not prepared to go. Having no reason to suppose that further negotiations would alter this commitment, he apparently thought his message to Hitler would support it.[98] Thus, his appeal was an attempt to prevent war (admittedly without further involving the United States) by pressur-

---

[94] Haight, "France, the United States, and the Munich Crisis," 355–56.

[95] Offner, *American Appeasement*, 267.

[96] See his remarks on September 16 comparing the British and French to Judas Iscariot and his attempts to advise the British about the proper strategy for conducting the war on September 19.

[97] Contrary to Offner's argument, when Roosevelt sent his message he had no reason to believe that Daladier and Chamberlain intended to give up more than they already had. The only suggestion that this might be so was contained in Bullitt's cable describing Bonnet's maneuvers in support of further appeasement, the importance of which Bullitt himself discounted. Kennedy's later call indicated Chamberlain's belief that he would have to fight, however reluctantly, and Bullitt's final telegram emphasized Daladier's readiness to do so as well. Moreover, as Moffat noted, Chamberlain's speech had left a similar impression. Hooker, *Moffat Papers*, 215. Bullitt to Hull, Sept. 27, 1938, *FRUS*, 1938, 1:680–81, received at 2:30 p.m.; Memorandum of a Telephone Conversation between Kennedy and Welles, Sept. 27, 1938, ibid., 679–80. See also Haight, "France, the United States, and the Munich Crisis," 354–55. Note also that in Ickes's account of the September 27 cabinet discussion of possible American moves, there is not the slightest suggestion that supporting appeasement was one of them. See above.

[98] Ickes's account of the cabinet's discussion of the second message supports this contention. See below.

ing Hitler into a peaceful settlement along already agreed lines. A subsidiary aim was probably, as Ickes believed, to create a record that could be used to assign blame should this effort fail.

The Denoument

The period of anxious waiting for Hitler's reply ended on the morning of September 28. At 10:30 a.m., Berle recorded in his diary Hitler's invitation to Britain, France, and Italy to meet him to discuss the Czech crisis: "The break! Thank God."[99] Roosevelt was also relieved by the news, writing to Margaret Suckley, "Could anything bring a more perfect morning!—It is too early to tell but it *looks* like no war." At 1 p.m. he sent his famous two-word message to Prime Minister Chamberlain: "Good Man."[100]

Although the terms of the settlement were not made known until September 30, emotionally the crisis ended with the announcement of the agreement to meet. In comparison with that achievement, the settlement itself had almost come to seem incidental. What little concern remained about matters of substance was rapidly engulfed by universal rejoicing over a procedural victory: Hitler had agreed to a peaceful meeting rather than war to achieve his ends. Ironically, in the widespread atmosphere of relief that war had been averted, few seemed to notice that the issue over which it had nearly been fought (the conditions under which the Czechs would give up the Sudetenland) had been all but forgotten.

ANALYSIS

What most obviously requires explanation in this episode is Roosevelt's dramatic reversal of preferences about intervening, though several other features of his decision-making also merit attention. In particular, the effect of the decision environment on his behavior must be considered. At the very least, having to make decisions in the midst of an international crisis subjected Roosevelt to the pressure of time. For that reason, as well

[99] Berle, *Navigating*, 188.

[100] Hull to Kennedy, Sept. 28, 1938, *FRUS*, 1938, 1:688. While the meaning of this message has been debated, most agree with Langer and Gleason that it signaled relief at the continuance of negotiations rather than approval of the policy of appeasement. *Challenge*, 34. Offner disputes this interpretation. Haight, on the other hand, believes that at this point Roosevelt "assumed that Chamberlain still stood with Daladier as an opponent to capitulation. . . . He expected Chamberlain to negotiate at Munich on the basis of 'reason and equity.'" Offner, *American Appeasement*, 269; Haight, "France, the United States, and the Munich Crisis," 356 n. 132. See also Haight, *American Aid*, 22; and Francis L. Loewenheim, "The Untold Story of FDR and Munich—And Its Cover-up," *Houston Chronicle*, Oct. 1, 1978, 24, who agrees with Offner.

as because of the gravity of the issues involved, the question of whether and in what way stress played a role must be addressed.

Accounting for the Preference Change

Why had preventing war become so important to Roosevelt that he was eager to intervene where he had previously been reluctant to? The obvious explanation is that his preference reversal was a rational response to new information altering the expected utility of intervention. But while one or more changes in the environment—in the value of the outcome of war, its probability, or the risks of intervention—could conceivably have triggered such a shift, none of these factors had changed sufficiently to justify Roosevelt's reversal of preferences.

If, for example, Roosevelt's post-Godesberg belief that an outcome of war would now be a loss had been based on new information about its costs to the United States, it would have been rational to intervene to prevent it, even at some risk. The crisis, however, did not provide any new information about the value of the war.[101] No matter how certain or imminent general war in Europe became after Godesberg, it was no more of a threat to the United States than it had been when it was merely probable. No one imagined for a moment that America would be directly threatened by it—certainly not Roosevelt, who firmly believed Britain and France would win. Yet despite his unaltered belief that the democracies would emerge victorious, Roosevelt behaved as though war had become a direct threat.

What is embarassing to a rational-choice explanation is that after Godesberg Roosevelt redefined essentially the same objective situation as a loss. Not only was there no change in Roosevelt's perception of the value of war, his conception of the risks involved in intervening also remained unchanged. With respect to the risk of failure, nothing had occurred at Godesberg that entitled him to infer that he could now act more effectively than he might have earlier. Although he believed that Czech agreement to the substance of Hitler's demands removed any rational basis for waging war, the Führer had provided nothing but evidence that he was unreasonable in the extreme.[102] Nor had anything

[101] The reports emphasizing the dreadful consequences of war for European civilization might conceivably be viewed as new information that changed Roosevelt's valuation of the outcome of war. Such arguments, however, were not new to Roosevelt and he had ignored them earlier. Cf. Bullitt's letter of May 20.

[102] Haight suggests that what helped Roosevelt to decide to intervene was not only Bullitt's emphasis on the seriousness of the situation but also the impression he gave that the democracies were now prepared to act with resolve. However, the cable conveying this idea

changed on the American side of the equation to allow him to suppose that he had the means to act more effectively. Nothing that happened at Godesberg in any way altered the fact that the United States would under no circumstances intervene militarily in the Czech crisis, or even threaten to do so.

Even after he had made the decision to intervene, Roosevelt still seems to have considered it a risky choice. The amount of effort he put into learning whether his second intervention had been successful, as well as the considerable anxiety this issue seemed to cause him, suggests that he was aware that move could well have failed. In fact, he seems to have been seeking reassurance that the risk he had taken had produced results.[103]

Not only did Roosevelt still worry about the risk of failure, he also remained concerned about the domestic risks, as shown by his acquiescence to Hull's and Davis's reservations during the drafting of his first appeal and confirmed by the testimony of Moffat and Welles. In planning for his second intervention, Roosevelt showed sensitivity to the domestic risks by supporting Hull's wish to omit any mention of American participation in a proposed conference.[104]

The changes in Roosevelt's assessment of the probability of war were also insufficient to justify his preference reversal. While his decision to intervene might have been an appropriate response to the increased likelihood of war, neither of his two shifts toward a heightened expectation of war was accompanied by a change from inaction to intervention. After Berchtesgaden, when he first came to expect war, he seemed quite relaxed, reacting not by trying to prevent it but by attempting to influence the way it would be fought. Moreover, even his post-Godesberg diagnosis that war was imminent did not immediately move him to act. As late as the afternoon of September 23, he still believed that the democracies could win if they followed his strategic advice and showed neither a sense of an immediate threat to American security nor a desire to inter-

---

was not received until 9:30 p.m., well *after* Roosevelt had made his first decision to intervene. See above. Haight, "France, the United States, and the Munich Crisis," 353; Bullitt to Hull, Sept. 25, 1938, *FRUS*, 1938, 1:656–57.

[103] See below, chap. 5.

[104] Roosevelt may have perceived that intervention involved significant domestic risks because it meant taking a public stand. While he was frequently prepared to engage in diplomatic activity that seemed risky enough to others (e.g., his talk with Lindsay), he was exceedingly cautious about what he did in public. As Hull had pointed out, Roosevelt's public involvement during the Munich crisis might have stirred up isolationist sentiment, raising alarm that he was embarking on an activist course that would take the United States into war. (For evidence of Roosevelt's habitual caution about taking public positions, see the discussion of his decision-making before and during the Nine Power Conference in Brussels in the fall of 1937 above, and Farnham, "Value Conflict," appendix.)

vene in the crisis. Although Roosevelt had clearly assimilated the information that war was imminent, he apparently did not believe that this called for a policy shift.[105] Thus, an explanation for his behavior must be sought elsewhere.

One possibility is that in line with the predictions of prospect theory, Roosevelt's preference reversal was a consequence of his reframing of the decision problem. A decision frame is "the decision-maker's conception of the acts, outcomes and contingencies associated with a particular choice" and it in part determines how people see the consequences of choice. When the same decision is framed differently, preferences between options have been shown to reverse, despite rational-choice theory's requirement that they should not.[106] In particular, whether an outcome is framed as a gain or a loss has a profound impact on preferences and risk taking.[107]

[105] I am indebted to Eldar Shafir for pointing out that the slight increase in the probability of war between the afternoon of the twenty-third and the morning of the twenty-fifth is insufficient to account for the dramatic reversal in Roosevelt's policy preferences that occurred that day. That small change in probability had a much greater impact on his decision-making than rational-choice theory would predict. Moreover, neither Roosevelt's perception of the increased likelihood of war nor its imminence afforded adequate justification for either the feeling that the United States had become directly threatened or the belief that American action might now be effective in ending the crisis.

[106] Amos Tversky and Daniel Kahneman, "The Framing of Decisions and the Psychology of Choice," *Science* 211 (1981): 453, 457; Daniel Kahneman and Amos Tversky, "The Psychology of Preferences," *Scientific American* 246 (1982): 166. Some of these effects are also discussed in Daniel Kahneman and Amos Tversky, "Prospect Theory: An Analysis of Decision Under Risk," *Econometrica* 47 (1979): 263–92. There has been some experimental confirmation of the idea that the framing of a decision problem can affect choice decisions. See Mark A. Davis and Philip Bobko, "Contextual Effects on Escalation Processes in Public Sector Decision Making," *Organizational Behavior and Human Decision Processes* 37 (1986): 125–26, 133–34; Max H. Bazerman, "Negotiator Judgement," *American Behavioral Scientist* 27 (1983): 214; Irwin P. Levin, Richard D. Johnson, Craig P. Russo, and Patricia J. Deldin, "Framing Effects in Judgment Tasks with Varying Amounts of Information," *Organizational Behavior and Human Decision Processes* 36 (1985): 262–77; and Shapira, "Making Trade-offs," 334, 344–48, 350.

[107] People evaluate prospective outcomes against a neutral reference point, usually the status quo. Outcomes that lie above the reference point are viewed as gains, while those below it are seen as losses. Framing an outcome as a loss rather than a gain changes the way people respond to it, even to the point of causing them to reverse their order of preference among equivalent options. In particular, they are likely to be risk averse when it is matter of achieving a gain but risk acceptant when striving to avoid a loss. Amos Tversky and Daniel Kahneman, "Rational Choice and the Framing of Decisions," *Journal of Business* 59 (Oct. 1986): S253, S258; Kahneman and Tversky, "Prospect Theory," 276, and "Psychology of Preferences," 160, 162; Tversky and Kahneman, "Framing," 456; George A. Quattrone and Amos Tversky, "Contrasting Rational and Psychological Analyses of Political Choice," *American Political Science Review* 82 (1988): 719–36. See also Abelson and Levi, "Decision Making" 247–48; and George A. Quattrone and Amos Tversky, "Causal versus Diagnostic Contingencies: On Self-Deception and on the Voter's Illusion," *Journal of Person-*

After Godesberg there was at least one major change in the way Roosevelt framed his decision that could have led to his preference shift: he had come to view the impending war in Europe as a loss for the United States—not that he had previously seen it as a gain, but neither had the prospect greatly disturbed him. By September 25, however, he unquestionably saw it as a potential catastrophe, although there is not the slightest evidence he believed that it would actually threaten the United States.[108] On the contrary, he had come to view war as a loss without having changed his mind about its actual costs.

Roosevelt's increased willingness to intervene in the crisis as a consequence of perceiving war as a loss may also have been reinforced by what Tversky and Kahneman call the "certainty effect," or a tendency to overweight outcomes that are considered certain relative to those that are merely probable. (For example, losing ten dollars with certainty seems more than twice as bad as a 50 percent chance of losing ten dollars.)[109] Since, after Godesberg, Roosevelt viewed war as a virtual certainty, this effect could have made it seem worse than when he thought it merely probable. His growing conviction that war was inevitable exacerbated his perception of it as a loss for the United States. Moreover, the certainty effect may have combined with the pseudo-certainty effect to reinforce his sense of threat.[110]

Roosevelt's frame change, reinforced by the certainty effect, transformed what had been merely a potential problem for American foreign policy into a serious loss that was bound to occur. Furthermore, because this reframing caused him to view the crisis from a different point of reference, it could also have been responsible for his reversal of preferences, even though the threat to the United States had not actually increased. As Jervis points out, "losses which are quite certain will be avoided even if they are relatively slight."[111] Moreover, since "the framing of an action sometimes affects the actual experience of its out-

---

ality and Social Psychology 46 (1984): 237–48. For a general discussion of framing and prospect theory, see appendix A.

[108] This interpretation is supported by the fact that from this point forward, Roosevelt's behavior exhibited all the characteristics that, according to Raymond Cohen, identify a decision-maker who has perceived a threat. Raymond Cohen, Threat Perception in International Crisis (Madison, Wisc.: University of Wisconsin Press, 1979), 4, 24.

[109] Kahneman and Tversky, "Prospect Theory," 265; Tversky and Kahneman, "Rational Choice," S263–70; Baruch Fischoff, "Strategic Policy Preferences: A Behavioral Decision Theory," Journal of Social Issues 39 (1983): 144.

[110] People tend to treat extremely likely but uncertain outcomes as though they were certain. Thus, as the probability of war rose after Godesberg, Roosevelt may first have converted it into a certainty in line with the pseudo-certainty effect and then overweighted it because of the certainty effect. Tversky and Kahneman, "Rational Choice," S268.

[111] Robert Jervis, "The Political Implications of Loss Aversion," unpubl. ms., 1989, 6. See also his article with the same title in Political Psychology 13 (June 1992): 190.

comes,"[112] framing the European crisis so that the outcome of war was a loss for the United States could have changed the way Roosevelt experienced the consequences of nonintervention, which in turn altered his assessment of the alternatives. Thus, he came to prefer acting to end the crisis before it eventuated in war to the passive stance he had adopted when he regarded war as another's loss. Viewing the impending war as in some sense a threat to the United States, he was no longer evaluating the alternatives as a mere observer but as a sort of participant.[113] Reframing the war as a loss for the United States meant reframing the crisis as an American one.

As prospect theory predicts, in deciding to act to avert the war he now viewed as a loss, Roosevelt became risk acceptant. That is, he was willing to incur the two risks he had previously avoided: the chance that his intervention might be ineffective, or even have an adverse impact on the crisis, and the danger that such action might provoke "untoward domestic effects." Finally, a prospect-theory explanation of Roosevelt's behavior is supported by his apparent lack of awareness that he was in fact framing the crisis differently. At no time did he link his decision to intervene in the crisis to a change in his feelings about the significance of war. Indeed, he seems not to have noticed that they had changed, nor to have recalled that only days earlier he had not thought a European war a calamity that he wished to intervene to prevent.[114]

If Roosevelt did not initially view war in Europe as a serious threat to the United States, why did he do so after Godesberg? What caused him to change his reference point so that he now counted war as a loss? Unfortunately, prospect theory does not offer many clues about what causes decision frames to change. Nor do the laboratory experiments on framing shed much light on this question. The experimenter alone manipulates the frame, providing subjects with both the original and altered version, the differences between the two being purely cognitive.

The Munich case, however, suggests that in the real world at times something more than cognition may be involved. In particular, Roose-

---

[112] Tversky and Kahneman, "Framing," 458.

[113] The change in Roosevelt's behavior after his frame change also accords with Hermann's finding of striking differences in perspective between participants and observers during a crisis simulation, with important implications for their decision-making behavior. Charles F. Hermann, "Threat, Time, and Surprise: A Simulation of International Crisis," in *International Crisis* ed. Charles F. Hermann (New York: Free Press, 1972), 208.

[114] "Decision-makers are not normally aware of the potential effects of different decision frames on their preferences." Ibid., 457–58. Roosevelt's behavior is also in line with Tversky and Kahneman's perception that, unless a conscious effort is made, decision-makers may not be able to anticipate how they will feel about a future experience. See Daniel Kahneman and Amos Tversky, "Choices, Values, and Frames," *American Psychologist* 39 (1984): 349–50.

velt's frame change appears to have been triggered by the strong emotions he experienced after the Godesberg meeting. That is, he reframed the crisis as a matter of direct concern to the United States only after the idea of impending war had become emotionally compelling to him.[115] This hypothesis is supported by several considerations. First of all, from a purely cognitive perspective, Roosevelt's reframing of the problem posed by the crisis is puzzling. The cognition that war was a virtual certainty was not sufficient to provoke either a perception of threat or a desire to intervene, which manifested itself only after nearly two days had passed. Moreover, the entire period in which the frame change occurred was, as Ickes has testified, generally a time of great emotion as Americans observed Europe's headlong rush toward war.[116] Finally, in the brief period between the initial reports from Godesberg and his decision to intervene, Roosevelt received numerous affect-laden communications, many of them from Bullitt and Kennedy who, emotionally at least, had already adopted the perspective of the parties to the crisis.

Unlike his two ambassadors, before Godesberg Roosevelt did not dwell on the disastrous immediate consequences of a general European war. Rather, as his remarks to Lindsay suggest, he was thinking in a general way about the eventual implications for the United States should an unappeasable and aggressive Hitler prove successful in Europe. This difference in focus may account for the contrast between Roosevelt's curiously detached attitude toward the anticipated conflict and Bullitt's and Kennedy's emotional responses. The idea of impending war seems to have lacked emotional reality for him. This detachment, as well as his continued refusal to intervene despite the imminence of war (both of which he exhibited as late as the afternoon of September 23), offers a striking contrast to the anxiety Morgenthau described to his staff early on the twenty-sixth. Roosevelt's preference shift was thus not the culmination of a gradual process of reevaluation but an immediate response to a sudden change in mood most probably induced by the emotionally charged communications he was receiving from Europe.

Indeed, the messages that bombarded Roosevelt from the twenty-third to the twenty-fifth of September were increasingly dramatic. Among other things, they predicted a war that would spell the end of European

---

[115] This may have been true of other members of the administration as well. See above.

[116] The emotional impact of the Munich crisis may have been a major contributor to the panic generated by Orson Welles's contemporary radio drama about a Martian invasion. As Heywood Broun analyzed it at the time, "I doubt if anything of the sort would have happened four or five months ago. The course of world history has affected national psychology. Jitters have come home to roost. We have just gone through a laboratory demonstration of the fact that the peace of Munich hangs over our heads, like a thundercloud." Philip Klass, "Wells, Welles and the Martians," *New York Times Book Review*, Oct. 30, 1988, 1. See also Hadley Cantril, *The Invasion from Mars* (Princeton: Princeton University Press, 1940).

civilization, underlined Hitler's brutality and intransigence, described Chamberlain's growing pessimism, conveyed the heartrending pleas of the Czechs for help, and—from Bullitt in particular—urged in the strongest possible terms American action to avoid the tragedy. Moreover, the emotional impact of these messages could only have been magnified by the highly stressful atmosphere produced by the continuing crisis, as well as by the increasing vividness, extremity, and frequency of the information itself.[117] These communications seem to have focused Roosevelt's attention primarily on the dreadful consequences of the impending conflict, making it emotionally real to him. Thus, by September 25, he not only *believed* that war was bound to occur, he had also begun to *feel* that it would be so terrible that he had to stop it.

Strong emotion, then, apparently lay behind Roosevelt's transformation from a detached observer of the crisis to a sort of participant. In the language of prospect theory, as he became increasingly affected by the emotional impact of the news from Europe, he began to experience the prospect of war as a loss. This in turn led him to understand the choice of whether or not to intervene in a fundamentally different way, and, as a consequence, to want to prevent the war rather than merely to advise others on how to fight it. As Kahneman points out, "Losses . . . compounded by outrage are much less acceptable than losses . . . caused by misfortune or by legitimate actions of others."[118]

This process continued on the twenty-fifth itself. Already desiring to act, Roosevelt experienced another day of great emotional tension that finally culminated in his decision to intervene. Even after he made that choice, however, the psychological pressure continued to build. September 26 began as a day of anxious waiting for Hitler's response to his message and ended with disappointment at the Führer's violent speech and unyielding reply. That Roosevelt's feelings had by this time become deeply engaged is shown by his account of his emotional reaction to Chamberlain's speech during the September 27 cabinet meeting, his letter on the twenty-sixth to his cousin, and reports of the tension that characterized the drafting of his second appeal, particularly his display of anger at the news that Hitler might be preparing to march immediately.[119] Clearly, outrage at Hitler's behavior and great sympathy for the democ-

---

[117] I am indebted to Carol Dweck for pointing out that the way the information was presented, as well as its nature, could have affected what sort of emotional response it engendered. On the increased flow of information during a crisis, see Raymond Cohen, *International Politics, the Rules of the Game* (New York: Longman, 1981), 141.

[118] Daniel Kahneman, "References Points, Anchors, Norms, and Mixed Feeling," *Organizational Behavior and Human Decision Processes* 51 (1992): 304.

[119] As Berle described it, "the President came up, all standing, and said in that case he would go on the air to tell the facts to the American people." *Navigating*, 188.

racies had joined Roosevelt's already considerable anxiety about the consequences of war.

Roosevelt's awareness of the imminence of war may also have added to these negative emotions. The imminence of a threatening event may generate greater emotion and stress than certainty alone does, and for Roosevelt the war that had seemed certain after Berchtesgaden, after Godesberg appeared imminent as well.[120] While that was not in itself sufficient to cause him to decide to intervene, by increasing the salience of war it may well have exacerbated the effect of the emotions that did. Not only might this awareness have heightened the painful emotions Roosevelt felt, it could also have intensified his stress by adding the pressure of time.

In any event, there is considerable empirical evidence pointing to strong emotion as the crucial element in Roosevelt's post-Godesberg change of frame and subsequent reversal of preferences. Moreover, while the idea that affect can motivate cognitive change has received ample theoretical support,[121] the reverse can occur as well. That is, a change of frame can affect the emotions experienced by the decision-maker. In fact, Tversky and Kahneman themselves usually speak of changes in emotional response as the *outcome* of frame changes rather than their cause;[122] clearly this could have occurred in Roosevelt's case. Framing the crisis as in some sense his own could have intensified the emotional involvement that caused the frame to change in the first place. This, in turn, could have reinforced the new frame in which the outcome of war was seen as a loss.[123] Again, the literature on the relationship between affect and cog-

---

[120] Janis and Mann, *Decision-Making*, 54, 59. I am indebted to Alexander George for pointing out that imminence may have a different impact on a decision-maker's assessment of threat than certainty.

[121] Martin L. Hoffman, "Affect, Cognition, and Motivation," *Handbook of Motivation and Cognition*, ed. E. Tory Higgins and Richard M. Sorrentino (New York: Guilford Press, 1986), 1:260. For Hoffman's view of the ways affect may influence information processing, see 245–46. There is also a body of theory that suggests that negative emotion encourages more analytic processing. Even those who hold this view, however, note the possible "interference effects of negative affect." See Norbert Schwarz, "Feelings as Information," in ibid., 2:551. See also George E. Marcus, W. Russell Neuman, Michael MacKuen, and John L. Sullivan, "Dynamic Models of Emotional Response: The Multiple Roles of Affect in Politics," paper delivered at the International Society of Political Psychology, Cambridge, Mass., July 1993.

[122] Tversky and Kahneman, "Framing," 458; Kahneman and Tversky, "Choices, Values, and Frames," 348–50.

[123] It is a commonly held view that a decision-maker's personal experience of a crisis generates considerable emotion and stress. Morgan, for example, defines a national-security crisis as "a severe threat to important values which, for the decision maker, means an increase in emotional intensity." Patrick Morgan, *Deterrence: A Conceptual Analysis* (Beverly Hills: Sage Library of Social Science, 1977), 168. See also Ole R. Holsti, *Crisis, Escala-*

nition supports the notion that a change in cognition can result in changes in affect.[124] Moreover, evidence that the causal connection runs in both directions has led a number of scholars to conclude that, as in Roosevelt's case, these processes are mutually reinforcing.[125]

Thus, the news from Godesberg may have touched off a complex interaction between cognition and affect that transformed Roosevelt from a somewhat detached observer into a kind of participant. He had come to feel that war would be a loss, not only for Europe, but for the United States as well, and in this sense the crisis had moved, at least in emotional terms, from being another's to being his own. As a consequence, Roosevelt reversed his preferences and chose to intervene.

Decision-Making during the Crisis

Did the strong emotion which caused a dramatic, and quite irrational, change of preference in the midst of the crisis lead to other changes in Roosevelt's information processing? Somewhat surprisingly, apart from that preference shift, Roosevelt's behavior was remarkably consistent throughout the crisis, both before and after Godesberg.

In fact, Roosevelt's decision-making behavior during the Munich crisis exhibited many of the features that characterized it from 1936 to 1938. However strong the emotion that led to his frame change and preference reversal, it did not cause him to abandon his fundamentally political approach to decision-making, even after reframing the crisis. For one thing, he displayed a characteristic eagerness to act. During the crisis, as before, when he perceived a problem, he was anxious to do something about it, at times even seeking to take action when there was no particular external pressure to do so. In the summer of 1938—though ultimately frustrated in his attempt to influence the Sudeten crisis by his own uncertainty as well as suspicion about British and French motives—Roosevelt's desire to act manifested itself in the Kingston speech and his plan for instituting countervailing duties. Later, during the first phase of the crisis, even when he

---

tion, *War* (Montreal: McGill-Queens University Press, 1972), and "Crisis, Stress and Decision-Making," *International Social Science Journal* 23 (1971): 53–67; Holsti and George, "Effects of Stress," 255–319.

[124] Hoffman, "Affect, Cognition, and Motivation," 244.

[125] Richard M. Sorrentino and E. Tory Higgins, "Motivation and Cognition," in Higgins and Sorrentino, *Handbook*, 1:12, 8. For opposing views, see Robert B. Zajonc, "Feeling and Thinking: Preferences Need No Inferences," *American Psychologist* 35 (1980): 151–75; and Richard S. Lazarus, "Thoughts on the Relations Between Emotion and Cognition," *American Psychologist* 37 (1982): 1019–24. For an attempt to reconcile such differences, see Joel Weinberger and David C. McClelland, "Cognitive versus Traditional Motivational Models," in Higgins and Sorrentino, *Handbook*, 2:562–97.

could not see what action to take, he attempted at least to influence the manner in which any conflict would be fought. Moreover, after Godesberg, when he had reframed the problem so that intervention now seemed appropriate, he showed every sign of relief at having the chance to act, telling Hull that he "believed with Bullitt that something should be done, even if it were not successful," and giving Berle the impression that he "certainly wanted action."[126]

Finally, while obviously pleased that war had been averted, Roosevelt was clearly anxious to establish the effectiveness of his own intervention. Although he received a number of cables on September 28 praising his message and testifying to its efficacy, he was apparently not altogether reassured (perhaps because Ambassador Wilson's account of the events leading up to Hitler's invitation to Munich stressed Mussolini's critical role while neglecting to mention Roosevelt's). Queries on this subject began to go out from the State Department to various embassies almost immediately, continuing into late October.[127]

Roosevelt's desire for effective action was invariably accompanied by another hallmark of the political approach: a dominant concern with acceptability. He was unwilling to violate previously established domestic constraints, no matter how much he desired to act, and no matter how great the emotion of the moment.[128] Thus before and during the crisis he paid close attention to appearances. As during the Nine Power Conference, he was determined not to allow the British and French to manipu-

[126] Hull, *Memoirs*, 1:591; Berle, *Navigating*, 188–89. Cole supports this interpretation. *Roosevelt*, 284. See also Alsop and Kintner, *American White Paper*, 8.

[127] Bullitt to Hull, Sept. 28, 1938, *FRUS*, 1938, 1:691–92; Kennedy to Hull, Sept. 28, 1938, ibid., 692–93; Wilson to Hull, Sept. 29, 1938, ibid., 698–99; Hull to Phillips, Sept. 30, 1938, ibid., 701–2; Welles to Wilson, Oct. 18, 1938, ibid, 724–25; Wilson to Welles, Oct. 20, 1938, ibid., 725; Hull to Wilson, Oct. 20, 1938, ibid., 725–26; "Sumner Welles, Under Secretary of State, to Roosevelt, October 22, 1938," (informing the president that he had telegraphed Wilson, asking him for the information he required), Schewe 7: no. 1361; "Hugh R. Wilson, Ambassador to Germany, to Sumner Welles, Under Secretary of State," Oct. 20 and 21, 1938, Schewe, no. 7: no.s ibid., no.s 1367a,b. What is important about this episode is the fact of Roosevelt's concern itself. However, it is interesting to note that most scholars agree that his interventions did not have a crucial influence, although Offner at least credits them with having reinforced the efforts of others. See Dallek, *Franklin D. Roosevelt*, 166; Blum, *Morgenthau Diaries*, 1:521; Langer and Gleason, *Challenge*, 34; Taylor, *Munich*, 890–91; Cole, *Roosevelt*, 287; Hugh R. Wilson, *A Career Diplomat* (New York: Vantage Press, 1960), 57–58; Edward L. Henson, Jr., "Britain, America, and the Month of Munich," *International Relations* 2 (1962): 299; and Offner, *American Appeasement*, 270–71. Roosevelt himself seems to have been convinced that his appeals had a significant impact. See James Farley, *Jim Farley's Story* (New York: McGraw-Hill, 1948), 197–98; and Roosevelt interview, Dec. 12, 1939, Alsop Papers.

[128] According to Alsop and Kintner's graphic account, Roosevelt "fumed sometimes at the necessity for caution," but always recognized that action was quite impossible if it depended on making a commitment. *American White Paper*, 8.

late the United States into taking the lead or seeming responsible for their actions. Hence, when he became suspicious of their motives, he abandoned his plan for countervailing duties and rebuffed Bonnet's attempt to depict the United States and France as "comrades in arms." Also reminiscent of his policy during the 1937 Far Eastern crisis was his insistence to Lindsay on September 19 that his support for a blockade against Germany and Italy was contingent on its being conducted so that honoring it would be acceptable in the United States, emphasizing in particular that there should be no mention of sanctions. In fact, Roosevelt's entire conversation with Lindsay is notable for his consistent attention to the requirements of domestic acceptability. Moreover, his concern for appearances was undiminished by his decision to intervene in the crisis, as is shown by his refusal on September 26, at the height of both his sympathy for the democracies and his desire to act positively, to allow Chamberlain's radio speech to be broadcast directly to the United States.[129] It is also suggested by Ickes's impression that Roosevelt's second message to Hitler was intended to establish a record, clarifying the situation and establishing a basis for assigning blame should all attempts at peaceful settlement fail.

This concern with acceptability also showed itself in Roosevelt's sensitivity to the potential reactions of various groups and individuals. Especially in his efforts to intervene diplomatically in the crisis, he was constantly aware of both the danger of transgressing the limits of domestic public opinion and the need to consider acceptability to key members of his administration. When information or advice about the reactions of either of these groups was offered, he was attentive; when it was not, he sought it out. In fact, his acquiescence to changes in his two messages seems to have been motivated as much by a desire to make them acceptable to his advisers as to the public. As well as heeding Hull's freely proffered reservations on both of these occasions, Roosevelt solicited the views of the rest of his cabinet, individually and collectively. Moreover, when he canvassed them about various alternative possibilities for his second message, he appears to have been seeking their views on the domestic acceptability of these options as well as their opinions on the merits.

These attempts to calculate what the public and members of his own administration would support suggest that Roosevelt was employing an acceptability criterion to evaluate the alternatives. As the political approach to decision-making predicts, acceptability seems to have functioned as an unavoidable constraint and a prior concern. Those measures

---

[129] Memorandum of a Telephone Conversation between Welles and Kennedy, Sept. 26, 1938, *FRUS*, 1938, 1:660–61, 1:30 p.m. See also Hull, *Memoirs*, 1:593.

(a presidential offer of arbitration and American participation in an international conference) that were completely unacceptable to Roosevelt's top advisers, or deemed by them to be unacceptable to domestic opinion, were rejected at once without further consideration of their other possible advantages.

On other occasions, rather than discarding a seemingly unacceptable option, Roosevelt used one of the classical political strategies to improve its acceptability to the point where the constraint could be satisfied. For example, with respect to Hull's objections to Bullitt's Pointe de Graves speech, Roosevelt himself reworked the offending statement until he had a compromise that satisfied both Bullitt and Hull. Moreover, each of his two decisions to make an appeal during the crisis represented a compromise directed at improving acceptability: he removed the provision most worrisome to Hull from each message so that the secretary could countenance sending it. Finally, Roosevelt's blockade strategy had many of the features of a transcendent solution: not only did it overcome the conflict between the supposed weakness of the democracies and their apparent need to fight a war, but it also transcended the conflict between America's neutrality laws and Roosevelt's desire to help Britain and France.[130]

Though he was clearly attentive to the requirements of domestic acceptability, however, it would be wrong to see Roosevelt's behavior during the crisis as driven primarily by the exigencies of domestic politics. In the first place, there is no evidence to support the argument that domestic constraints caused him to act much less vigorously than he desired. Before the crisis, his reluctance to act was due at least as much to his uncertainty about the proper course to take and his suspicion that the democracies were trying to use the United States for their own purposes as to a concern about the sensitivities of the isolationists. Even after Godesberg, when he very much desired to prevent war, Roosevelt did not consider making a serious deterrent threat, or even supporting the democracies publicly, and he seemed genuinely sympathetic to the reservations of others such as Hull and Davis about American participation in an international conference.

Furthermore, both before and after Godesberg, Roosevelt was willing to push to a considerable degree against whatever domestic constraints he perceived. Although he expressed the fear that public knowledge of his conversation with Lindsay could lead to his impeachment, he proceeded with that conversation nonetheless. Moreover, he allowed Bullitt to give substantially the speech he desired at Pointe de Graves, and later issued

---

[130] The strategies of procrastination, minimal decisions, and sequencing were not in evidence during the Munich crisis. Possibly the sense of urgency and short time available during a crisis make such strategies unappealing to all but impaired decision-makers.

his two appeals despite Hull's continuing objections. While acceding to modifications of these appeals on the grounds of domestic acceptability, Roosevelt did not back down on the issue of sending them in the first place. As before, he showed a willingness to stretch the limits of domestic acceptability, albeit cautiously. In line with the expectations of the political approach to decision-making, he consistently attempted to reconcile the need for domestic acceptability with the requirements of foreign policy. As Welles remarked to the French ambassador, Roosevelt was trying to strike a balance between his desire to bring "the weight of the United States to bear upon the European crisis" and his wish to avoid stirring up isolationist feeling.[131]

Even if Roosevelt persisted in his essentially political approach to decision-making, it is possible that emotion strong enough to cause him to reverse preferences in mid-crisis affected his information processing in other ways. To determine whether this was the case, we can briefly review his behavior at the five stages of decision-making.

With respect to diagnosis and revision, Roosevelt seems generally to have conformed to a rational standard, particularly in his response to new information. Throughout the crisis, he displayed neither the tendency to assimilate new information to preexisting beliefs predicted by the intuitive approach, nor the cognitive rigidity under conditions of stress and short time the motivational approach expects, showing his openness to new and discrepant information in several ways.[132] For example, despite his conviction that the British and French were appeasers who were more than willing to betray the Czechs, he readily accepted reports from Bullitt and Kennedy that this had changed after Godesberg and revised his estimate of how the Allies were likely to behave. Similarly, as he received new information about the likelihood of war, he responded by altering his expectations. His lack of cognitive rigidity is shown by his timely response to cues throughout the crisis, accepting, and even seeking out, critical appraisal of the options.

Although Roosevelt's behavior did not show the sort of impaired processing predicted by the intuitive and motivational approaches for diagnosis and revision, his decision-making during search may have been less analytical. Particularly striking is his reliance on previously considered, and therefore easily available, alternatives at all stages of the Munich crisis. In the summer of 1938, when he sought to affect the growing crisis by attempting to deter Hitler, he resurrected the notion of economic mea-

---

[131] Haight, "France, the United States, and the Munich Crisis," 356 n. 29.
[132] See appendix A.

sures against Germany, especially countervailing duties, which had surfaced first in 1936 and again during the *Panay* Incident. During the initial phase of the crisis, when he believed the democracies would be forced to fight Hitler, he advanced three other policies with a considerable history: a strategic blockade such as he had contemplated as early as March 1935 and which had reappeared in the Quarantine Speech and during the Nine Power Conference and the *Panay* Incident; expanding the democracies' air forces, an idea he had supported at least since his conversation with La Grange in January 1938; and the notion that the United States would provide substantial aid to the democracies in the event of war, stretching or circumventing the neutrality laws should that prove necessary. Finally, after deciding to intervene directly in the crisis, Roosevelt turned to a number of other ideas he had entertained throughout the 1930s, such as appealing to the ideals of peaceful settlement of disputes and meaningful negotiations, and he resurrected the notion of an international peace conference, which had been in his mind at least since the Welles Peace Plan.

Despite the questions that Roosevelt's resort to only familiar and easily available alternatives raises, however, his behavior may not have been irrational in the context of a crisis. Under conditions of short time, such a strategy may be appropriate because the costs of an extensive search for new options may outweigh its possible benefits (if it is feasible at all).

Turning to the quality of evaluation, it is clear that the crucial policy evaluation about whether or not to intervene directly in the crisis was biased. In less complex evaluations concerning implementation, however, Roosevelt retained or ruled out alternatives largely on the basis of whether or not they fit the needs of the situation while also remaining within the bounds of domestic acceptability. In his assessment on September 25 he did little more than screen a State Department draft appeal for its acceptability to Hull, and by extension to domestic public opinion, since fears about that were at the heart of the secretary's objections. In formulating the September 27 message, as well as focusing on domestic acceptability, he was concerned to some extent with the substance of the foreign-policy problem. Thus, when the wisdom of calling for an international conference was questioned, he sought additional information in the form of opinions from Chamberlain and Daladier. Moreover, in what was in many respects a pretty fair approximation of an analytic-group process, Roosevelt solicited his cabinet's assessment of the options. All the available alternatives were presented for examination, even one calling for an international conference including the United States of which Hull (and possibly Roosevelt himself) disapproved; neither Roosevelt nor Hull gave any indication of his own preferences; and the participants apparently felt able to express themselves freely.[133] Even in this exemplary proceeding, however, the options were first screened for acceptability.

In general, then, as the political approach to decision-making predicts, Roosevelt's evaluation during the Munich crisis relied on quasi-rational processes, with considerable attention to acceptability. Acceptability in fact functioned as an unavoidable constraint, as well as a prior concern, and was apparently not traded off against other values. Considering that the alternatives were familiar options previously assessed for substance, however, an emphasis on acceptability probably made sense. If an option has already been evaluated for substance, it may be rational to assume that one need only assess acceptability, especially given the short decision time in a crisis.[134] Moreover, it must be remembered that these decisions were largely about implementation and the alternatives were standard procedures (recommending negotiations, good offices, international conferences, etc.) that do not require a great deal of evaluation on their merits. Moreover, Hitler's agreement to any one of them would have served Roosevelt's purposes equally well. Hence, he needed only to assess their domestic acceptability. While the relative effectiveness of such options as tools of diplomacy was well understood, whether any of them would be acceptable was not. All of this suggests that the rationality of evaluative processes may be quite context dependent. In particular, the rationality of relying on previously evaluated alternatives may depend on both the nature of the decision and the circumstances surrounding it.

Finally, with respect to the choice process, Roosevelt chose the alternatives he judged to achieve the best balance between the needs of the international situation and the requirements of domestic acceptability. Despite his obvious desire to act, there is no evidence that he was tempted to bolster an inferior option in order to do so.[135]

That Roosevelt's information processing was apparently not otherwise impaired by an amount of stress sufficient to cause a frame change and preference reversal poses a challenge to Janis and Mann's decisional-conflict model of decision-making. Many of the variables associated with biased information processing, such as significant negative emotion and time pressure, were present during the crisis, and Roosevelt evidently experienced considerable stress, which critically affected his cognitive processes. What is embarassing for the decisional-conflict model, more-

[133] For a more detailed account of this incident, see Farnham, "Value Conflict," 427–28. For an analysis of biased group processes see Irving L. Janis, *Groupthink*, 2d ed. (Boston: Houghton Mifflin, 1982).

[134] It would also be rational to use such alternatives without evaluating them further except for acceptability, if the primary purpose of an action was, as Ickes suggested with respect to the September 27 appeal, merely to assign blame in the event of failure.

[135] See appendix A.

over, is not just that it fails to predict this particular kind of response to stress, but also that Roosevelt did not otherwise react to stress in the ways it does predict. Contrary to the expectations of the model, there is not slightest indication that the need to make a painful decision was the source of Roosevelt's negative emotion and stress. Nor did he show the least disposition toward defensive avoidance. Furthermore, apart from triggering the frame change, there is no evidence that his stress resulted in the kind of biased information processing and cognitive rigidity predicted by the decisional-conflict model.

Janis and Mann might argue that Roosevelt experienced sufficient stress to result in "vigilant information processing" but not enough to cause impaired processing.[136] At the very least, however, his behavior raises the question of how much is enough. If a decision-maker can experience a level of stress sufficient to trigger an unacknowledged frame change that then motivates him to act in a way he had previously thought unwise, yet leaves the general quality of his information processing unaffected, just what does it take to activate the pattern Janis and Mann predict? The question is all the more compelling because it cannot be answered by pointing to individual differences. However high Roosevelt's tolerance for stress may have been, he was clearly subject to it on this occasion.[137]

CONCLUSION

Roosevelt's behavior during the Munich crisis shows that the gap Charles Hermann found between participants and observers in a crisis situation may, under certain circumstances, be narrowed. In effect, a third-party observer of a crisis can be transformed into a sort of participant, who *feels* involved and as a consequence behaves differently. The Munich episode also shows that a crisis can affect decision-making behavior by reducing uncertainty. Roosevelt's frame change after Godesberg, for example, removed his doubt about the proper course to follow. Moreover, while that kind of subjective reduction of uncertainty is hardly the result of rational processing, the experience of a crisis can reduce uncertainty in ways which are not biased. By furnishing the decision-maker with new information, a crisis may serve as a true learning experience.

What the Munich case also demonstrates, however, is that the lessons of a crisis may not be immediately apparent. The Munich crisis ulti-

---

[136] Appendix A.

[137] For other criticisms of the utility of this model for explaining crisis behavior, see Morgan, *Deterrence*, 177–79; and Ariel Levi and Philip E. Tetlock, "A Cognitive Analysis of Japan's 1941 Decision for War," *Journal of Conflict Resolution* 24 (1980): 195–211.

mately provided Roosevelt with the information that allowed him to re-solve his uncertainty about the nature of the challenge posed by Hitler that had plagued him throughout the 1930s, and in this sense represents a genuine turning point in his prewar foreign policy. Nevertheless, he did not fully absorb its lessons until some time after the crisis had ended. In order to see the full impact of the Munich crisis on Roosevelt's decision-making, we must turn to its aftermath.

CHAPTER V

Assessing the Munich Crisis

WHILE SOME ARGUE that Roosevelt approved of the Munich agreements, the evidence that he was far from satisfied with the outcome is overwhelming. As he pointed out in a meeting with key members of his administration on November 14, 1938, "the recrudescence of German power at Munich had completely reoriented our own international relations; . . . for the first time since the Holy Alliance in 1818 the United States now faced the possibility of an attack on the Atlantic side in both the Northern and the Southern Hemispheres."[1]

Based on his experience of Munich, Roosevelt had concluded that a Europe dominated by Hitler would eventually pose a grave threat to American security. While influenced to some extent by new insights into German capabilities, his perception of threat after Munich was primarily triggered by a reassessment of Hitler's intentions in the light of his behavior during the crisis. Applying a political standard, Roosevelt interpreted his extreme disregard for the values and processes associated with political accommodation as an indication of unlimited aims that could never be satisfied by normal diplomatic means. Sooner or later, Germany was bound to threaten the United States.

Roosevelt's decision-making after Munich divides into two stages. The first stage from September 30 to October 7 was a transitional period during which he and others continued to react to the crisis, remaining involved with it cognitively and emotionally. Despite conscientious attempts by the diplomatic corps to consider the wider import of what had just taken place, the main focus of attention for most government officials, including Roosevelt, was the war that had so narrowly been

---

[1] "Meeting at the White House, Dictated by Mr. Oliphant, November 14, 1938," Morgenthau Diary, 150:338, FDRL (hereafter Oliphant, "Meeting"). This is a firsthand report by a participant in the November 14 White House meeting. The other firsthand account is that of General H. H. Arnold, Chief of the Air Corps, "November 15, 1938, Memorandum for the Chief of Staff," PPF1-P, Box 118, Special Conferences Folder, FDRL (hereafter Arnold, "Memorandum"). See also Roosevelt's remarks on the meeting at a press conference the following day, "Press Conference in the White House, November 15, 1938, 4:08 p.m.," Schewe, 7: no. 1409. For other accounts of this meeting, see H. H. Arnold, *Global Mission* (New York: Harper and Brothers, 1949), 172–73; Blum, *Morgenthau Diaries*, 2:48–49; Haight, *American Aid*, 58–59; Langer and Gleason, *Challenge*, 38–39; Forrest Pogue, *George C. Marshall* (New York: Viking, 1963), 1:322–23; Watson, *Chief of Staff*, 136–39.

averted. Following this initial postcrisis phase, a more protracted period of decision-making occurred as Roosevelt began to view the crisis in long-term perspective, assimilating the information it had provided and evaluating its significance for the United States. It was during this period of assimilation, extending roughly from October 8 to November 14, that significant changes in diagnosis and policy occurred.

POSTCRISIS TRANSITION, SEPTEMBER 30–OCTOBER 7

At the highest echelons of the Roosevelt Administration, the initial response to the end of the Munich crisis was relief tempered only slightly by occasional misgivings. The President himself publicly expressed his relief that the crisis was over with some feeling, and the Secretary of State's response, although more subdued, reflected a similar attitude.[2] Other members of the administration were less restrained. Ambassador Kennedy declared to Lord Halifax on September 29 that he was a "warm admirer of everything the Prime Minister had done," and Ambassador Bullitt was even more effusive, rushing to Bonnet's apartment after the signing of the Munich agreement "with tears in his eyes and his arms full of flowers, to convey 'le salut fraternel et joyeux de l'Amerique.'"[3]

While Bullitt's reaction was extreme, even those with reservations about Munich were not at first inclined to criticize, believing that little else could have been done. Ickes, for example, though doubtful that Hitler would be satisfied with attaining his goals in the Sudetenland, observed that the cost of a war in Europe would have been "terrific," and concluded that if France and Britain used the time gained to rearm, they would be in a better position to meet future German aggression.[4]

For others, relief was accompanied by optimism about agreement on broader issues. On the grounds that Hitler had declared Germany "satisfied" and would prefer domestic progress to enormous military expenditures, Berle thought the time ripe for a disarmament effort in which the United States should participate.[5] Welles agreed, declaring, as the disapproving Hull recalled it, that "today, perhaps more than at any time during the past two decades, there was presented the opportunity for the establishment by the nations of the world of a new world order based

[2] "Press Conference, in the White House, September 30, 1938, 10:45 a.m.," Schewe, 7: no. 1317; statement issued by the Department of State, Sept. 30, 1938, *FRUS*, 1938, 1:703.

[3] Kaufmann, "Two American Ambassadors", 661–62.

[4] Ickes, *Diary*, 2:480. The entry is for September 30, 1938. Morgenthau took a similar position. See Blum, *Morgenthau Diaries*, 1:522.

[5] Berle to Hull, Sept. 30, 1938, Berle Papers, Diary, Box 210, FDRL. Alsop and Kintner, *American White Paper*, 14.

upon justice and upon law."[6] Roosevelt, too, seemed optimistic about the possibility of future agreements with Hitler, writing to Chamberlain on October 5,

> I fully share your hope and belief that there exists today the greatest opportunity in years for the establishment of a new order based on justice and on law. Now that you have established personal contact with Chancellor Hitler, I know that you will be taking up with him from time to time many of the problems which must be resolved in order to bring about that new and better order.[7]

In fact, Roosevelt claimed retrospectively that his initial postcrisis thoughts were of disarmament, telling Joseph Alsop on December 23, 1939, "After Munich we made disarmament feelers, but . . . [we] could not arouse interest in any country, 'they just smiled and said it was a crazy dream of those Americans.' "[8]

This cautious optimism was not to last. Indeed, even during this week of presidential relief, discordant notes were being sounded. The first rumblings were heard as early as September 30 as the Czechs expressed bitterness at their betrayal by France and Britain, and the French ambassador declared "that the results of the Munich meeting caused him as much anxiety as relief."[9] Such reservations were strongly seconded by Messersmith in a memo transmitted to Roosevelt on October 1. While professing to share in the general rejoicing at averting hostilities, the assistant secretary remarked pointedly that any "optimism and relief" should be "seriously tempered" by the realization that if "the desire to avoid the war with which Hitler is threatening Europe and the world" results in "too far-reaching concessions . . . we should only have put Germany in a position to carry through successfully the war which she

[6] Hull, *Memoirs*, 1:596. Such optimism was not confined to the State Department. On October 5, the American military attache in Germany wrote, "Germany wants a period of peace,—not a few months, but several years at least, and probably a decade. Germany is even more pleased over peace with France and England than she is over the acquisition of the Sudetens." Report by Military Attaché in Germany (Smith), Oct. 5, 1938, *FRUS*, 1938, 1:716–19. This report was not transmitted by the War Department to the State Department until October 19.

[7] Cited in Langer and Gleason, *Challenge*, 35.

[8] Verbatim transcript of an interview with Roosevelt, Dec. 23, 1939, Alsop papers. See also Alsop and Kintner, who quote the President as saying "only a few days after Munich," that "The acid test . . . is whether anyone is ready to disarm." *American White Paper*, 14. While no other confirmation of these disarmament feelers has been found, Alsop and Kintner argue that Roosevelt communicated on this issue with his emissaries, as he so frequently did, by telephone. Given the brevity of his interest in the subject, it is not surprising that no mention of it appears in the diplomatic traffic.

[9] Kirk (Charge in the Soviet Union) to Hull, Sept. 30, 1938, *FRUS*, 1938, 1:708; Memo by Green (Chief of Office of Arms and Munitions Control), ibid., 708–9.

intends to fight and which she is not in a position to wage successfully now." Alone at this early date, Messersmith linked the German danger directly to the security of the United States. Observing that it was extremely unrealistic to believe Hitler's territorial ambitions had been satisfied at Munich, he warned that any arrangements which were dominated by the desire for peace at any price "will have the most far-reaching consequences for us [and] . . . we shall ourselves eventually be faced by war which will become just as imminent a threat as that which has faced Europe in the last days."[10]

Two days later, Roosevelt received dramatic support for Messersmith's analysis when Bullitt conveyed Daladier's deeply pessimistic assessment. Reciting the now-familiar tale of Hitler's disgraceful behavior during the crisis, Daladier flatly rejected the notion that the Führer's territorial ambitions had been satisfied, predicting that "within 6 months France and England would be face to face with new German demands."[11] Furthermore, a number of Roosevelt's ambassadors, with the notable exception of Kennedy, made similar assessments. From Czechoslovakia, Carr denounced Hitler's reply to the President's second note as "a mixture of half truths and misstatements of fact," and, in terms that left no room for doubt, put the onus for instigating the Sudeten crisis on Hitler. Looking toward the future, the ambassador to Poland also foresaw trouble: "I am personally inclined to feel Hitler's voracious appetite will have been only whetted by his recent gains. Moreover, I am aware that official circles here feel there are as yet no tangible grounds for a belief that Hitler has altered his determination to continue driving eastward and southeastward."[12]

While it is impossible to determine Roosevelt's immediate reaction to

[10] Hull to Roosevelt, Oct. 1, 1938, transmitting Messersmith to Hull, Sept. 29, 1938, ibid., 704–7. This memorandum was written after the announcement of the Munich meeting but before its results were known. Hull, too, claimed to have been skeptical about the prospects of the Munich agreement, declaring in his memoirs that, unlike Welles, he saw it as "only a momentary solution." Although Hull's account of his own views is retrospective, it is supported by the alacrity with which he transmitted the Messersmith memorandum to Roosevelt. *Memoirs*, 1:595–96. For a contrary view of Hull's response, see Offner, *American Appeasement*, 268–69.

[11] Bullitt to Hull, Oct. 3, 1938, *FRUS*, 1938, 1:711–12. See also Haight, "France, the United States, and the Munich Crisis," 358.

[12] Carr to Hull, Sept. 28, 1938, *FRUS*, 1938, 1:689–91; "Anthony J. Drexel Biddle, Jr., Ambassador to Poland, to Roosevelt, October 6, 1938," Schewe, 7: no. 1328. (The exact date on which Biddle's letter was received is not known.) See also Wilson to Hull, Oct. 5, 1938 (received Oct. 6), *FRUS*, 1938, 1:713–15. Other ambassadors were even more emphatic: "Hitler's program, wrote Josephus Daniels, envisaged control of all territory from Berlin to Baghdad. Joseph Davies was of the opinion that the Fuehrer had crossed the Rubicon and could not stop. Germany was guided by a will for conquest, he observed, not a will for peace. Dictators ride bicycles, he concluded, and are unable to stand still." Kinsella, *Leadership*, 125.

these somber communications, the brevity of his post-Munich optimism suggests that they had an impact. Nevertheless, in the first week after the crisis there was little in his behavior to forecast the dramatic change in attitude he unveiled at the November 14 meeting.

Alsop and Kintner interpreted the optimism of the president and his key advisers "in that puzzling time after Munich," as an inclination "to shrink from their thorny task."[13] Looked at in context, however, their behavior reflects not so much a disposition to avoid future responsibility as a tendency to remain focused on the recent past. Though the Munich crisis ended on September 30, for several days it continued to occupy the center of their attention.

The spasm of relief felt by many during this period was in large measure a reaction to the emotional intensity of the crisis itself. It had been a "violently unsettling" experience, with many fearing it would end in a war destroying European civilization, and being spared that catastrophe seems to have generated a sort of euphoria.[14] Bullitt, in the same letter to Roosevelt in which he conveyed with utmost seriousness alarming figures about German air superiority, was positively giddy with relief over Hitler's invitation to Munich: "I am so relieved this evening that I feel like embracing everyone and wish I were in the White House to give you a large kiss on your bald spot. Love, good luck, and hurrah."[15] Roosevelt himself, though considerably more restrained, expressed the emotion of the moment in a letter to Margaret Suckley about his forthcoming visit to Hyde Park: "I'm getting a little incoherent—so would you if *you* were *I*—But it's a nice feeling and has lots of possibilities just like the European situation at this moment!"[16]

Supporting the idea that Roosevelt's optimism was only a temporary reaction to a traumatic experience is the fact that it was clearly a departure from both his earlier and his later responses. While the emotion of the moment had overwhelmed the more pessimistic evaluation of the future he had made during the crisis,[17] the likelihood that this was primar-

---

[13] Alsop and Kintner, *American White Paper,* 13–14.

[14] Ibid., 12. See also Bullitt's May 20 letter to Roosevelt, above; Dallek, *Franklin D. Roosevelt,* 171; and Langer and Gleason, *Challenge,* 35.

[15] "William C. Bullitt, Ambassador to France, to Roosevelt, September 28, 1938," Schewe, 7: no. 1306.

[16] Ward, *Closest Companion,* 126.

[17] See, for example, Roosevelt's letter to Phillips on September 15, his remarks to Lindsay on September 19 about Hitler's appetite for aggression, and his prediction to his son Elliot after the dispatch of his second note to Hitler that "Sooner or later there's going to be a showdown in Europe." "Roosevelt to Phillips, September 15, 1938," Schewe, 7: no. 1277; Lindsay to Halifax, (Received Sept. 20), *DBFP,* Series 3, 7:627; and Elliot Roosevelt,

ily a reaction to, in Secretary Hull's words, the "immediate peace results" of the Munich conference rather than an endorsement of the substance of the agreements, is suggested by the speed with which his optimism was replaced by a more sober assessment.

Nevertheless, although Roosevelt had learned a great deal from the Munich crisis he did not fully assimilate its lessons until the strong emotions generated by the crisis and its denouement had dissipated. This suggests that decision-makers may react to the experience of a crisis itself as well as to the substantive issues, a response that can temporarily mask its wider lessons. In Roosevelt's case, Godesberg changed his perception of Hitler almost immediately, but he did not fully absorb all he had learned until the crisis had lost its cognitive and emotional immediacy— hence his initial postcrisis optimism about the prospects of international cooperation, which metamophosized first into uncertainty and ambivalence and then into a new diagnosis that was a complete reversal of his initial position.

CRISIS AFTERMATH, OCTOBER 8–NOVEMBER 14

I am not sure now I am proud of what I wrote to Hitler in urging that he sit down around the table and make peace. That may have saved many, many lives now, but that may ultimately result in the loss of many times that number of lives later.[18]

As the Munich crisis receded into the past, Roosevelt began to assess the significance of the new situation in Europe. Uneasy about the wisdom of the Munich settlement, he worried that it might have avoided war in the present only at the cost of serious future problems. While he did not formally state his concern about the consequences of the Munich settlement until November 14, disillusionment had set in well before. Though we cannot pinpoint the exact date, his post-Munich optimism seems to have evaporated by at least October 9,[19] when Ickes reported:

As He Saw It (New York: Duell, Sloan, and Pearce, 1946), 4. See also the views that Bullitt expressed to the president on September 28, two days before he smothered Bonnet with flowers and congratulations "Bullitt to Roosevelt," Schewe, 7: no.s 1306, 1306a.

[18] Franklin D. Roosevelt, November 14, 1938, cited in Oliphant, "Meeting."

[19] On October 4, despite Admiral Leahy's reservations, Roosevelt approved Hull's September 27 request to allow the French to test-fly several American planes being built under contract to the Navy, which suggests that he may have abandoned his postcrisis optimism even earlier. "Cordell Hull, Secretary of State, to Roosevelt, September 27, 1938," Schewe, 7: no. 1301; "Admiral William D. Leahy, Chief of Naval Operations, to Roosevelt, Septem-

I have it from the President that he expects some such move as the following in the near future: Germany will be wanting colonies and in the process of satisfying its appetite it is suggested that England will offer her Trinidad and prevail upon France to offer Martinique. This would give Germany strong outposts on our eastern coast as well as the coasts of Central and South America. . . . The President has made up his mind that if any such thing as this happens, the United States Fleet will forthwith be sent to take both of these islands.[20]

At the same time, Roosevelt reacted with dispatch to a considerably less dramatic German move than the one he predicted to Ickes. On October 9, Hitler called for increasing German arms on the grounds that Chamberlain's promises could not be trusted because he might be replaced by those who had denounced the Munich settlement. On October 11, Roosevelt responded to these "ominous remarks" by announcing a three-hundred-thousand-dollar increase in national-defense expenditures.[21]

Roosevelt's awareness of the alarming implications of Hitler's behavior was reinforced by mounting concern within his administration. Messersmith's and Bullitt's earlier pessimism, for example, was echoed by a lengthy memorandum from the consul at Geneva, stating that the Munich settlement could "only lead to a temporary *detente*" and predicting "a recurring series of crises within the relatively near future which may or may not lead to war in Europe."[22] After a firsthand briefing from Bullitt on October 13, there is little doubt that the last vestige of presidential optimism had disappeared.[23]

---

ber 29, 1938," ibid., no. 1312; "Cordell Hull, Secretary of State, to Roosevelt, October 3, 1938," ibid., no. 1324; Haight, *American Aid*, 17.

[20] Ickes, *Diary*, 2:484. Ickes agreed completely, stating a rather different opinion of the Munich agreement from the one he had given on September 30: "There is a growing impression that the Czechoslovak solution was a totally disgraceful thing and the President may want to dissociate himself from too close a connection before he is through with it." Ibid., 483. See also Roosevelt's letter to Arthur Bliss Lane on October 10, below.

[21] Langer and Gleason, *Challenge*, 37. See also Dallek, *Franklin D. Roosevelt*, 171.

[22] Bucknell to Hull, Oct. 12, 1938, *FRUS*, 1938, 1:86–92. Biddle's letter of October 6, which had probably reached the President by this time, was followed by another on October 15 reiterating that he still perceived "no tangible grounds for hope that the Munich Conference might lead to a general European appeasement and pacification." Rather, Europe was "passing through a period of armed truce." "Anthony J. Drexel Biddle, Jr., Ambassador to Poland, to Roosevelt, October 15, 1938," Schewe, 7: no. 1355.

[23] See Press Conference, Oct. 14, 1938, *Complete Presidential Press Conferences of Franklin D. Roosevelt* (New York: Da Capo Press, 1972), 12: no. 491; Watson, *Chief of Staff*, 131–32. According to Langer and Gleason, "The reports submitted by Ambassador Bullitt during his visit to Washington in October 1938, probably clinched the matter and dispelled all further hopes of success through appeasement." *Challenge*, 37–38.

Since the evidence is compelling that within two weeks of the end of the crisis Roosevelt had been thoroughly purged of any hopeful feelings he may have had about the Munich settlement, it is something of a mystery that so many have thought otherwise. In fact, the notion that he regarded the outcome of the crisis with equanimity rests largely on a letter he wrote to Phillips on October 17. Offner, for example, uses this letter, in conjunction with another to MacKenzie King, as proof that Roosevelt remained sanguine about the Munich agreements for a considerable period of time:

> There is no reason to believe . . . that the [Munich] settlement, or events of the next few weeks, disappointed Roosevelt. On October 11 he wrote the prime minister of Canada, MacKenzie King, that he rejoiced that war had been averted. Explicitly and plainly he told Phillips six days later: "I want you to know that I am not one bit upset over the final result."[24]

The problem with Offner's argument is that this sentence does not refer to the Munich settlement. Rather, it is a response to an October 1 letter from Phillips apologizing for his conduct during the crisis and offering his resignation.[25] In his anxiety about the effectiveness of his September 27 appeal to Mussolini, Roosevelt had reprimanded Phillips for being out of Rome and unable to deliver his message the moment it arrived.[26] Phillips, while stating his conviction that Mussolini had learned

[24] Offner, *American Appeasement*, 268. Offner repeated this view in "Misperception and Reality," 613 n. 21. The tone of Roosevelt's letter to King is less optimistic than Offner suggests. For example, Roosevelt observed:

> "I am still concerned, as I know you are, when we consider prospects for the future. I cannot help but feel that unless very soon Europe as a whole takes up important changes in two companion directions—reduction of armaments and lowering of trade barriers—a new crisis will come. If Hitler means what he said so definitely, he will have to go along and if he did not mean what he said, he will not go along."

PL, 1938, 2:816; Langer and Gleason, *Challenge*, 35. Loewenheim, Drummond, and Graebner also cite Roosevelt's reply to Phillips in support of the contention that he continued to feel positive about Munich in mid-October. Loewenheim, "Illusion," 177–220; Drummond, *Passing of American Neutrality*, 78; Norman A. Graebner, *Foundations of American Foreign Policy: A Realist Appraisal from Franklin to McKinley* (Wilmington, Del.: Scholarly Resources, 1985), 54. See also Robert E. Herzstein, *Roosevelt and Hitler* (New York: Paragon House, 1989), 217.

[25] An account of this episode was given by Edward Henson, who found Phillips's original letter and realized that the first sentence of Roosevelt's reply referred to its contents rather than the outcome of the Munich crisis. He did not, however, relate his insight to the controversy about about Roosevelt's assessment of the results of Munich and his article was apparently not known to the authors just cited. The sole reference to it since its publication is in Marks's *Wind Over Sand*, 146. Henson, "Britain, America," 299–300.

[26] Hull to Phillips, Sept. 30, 1938, *FRUS*, 1938, 1:701–2. The only evidence of this presidential reprimand is in Phillips's own letter to Roosevelt: "I have this morning received

the substance of the president's message before 10 a.m. on the twenty-eighth, offered an abject apology and his resignation.[27]

This context makes it abundantly clear that the first sentence of the October 17 letter is not a reference to the Munich crisis but a response to this apology. Roosevelt begins by saying, "Yours of September twenty-ninth and October first have just come and I want you to know that I am not a bit upset over the final result." He then goes to great pains to reassure Phillips that his message did have an impact on Mussolini and that, therefore, no harm was done by Phillips's absence from Rome. The letter ends with a friendly reference to Phillips's mission, and his offer of resignation is simply ignored. Nowhere is there any mention of the Munich agreements, and there are no grounds whatever for supposing that Roosevelt's opening sentence was intended to express approval of them.[28]

All the evidence indicates that within at least two weeks after the crisis, Roosevelt had become thoroughly disillusioned with the Munich settlement. Moreover, by October 26 his reservations were sufficiently well established to state publicly:

It is becoming increasingly clear that peace by fear has no higher or more enduring quality than peace by the sword. There can be no peace if the reign of law is to be replaced by a recurrent sanctification of sheer force. There can be no peace if national policy adopts as a deliberate instrument the threat of war.[29]

---

your message through the State Department and I accept your reprimand as fully deserved. It is only too true that I should not have left Rome." "Phillips to Roosevelt, October 1, 1938," Schewe, 7: no. 1318.

[27] "There is nothing to add except once more to express my profound sorrow that I have failed you in this instant [sic]. It may well be that as a result you have lost confidence in me and, if so, do not hesitate to tell me and my resignation will follow immediately." Phillips to Hull, Oct. 1, 1938, *FRUS*, 1938, 1:702–3; "Phillips to Roosevelt, October 1, 1938," Schewe, 7: no. 1318.

[28] "Roosevelt, Hyde Park, to William Phillips, Ambassador to Italy, October 17, 1938," ibid., no. 1360. Jim Farley's memoirs contain an account of this incident that, although somewhat garbled, confirms Roosevelt's awareness of Phillips's remorse. *Jim Farley's Story*, 197.

[29] "Radio address to the Herald-Tribune Forum," *PPA* 7 (1938):563–66. In his memoirs Secretary Hull specifically relates this passage to the President's disillusionment with Munich. Hull, *Memoirs*, 1:596–97. The day after Roosevelt's speech, Secretary of the Navy Edison sounded the same note of disillusionment. *New York Times*, Oct. 28, 1938. Edison's subsequent recollections support the idea that not long after Munich the President had come to expect war: "From Munich onwards, according to Edison, the Navy was continuously engaged in an effort 'to speed up the tempo.' He and the President wished to have everything in readiness, for they both feared war. They often discussed it." "Interview with Edison," n.d., Alsop papers. Although this interview is undated, it is clearly one of the interviews for *American White Paper*, most of which were done between October and December 1939.

In less than a month after his initial burst of relief that war had been averted at Munich, then, Roosevelt had come to believe that the danger was greater than ever, a theme he would sound with increasing urgency in the months to come. In his State of the Union message on January 4, 1939, he warned that "A war which threatened to envelop the world in flames has been averted, but it has become increasingly clear that peace is not assured."[30]

Evaluation of Germany

Roosevelt's disillusionment about the prospects for peace was rooted in a reassessment of Germany stimulated by his experience of the Munich crisis. In terms of the capabilities, Munich convinced him that air power would dominate any future conflict. This made Germany seem even more formidable and magnified the risk that she might prevail in a European war. Moreover, Roosevelt feared that the ensuing shift in the balance of power would be detrimental to the United States, which would be endangered not only by Germany's acquisition of the democracies' resources but also by the disappearance of the buffer they had traditionally provided. In terms of intentions, as a result of Hitler's behavior during the crisis, the President judged him to be both intransigent and implacably aggressive. From Munich on, Roosevelt was persuaded not only that Germany was capable of endangering American security, but also that she would eventually do so.

In the months immediately preceding the crisis, Roosevelt had received a number of communications emphasizing German military superiority and predicting that the impact of air power in the next war would be both catastrophic and decisive.[31] On May 12, for example, Bullitt wrote that British and French aircraft production combined did not begin to

[30] *Peace and War*, 449.

[31] In the year before Munich, Roosevelt received numerous reports from Charles Lindbergh and others emphasizing Germany's striking advances in military aviation. Lindbergh played a crucial role in the pre-World War II development of a widespread belief in German air superiority. He was first brought into the picture by Major Truman Smith, the American military attaché in Berlin, who arranged for his information gathering trips to Germany in 1936, 1937, and 1938. Cole, Lindbergh, 31–37. See also Taylor, *Munich*, 754–65; Charles A. Lindbergh, *Wartime Journals of Charles A. Lindbergh* (New York: Harcourt Brace Jovanovich, 1970), 71, 73; Harold Nicolson, *Diaries and Letters, 1930–1939*, ed. Nigel Nicolson (New York: Atheneum, 1966), 343; David Kahn, "United States Views of Germany and Japan in 1941," in *Knowing One's Enemies: Intelligence Assessment Before the Two World Wars* ed. Ernest R. May (Princeton: Princeton University Press, 1984), 491; Walter S. Ross, *The Last Hero: Charles A. Lindbergh* (New York: Harper and Row, 1968), 274–76.

approach the German effort. On May 20 he forecast the certain "slaughter of the entire younger generation of France" and the leveling of all its cities. On June 23, Roosevelt received Glenn Martin's account of a recent visit to a number of European airplane factories. Martin underlined German power and French weakness and concluded that "Germany is greatly superior to England and France in so far as air power is concerned and that the superiority is rapidly increasing." (This was marked in the margin with a double line, probably by Roosevelt.)[32] This report was reinforced by another from Hugh Wilson that was even more striking because it was based on discussions with a number of professional observers (the American military attachés, especially the air force attaché) as well as several American manufacturers and experts, and because it emphasized the vulnerability of the United States itself.[33]

At first Roosevelt resisted the conclusion to which these reports led. Although he sent Harry Hopkins to the West Coast in early September to survey the aircraft industry following a bellicose speech by Hitler,[34] until well into the crisis he continued to believe that the democracies would win any future war, German air power notwithstanding. As the crisis wore on, however, Roosevelt began to understand the role that percep-

---

[32] "William C. Bullitt, Ambassador to France, to Roosevelt, May 12, 1938," Schewe, 6: no. 1086; "Louis Johnson to Marvin McIntyre, June 23, 1938," transmitting a "Memorandum to the Assistant Secretary of War" from Colonel Burns about Martin's visit, PSF, Departmental, Box 105, Folder: War Department: Louis Johnson, 1937–40, FDRL. Both before and after Munich, in addition to using the State Department and armed services to gain information, Roosevelt called on a number of American aircraft producers to tour the British, French, and German aviation industries. Haight, *American Aid*, 15, n. 29.

[33]
> The conclusions reached from these talks are startling to any one used to thinking that France, England and the United States, especially the United States, held at least a small margin of superiority over Germany. . . . American visitors who know something about our own industry . . . at first . . . find it hard to believe and grasp, but they go away convinced of the truth of what I have said.

"Hugh R. Wilson, Ambassador to Germany, to Roosevelt, July 11, 1938," Schewe, 6: no. 1199. Also in Wilson, *Career Diplomat*, 39–40. Weinberg believes that Wilson, in making this report to Roosevelt, contributed to the scare over the German air force. Weinberg, *Foreign Policy of Hitler's Germany*, 254. For other disturbing reports, see "William C. Bullitt, Ambassador to France, to Roosevelt, August 17, 1938," Schewe, 7 no. 1231; and Dallek, *Franklin D. Roosevelt*, 163 n. 34.

[34] According to Hopkins, Roosevelt was sure that the United States would get into the war and would need air power to win. However, since Hopkins' account was written after Pearl Harbor, it may represent a considerable overstatement of the president's earlier views. Robert Sherwood, *Roosevelt and Hopkins* (New York: Harper and Brothers, 1948), 110; and Jack Raymond, *Power at the Pentagon* (New York: Harper and Row, 1964), 26. That Hopkins was sent to visit a number of airplane factories in California, however, is confirmed by Morgenthau, who learned of it in a meeting on November 12, 1938. "Presidential Diary," November 13, 1938, 1:0052–55.

tions about air power were playing. On September 20, for example, Bull-itt declared, "The moral is: If you have enough airplanes you don't have to go to Berchtesgaden," and the French ambassador attributed French handling of the crisis to the unfavorable balance of air forces, telling Moffat that it was "due to the fact that France was not prepared to fight. Her inferiority in the air made this out of the question."[35] On September 22, Lindbergh also offered the American commander-in-chief considerable food for thought, noting that while the United States was the "only country in the world capable of competing with Germany in aviation, . . . [she] is rapidly cutting down the lead we have held in the past. In numbers of fighting planes she is already ahead of us."[36]

In the end, possibly owing to the cumulative impact of these communications, Roosevelt's skepticism about the potency of military aviation began to erode, and he came to believe that it underlay Germany's success. Thus, on September 23, discussing the likelihood of war with his cabinet, he expressed considerable anxiety about the role of air power.[37] Although he repeated on September 27 his view that the democracies could win a war with Germany, he had clearly become concerned about the effect of air power in general and the influence of German strength in particular.[38]

Between the end of the crisis and the announcement of his new diagnosis on November 14, Roosevelt's growing belief in the potency of air power and worries about the consequences of Germany's dominance received considerable reinforcement. Arguably one of the greatest influences on his thinking was Bullitt's dramatic letter of October 3 and his briefing on his return home in which he conveyed French opinion of German strength in the strongest possible terms.[39] In addition to Bullitt's

[35] "Bullitt to Roosevelt, September 20, 1938," Schewe, 7: no. 1288; "Memorandum by Moffat, September 20, 1938," ibid., no. 1289a.

[36] Kennedy to Hull, Sept. 22, 1938, FRUS, 1938, 1:72–73. On Lindbergh's activities in Britain during the Czech crisis, see Taylor, Munich, 849–52.

[37] Ickes, Diary, 2:473–74.

[38] Apart from Roosevelt's September 23 remarks to the Cabinet, there is no evidence pinpointing the precise moment this change occurred. Haight cites a September 29 report of the British air attaché in the United States to show that by the end of the Munich crisis Roosevelt believed that air power was the basis of German dominance. In looking at Haight's source, however, it is not clear whether this opinion is the attaché's or that of the authors who cited his report orginally. The attaché's evidence for his views is equally unclear. Haight, American Aid, 18–19; H. Duncan Hall, North American Supply (London: Her Majesty's Stationery Office, 1955), 106–7. The experience of the crisis, however, did lead others to this opinion. Both Bullitt and Ickes, for example, came to believe that if the crisis had ended in war, German preponderance in the air would have been decisive. "William C. Bullitt, Ambassador to France, to Roosevelt, September 28, 1938," Schewe, 7: no. 1306, 1306a; Ickes, Diary, 2:480.

[39] Watson, Chief of Staff, 132. Bullitt repeated such views throughout his stay in the

report, Roosevelt saw similar analyses of the situation, the most trenchant of which argued that had the crisis ended in war,

> the first great battle would have been in the air. Everything goes to point out that in this respect Germany was superior in numbers and ability to reproduce airplanes. Any nation which gains supremacy in the air and can keep it, places the other nations at a disadvantage because it would be impossible to build either airplanes or defences when the factories are subject to constant raiding by a superior air force.[40]

Certainly, by the time of the November 14 White House meeting, Roosevelt had developed the conviction that air power was the essential means to counteract German strength.[41] In the weeks that followed, he continued to express the belief that German dominance in the air had been the basis of her superiority during the crisis, telling Ambassador to Mexico Josephus Daniels on January 13, 1939, that at the time of the Munich crisis,

> Germany and Italy had 13,000 effective combat planes. Together Britain and France had only 1,900 that were ready. . . . The British said they had power to ward off the first 2 or 3 attacks, but their munitions and resources could not resist after the first 500 German bombing planes. This knowledge

---

United States. See his statements to Ickes in early December 1938 and late January 1939, *Diary*, 2:519–20, 562. On Bullitt's visit see Gordon Wright, "Ambassador Bullitt and the Fall of France," *World Politics* 10 (Oct. 1957): 70; Haight, *American Aid*, 358. In his October 3 letter, Bullitt quoted Daladier as saying that "in his opinion the single thing which counted today was not diplomatic negotiations but strengthening of the military forces of France especially in the field of air armament." Bullitt to Hull, Oct. 3, 1938, *FRUS*, 1938, 1:712. On September 28 Bullitt had written Roosevelt in a similar vein about the need for France to build an air force in order to be prepared for Hitler's next ultimatum. "William C. Bullitt, Ambassador to France to Roosevelt," Sept. 28, 1938, Schewe, 7: no.s 1306, 1306a.

[40] "Memorandum, October 11, 1938," Schewe, 7: no. 1345. On October 31, Roosevelt received another memorandum from a key figure in the aircraft industry, confirming Germany's superiority in the air. Louis Johnson to Roosevelt, Oct. 31, 1938, transmitting a confidential report by Lawrence D. Bell of the Bell Aircraft Corporation, and summary of the report dated Sept. 12, 1938. PSF Departmental, Box 102, War Department, 1938 folder, FDRL.

[41] Roosevelt

> outlined the necessity for having a large mass of airplanes in being, together with a large productive capacity to be available as a striking force to back United States foreign policies. Referring to Hitler, he went into details [*sic*] to show why even though a 400,000 manned army were in being and were well equipped it would not be considered in the light of a deterrent by any foreign power, whereas a heavy striking force of aircraft would.

Oliphant, "Meeting"; Press Conference in the White House, November 15, 1938, 4:08 P.M.," Schewe, 7: no. 1409.

made Chamberlain capitulate at Munich. . . . When I expressed some doubt as to the great superiority of the totalitarian countries, he said he was so convinced of its accuracy that if he had been in Chamberlain's place he would have felt constrained to have made terms to prevent the war for which Germany was fully prepared.[42]

Roosevelt's concern about German prowess in military aviation influenced both his diagnosis of the German threat and the policies he developed to meet it.[43] Moreover, his worries went far beyond air power. In his view, the Munich crisis had contributed to a measurable improvement in Germany's position relative to Great Britain and France, materially and psychologically.

During the crisis itself, Roosevelt had already begun to assess the implications of a German victory for power relations in Europe, predicting at the outset that the Czech crisis would result in the growth of German power. In the aftermath of the crisis, the theme of growing German strength remained prominent. Bullitt first sounded the alarm on October 3 when he transmitted Daladier's view that Munich had been an "immense diplomatic defeat for France and England," which would result in a "fatal situation within the next year," unless France could "recover a united national spirit."[44] Within the administration, Morgenthau was quick to call Roosevelt's attention to the political conclusion to which these strategic considerations pointed.[45] On the diplomatic front Ambassador Pell, scanning the post-Munich political and military landscape,

[42] Kilpatrick, *Roosevelt and Daniels*, 181–82.

[43] On January 31, 1939, Roosevelt told the Senate Military Affairs Committee that if Germany and Italy beat Britain and France in a future war, "it would be primarily because of the air force." "Conference with Senate Military Affairs Committee, in the White House, January 31, 1939, 12:45 P.M.," Schewe, 8: no. 1565. During talks with Anthony Eden in December 1938, the British Embassy reported, the president had "harped on the great inferiority in Air Power of Great Britain and France as compared with Germany" and urged Britain "to do everything possible to strengthen its air power." Cited in Cole, *Roosevelt*, 302.

[44] Bullitt to Hull, Oct. 3, 1938, *FRUS*, 1938, 1:711–12.

[45]

Who in France as late as 1930 would have dreamt that in less than a decade that great democratic nation was to become a second-rate power, shorn of influence in central Europe, dependent upon a grudging and demanding ally for security? Who would have expected that Great Britain's might would be challenged in the Mediterranean, that her economic interests would be brushed aside in China, and that the Premier of England would hurry to Hitler to plead that he be not too demanding or impatient, and to plead, moreover in humble tones lest the dictator take umbrage and demand more?

"Henry Morgenthau, Jr., Secretary of the Treasury, to Roosevelt, Hyde Park, October 17, 1938," Schewe, 7: no. 1358. See also Blum, *Morgenthau Diaries*, 1:527.

delivered "a fair statement of the cost to Great Britain and France of the conference." While conceding that both their armies and the British fleet were in fairly decent shape, the ambassador noted other striking military deficiencies as well as political consequences that were even more discouraging.[46] Eventually, Roosevelt himself adopted a similarly bleak assessment of Munich's impact on the relative power of Germany and the democracies. Speculating to the Senate Military Affairs Committee on January 31, 1939, about the outcome of a German thrust to the west, he remarked, "It is a fifty-fifty bet that [Britain and France] would be put out of business and that Hitler and Mussolini would win."[47]

In addition to augmenting her political and military power as a consequence of Munich, Germany had gained a distinct psychological advantage due to the emergence of considerable skepticism about the will of Britain and France to withstand pressure from the dictators.[48] This judgment was reinforced by the fact that Hitler's behavior during the crisis encouraged no similar doubts about his will to prevail. The perception that the British and French had demonstrated weakness and worse by their actions at Munich translated into a conviction that, all protestations to the contrary, they would continue to appease the dictators. Even Bullitt, while urging Roosevelt in October to support the democracies, was unsure that they would actually fight.[49] Roosevelt, according to his own testimony, not only shared this belief but retained it right up to the beginning of World War II. Asked whether he had credited Lord Lothian's January 1939 declaration that appeasement was dead in England, Roosevelt replied, "No. . . . I took Lothian's description that England would not appease with a grain of salt and wanted more proof. I continued to

---

[46] In most other countries the prestige of Great Britain and France has fallen tremendously. In Portugal the Italians openly and the Germans somewhat more modestly look on the Munich conference as a second Canossa, a great victory for the Dictators and a crushing defeat for England. They seem to think that they can without real danger continue indefinitely to nibble at the strength and prestige of Great Britain.

"Pell to Roosevelt," Schewe, 7: no. 1366.

[47] "Conference with Senate Military Affairs Committee, January 31, 1939," Schewe, 8: no. 1565.

[48] This view was expressed with some feeling by Claude Bowers: "The reaction to reality [in Britain] since the Munich betrayal of democracy is one of shame and resentment. Of course the same is true in France, though here the feeling is that France has been so hopelessly betrayed that she has sunk to a Second Class Power and has no friends." "Claude G. Bowers, Ambassador to Spain, St. Jean de Luz, France, to Roosevelt, October 24, 1938," ibid., 7: no. 1368. Pell reflected a similar lack of confidence in British capacity to withstand pressure from Hitler. Ibid., no. 1366.

[49] Wright, "Ambassador Bullitt," 70.

take to British professions of being willing to fight, also with a grain of salt. And I continued skeptical through the Spring and even down to August and the beginning of the war."[50]

Thus, not only did the Munich experience persuade Roosevelt that air power was the dominant component of national power and reinforce his belief that Germany enjoyed absolute superiority, it also convinced him that she had acquired political and psychological advantages over the democracies which rendered her superior to them in other respects. As a consequence of Munich, in fact, Roosevelt believed that the European balance of power had shifted. His understanding of German capabilities does not, however, explain why he also came to believe that Germany actually *would* threaten the European democracies and the United States. After all, before Munich Roosevelt had assumed neither that having the capacity to attack America would cause Germany to do so, nor that her military advantage would necessarily prevent her from cooperating with the democracies in the cause of peace. The explanation for Roosevelt's perception of threat in the aftermath of the Munich crisis lies elsewhere —in his reassessment of Germany's intentions.

Munich enabled Roosevelt to settle in his own mind the nature of the challenge posed by the dictators. For one thing, he no longer seriously entertained the possibility of working with Hitler in the interests of peace generally. The Führer's performance during the crisis raised questions about his character and political style that made it impossible for Roosevelt to persist in his intermittent optimism about dealing with him on a cooperative basis. Moreover, Roosevelt finally came to believe that Germany could not be satisfied by diplomatic adjustment of her legitimate grievances. However much had been gained at Munich, Hitler would move again. The question was not whether, but when.

The first aspect of Roosevelt's diagnosis of German intentions reflected

[50] Verbatim transcript of interview with Franklin Roosevelt, Dec. 23, 1939, Alsop papers. This retrospective account is confirmed by Ickes, who noted in his diary that on January 28, 1939, the president described having told Lord Lothian "recently" that he would do nothing for Britain if she

> cringed like a coward. The President thinks that Great Britain is suffering from an inferiority complex. For the first time she is being out-maneuvered at the council table. Her fleet is helpless and she has neglected to build enough airplanes. She has fooled herself with respect to Spain. The wealthy class in England is so afraid of communism, which has constituted no threat at all in England, that they have thrown themselves into the arms of Nazism and now they don't know which way to turn.

Diary, 2:571. See also Roosevelt's letter to Roger Merriam, Feb. 15, 1939, Schewe, 7: no. 1594. Ickes confided his own doubts about whether the democracies would stand up to the dictators to his diary on January 29, 1939. *Diary*, 2:569.

an assessment of Hitler's character, which led to the conviction that something about the man himself precluded decent relations. The dramatic demonstration of the Führer at his worst during the crisis had finally overcome Roosevelt's characteristic openness, along with the lingering hope (which had persisted well into 1938) that Germany might yet be induced to cooperate at some level.[51] The colossal character flaws revealed by Hitler's behavior at Munich added up to the disquieting picture of an individual whose demands were unreasonable, whose methods were gratuitously offensive, and who respected neither the rights nor the interests of others. As Bullitt related Daladier's assessment, "Hitler at the present time would accept nothing except the absolute humiliation of every nation on earth. He desired by such humiliation to make his wish law in Europe."[52]

Although there had been intimations of these attitudes early in the crisis,[53] Godesberg confirmed Hitler's intransigence and demonstrated the impossibility of working with him even on the basis of near capitulation.[54] The conditions he laid down as the price of peace were so extreme that there was no honorable way of meeting them.[55] His unwillingness to cooperate manifested itself in an unyielding response to both Roosevelt's

[51] Roosevelt's tolerance of diversity was deeply ingrained. As Berle described it, "Nothing was alien to him. . . . He was tolerant of many things which shocked me: the crude and bitter intrigues of the European powers often directed against us; the corruption of some of his Tammany friends; the bickering and self-seeking which went on all around him." Quoted in Arthur Schlesinger, Jr., "Getting FDR's Ear," *New York Review of Books* 36 (Feb. 16, 1989): 23.

[52] Bullitt to Hull, Sept. 27, 1938, *FRUS*, 1938, 1:686.

[53] See, for example, Wilson to Hull, Sept. 18, 1938, ibid., 612–14; and Bullitt to Hull, Sept. 19, 1938, ibid., 615–18.

[54] As Stromberg has pointed out, by the time of the Godesberg meeting, the principle that Germans would be incorporated in the Reich had been conceded. "What Munich really exposed was not that Germany wanted Czechoslovakia and could get it but that Hitler's arrogance and greed were such as to preclude a gentlemanly transfer of power." *Collective Security*, 123. The sheer volume of negative reports of Hitler's behavior in the wake of Godesberg is striking, and the overwhelmingly unfavorable impression it conveyed could only have reinforced Roosevelt's earlier feelings of distaste. That meeting proved to be a turning point in others' evaluation of Hitler as well. Lord Lothian, for example, told the House of Lords in April 1939 that "it was only on his return in October [1938], when he learnt how Hitler had behaved in his negotiations with Chamberlain, that he came, for the first time, to suspect the man's real character. It was the Godesberg conference . . . which set him thinking that Germany no longer had right on her side." James R. M. Butler, *Lord Lothian* (London: Macmillan, 1960), 226.

[55] Bullitt declared that Hitler's terms for Czechoslovakia at Godesberg were "virtually those imposed on a defeated German Army for evacuation of northern France," and Carr likened them to "demands of victorious nations over vanquished." Bullitt to Hull, Sept. 25, 1938, *FRUS*, 1938, 1:648–49. See also Carr to Hull and Kennedy to Hull, Sept. 24, 1938, ibid., 642–44; Carr to Hull, Sept. 25, 27, 1938, ibid., 649–50, 679; and Bullitt to Hull, Sept. 26, 1938, ibid., 668.

first peace appeal and Chamberlain's note.[56] Not only did Hitler regard his demands as absolute, he was more than willing to go to war to satisfy them, and what had seemed a frightening possibility before Godesberg became a near reality thereafter.[57] Worse yet, this bellicosity was completely gratuitous, leading Roosevelt to conclude that war would be Hitler's fault alone.[58] This in turn had considerable influence on Roosevelt's emotional response to him.

In addition to these negative cognitions, the experience of Munich had generated in Roosevelt and others a host of unpleasant emotions. Hitler's apparent abnormality elicited uneasiness and frustration, his uncivilized behavior caused revulsion. Contemporary observers consistently voiced the opinion that there was something incomprehensible about him. As Ambassador Wilson saw it, he was "a man apart whom it seems almost impossible to judge by customary standards," a difference so pronounced that many resorted to the vocabulary of mental illness to describe him.[59] Thus, Ickes reacted to Hitler's speech of September 26 by noting that he "ranted and raved for over an hour. At times he seemed almost incoherent."[60]

Hitler's behavior was not only puzzling, it provoked anger and ex-

[56] Ambassador Kennedy described Hitler's reply to Chamberlain's note as "completely and definitely unsatisfactory," giving not the slightest hint of an inclination to compromise. Kennedy to Hull, Sept. 27, 1938, ibid., 673. See also Bullitt to Hull, Sept. 27, 1938, ibid., 673–74. Hitler's refusal to compromise was, of course, thrown into high relief by the strenuous efforts at accommodation of the other participants.

[57] For pre-Godesberg reports of Hitler's willingness to go to war, see Kennedy to Hull, Sept. 17, 1938, Wilson to Hull, Sept. 18, 1938, and Bullitt to Hull, Sept. 19, 1938, ibid., 609–18. For opinion after Godesberg, see the telephone call from Bullitt on September 23, 1938, "Memorandum to Roosevelt, September 23, 1938," Schewe, 7: no. 1294; and Bullitt to Hull, transmitting Daladier's view of the matter on September 27, 1938, *FRUS*, 1938, 1:686–88.

[58] As the United States minister to Czechoslovakia pointed out, "a peaceful settlement with the Praha Government conceding substantially all Sudeten demands was in sight as a result of the Runciman mission and could have been concluded had Germany shown a sincere desire to have such an agreement made." Thus, "If war now comes the responsibility for creating it . . . may be placed directly upon Hitler and his advisers," Carr to Hull, Sept. 28, 1938, ibid., 690–691. Roosevelt's recognition that Hitler was the sole obstacle to a peaceful settlement is suggested by the fact that his second appeal was directed to him alone. See Welles's remarks in a telephone conversation with Bullitt on September 27, Bullitt to Hull, ibid., 675–76

[59] Wilson to Hull, Oct. 5, 1938, ibid., 715.

[60] A few days later, Ickes referred to Hitler as a "maniac," and observed that, if Britain and France rearmed, they might be better able to deal with Germany should he go "berserk" again. *Diary*, 2:477, 480. In the same vein, see Roosevelt's remarks to Arthur Sweetzer about Hitler's performance at his meeting with the Austrian Chancellor, which left Sweetzer with the impression "that the Chief Executive seemed to think you could do very little with such a man." Kinsella, *Leadership*, 109. See also Cadogan's characterization of Hitler after his reply to the British note of September 24.

treme dislike.[61] Particularly after Godesberg, he was perceived to be rude, uncivilized, and violent. Roosevelt himself compared the emotional impact of Hitler's tirade on September 26 to that of Chamberlain's speech of the following day and showed "real anger" during the drafting of his second message when he heard that Germany might march that night, "forcing a war to no purpose."[62]

The emotions provoked by Hitler's behavior during the crisis reinforced Roosevelt's belief that the Führer could not be relied upon to cooperate with other states in the interests of peace, a conviction he retained in the immediate aftermath of Munich, as shown by his highly negative reaction to Kennedy's Trafalgar Day speech on October 19 which recommended that the democracies and dictatorships "bend their energies toward solving their common problems by an attempt to reestablish good relations on a world basis." Roosevelt responded with a radio address designed to undo the damage caused by this speech and bypassed Kennedy as a channel of communication with the British from that point forward.[63]

Roosevelt's belief that it was impossible to work with Hitler in any meaningful way persisted after the crisis, as did his emotional reaction to Hitler's behavior, fueled by new outrages. On November 15, 1938, for example, he publicly expressed his revulsion at the events of Kristallnacht.[64] In the months leading up to the German takeover of Czechoslovakia, he continued to receive reports of Hitler's irrationality that only reinforced his earlier impression,[65] and at the end of January 1939, he

[61] Even Chamberlain was revolted by Hitler's personal qualities. See above.

[62] See above for Bullitt's impression of Hitler's response to Chamberlain.

[63] Quoted in Cole, *Roosevelt*, 289–90. According to Koskoff, Roosevelt revised the draft of his speech prepared by Berle and Moffat to make it stronger. Koskoff, *Joseph P. Kennedy*, 159. See also Hull, *Memoirs*, 1:596.

[64] "I myself could scarcely believe that such things could occur in a twentieth-century civilization." "Statement by President Roosevelt, November 15, 1938," *Peace and War*, 439. See also Schewe, 7: no. 1408. The majority of Americans were coming to similar views as a result of Munich and Kristallnacht, a change reflected in the Fortune polls. While 62 percent of Americans were neutral toward Germany in October 1937, after Munich 56 percent favored a boycott of German goods, a figure which rose to 62 percent after Kristallnacht. By February 1939, 69 percent favored extending all aid short of war to Great Britain. This is particularly striking in view of the fact that "American public opinion in regard to the foreign policy of the United States remained virtually unaffected by international developments from the fall of 1935 until after the Munich crisis in September 1938." Jacob, "Influence of World Events," 48. See also Jonas, *Isolationism*, 211–12.

[65] For example, Lord Halifax asked Mallet to inform Roosevelt that Hitler might launch a "desperate coup" against the Western powers, noting that such a move was consistent with his "mental condition, his insensate rage against Great Britain and his megalomania." Halifax to Mallet, Jan. 24, 1939, *DBFP*, Series 3, 4:5. See also Arthur Murray's December 15 report on Hitler's mental condition. "Arthur Murray, London, to Roosevelt, December 15, 1938," Schewe, 7: no. 1481; and Viscount Elibank, "Franklin Roosevelt, Friend of

conveyed in no uncertain terms his impression of the Führer's instability to the Senate Military Affairs Committee:

> if this wild man—well, some people say it is paranoia, other people say he is a Joan of Arc . . . , as Schuschnigg said after the famous visit to Berchtesgaden, . . . Hitler, walking up and down the room for about eight hours, pounding the table and making speeches, only mentioned two people in his entire conversation. One was Julius Caesar and the other was Jesus Christ. He kept on talking about those people in such a manner as to indicate that he believes himself to be a reincarnation of Julius Caesar and Jesus Christ. What can we people do about a personality like that? We would call him a "nut." But there isn't any use in calling him a "nut" because he is a power and we have to recognize that.[66]

Abandoning all hope of cooperating with Hitler is not, of course, the same as perceiving a threat to American security, and Roosevelt's diagnosis of threat was also linked to his newfound belief that Germany's aims were unlimited. Munich was a turning point in the development of his understanding of the extent of Hitler's will to dominate. Concern on this score grew with the crisis itself. In a letter to Phillips on September 15, Roosevelt alluded to the inevitability of future conflict even if Chamberlain's current endeavors proved successful. On the nineteenth he developed this theme for Lindsay, telling him that "even if Czechoslovakia did acquiesce in the demands made, . . . he was sure that other demands would follow elsewhere."[67]

In the aftermath of the crisis, two schools of thought emerged about the intentions of the dictators. As Wilson noted:

> There are many who feel that their "victory" in the game of great power politics will be a precursor of violent demands in all directions on the part of Berlin and Rome under the guise of proceeding by "negotiations." On the

---

Britain," *Contemporary Review* 187 (1955): 367. In January 1939, when Roosevelt "twitted Lord Lothian with his confidence in Hitler two years ago, . . . Lothian now admitted that 'no one could talk to Hitler.'" (The president found this conversation interesting enough to repeat to Ickes on January 28.) Butler, *Lord Lothian*, 227; Ickes, *Diary*, 2:571.

[66] According to a participant in the conference, "The President apparently was quite aggressive in his dislike for Hitler." "Conference with the Senate Military Affairs Committee, Jan. 31, 1939." Interview with Senator Warren Austin, Dec. 8, 1939. Alsop papers. Note also Murray's later comment to Halifax on March 1, 1940 that Roosevelt was not normally given to hatred but "hates violently everyone and everything to do with the Nazi Regime." Elibank, "Franklin Roosevelt," 368.

[67] "Roosevelt to Phillips, September 15, 1938," Schewe, 7: no. 1277; Lindsay to Halifax, Sept. 20, 1938, *DBFP*, Series 3, 7:627. For evidence of this point of view within the administration see Ickes, *Diary*, 2:468–69, 480; Messersmith's memorandum of September 29 and Bullitt's letter of October 3, Bullitt to Hull, Oct. 3, 1938, *FRUS*, 1938, 1:704–7, 711–12.

other hand there are those . . . who believe . . . that Hitler feeling that he has righted Versailles injustices . . . is . . . under the "spell" of a, for him, new international experience at Munich and that he will endeavor to continue in a spirit of adjustments by conciliation.[68]

Most of Roosevelt's advisers leaned toward the first opinion, and once his postcrisis optimism had dissipated, he too returned to the negative evaluation of German intentions that he had developed during the crisis.[69] As his remarks to Ickes indicate, by October 9 he had come to expect German moves directed at satisfying her appetite for colonies. Nor was this the only area in which Roosevelt anticipated trouble. Writing to Lane on October 10, he predicted that "the expansion of Germany may well come into conflict with Italian interests in Yugoslavia." Moreover, Lord Elibank, who visited him at Hyde Park from October sixteenth to the twenty-fourth, has stated unequivocally that "to Roosevelt's mind, it was by that time a *certainty* that Germany definitely intended to launch another war upon civilization."[70]

In the coming months, Roosevelt remained convinced of the aggressive aims of the dictators, telling the Senate Military Affairs Committee on

[68] Wilson to Hull, Oct. 6, 1938, ibid., 1:715.

[69] Pell stated the common conclusion more colorfully than most: "Will Hitler use his increased strength to demand even greater concessions within a year or have they crammed him so full that he will forever hate the sight of food? My observation of small boys at Christmas parties has lead [sic] me to the conclusion that a surfeit seldom kills." "Pell to Roosevelt, October 21, 1938," Schewe, 7: no. 1366. See "George S. Messersmith, Assistant Secretary of State, to Cordell Hull, Secretary of State, September 29, 1938," ibid., no. 1319a; "Morgenthau to Roosevelt, October 17, 1938," ibid., no. 1358; "Biddle to Roosevelt, October 15, 1938," ibid., no. 1355; and "Bowers to Roosevelt, October 24, 1938," ibid., no. 1368. Kennedy, on the other hand, lent a sympathetic ear to the views of the British foreign minister, Lord Halifax, reporting that he "does not believe that Hitler wants to have a war with Great Britain and he does not think there is any sense in Great Britain having a war with Hitler unless there is direct interference with England's Dominions." Kennedy to Hull, Oct. 12, 1938, *FRUS*, 1938, 1:722.

[70] "Roosevelt to Arthur Bliss Lane, Minister to Yugoslavia, October 10, 1938," Schewe, 7: no. 1335; Elibank, "Franklin Roosevelt," 364. Official American policy was apparently based on similar assumptions. See Halifax to Mallet, Jan. 24, 1939, Mallet to Halifax, Jan. 27, 1939, *DBFP*, Series 3, 4:5, 27; and Juliusz Lukasiewicz, *Diplomat in Paris, 1936–1939* (New York: Columbia University Press, 1970), 168. Roosevelt also received a number of reports during this period expressing the opinion that the Germans were irrevocably bent on domination. Even Kennedy eventually came around to this view, which he conveyed to the President on his return home in December. See Kaufmann, "Two Ambassadors," 664–65; Beschloss, *Kennedy and Roosevelt*, 181–82, 184, 185; and Farley, *Jim Farley's Story*, 158. For a range of opinion along similar lines, see Moffat, Memorandum, Dec. 22, 1938, *FRUS*, 1938, 1:735–36; "Herbert C. Pell, Minister to Portugal, to Roosevelt, February 11, 1939," Schewe, 7: no. 1588; "Anthony J. Drexel Biddle, Jr., Ambassador to Poland, to Roosevelt, March 11, 1939," ibid., no. 1634; Butler, *Lord Lothian*, 227; and Kinsella, *Leadership*, 130–31.

January 31, 1939, that in the years after the signing of the Anti-Comintern Pact by Germany, Italy, and Japan "that pact has been strengthened almost every month, not only by aggression but by a better understanding between the three of them. There exists today, without any question . . . what amounts to an offensive and defensive alliance."[71]

The Threat to American Security

Were Great Britain to be defeated, a tremendous, indeed a decisive, alteration in the balance of world forces, military, moral and political, would occur to the grave disadvantage of the United States. . . . The world, in fact, outside America would be totalitarian and she would be unable to do anything effective to prevent it. . . . America, alone in a jealous and hostile world, would find that the effort and cost of maintaining "splendid isolation" would be such as to bring about the destruction of all those values which the isolation policy had been designed to preserve.[72]

Based largely on his reassessment of German intentions, Roosevelt had come to believe not only that the hope of cooperating with Hitler was illusory and that his aims were unlimited, but also that Germany posed a threat to American security. While he had expressed similar fears earlier, the experience of the Munich crisis gave them an immediacy that had been lacking. As Roosevelt observed to Ambassador Pell on November 12, 1938, "The dictator threat is a good deal closer to the United States and the American Continent than it was before." This, as he had already pointed out in a press conference on October 14, required a "complete restudy of American national defense."[73]

[71] "Conference with the Senate Military Affairs Committee, Jan. 31, 1939." See also Senator Austin's impression of Roosevelt's remarks to this group. Interview with Joseph Alsop on Dec. 8, 1939, Alsop papers. Other evidence of Roosevelt's views on the subject can be found in the Alsop interview with Secretary of the Navy Edison, in which the secretary stated that "about the time of the new year," Roosevelt told him "I have it in mind that we are not going to get through the summer without seeing the world in a hell of a lot of trouble." Ibid. For similar remarks by the president throughout this period, see Farley, *Jim Farley's Story*, 158 (Dec. 28, 1938); Kilpatrick, *Roosevelt and Daniels*, 181–83 (Jan. 14, 1939); Ickes, *Diary*, Jan. 28 and Feb. 7, 1939, 2:571, 576; and Roosevelt's own press conference on February 18, *PPA* 8:140.

[72] "Memorandum from Joseph P. Kennedy, Ambassador to Great Britain, [March 3, 1939]," Schewe, 8: no. 1616a. See also Beschloss, *Kennedy and Roosevelt*, 181–82.

[73] Roosevelt to Pell, Nov. 12, 1938, *PL*, 2:826; Press Conference, Oct. 14, 1938, *Presidential Press Conferences* 12: no. 491. In his interview with Alsop and Kintner, Roosevelt indicated that he did not develop these views until November or December (Interview with Roosevelt, Dec. 23, 1939). This statement is belied by his remarks at the October 14 press conference. Responding to a question about the origins of the decision to reorganize the

The challenge to American security had three aspects. First, Roosevelt feared that the United States might find itself facing the dictators isolated and alone. Second, he saw Latin America as the target of military as well as economic and political threats. Finally, he believed that the physical security of the United States itself was in jeopardy.[74]

Even before Munich, Assistant Secretary Messersmith had predicted that the United States could not escape the consequences of a German victory in Europe, one of which was that she would be left to face the dictators alone. After the crisis, Roosevelt shared this view. As early as October 26, he publicly expressed his sense that none could escape from "the disaster of war. . . . The impact of such a disaster cannot be confined," and in the weeks between Munich and the German takeover of Czechoslovakia he returned repeatedly to this theme.[75] In his State of the Union address on January 4, he spoke of the ideological isolation that the victorious totalitarian states could impose, concluding that "We, no more than other nations, can afford to be surrounded by the enemies of our faith and our humanity."[76] Later that month, he expanded on more material consequences, asserting at a Cabinet meeting on January 27 that "If Hitler breaks loose, . . . and if he attains his objective, this country is going to suffer tremendously." At lunch with Ickes the following day, Roosevelt

> developed the theory that our first line of defense is really the small countries of Europe that have not yet been overwhelmed by the Nazis. He seriously thinks that if Hitler extends his power over these small countries and then uses the economic weapon that will be his, he will be striking a serious blow at us without ever a thought of trying to land a soldier on our shores.[77]

Roosevelt also saw German actions in Latin America as potentially threatening American security. On November 15, 1938, he told the

"whole national defense picture," Roosevelt said, "It has been in progress for about a year and it has, in a sense, been forced to a head by events, developments and information received within the past month."

[74] Reynolds describes Roosevelt's post-Munich perception of the German threat in similar terms. *Creation*, 40–41.

[75] "Radio Address, October 26, 1938," 565. See also Alsop and Kintner, *American White Paper*, 16, and Morgenthau's letter to the president, Oct. 17, 1938, Schewe, 7: no. 1358. Iriye argues that Munich exposed the links between European developments and the East Asian crisis, raising the fear that, "the aggressive nations, in particular Germany and Japan, might band together and collectively menace the status quo and peace in the whole world." Akira Iriye, *Across the Pacific: An Inner History of American-Asian Relations* (New York: Harcourt, Brace, and World, 1967), 202–3.

[76] "Address Delivered by President Roosevelt to the Congress, January 4, 1939," *Peace and War*, 448.

[77] Ickes, *Diary*, 2:568, 571. This idea later became notorious when Roosevelt tried to convey it to the members of the Senate Military Affairs Committee. See below, chap. 6.

press, "As a result of world events in the last few years, and as a result of scientific advancement in waging war, the whole orientation of this country in relation to the continent on which we live . . . has had to be changed."[78] This was because German rearmament, coupled with the development of the long-range bomber, had made it possible for her to invade the Western hemisphere "via the unprotected bulge of Western Brazil."[79]

Framing the German threat to Latin America in military terms was something of a departure for Roosevelt. Before Munich, he and others had seen the threat as primarily political and economic, but during the crisis this began to change.[80] For example, on September 23 Secretary Hull, presumably with Roosevelt's acquiescence, told the Cabinet that a victorious Axis in Europe might lead "to attempts to penetrate South America," in which case "the United States would have to go to [its] defense."[81] In the aftermath of the crisis, although concern about the economic and political threat to Latin America also intensified,[82] the mil-

---

[78] "Press Conference in the White House, November 15, 1938, 4:08 p. m.," Schewe, 7: no. 1409. For an account of the German threat to Latin America in terms of both intentions and capabilities, as well as the perceptions of American leaders about it, see Frye, *Nazi Germany*, 186–92. For contemporary discussion of the Axis threat to South America, see Carlton Beals, "Totalitarian Inroads in Latin America," *Foreign Affairs* 17 (1938): 78–89; and Percy W. Bidwell, "Latin America, Germany and the Hull Program," *Foreign Affairs* 17 (1939): 374–90.

[79] Stetson Conn, "Changing Concepts of National Defense in the United States, 1937–1941," *Military Affairs* 28 (1964): 3. Roosevelt referred explicitly to this reasoning in his November 15 press conference, basing his analysis of the threat primarily on developments in aircraft. "Press Conference, November 15, 1938," Schewe, 7: no. 1409. See also George Questor, *Deterrence Before Hiroshima* (New York: John Wiley and Sons, 1966), 130.

[80] A discussion between Welles and Ickes on April 1, 1938 illustrates these traditional interpretation of the threat to Latin America. Ickes, *Diary*, 2:352–53. While Roosevelt did mention the possibility of a military threat to Latin America as early as April 1938, he was thinking of local revolutions sponsored by the fascist dictators following the model of the Spanish Civil War. Another contemporary scenario for this type of Axis military penetration of Latin America may be found in Watson, *Chief of Staff*, 87. See also Wesley Frank Craven and James L. Cate, ed., *The Army Air Forces in World War II* (Chicago: University of Chicago Press, 1948–1955), 117–21.

[81] Ickes, *Diary*, 2:473–74.

[82] See "Morgenthau to Roosevelt, October 17, 1938," 3. Other expressions of concern may be found in "Messersmith to Hull, September 29, 1938," 5; Schewe, 7: no. 1319a; Ickes, *Diary*, 2:497; "Claude G. Bowers, Ambassador to Spain, St. Jean de Luz, France, to Roosevelt, October 24, 1938," Schewe, 8: no. 1368. The October 11 memorandum stressed the economic and political threat, although it also mentioned the possibility that successful fascist penetration in those areas might lead to German and Italian acquisition of bases in the region. "Memorandum, October 11, 1938," ibid., no. 1345. In the following weeks, Roosevelt received ample evidence of German efforts to undermine the Latin Americans politically. See, for example, the reports dealing with such activities in Brazil and Venezuela (Nov. 17, 18, 21, Dec. 10, 15, 1938), Schewe, 8: no.s 1412, 1412a, 1413, 1413a, 1471, 1482, 1422.

itary threat was now of paramount concern, and Roosevelt began to think of preparing for it almost immediately. As Morgenthau remarked to his staff on October 14, the President's plan for an extended air force included enough planes to "take care of the whole South American continent too."[83] And as his statements in January 1939 to the Senate Military Affairs Committee and Josephus Daniels attest, Roosevelt's concern about the German military threat to Latin America persisted well after the November 14 conference.[84]

Roosevelt's fears about the German military threat to the Western Hemisphere were not confined to Latin America. In his November 14 presentation to key members of his administration he warned that the United States "now faced the possibility of attack on the Atlantic side in both the Northern and the Southern Hemispheres," and many of his post-Munich references to the security of South America were accompanied by similar expressions of concern.[85] Observing that Brazil was "half way to Europe," Roosevelt had alluded to a potential threat from Latin America as early as April 20, 1938. Aware of the capabilities of modern aircraft, he had since the end of 1937 come to view Brazil as a virtual launching pad for an attack on the United States.[86]

In addition to exacerbating fears about attack from the south, the Munich crisis raised the specter of losing the protection that the existence of powerful European democracies had traditionally conferred. As William Allen White expressed this new feeling of American vulnerability to Lord Lothian,

[83] "Morgenthau Diary," 146:293. See also Roosevelt's remarks to Ickes on October 9, above.

[84] "Conference with the Senate Military Affairs Committee, January 31, 1939," 10–11. Kilpatrick, *Roosevelt and Daniels*, 182–83. On February 22, 1939, General Arnold told Congress that Germany had 1700 planes that were able to fly from the west coast of Africa to the east coast of South America. Kahn, "United States Views," 492. By February 1939 the military had begun to take account of the security threat to Latin America in their planning. See Watson, *Chief of Staff*, 153.

[85] Oliphant Meeting," 338. See also Arnold, "Memorandum," 1. Thompson argues that "The threats to the security of the continental United States postulated by Roosevelt and others in this period were obviously and explicitly part of their battle against isolationism" and for that reason were greatly exaggerated. That the security argument was an acceptable way of presenting the case against isolationism, however, does not mean that Roosevelt did not believe it. He based his evaluation in part on an assessment of Hitler's intentions, and he was hardly alone in accepting both exaggerated reports of German air strength and the idea that America's ocean barriers could now be breached. Furthermore, not everyone agrees that it was altogether irrational to perceive a potential threat to American security even at this early date. See, for example, Heinrichs, *Threshold*, 4; John A. Thompson, "The Exaggeration of American Vulnerability: The Anatomy of a Tradition," *Diplomatic History* 16 (Winter 1992): 34–35 (see also 28–30, 34–36).

[86] "Press Conference, April 20, 1938," Schewe, 7: no. 1031. David Haglund, "George Marshall and the Question of Military Aid to England," *Journal of Contemporary History* 15 (1980): 747. See also Craven and Cate, *Army Air Forces*, 119.

In the matter of relations with Great Britain, . . . we have come into a new sense of insecurity since Munich. Probably that insecurity has been there for several years, but the sense of it has not been made plain until now. Now we know that for the first time in a hundred years the United States is out on its own. We no longer lie under the protection of the British fleet. That protection has been "a very present help in trouble." I believe it has been the keynote of our foreign policy. Now we know that we must walk alone. And we are going in fear and trembling.[87]

Roosevelt's apprehension about what would happen if America could no longer rely on British protection is most clearly seen in his activities after the crisis, particularly the whirlwind series of moves directed at developing and implementing the policy of aiding the European democracies with airplanes he initiated immediately following Bullitt's personal report on October 13.[88] In the weeks after the November 14 White House conference, his concern was expressed in his remarks to the Senate Military Affairs Committee at the end of January and reinforced by Lord Lothian, who advised him that "Britain has defended civilization for a thousand years. Now the spear is falling from her hand and it is up to you to take it and carry on."[89] Although Roosevelt expressed considerable irritation with this formulation,[90] he could not entirely avoid the knowledge that he might have little choice but to accept Lothian's challenge,[91] and he voiced his new sense of threat on more than one occasion. In his State of the Union message, for example, he discussed American defense needs in terms suggesting the need to prepare for direct attack. And in his defense message of January 12, 1939, he reminded Congress that while there was no intention of participating in a European war, should the worst occur, "we cannot guarantee a long period, free from attack, in which we could prepare."[92]

[87] *Selected Letters of William Allen White, 1899–1943*, ed. Walter Johnson (New York: Henry Holt, 1947), 394.

[88] See below.

[89] "Conference with the Senate Military Affairs Committee, January 31, 1939," 9; Ickes, *Diary*, 2:571.

[90] "Roosevelt to Roger Merriam, February 15, 1939," Schewe, 8: no. 1594.

[91] According to Polish Ambassador Lukasiewicz's account of Bullitt's views on the latter's return from the United States in January 1939, "Those in authority [in the United States] are of the opinion that, should war break out between Britain and France on the one side and Italy and Germany on the other, and should Britain and France suffer defeat, the Germans would directly threaten the real interests of the United States on the American continent." Lukasiewicz, *Diplomat in Paris*, 168.

[92] "Address by Roosevelt to the Congress, January 4, 1939," *Peace and War*, 450; "Message of President Roosevelt to the Congress, January 12, 1939," ibid., 451. American military planners had become sensitive to the new threat even before Roosevelt made his presentation on November 14. As Matloff and Snell note, one of the consequences of the

ANALYSIS

As we have seen, the change in Roosevelt's understanding of German capabilities was not the primary cause of his perception of a security threat in the aftermath of the Munich crisis. Well before the crisis, he had come to believe that advances in aviation technology gave Germany the ability to harm the United States. Similarly, while his post-Munich perception that Germany was in a better position to dominate Europe reinforced this evaluation of German capabilities, it did not in itself lead to the belief that she now posed a direct threat to American security. Rather, Roosevelt's post-Munich diagnosis of German intent was considerably more consequential for his perception of threat. The crisis dispelled his uncertainty about how to evaluate Hitler, and he now believed that given the chance Germany not only could, but would, eventually threaten the United States.

Why the crisis should have caused him to form this impression, however, is not immediately obvious. Munich by no means affected everyone's understanding of German intentions. Some had long felt that Hitler's ambitions knew no bounds and that he was fundamentally untrustworthy. Messersmith, for one, had often advanced the view of German intentions that Roosevelt did not adopt until after the crisis. Others required considerably more evidence than Hitler's behavior at Munich to reach the same conclusion. The diagnosis Assistant Secretary Berle arrived at only after the Germans marched into Prague in 1939, for example, strikingly mirrors the one Roosevelt developed in the aftermath of Munich.[93]

What was it about Hitler's behavior at Munich that led Roosevelt to believe he would eventually threaten the United States? In fact, that conclusion was rooted in a judgment about process: it was primarily Hitler's unconcealed disdain for the processes of accommodation that are the essence of democratic politics that led Roosevelt to conclude that the Führer could not be trusted and would eventually threaten the United

---

Munich crisis was that "the American military staff extended the scope of war planning to take account of the reassertion of German imperial aims." Maurice Matloff and Edwin M. Snell, *Strategic Planning for Coalition Warfare, 1941–1942* (Washington, D.C.: Department of the Army, 1953), 4–5. See also Watson, *Chief of Staff*, 97–98.

[93] See below. As Jervis points out, the belief that Hitler could be appeased was in many ways more reasonable than the idea that he would want to wage a cataclysmic war for world dominance: "Common sense indicated that while Hitler was an evil tyrant, he would be content with regaining Germany's pre-1914 position. Indeed, until he took over the non-German portions of Czechoslovakia in March 1939, all his behavior could be explained by his drive for this goal." Robert Jervis, "Intelligence and Foreign Policy: A Review Essay," *International Security* 11 (1986): 151.

States.[94] Throughout the crisis, but particularly at Godesberg, Hitler had shown repeatedly that his ambition knew no bounds, that he had no respect for the legitimate interests of others, no desire to settle disputes peacefully, no regard for the rules of the game, and no use for compromise. Indeed, he had specifically refused Roosevelt's own appeal to find a peaceful solution in a manner the president found "truculent and unyielding." Worse yet, not only were his aims unlimited, but he was willing, perhaps even eager, to gain them by force. Munich showed that Hitler lacked all respect for the principles at the heart of Roosevelt's own belief system, principles to which he had repeatedly asserted his dedication during the Munich crisis itself.[95]

A number of other considerations point to Roosevelt's perception of Hitler's political creed and modus operandi as the critical factor in his expectation of future trouble. For one thing, as the crisis wore on, his feelings toward Britain, France, and Germany varied with his assessment of their willingness to compromise, a standard he used increasingly in assigning blame for the slide toward war. Although initially angered by the democracies' lack of resolve, having compared their strenuous efforts to settle the crisis to Hitler's intransigence, Roosevelt ceased to criticize them; after Godesberg there is no doubt that his anger was reserved for Hitler alone. Secondly, neither ideology nor Hitler's status as a dictator can explain Roosevelt's post-Munich assessment of his aggressiveness. Not only did Roosevelt steadfastly refuse to render such a judgment be-

---

[94] Roosevelt's perception of threat on this basis is the other side of the coin of the "democratic peace" thesis. As Russet states it, one of the explanations for peace between democracies is that "the *culture, perceptions, and practices* that permit compromise and the peaceful resolution of conflicts without the threat of violence within countries come to apply across national boundaries toward other democratic countries." Bruce Russett, *Grasping the Democratic Peace* (Princeton: Princeton University Press, 1993), 31.

[95] "I earnestly repeat that so long as negotiations continue, differences may be reconciled. Once they are broken off, reason is banished and force asserts itself." Roosevelt to Hitler, Sept. 26, 1938, *FRUS*, 1938, 1:658. Roosevelt's attachment to these processes sprang from

> his deepest political instincts and intuitions. By temperament, as well as conviction, he was committed to the tactics of moderation and toleration and compromise within an overall strategy of the golden mean or middle way. His tacit assumption was that a democratic society generally demands as the price of its survival the acceptance of halfway measures and imperfect solutions and that its survival is an absolute value well worth the sacrifice of relative ones. Hence his abhorrence of extremism, whether of left or right.

Davis, *FDR* 1:625. Roosevelt himself remarked to Averill Harriman, "You know, Averill, I am by nature a compromiser." Judge Rosenman also noted Roosevelt's great "capacity for compromise." W. Averell Harriman and Elie Abel, *Special Envoy to Churchill and Stalin, 1941–1946* (New York: Random House, 1975), 4; Hull, *Memoirs*, 1:592; Rosenman, "Franklin Roosevelt," 360.

fore Munich despite the obvious presence of both factors, he also had no difficulty working with leaders who espoused fascism like Mussolini, or with brutal dictators of a different ideological stripe, like Stalin. During the Munich crisis, though, Roosevelt began to distinguish between Hitler and Mussolini in a way he had not previously.[96] Particularly after Godesberg, he assigned blame for the imminence of war to Hitler, while simultaneously expending considerable energy to persuade Mussolini to intervene to preserve the peace, and he continued to differentiate between the two dictators after the crisis was over.[97]

Roosevelt not only distinguished between Mussolini and Hitler despite their similar ideologies, but he regarded Stalin differently as well. As Alexander George has noted, several aspects of Roosevelt's belief system encouraged this. For one thing, he thought that Russian totalitarianism was less dangerous than the German variety because the Soviet Union had not "sought world conquest through military aggression." Even more striking, his belief in the possibility of gaining "Stalin's trust" and establishing "mutual confidence" was based on a perception that Stalin was "a fellow 'politician' with whom 'arrangements' [could] be made through personal diplomacy."[98]

After Munich Roosevelt put Hitler into a special category. As unsavory as Stalin and Mussolini were, he could work with them. They might, at least observe those processes of political accommodation Roosevelt considered essential, whereas Hitler, as he proved at Munich, would not. In the aftermath of the crisis, Roosevelt explicitly acknowledged the importance of these processes, declaring in a radio address that good relations among nations required "certain fundamental reciprocal obligations" and "a deliberate and conscious will that such political changes as changing needs require shall be made peacefully."[99] The implications for

[96] Roosevelt told the Senate Military Affairs Committee in January 1939 that he had made such a distinction "beginning about three years ago." However, there is ample evidence that Roosevelt seemed at least as anxious to induce Hitler to cooperate in the interest of peace during that period as he was to involve Mussolini. Thus, his statement must be taken as an indication of his post-Munich views rather than as a reflection of his attitude from 1936 to 1938. "Conference with the Senate Military Affairs Committee, Jan. 31, 1939" Schewe, 8:4.

[97] In an interview with the Italian ambassador, Prince Colonna, in April 1939 Roosevelt supported the British effort to separate Italy and Germany. Later that month, and again in May, he made additional appeals to Mussolini to distance himself from Hitler. Not until Italy invaded France in June 1940 did Roosevelt finally abandon his belief that Mussolini was somehow different from Hitler and might yet be induced to cooperate in the interests of peace. Dallek, *Franklin D. Roosevelt*, 183–84, 220–21, 228.

[98] George, Alexander, "Roosevelt's Image of the Soviet Union," unpubl. supplement to a lecture, n.d.

[99] "Radio Address to the Herald-Tribune Forum, October 26, 1938," PPA 7:564.

American policy, which George Messersmith was again quick to spell out, were clear:

> The Germany with which certain arrangements could have been made under Streseman and Bruning is a different Germany from the one we have to deal with under Hitler today in many ways. And arrangements which were then possible, and which would have been constructive, are today impossible until there is a regime of law and order in Germany.[100]

Similarly, in Roosevelt's first post-Munich State of Union address, a speech notable for the strong sense of threat it conveyed, he went even further in connecting the systematic violation of these processes to the threat of war, observing that "no nation can be safe in its will to peace so long as any other single powerful nation refuses to settle its grievances at the council table." Noting the existence of truly awesome capabilities for destruction, Roosevelt seemed nevertheless to emphasize that the threat to security stemmed primarily from the refusal of powerful states to play by the rules and to cooperate with others.[101]

What finally led Roosevelt to conclude that American security was directly threatened by Germany, then, was not so much that the crisis reinforced his perception that Germany had the capacity to endanger the United States, but the conviction he developed that she actually would be inclined to do so. This assessment of hostile intent, based on the violation of an essentially political norm, was at the heart of Roosevelt's post-Munich understanding of the international situation. The puzzle for decision-making theory is why intent was so prominent in Roosevelt's perception of threat and why political factors were so influential as indicators of intent.

Theories of Decision-Making

Clearly, the motivational approach to decision-making is no help in explaining Roosevelt's post-Munich diagnosis of threat. According to the theory of defensive avoidance, his awareness of strong domestic opposition to American involvement in international conflict should have led him to try to escape the knowledge that Germany threatened the United States.[102] Like Chamberlain, he should have ignored or played down

---

[100] "Messersmith to Hull, September 29, 1938," Schewe, 7: no. 1319a.

[101] "Address Delivered by President Roosevelt to the Congress, January 4, 1939," *Peace and War*, 449. See also "Radio Address to the Herald-Tribune Forum, October 26, 1938," *PPA* 7:564.

[102] Janis and Mann discuss defensive avoidance only at the evaluation stage of decision-making, but the theory does make predictions about information processing generally that

signs that it was impossible to work with Hitler. At no time, however, either before or during the crisis, did Roosevelt avoid any of the evidence presented to him or reject the conclusions to which it led. Rather, he attended to mounting evidence that supported a negative view of Hitler and made his appraisal of threat on the basis of it. Moreover, while the emotion generated by the crisis produced feelings of relief and optimism at its end, within a week Roosevelt had overcome those feelings and accepted the unpleasant conclusions to which the evidence led. Nor did the emotion Roosevelt experienced during and after the Munich crisis adversely affect his ability to process information. Not only did his negative feelings about Hitler reinforce rather than contradict his cognitions, but both combined to foster a new view of Hitler supplanting the previously accepted one.

Roosevelt's behavior in diagnosing the post-Munich international situation also attained a considerably higher level of performance than intuitive theories predict. He was not only open to new information, but before settling on a diagnosis consulted a wide range of opinion from an impressive variety of sources, attending both to analyses that reflected optimism about the future from Welles, Kennedy, and Berle, and those from Bullitt and other ambassadors, Messersmith, Morgenthau, Ickes, Edison, and Hull that warned of the German threat.

Nor is there any sign of premature cognitive closure in Roosevelt's diagnosis. His optimism in the week after the crisis indicates that he did not immediately make up his mind about a German threat to American security. Considering the entire period from 1936 to 1938 during which he experimented with a number of different policies at least partly to determine whether or not cooperation with Hitler was possible, moreover, Roosevelt can hardly be accused of rushing to judgment.

It is equally clear that Roosevelt was not overly influenced by vivid or dramatic information. While there was some contemporary speculation that Bullitt's October 13 presentation carried undue weight, in fact Roosevelt had abandoned his mood of optimism before the ambassador's return. Moreover, Bullitt's analysis was fully compatible with most of the reports Roosevelt received in the aftermath of the crisis, including one on October 12 from Bernard Baruch, who had also just returned from Europe. Dramatic as it was, Bullitt's visit seems principally to have reinforced views Roosevelt was already in the process of adopting.[103]

---

relate to diagnosis, such as those dealing with the way in which new information is handled. Janis and Mann, *Decision-Making*, 76. Janice Stein has attempted such an extension of the theory, "Deterrence and Reassurance," Committee on the Contribution of the Behavioral Sciences to the Prevention of Nuclear War, National Research Council, June 1987, 20, 22.

[103] For an account of Baruch's meeting with the president, see Baruch, *Public Years*, 274–76; and Margaret Coit, *Mr. Baruch* (Boston: Houghton Mifflin, 1957), 466–69. Roo-

Roosevelt also avoided two cognitive shortcuts that might seem particularly likely. For one thing, he rejected the obvious lesson of history offered by World War I.[104] For another, although he applied a political standard in evaluating Hitler's capacity for future cooperation, the length of time he took to diagnose the German threat, the quantity of information he considered, and his postcrisis optimism despite ample evidence of Hitler's disdain for the processes of political accomodation during the crisis, argue against the notion that his diagnosis was scripted or schema driven.[105]

For the most part, then, Roosevelt's post-Munich assessment of Hitler's intentions seems generally to have conformed to a rational standard. He was open to new information about Hitler's behavior and, after attending to several different explanations, interpreted it, with some justification, as indicating a potential threat to American security.[106] In one area, however, the quality of Roosevelt's post-Munich diagnosis of the security threat may be open to question. During the course of the crisis, his initial resistance to the notion that air power was in some sense dominant and that Germany's commanding lead in it could have a decisive impact in Europe evaporated. Could Roosevelt's acceptance of a view he had rejected previously have been due to the vivid accounts he received concerning the role of air power during the crisis? The question is important because it is generally agreed that the beliefs Roosevelt adopted were based on several misconceptions fostered by Lindbergh and others about the absolute strength of Germany's air force, its mission, and its ability to

---

sevelt himself denied that Bullitt had had any extraordinary influence. "Conference with the Senate Military Affairs Committee, January 31, 1939," Schewe, 7: no. 1565.

[104] World War I was seen by many as a war that could have been avoided, and isolationists based their diagnosis of the situation in 1938 on its lessons. Roosevelt, however, seems to have been immune to that particular lesson of history, refusing steadfastly to acknowledge a parallel between the late 1930s and the years from 1914 to 1917. (He observed to Ambassador Phillips at the beginning of the Munich crisis, that the situation was "very different from 1914.") Moreover, he consistently failed to sympathize with the argument that American's participation in the war could have been avoided if only she had behaved differently. Robert Jervis, "Perceiving and Coping with Threat," in *Psychology and Deterrence*, ed. Jervis et al. (Baltimore: Johns Hopkins University Press, 1985), 22; "Roosevelt to Phillips, September 15, 1938," Schewe, 8: no. 1277; Dallek, *Franklin D. Roosevelt*, 10. For the views of the isolationists at this time, see Cole, *Roosevelt*, chaps. 11 and 12.

[105] See appendix A.

[106] The Munich experience had several features that psychologists believe encourage rational procedures. The crisis was a dramatic and important event of the sort that commands attention and may serve as an inducement to greater concentration and more careful processing. Moreover, the rate at which information comes in affects its reception. If discrepant information arrives in large batches, as it did during the Munich crisis, it is more likely to be heeded. Jervis, *Perception*, 195, 308–10

prevail over the democracies.[107] In reality, "Germany could not have defeated one of its major opponents by an aerial campaign."[108]

Despite what is now known about German air-force capability, however, the erosion of Roosevelt's skepticism about it was based on what seemed to be substantial evidence. He received reports from a wide variety of sources about the power of military aviation, as well as Germany's decisive lead in it, and all of them suggested that Germany's success in the crisis negotiations was highly correlated with her perceived superiority in the air. Roosevelt thus became sensitized to the political significance of Germany's lead in the air on the basis of fairly solid evidence that it had been behind her achievements at Munich. As his subsequent statements indicate clearly, the ability of an air-force capability to influence political behavior impressed him at least as much as its military advantages.

The most damaging thing that can be said about the change in Roosevelt's attitude toward air power is that his observation of its political impact may have heightened his perception of its military importance. Again, however, almost all the apparently reliable analyses he received during and after the crisis emphasized the military value of Germany's preeminence.[109] While his change of heart was undoubtedly based on misinformation, it is difficult to attribute to bias.[110]

---

[107] In October 1937, Lindbergh and the American military attaché in Berlin, Truman Smith, wrote a report on German air power that stressed Germany's superiority over Britain and France. As Smith admitted years later, this report suffered from a "most significant omission" in neglecting to note that this impressive German air force was primarily "designed to operate in close support of Germany's ground armies." Like Lindbergh's later reports, it failed to point out that the Germans were not "building the strategic heavy bomber force needed if Hitler intended decisive operations against England—or against the United States." While it is not known if Roosevelt saw this first report, the one he did see in February 1938 suffered from the same failings. Cole, *Lindbergh*, 31–37.

[108] Herbert Dinerstein, "The Impact of Air Power on the International Scene, 1933–1940," *Military Affairs* 19 (Summer 1955): 66; see also 65–71. On this point, see also Uri Bialer, *The Shadow of the Bomber: The Fear of Attack and British Politics, 1932–1939* (London: Royal Historical Society, 1980), 157–59; and Kahn, "United States Views, 492.

[109] Taylor suggests the close connection between perceptions of the military and political effects of German air power: "Munich was a German military triumph . . . and the prime instrument of that triumph was the German Air Force: the *Luftwaffe*. It is a remarkable fact that Munich was the only victory of strategic proportions that the Luftwaffe ever won. . . . At the time of Munich, the Luftwaffe was the psychological spearhead of German power." Taylor, *Munich*, xv.

[110] This is not the case for some European statesmen. For example, Daladier's position on the quality of the French air force underwent a rather interesting reversal: "When he felt that France could not fight, then the French air force was terrible. When he felt that France had to fight, then the French air force was not so bad, and, quite without basis, he included 5,000 Russian planes on the French side." Dinerstein, "Impact of Air Power," 70. For a discussion of British perceptions of German air strength in terms of motivated misperception, see Robert Jervis, "Deterrence and Perception," *International Security* 7 (1982): 14–17.

Even though the processes Roosevelt used to diagnose the German threat met a fairly high standard of rationality, however, the analytical approach cannot completely account for his conclusion. Nothing in analytic theories of decision-making allows them to explain either why he relied so heavily on intent to diagnose threat, or why Hitler's performance at Munich was crucial to Roosevelt's assessment of aggressive intent.

The political approach to decision-making, however, specifically expects the imperatives of the political context to influence the choice of evidence. Thus, it would not find surprising a disposition to look at intentions. While political decision-makers need information about capabilities to judge whether or not security *can* be endangered, this may not be sufficient for them to conclude that it *will* be. Their orientation toward achieving their goals through political accommodation may make them slow to assume that possessing a capability to apply force forecasts its use, leading them instead to seek additional information about intentions.

As to the kind of information political decision-makers find enlightening, the political approach suggests that they may see disdain for procedures essential to the peaceful adjustment of differences as diagnostic of aggressive intent. This is due both to the belief that political action is unlikely to be truly effective unless a decision is at least minimally acceptable—even to the losers—and to the conviction that, where there is substantial disagreement, procedures that afford the interests of others a modicum of respect are a condition of acceptability. Indeed, willingness to employ such procedures is itself a sign of the acceptance of limited aims, and political decision-makers may infer that those who disdain them are not interested in *political* action at all, but are willing to gain their ends by action of a very different sort.[111] The systematic violation of these processes may thus be taken to mean that a military capability is actually likely to be used.

This hypotheses is supported by Raymond Cohen's analysis of threat perception. In particular, Cohen's findings establish a connection between the violation of a norm and an expectation of future aggression.[112]

---

[111] On the importance political decision-makers attach to procedural legitimacy, see appendix B.

[112]
The crucial inference, central to the appraisal of threat, is found in the recurrent argument that the opponent had in some way betrayed a trust or undertaken an illegitimate and unpermissable action—that he had somehow infringed a norm of behavior—and that, *as a consequence of this,* he had ceased to be bound by existing restraints and was to be considered as bent on a policy of aggressive domination gravely damaging to the interests of the observing actor.

Cohen, *Threat Perception*, 165–71. In a slightly different application of Cohen's insight, Jervis argues that "perceptions of threat are often determined less by *what* the

Thus, Roosevelt's observation of Hitler during the crisis did not merely result in generalized uneasiness about the future, but led him specifically to expect the systematic violation of the processes on which peaceful adjustment of differences depends. As Cohen predicts, the application of a political norm laid bare for him a direct connection between the violation of that norm and the probability of future aggression.[113]

That Roosevelt was employing a political norm also explains the timing of his diagnosis of the German threat. He did not make this assessment before Munich because he did not yet have conclusive evidence that Hitler lacked all respect for the processes of political accommodation. In this, he differed from Messersmith, who became convinced of Hitler's aggressive intentions on the basis of his words.[114] Roosevelt apparently required action as well.

After Munich, however, Roosevelt did not need to wait for further developments. Others, such as Chamberlain and Berle, did not make this judgment until the Germans marched into Prague in March 1939 because they were applying the norm of national self-determination. It took six months and a military takeover before they realized that the principle that allowed them to condone Hitler's behavior was not the one on which he was acting.[115] Roosevelt, having seen Hitler's extreme disregard for the processes of political accommodation at Munich, did not need to wait for him to seize territory occupied by non-Germans in order to conclude that he would threaten the rights of others.

Of course, Roosevelt was not alone in being less than sanguine about the future after Munich.[116] For the most part, however, this judgment reflected the inclusion of an additional value, such as civility or fair play, while Roosevelt's abrupt change about the possibility of working with

---

other does than by *how* the other does it." Jervis et al., *Psychology and Deterrence,* 14–15.

[113] T. W. Mason's characterization of the "political dimension" of Hitler's strategy suggests that this norm was effective in penetrating to the heart of his policy: "The Foreign Policy of the Third Reich was dynamic in character, limitless in its aims to achieve domination and entirely lacking a conception of an 'ultimate status quo.'" Quoted in Barry R. Posen, *Sources of Military Doctrine* (Ithaca, N.Y.: Cornell University Press, 1984), 179.

[114] "I myself never have been able to understand why these illusions [about Hitler's intention to honor his agreements] should persist when Hitler himself in his book and in the statements which he has made privately and semi-publicly has never left any doubt as to his political practice according to which agreements are valid only as long as he believes they should be kept." Memorandum by Messersmith to Hull, Feb. 18, 1938, *FRUS,* 1938, 1:18.

[115] In Chamberlain's case at least, this misperception appears to have been motivated. After Godesberg, Chamberlain resolutely refused to measure Hitler's behavior against a political norm, maintaining that "the difference between Berchtesgaden and Godesberg was one only of degree," and giving a "fanciful portrayal of a meeting that one can at best describe as a diplomatic disaster." Murray, *Change,* 206–7.

[116] See, for example, the post-Godesberg reactions of a portion of the British Cabinet. Taylor, *Munich,* 928; Murray, *Change,* 206–8.

Hitler reflected *the application of a political norm, the violation of which forecast a pattern of future behavior.*[117] Again it is instructive to compare Roosevelt to Chamberlain who, even having experienced Hitler's methods at firsthand, not only failed to apply a political norm, but also apparently misdiagnosed domestic opinion.

As a result of the Munich crisis, then, Roosevelt was at last able to reach closure about the German threat to American security. The uncertainty about how to evaluate Hitler that had plagued him from 1936 to 1938 had evaporated. The experience of the crisis had taught him that Hitler had the will, as well as the ability, to do harm. Moreover, changes in technology had made America increasingly vulnerable to German power. Due to the rise of the long-range bomber, America's ocean barriers would no longer protect her from attack, and she was at risk both directly and via Latin America. Nor, if Hitler were to be victorious in Europe, could the United States count on her other traditional source of protection, the power of the European democracies, most importantly the British fleet. The conclusion Roosevelt drew from this new diagnosis was the obvious one: Hitler must be prevented from controlling Europe.

---

[117]
The essence of Chamberlain's tragedy was that, having pursued a course that revealed the nature of Nazi policy, he refused to recognize that reality. . . . Ironically, the conciliatory nature of appeasement and the blatant, cynical Nazi response convinced most British that Hitler and his regime were malicious and dangerous. At Godesberg appeasement reached a dead end. Had Chamberlain recognized that fact, he would have had little difficulty in persuading his ministers and the country to resist.

Ibid., 214.

Dealing with the Consequences of Munich

ONCE ROOSEVELT'S post-Munich evaluation of the international situation had convinced him that German domination of Europe would pose a direct threat to the United States, his problem became how to deal with it. Establishing the nature and timing of his solution, however, is far from simple. Not only is the idea that Munich triggered significant policy decisions itself controversial, but even those who believe the crisis led to policy changes disagree about their nature.[1] Worse yet, the President's own testimony on the subject is thoroughly misleading.

Roosevelt offered at least two accounts of his response to the events of Munich. On December 28, 1938, reviewing for Jim Farley "the world-shaking events of the closing year," he declared that "the answer was adequate defense, amendment of neutrality legislation, and serving notice on dictators that 'if another form of government can present a united front in its attack on a democracy, the attack must and will be met by a united democracy.'"[2] A year later, he reported to Alsop and Kintner that although his first thoughts after the crisis were of disarmament, since this exercise in optimism met with a negative response, we the United States

> had to proceed on the basis that there would be no disarmament. We had to put our own house in order, be prepared by increasing our own armaments. We had to overall [sic] our entire preparedness in the light of Munich. After Munich, then our general policy was as follows: First, place more emphasis on the North-South axis; Second, Revise the neutrality act; Third, Use our diplomatic influence to hamper the aggressors.

Roosevelt even provided a timetable: "We reached the decision to try disarmament in October, and in November we decided on the North-South axis and revision of the neutrality law."[3]

---

[1] Burns, for example, argues that while Roosevelt believed the Nazis would ultimately have to be restrained, "these were private sentiments. . . . Unwilling to throw his weight into the balance, the President was still confined to a policy of pinpricks and righteous protest. No risks, no commitments, was the motto of the White House." *Lion*, 385.

[2] Farley, *Jim Farley's Story*, 162–63.

[3] Interview with Franklin Roosevelt, Dec. 23, 1939, Alsop papers. Roosevelt also said that after his disarmament scheme failed, he had reverted to his quarantine idea: the United States "put out feelers but they got no where [sic], because the little nations were scared of Germany and feared her displeasure." Ibid. Unfortunately, this account cannot be taken at face value. Not only is there no independent confirmation that such a policy was actually

Thus did the President present a neat package of complimentary policies to deal with the situation facing him in the aftermath of the Munich crisis. Unfortunately, this "definitive" account is flatly contradicted by his own activities during the critical five-week period following the post-Munich euphoria. Roosevelt's behavior between the end of the Munich crisis and the November 14 meeting where he announced his intentions to key members of his administration shows clearly that the policy of aiding Britain and France, primarily with planes, dominated his thinking from the outset and that the other steps he cited (including neutrality revision, rearmament, hemisphere defense, and measures short of war) were subsidiary or peripheral. Furthermore, the tenacity with which he adhered to his chosen policy in the face of both the domestic challenges it provoked and the external challenge posed by the German takeover of Czechoslovakia in March 1939 confirms his attachment to it and establishes his statements about aiding the democracies as a good deal more than idle speculation.[4] Indeed, although its form changed in response to new problems, that policy remained Roosevelt's principal response to the German threat right up to America's entry into the war in December 1941.

The critical question, then, is what led Roosevelt to choose aid to the democracies in the first place and defend it so vigorously thereafter, especially since it was not necessarily the optimal choice from either the international or the domestic perspective. The answer lies in his perception that this policy allowed him to transcend the value conflict between peace and security that had become his central policy dilemma. That belief explains not only Roosevelt's attachment to aiding Britain and France, but also his attitude toward rearmament and his approach to neutrality revision.

"MOVING AWFUL FAST WITH THE PRESIDENT"— OCTOBER 8–NOVEMBER 14, 1938.[5]

Roosevelt's activities in mid-October 1938 revolved around two key events, neither of which he saw fit to mention to Alsop and Kintner. The first was Bullitt's personal report on the European situation, the second a

---

pursued, but also Roosevelt's testimony is contradicted by the only evidence that does touch on the subject. On October 8, 1938, he threw cold water on a suggestion made by Mexican President Cardenas to establish "now, before the war, a boycott against the aggressor countries." While expressing "great interest" and "much appreciation" for Cardenas's ideas, Roosevelt replied that "that by reason of the fact that the immediate danger of an outbreak of war in Europe would seem to have been averted there is no immediate occasion for a decision to be reached upon them." "Lazaro Cardenas, President of Mexico, to Roosevelt September 28, 1938," and "Roosevelt to Lazaro Cardenas, President of Mexico, October 8, 1938," Schewe, 8: no.s 1331a, 1334.

[4] As Donald C. Watt maintains, for example. *How War Came* (New York: Pantheon, 1989), 129–30.

[5] "Morgenthau Diary," Oct. 20, 1938, 146:284.

five-day meeting with several key advisers at Hyde Park that made clear both the scope of Roosevelt's plans to aid the democracies and his sense of urgency about getting them underway.

On returning from France, Bullitt went directly to the White House, where on the night of October 13 he held an extended conversation with the president. While no firsthand account of this meeting exists, we can piece together a fair idea of what took place. To begin with, there is the ambassador's own testimony that he planned to discuss "the aviation position and ways and means of remedying it" with the President when he arrived home.[6] That he did so is confirmed by Morgenthau's October 20 account of the origins of Roosevelt's thinking.[7]

Roosevelt, of course, was by no means unprepared for such a report. Not only was he fully aware of the attention air power had commanded throughout the crisis, he had subsequently received numerous reports stressing German air strength and urging American rearmament, and his sympathy with the efforts of the democracies to deal with this situation was reflected in his agreement on October 4 to allow French representatives to test-fly American planes. Moreover, on October 12 Bernard Baruch, who had also recently returned from Europe, informed Roosevelt of German military prowess and the role British and French lack of preparedness had played in the outcome of the Munich crisis, emphasizing the urgent need to build American defenses and impressing the president sufficiently for him to ask Baruch to brief the press.[8]

Whatever the extent of Roosevelt's previous concern, Bullitt's visit triggered a pronounced burst of presidential activity focused on air power.[9] It began with a press conference at which Roosevelt announced

[6] Bullitt to Hull, Oct. 3, 1938, *FRUS*, 1938, 1:712.

[7] "Now also very, very much in this room, Ambassador Bullitt comes back and he says the thing to do is to help France and England if she [*sic*] wishes to build plants in Montreal across from Niagara Falls across from Detroit, to produce a thousand planes a month." "Morgenthau Diary," Oct. 20, 1938, 146:288–89.

[8] For an account of Baruch's remarks to the press. See The *New York Times*, Oct. 14, 1938. Others had been thinking about the implications for the United States of the importance of air power at this time as well. See "Memorandum to the Military Attache, Berlin, Germany, October 7, 1938," "Memorandum from the Military Attache, Berlin, Germany, November 6, 1938," and "Johnson to Roosevelt, December 8, 1939," transmitting these two communications, PSF, Subject File, Box 116, Aviation—folder I. See also "Arnold to Lindbergh, October 8, 1938," Arnold Papers, container 16, Lindbergh folder, LC.

[9] According to Watson, Bullitt conveyed the French view that air power had been the source of Hitler's success and that the only way to prevent such victories in the future was "the development of American airplane production for Anglo-French purchase." Watson, *Challenge*, 132. Watson's source is General James H. Burns, who at the time was the executive officer of the assistant secretary of war, Louis Johnson, and was a participant in many of the conferences that took place subsequently. Watson's version of the meeting between Roosevelt and Bullitt has been accepted by most other analysts. See, for example, Bullitt, *For the President*, 302; Cole, *Roosevelt*, 302; and Pogue, *Marshall*, 1:322.

that he had "sat up last night hearing the European side of things from Ambassador Bullitt" and that "new developments in national defense require . . . a complete restudy of American national defense." While not specifically mentioning planes, Roosevelt left his audience with the "inescapable" impression "that he had in mind much heavier expenditures for both the army and the navy than heretofore indicated."[10] He also took pains to convey the impression that since a reevaluation of the American defense posture had only just begun, no conclusions about future requirements could yet be drawn.

Roosevelt's actions, however, suggest that he at least was quite clear about what was needed. On the very day he spoke to the press, he took several steps toward implementing a policy along the lines Bullitt had suggested. He raised the question of expanding airplane production with Assistant Secretary of War Johnson, and apparently approved Jean Monnet's impending mission "to study how the American aircraft industry could best serve France's need."[11] Roosevelt also spoke to the secretary of the treasury about financing his new policy, demonstrating in the process that he was contemplating an amount of money far exceeding anything previously imagined, particularly for airplanes.[12] As a consequence of Bullitt's report, "Roosevelt became convinced for the first time that American airplane production should be greatly stimulated with all possible speed," with the goal of creating "airplane production facilities whose output would go to Britain and France, enabling them to build up aerial fleets that might overawe Hitler or that, if war should come, could even help to defeat Hitler without American armed intervention."[13]

This interpretation is amply supported by the second event shaping Roosevelt's policy response to the Munich crisis—the series of meetings at Hyde Park. The president left Washington for Hyde Park on Sunday, October 16, and was joined on the train by his old friend Arthur Murray,

[10] Press Conference no. 491, Oct. 14, 1938, *Complete Presidential Press Conferences* 12: 155–59; *New York Times*, Oct. 15, 1938. Both Dallek, *Franklin D. Roosevelt*, 172, and Haight, *American Aid*, 27, cite these sources as evidence that Roosevelt said he would probably ask Congress for an additional $500 million in defense funds. In fact, this figure is mentioned in neither, and both show clearly that Roosevelt resisted all efforts to get him to commit to a figure.

[11] Ibid., 27, 48; and Dallek, *Franklin D. Roosevelt*, 172. See also Alsop and Kintner, *American White Paper*, 14. While Haight documents the moves of Assistant Secretary Johnson, he offers no evidence for his assertion that Roosevelt approved Monnet's mission. However, since Monnet did in fact go to Hyde Park to meet with Roosevelt on October 19, it is likely that Haight is correct on this point. Dallek's account relies on Haight.

[12] As Morgenthau recalled on October 20, "His original proposition to me was 500 million for Hopkins for the real needy, three billion dollars for airplanes, and a two billion dollar national defense tax. That was the original proposal Friday morning [Oct. 14]." "Morgenthau Diary, Oct. 20, 1938, 146:279.

[13] Watson, *Chief of Staff*, 132–33.

whose visit had been planned for some time. Bullitt and Morgenthau arrived the same day, and the Frenchman, Jean Monnet, came up on the nineteenth, by which time Harry Hopkins had also arrived. This guest list alone provides considerable insight into Roosevelt's concerns during this critical five day period. Having decided to respond to the German threat by increasing the democracies' air strength, he was clearly intent on working out the implementation of this policy—how to build the planes, how to pay for them, and how to get them into the hands of the British and French.[14]

On October 18, Roosevelt informed Morgenthau of the defense measures he was contemplating. As Morgenthau told his staff on returning from Hyde Park, the president was focused primarily on airplanes: "He is thinking in terms of our producing 15,000 airplanes a year for this country; give private industry 3,000 and we'll produce 12,000. He's thinking in terms of three shifts. . . .[and] eight plants located around the United States." Roosevelt wanted to raise airplane production drastically (from five to fifty planes a day), and to acquire one thousand antiaircraft guns.[15]

However, the President had more in mind in bringing the secretary of the treasury to Hyde Park than briefing him on the new defense program. In fact, Morgenthau and Hopkins were there to provide Roosevelt with ideas about financing that program and producing the aircraft he desired, and he had several extended sessions with both of them concerning these subjects. Hopkins was uniformly optimistic about building the required number of plants. Moreover, he saw the defense buildup as an opportunity to put people to work, both in the construction of the plants and in their later operation. Morgenthau, on the other hand, initially found the discussions somewhat frustrating and was particularly upset by the president's approach to financing. Roosevelt, he complained, woefully underestimated the costs of producing airplanes ($25,000 per plane as against the Treasury's figure of $100,000). Moreover, his approach seemed to Morgenthau unsystematic, even cavalier: "The President just takes a piece of paper like this, works it out on there and says, 'That's what we're

---

[14] Fortunately, an unusually rich variety of sources detailing the events of this week is available. See "Morgenthau Diary," Oct. 20, 1938, 146: 279–94 and Oct. 24, 1938, 147:185, 39–44; Elibank, "Franklin Roosevelt"; Cole, *Roosevelt*, 301–2; Divine, *Causes and Consequences*, 87–97; and Haight, *American Aid*, 25–33, and "Roosevelt as Friend of France." Haight bases his account on an interview with Monnet and on the Elibank papers, as well as on these other sources.

[15] Morgenthau also reported that the army and navy knew nothing of these plans, which is easy to believe considering the small part their needs played in the president's plans. Roosevelt intended to allocate to the navy only two or three hundred of the planes he wished to produce—and precious little else. "As far as the Navy is concerned, [the President] said they've got enough." Morgenthau Diary," Oct. 20, 1938, 146:283.

going to do.' Hopkins says, 'Well, I can do that.' . . . The thing is all in the air. When I talked to the President about taxes, he didn't seem interested." Despite these frictions, Morgenthau, Hopkins, and Roosevelt managed in a relatively short time to thrash out a plan. As the secretary graphically recounted how the final agreement was reached,

> I seldom travel so fast. I said a billion and a half for [Hopkins] and nothing for Ickes . . . plus 500 million for Agriculture gave us a total expenditure of seven and a half billion, and I said I recommended to the President he go before the country with a total expenditure of seven and a half billion, a five billion dollar tax program, or two and a half billion dollars deficit; that I could stand that; then that he should say to Congress, "If you want anything more above that for national defense, anything else, give me a tax." So I says, "Harry, will you take that?" . . . Harry says, "I'll be delighted to take that."

In the end, Morgenthau was left with a sense of optimism about finding a way to carry out Roosevelt's new program: "I'm all bucked up over this thing, because I think that [it] can be done and done right; I think he can go to the country with it, . . . raise the taxes, and . . . instead of having a four billion dollar deficit there's a chance of cutting it down maybe to two."

Morgenthau's satisfaction also came from his belief that expanded air power would be used for continental and hemisphere defense.[16] Roosevelt's objective in sponsoring the defense buildup, however, was more complex than the secretary imagined. In fact, he was determined to use it primarily to strengthen the European democracies, an aim suggested not only by the presence at Hyde Park of the main proponent of such a strategy, Ambassador Bullitt, but also that of Monnet, who had come to the United States as the emissary of Daladier.

Morgenthau was aware of Monnet's mission, Bullitt's advocacy of it, and Roosevelt's support for it.[17] The secretary believed, however, that

[16] "I'm tickled to death the President is thinking of making this country so strong that nobody can attack us. . . . The other thing he said is that we want enough planes to take care of the whole South American continent too, to be able to supply them with as many planes as they need." Ibid., 279–94; see also Haight, *American Aid*, 29–30.

[17]
Monnet was sent over here by Daladier and the Minister for Air of France with the idea that he could organize a corporation to build aeroplanes in Canada for France. . . . Bullitt told me that the President had been most frank with Monnet; that he had drawn a map and shown him just where outside of Montreal this plant should be located; had even told Monnet how many planes the English had built and how many the French had built in their respective countries, and that they should build a plant in Canada which would produce 1700 planes on an 8-hour shift and 5,000 planes on a 3-hour shift.

"Morgenthau Diary," Oct. 24, 1938, 147:185. This account was confirmed by Monnet. Haight, *American Aid*, 32.

the desire to expedite Monnet's plans marked the limits of that support. In fact, Roosevelt's objectives, like Monnet's instructions, were considerably broader, encompassing a level of cooperation far beyond building plants in Canada.[18] As his talks with Murray make abundantly clear, Roosevelt intended nothing less than backing the democracies with the full industrial potential of the United States.[19] In Murray's words,

> The President asked me, on my return to London, to convey . . . to the Prime Minister . . . an assurance—in the event of hostilities and the United States being neutral—of his desire to help in every way in his power. . . . He said he wished the Prime Minister to feel that he had, in so far as he, the President, was able to achieve it, "the industrial resources of the American nation behind him in the event of war with the dictatorships."

Roosevelt was particularly concerned with air power, and desired to ensure the democracies' command of an "overwhelming superiority." Quoting statistics about relative productive capability, he declared

> that his object would be—in the event of Great Britain being at war with the dictatorships, and the United States not being engaged—to do his best to provide partly-finished basic materials, which did not come within the Neutrality law, for an extra 20,000 to 30,000 'planes, to give the necessary overwhelming superiority over Germany and Italy.

After spelling out the precise nature of the materials he had in mind and expressing the hope that British and Canadian plants would eventually have the capacity to handle such materials, Roosevelt "said that the question of transporting the 'basic materials' across the Atlantic would also have to be considered." As a final gesture to the British, the president told Murray that he might assure the prime minister that "Great Britain could rely upon obtaining raw materials from the democracies of the world," adding that while his other assurances had to be kept secret, Chamberlain was free to publicize this one.[20]

When Murray and Roosevelt spoke again on October 23 the subject was Canada. The president proposed to appoint one of the assistant

[18] Monnet was charged principally with establishing "the possibility for manufacture in the United States of a maximum number of military planes." Ibid., 25.

[19] Roosevelt spoke with Murray at Hyde Park on October 21 and October 23. An account of both conversations is in Elibank, "Franklin Roosevelt," which is based on Murray's contemporary notes and two letters he wrote to the president reporting on the discharge of his commissions. "Arthur Murray, Ottawa, to Roosevelt, October 30, 1938," and "Arthur Murray, London, to Roosevelt, December 15, 1938," Schewe, 8: no.s 1377, 1481. See also Haight, *American Aid*, 30–31; and Cole, *Roosevelt*, 301.

[20] Elibank, "Franklin Roosevelt," 365–66. Roosevelt's statement concerning raw materials was omitted from this article, but Elibank referred to it in his December 15 letter, and according to Haight it is contained in the original copy of his contemporary notes. Schewe, 8: no. 1481; *American Aid*, 31, n. 18.

chiefs of the Bureau of Procurement as a liaison officer for his airplane program. The "most important object" of this liaison was to make it "possible for information as regards design, engines, and other aspects of aeroplane manufacture and programme, to pass confidentially between the United States, Canadian and British Governments, to the extent that each thought fit. Existing official channels . . . should not . . . be used for this purpose."[21]

Roosevelt's talks with Murray and Monnet make it abundantly clear that his primary concern was aiding the democracies and convey his determination that the outbreak of war should not put an end to his ability to do so. Contrary to his subsequent statement to Alsop and Kinter, however, this concern did not manifest itself in an effort to revise the Neutrality Acts. Rather, the whole thrust of his strategy was toward circumventing them.[22] In the immediate aftermath of the Munich crisis, neutrality revision apparently played no part in Roosevelt's plans to aid the democracies.[23]

The initial challenge to Roosevelt's post-Munich policy of assisting the democracies with planes came from the secretary of the treasury. Although unaware of the full scope of Roosevelt's plans, Morgenthau was uneasy about even the narrower objective of helping the French build airplane factories in Canada. Indeed, the secretary had expressed his reservations at Hyde Park, presenting Roosevelt on October 18 with a long memorandum arguing against American financing and concluding that building plants in Canada would be unnecessary and unwise. Morgenthau himself was "one hundred percent opposed to our doing anything."[24]

Roosevelt responded by calling Morgenthau in Washington on October 21 to tell him that his fears were groundless and ask for his help: "[The] President . . . told me that he had this talk with Monnet and Bullitt and that my particular worry that the French could not supply the

[21] Elibank, "Franklin Roosevelt," 364–65"; Haight, *American Aid*, 31.

[22] In his December 15 letter, Murray spoke of having communicated to Chamberlain "what was in your mind as to methods, outwith [sic] the Neutrality Law, for assisting towards superiority." Schewe, 8: no. 1481.

[23] Thus, Haight's inference that a State Department meeting about amending the Neutrality Act that took place on October 18 was at the behest of the president may be in error. Haight, *American Aid*, 27. Haight's source for this meeting is Hooker, *Moffat Papers*, 228 n. 70.

[24] "Memorandum dictated by Morgenthau, October 24, 1938," and "Memorandum from Mr. White to Secretary Morgenthau, October 18, 1938," "Morgenthau Diary," 147:185, 39–44; "Meeting October 20, 1938," ibid., 289–90. On the day after he saw the president, Morgenthau told Bullitt that he thought the scheme for vastly increased production of airplanes was "just cockeyed," and that he could not go along with it. Bullitt, Morgenthau noted, was "furious." Ibid., 291. See also Haight, *American Aid*, 29.

foreign exchange was nothing and that that had been taken care of and that he would like me to see these people."[25] This Morgenthau did on October 22, and although he voiced his reservations about the French capacity to pay for plant construction in Canada, he ended by formulating a plan based on the forced return of flight capital that would enable the French to do just that. Bullitt immediately labeled this idea "an absolute stroke of genius," and both he and Monnet appeared to be "simply beside themselves with joy," which may have contributed to the fact that thereafter Morgenthau seemed much mollified. Whatever the reason, from this point forward the secretary was willing to work closely with Monnet, and Bullitt was able to report with some satisfaction to Daladier on October 25 that "Monnet has been received by President Roosevelt and Secretary Morgenthau, who offered complete and close cooperation in studying the program of which we spoke in Paris."[26]

The first challenge to the President's policy of aiding the allies was thus overcome with little difficulty. The second, based on the military's instinctive suspicion of a defense plan that featured a massive buildup of planes and little else, was not so easily dispatched. Again Morgenthau was involved. On returning to Washington from Hyde Park, the secretary spoke about the president's plans with the Army Chief of Staff, who gave him with new grounds for concern. As Morgenthau told his staff on October 20,

> General Craig . . . is having lunch with me today, and I talked to him and he's terribly excited because he knows that what is being told the President is impossible. . . . Craig said last night . . . "What are we going to do with fifteen thousand planes?" . . . "Who you going to fight, what you going to do with them, with three thousand miles of ocean?"[27]

Impressed by the general's objections, Morgenthau determined to get at the truth by "going to school" with Generals Craig and Arnold to discover the basis for their concern.[28]

At this point Morgenthau attributed the differences between Roosevelt and the military primarily to misinformation.[29] He did not imagine that

[25] "Memorandum dictated by Morgenthau, October 24, 1938," 185. As Haight notes, Roosevelt's conversations with Murray also indicate that he "was apparently little affected by Secrtary Morgenthau's reaction against aiding the European democracies." *American Aid*, 30.

[26] "Memorandum dictated by Morgenthau, October 24, 1938," 187. See also Haight, *American Aid*, 33–38. For Monnet's subsequent efforts on his arrival home, see ibid., 38–40.

[27] "Morgenthau Diary," Oct. 20, 1938, 146:281–82.

[28] Ibid., 282–83, 288.

[29] As he told his staff, "We don't want the President to make a mistake. . . . And somebody has given the President a lot of misinformation . . .; he's just all wet on it." Ibid., 291, 294.

the real reason for the disparity of views was that Roosevelt's planning was driven by a different agenda altogether. The military, however, had begun to suspect just that, launching their effort to implement Roosevelt's defense expansion while he was still at Hyde Park.

Although the air force initially set its sights on many fewer aircraft than Roosevelt had in mind, it was soon engaged in upward revision. By October 25 the budget estimate for new planes submitted to the assistant secretary of war had risen from one thousand to two thousand five hundred.[30] As Watson points out, these revisions reflected considerable uncertainty and confusion, particularly as to how the funds should be allocated between ground forces and the air corps. However, the chief of staff at least was determined that a balance be maintained and undertook "to convince the Secretary, the Assistant Secretary, and the President's other advisers that the balanced force was a prime desideratum."[31]

Despite this opposition, Roosevelt persisted in his chosen course, and on October 25 appointed a committee composed of Assistant Secretary of War Johnson, Assistant Secretary of the Navy Edison, and Deputy Administrator of the Works Progress Administration Aubrey Williams, "to report steps necessary to increase military aircraft production."[32] He also continued to prod those at higher levels to move forward with implementing his policies. Thus, on November 12 (at 5 p.m. on a Saturday), he called Morgenthau, Hopkins, and Johnson to the White House to "talk . . . about the aviation program." Johnson reported that private industry could build eleven thousand planes "over and above commercial needs," and according to Morgenthau, the president planned to construct eight to ten plants that could produce ten thousand planes over two years (although initially putting only two into operation). This figure, the secretary felt, reflected a step toward realism on Roosevelt's part.[33]

[30] Watson, *Chief of Staff*, 134–35. For an account of various planning activities between October 19 and 25, see ibid., 134–36. On November 11, General Arnold again raised the goal to seven thousand planes. Ibid., 136; Haight, *American Aid*, 54.

[31] See his October 24, 1938, statement to the Bureau. Watson, *Chief of Staff*, 135; Haight, *American Aid*, 50. General Marshall took a similar position. Ibid., 51.

[32] The committee reported back on October 28, recommending "expansion of the commercial aircraft industry within two years from a current capacity of 2,600 to one of 15,000 planes a year, and for the creation within three years of government-built plants which would produce an additional 16,000 planes a year." Watson, *Chief of Staff*, 136. See also Haight, *American Aid*, 53. In the interim, on October 26, Roosevelt spoke publicly about the necessity "of increasing our own military and naval establishments," declaring that the United States "must be prepared to meet with success any application of force against us." "Radio Address to the Herald-Tribune Forum," *PPA* 7:565. See also Hull, *Memoirs*, 1:597.

[33] "In the month or so that the President has been discussing this thing, he is getting more and more practical about it, and, as Louis Johnson said, he has gone from 40,000 planes a year down to 10,000 planes in two years. So I think we have made some progress.

Roosevelt was also interested in exploring the financing of his expanded program, though Morgenthau found the discussion frustrating because he refused to commit himself to a special defense tax. The secretary was also troubled that Roosevelt seemed to be in such a hurry to implement his scheme and came away with the "feeling that the President was rushing the whole thing terribly and really wasn't interested in giving it anything like the time or thought it deserved." Apparently Roosevelt too was dissatisfied with the way things were going because he arranged another meeting for Monday, November 14. Morgenthau thought that its subject would be "method of procurement and what kind of law we need in order to operate [his] program."[34] Roosevelt, however, had in mind a far more ambitious agenda. In fact, he was moving even more rapidly than Morgenthau suspected to establish, once and for all, his post-Munich policy of aiding the democracies with air power.

As in the Hyde Park meetings, Roosevelt called key members of his administration together on November 14 neither to solicit their views about the significance of the Munich crisis nor to receive their recommendations about policies to follow in its wake. Rather, this distinguished group had been gathered solely to receive the benefit of *his* thinking and suggest ways of implementing the measures upon which he had already decided.[35] Roosevelt set forth a definitive statement of his policies, linked explicitly to his diagnosis of the German threat to American security, in a way that left no room for doubt that aid to the democracies was the cornerstone of his post-Munich policy.

After briefly reviewing the state of the air forces in being and the productive capacities of the United States, Great Britain, France, Germany, and Italy, Roosevelt set the tone for the gathering by declaring that as a consequence of technological advances in aviation and the "recrudescence of German power at Munich," the United States now faced the threat of attack in both the Northern and Southern Hemispheres. From this he concluded that America would require a "huge air force so that we did not need to have a huge army to follow that air force. . . . Sending

---

Morgenthau, Presidential Diary, Nov. 13, 1938, 1:0052–55. See also Haight, *American Aid*, 55.

[34] Morgenthau, Presidential Diary, Nov. 13, 1938, 1:0055.

[35] As Watson observed, "The President did most of the speaking, as if his mind had been made up by earlier discussion and appraisal." Watson, *Chief of Staff*, 137. In addition to the president, those present on this occasion were Morgenthau, Hopkins, Solicitor General Robert Jackson, Johnson (at that time acting secretary of war), General Counsel of the Treasury Herman Oliphant, Chief of Staff of the Army General Malin Craig, Deputy Chief of Staff George C. Marshall, General Arnold, Colonel Burns, Executive Assistant to Johnson, and the president's naval and military aides. Oliphant, "Meeting," 338. See also Arnold, "Memorandum," 1.

a large army abroad was undesirable and politically out of the question."
Building this air force was an immediate necessity because, under modern
conditions, there would be no such grace period as occurred in World
War I. Hence, "We must have resources, plans and equipment for putting
a large number of planes into actual operation on short notice."[36]

Roosevelt was adamant that air power alone would suffice to meet the
challenge, pointing out that "our only important need was anti-aircraft
equipment of the mobile sort and an abundance of aeroplanes. He said
there was little need of more battleships, forts, military posts and ammu-
nitions." Indeed, General Arnold drew the conclusion that "the President
did not seem to want an American air force at all, feeling that new bar-
racks in Wyoming 'would not scare Hitler'; what he wanted was
'airplanes—now—and lots of them.'"[37]

Roosevelt had two aims in proposing this expansion of air power. The
first was to protect the Western Hemisphere against attack,[38] the second
to deter Hitler, which he intended to accomplish principally by aiding the
European democracies. Thus, he declared: "When I write to foreign
countries I must have something to back up my words. Had we had this
summer 5000 planes and the capacity immediately to produce 10000 per
year, even though I might have had to ask Congress for authority to sell
or lend them to the countries in Europe, Hitler would not have dared to
take the stand he did."[39]

That aiding the democracies was Roosevelt's real objective explains his
neglect of all the components of an air force save the planes themselves.[40]
According to General Marshall's later recollection, "the President was all
for the increase in the air but he wasn't much for getting the men to man
the airships nor for the munitions and things that they required. He was
principally thinking at that time of getting airships for England and for
France." As Major Burns concluded, Roosevelt intended this aid to enable the democracies "to build up aerial fleets that might overawe Hitler

---

[36] Oliphant, "Meeting," 338. See also Arnold, "Memorandum," 1.

[37] Oliphant, "Meeting," 338. Arnold is quoted in William R. Emerson, "Franklin Roosevelt as Commander-in-Chief in World War II," *Military Affairs* 22 (1958):185, but see
also Arnold, *Global Mission*, 177, and "Memorandum," 1; and Watson, *Chief of Staff*,
138.

[38] Arnold, "Memorandum," 1. See also Pogue, *Marshall*, 1:323; Haight, *American Aid*,
58–59.

[39] Oliphant, "Meeting," 338. Note Roosevelt's casual use of the word "lend" in connection with supplying arms to the European democracies. This appears to be the debut of the
idea that surfaced dramatically, and apparently out of the blue, in December 1940 as Lend
Lease. Oliphant's account has been corroborated by other participants in the November 14
conference.

[40] Watson, *Chief of Staff*, 132–33.

or . . . , if war should come, . . . even help to defeat Hitler without American armed intervention."[41]

With respect to the number of planes, Roosevelt was thinking of building ten thousand as soon as possible and acquiring a capacity to build an additional ten thousand a year. In order to end up with the desired figure, however, he planned to inflate his request to Congress. As Arnold noted, "He figured that if he asked Congress for 20,000 airplanes, with a productive capacity of about 24,000, he would probably get an airplane strength of 10,000, with a productive capacity of about 10,000."[42]

Following Roosevelt's dramatic presentation, discussion turned to the details of financing, procurement, plant construction, and informing the public. Again, the president did more instructing than consulting. He was clearly well prepared and had an impressive command of even quite technical detail. In the matter of plant construction, Roosevelt advanced a plan similar to the one he had discussed with Morgenthau, Hopkins, and Johnson on November 12.[43] Although he disagreed initially with the other participants about the cost of building these plants, preferring a much lower figure, he eventually acceded to the general view.[44] As to financing the buildup, Roosevelt decided to allow the War and Navy

---

[41] Pogue, *Marshall*, 323; Watson, *Chief of Staff*, 138. That Roosevelt's plan included few planes for the navy also suggests that the new aircraft were intended primarily for use by the European democracies, since naval aircraft would presumably have played a crucial part in any serious defense of the Western Hemisphere. Interestingly enough, General Arnold's record of this meeting does not emphasize aid to Britain and France as a major aim of the expanded air force, seeing it as intended to deter an attack on the Northern and Southern Hemispheres. Since Oliphant, Marshall, and Burns had no problem detecting the President's purpose, it is possible that Arnold failed to pick it up because he had some difficulty perceiving that "his" planes were intended for the air forces of other countries. As the remarks quoted earlier demonstrate, the general soon got the point.

[42] Arnold, "Memorandum," 1. Oliphant's understanding of these figures was slightly different. According to his notes, "the discussion ended with agreement that we should have 10,000 with the capacity to produce 20,000 per year and, for political reasons, should ask Congress for 12,000 and 24,000 respectively." Oliphant, "Meeting," 339. See also Haight, *American Aid*, 56–57; and Watson, *Chief of Staff*, 137.

[43] Declaring his objective to be "a 2 year program, wherein we would get 8,000 airplanes from commercial plants, the balance from government owned plants. . . . He stated that it was desirable to bring into being plants sufficient to bring our total productive capacity up to 20,000 a year but they would not all be operated." Arnold, "Memorandum," 1–2; Oliphant, "Meeting," 339. Oliphant gives the total number of plants which the president intended to build as seven.

[44] "The President started with a figure as low as $1,000,000 and finally agreed to discuss the problem on the basis that the 7 plants would cost $70,000,000. He pointed out that Hopkins could build these plants without cost to the Treasury because it would be work relief which otherwise would have to be provided in any case." Ibid.; see also Arnold, "Memorandum," 2.

Departments to defend their current budgets and present a separate supplementary budget.

In line with his usual preference, the secretary of the treasury advocated putting "the whole program . . . before the country with all of its financial implications early in the session."[45] The available accounts do not give Roosevelt's response. However, earlier in the meeting he expressed reservations about the involvement of Congress, raising "the question as to how much he would be justified in doing on the program before Congress had a chance to act on it." With respect to the issue of informing the public, on the other hand, he seemed almost eager, declaring that he "must begin to lay the matter before the country."[46]

Finally, there can be no doubt that Roosevelt was intent on having his program implemented without delay, stating "that he would like to have a plan drawn up at once showing how much of this could be started now and outlining the steps to be taken to carry the thing through to its determination." Assistant Secretary Johnson, at least, seemed anxious to accommodate him, declaring that he could have the plan by November 19.[47]

Clearly, then, there was a distinct hierarchy among the policies Roosevelt announced on November 14. Although national and hemisphere defense were mentioned, they were not his primary objective; deterring Hitler was. Rearmament, far from being an end in itself, was largely intended to aid the democracies in achieving that goal.[48] Indeed, Roosevelt seemed to believe that deterrence might eliminate the need for a substantial defense effort altogether.[49] As many of those present surmised, the airplanes that were to be the main instrument of deterrence were not intended primarily for use by the United States itself. Rather, deterrence was to be accomplished by putting the planes in the hands of Britain and France. Thus, when Roosevelt spoke of needing planes to back up his words to Hitler, he referred to having the ability "sell or lend them to the countries in Europe." *This* was the capability he believed would have deterred Hitler during the Munich crisis.[50]

With respect to the broader range of foreign-policy strategies, Roosevelt also had a definite hierarchy in mind, and it was not the one he had

[45] Ibid.; Oliphant, "Meeting," 341.

[46] Ibid., 340–41.

[47] Arnold, "Memorandum," 3.

[48] As Emerson observes, "military strength was not Roosevelt's sole—or even his major—aim at the time. From the beginning of the rearmament program, Roosevelt sought, not rearmament, but the appearance of rearmament. He was concerned with the 'show-window,' not the 'stockroom.'" Emerson, "Roosevelt as Commander-in-Chief," 187.

[49] See Greenfield, *American Strategy*, 54.

[50] Oliphant, "Meeting," 338. See also Emerson, "Roosevelt as Commander-in-Chief," 187.

laid out for Farley and Alsop and Kintner. In fact, there is no evidence whatever to support his statements implying that in the immediate aftermath of the Munich crisis he was equally interested in hemisphere defense, neutrality revision, and other measures short of war. These were either subsidiary or subordinate to the goal of aiding the democracies and actually received scant attention. For example, his November 14 remarks indicating concern about the security of South America did not translate directly into a coherent policy of hemisphere defense. Such attention as he accorded hemisphere defense came considerably later.[51] The same can be said of the group of diplomatic and economic policies, somewhat loosely grouped together under the heading of "measures short of war," designed to demonstrate America's seriousness in supporting the democracies.[52] Apart from approving the decision to recall the American ambassador after the Kristallnacht violence, Roosevelt spent little time on such measures during the five week period before the November 14 meeting.[53]

Somewhat more surprisingly, Roosevelt also had little interest in neutrality revision. At the Hyde Park meetings he responded to concern about the impact of the neutrality laws on his ability to provide planes to the democracies with a scheme for circumventing, rather than repealing, them; the subject was not even mentioned at the November 14 conference.[54]

[51] The only references to hemisphere defense at the November 14 meeting occurred at the outset, when Roosevelt included the Southern Hemisphere with the Northern as an area that would need protection against attack, and at the very end, when "The President . . . disclosed the plans, next summer, for naval manoeuvers with Army observers, basing on Trinidad and working on the problem of keeping off an European fleet at a point well out in the Atlantic." Oliphant, "Meeting," 342; Arnold, "Memorandum," 1.

[52] Alsop and Kintner, *American White Paper*, 18. In his interview with these reporters, Roosevelt called using "our diplomatic influence to hamper the aggressors" one of his three principal post-Munich policies. Interview with Franklin Roosevelt, Dec. 23, 1939, Alsop papers.

[53] Divine, *Reluctant Belligerent*, 55; Langer and Gleason, *Challenge*, 36; Dallek, *Franklin D. Roosevelt*, 167–68. The principal supporter of measures short of war was Morgenthau, who, in his October 17 letter to the president, advocated that the United States "initiate effective steps to stop aggression by peaceful means." Hull, however, objected in early November to countervailing duties because they would be subject to "political interpretations," and the president declined to overrule him. As a consequence, by the time the Germans took over Czechoslovakia in March 1939, nothing had been done about instituting this policy. Morgenthau, "Letter to the President, October 17, 1938," Schewe, 7: no. 1358; Blum, *Morgenthau Diaries* 2:79–81. MacDonald argues that Roosevelt himself was unenthusiastic about Morgenthau's plans for economic action because "he needed support for his rearmament plans and dared not couple rearmament with offensive actions against Germany." Callum A. MacDonald, *The United States, Britain and Appeasement, 1936–1939* (London: Macmillan, 1981), 117, 120.

[54] That Roosevelt was not thinking seriously about neutrality revision at this time is also

An account of the policy process from October 8 to November 14, then, leaves little room for doubt that Roosevelt's primary response to the Munich crisis was aiding the European democracies with airplanes or that the other policies that were later prominently mentioned were secondary to that aim. In particular, the record of the Hyde Park meetings substantiates what was suspected by most of the participants at the November 14 conference: the president wanted to build airplanes; he meant them to be used as a threat to deter to Hitler; and he did not intend that threat to be delivered directly by the United States.

DOMESTIC CHALLENGES: THE NATURE AND PURPOSE OF REARMAMENT, NOVEMBER 14, 1938–MARCH 15, 1939

This program was immediately challenged in both the War Department and Congress, and Roosevelt's response again shows the depth of his commitment both to planes and to getting them to the democracies. As before, he was willing to make a fight for one thing and one thing only, planes for Britain and France.[55] As well as confirming the original policy hierarchy, moreover, these domestic challenges forced Roosevelt to explain his program to an ever-widening audience, first within the executive branch, then to the Congress and the public at large. Not wishing to publicize aid to the democracies, he disliked the confrontation with Congress intensely, but was willing to engage in it when his chosen policy was threatened. Caution may have induced Roosevelt to try to obscure his real purpose; it did not cause him to abandon it.

The initial challenge to Roosevelt's announced program came from the War Department and was directed at both its emphasis on building planes and using them to help the democracies. With respect to the former, the military objected that the president's policy would create an imbalance in the armed forces as a whole as well as within the air force itself. Problems in this quarter surfaced as early as the November 14 meeting, as General Marshall voiced his reservations about Roosevelt's

---

shown by his choice of visitors at Hyde Park. Having a clear idea of what he wanted to accomplish, he brought with him only those who could be helpful to him in working it out: Morgenthau and Hopkins to finance his military expansion and build plants, and Bullitt and Monnet to plan for getting the arms to the democracies. On neither that occasion nor the November 14 meeting did Roosevelt invite the representatives of the State Department who would have had to play a major role in securing repeal of the neutrality laws.

[55] "Rightly or wrongly, [Roosevelt] was convinced that aircraft held the key to the diplomatic situation in Europe and the depth of his belief was shown by his willingness in 1939 and 1940 to buck isolationist sentiment on this point almost alone. 'Planes—now—and lots of them' remained his constant theme." Emerson, "Franklin Roosevelt," 186.

plan. The other participants were apparently more reticent.[56] They did not remain so for long.

Acting Secretary of War Johnson fired the opening salvo for balanced forces, directing the chief of staff on November 15 to prepare a detailed budget for a two-year period. Johnson's instructions went considerably beyond the " 'airplanes-only' program which the President had originally specified. . . . The objectives were not only 10,000 planes but immediate supplies for the Protective Mobilization Plan force and also industrial preparedness for a much larger eventual force." Also ignored was Roosevelt's $500 million spending limitation.[57]

The chief of staff's response on December 17 indicated a desire for balance in both the air force and the army itself and pulled no punches in stating the army's reservations about the president's program.[58] Citing the increasing urgency of American military obligations not only in the United States but in the entire Western Hemisphere and the fact that the army was too weak to meet them, it outlined a host of requirements for obtaining "a balanced military force that could command respect."[59]

When Roosevelt became aware of this activity, he called another meeting in late December to deal with the military's demands. On this occasion, he "informed them sharply that . . . it was extremely doubtful whether he could ask Congress for more than $500,000,000 in new armament money for the coming fiscal year: he had stated his desire to spend that upon the production of Army-type airplanes . . . and he was being offered everything except airplanes."[60] There followed "a careful and thorough discussion of the armed forces' low state and, more particularly, of the futility of producing planes over a long period without

[56] Pogue, *Marshall*, 1:323. General Arnold does not mention any opposition. Oliphant's memo says only that Roosevelt "asked the Army and Navy men how many planes they thought we needed. Obviously they had not been thinking in terms of figures as large as the President had in mind." Oliphant, "Meeting," 338.

[57] Watson, *Chief of Staff*, 139–40. See also Haight, *American Aid*, 59–60. At the same time, General Arnold began his struggle to obtain a balanced air force, demanding "not only planes but also productive capacity, pilots, mechanics, air bases, and an adequate training program." Ibid., 62–63.

[58] Watson, *Chief of Staff*, 140–41. According to Haight, this memorandum was intended to provide the rationale for a $2 billion rearmament proposal focused on balanced forces that was sent to the president by the chief of staff on December 1. After Roosevelt objected to this proposal on December 10, Johnson asked the chief of staff to send a justification of it to the White House. *American Aid*, 60–61.

[59] Watson, *Chief of Staff*, 141–42. As Watson points out, the navy had its own long list of needs. The Roosevelt Library contains the responses of the services to Roosevelt's November 14 requests, including the chief of staff's memo of December 1 and a navy report on establishing additional submarine, destroyer, mine, and naval bases. Folder 1, PSF, Subject, Box 116, Aviation, FDRL.

[60] Watson, *Chief of Staff*, 142–43.

producing trained pilots and crews and air bases at an appropriate pace."
Apparently impressed by these arguments, Roosevelt agreed to a new
division of the $500 million pie that left only $180 million for three
thousand "combat planes with which to impress Germany" ($200 mil-
lion would be allotted to nonair armaments and $120 million to air bases
and "other non-plane air items").[61] Subsequently, he attempted to stick
with this figure despite the air corps' insistence that a considerable portion of the funds for planes go to building trainers, not combat planes.
Although he apparently did not prevail in this either, Roosevelt continued to push for combat planes even after sending the supplementary ap-
propriations bill of $500 million to Congress on January 12.[62]

In his public statements, Roosevelt consistently played down the need
for a huge across-the-board rearmament effort, emphasizing instead the
desirability of selectivity and the need to concentrate on building airplanes. For example, he told the press on January 4, 1939, that he saw
"no reason at this time . . . why, since things are moving awfully fast in
the world, we should lay down an enormous five-year or ten-year program for national defense." A few days later, he used much of his January 12 message presenting the supplementary defense bill to Congress to
explain why the bulk of the funds ought to go toward building aircraft.[63]
Thus, although the determined opposition of the military ultimately
forced him to compromise on his airplane program, the fight he waged
for it shows the degree of his commitment.

Not only was Roosevelt determined to build airplanes, he was equally
resolved that a good proportion of them should go to the European democracies. This provoked the second round of military challenges to his
post-Munich policies, which began when Monnet returned from France
on December 16, 1938. He had been authorized to buy one thousand
planes, a mission that Roosevelt officially approved on December 17,
assigning Morgenthau to expedite it.[64] Morgenthau had his work cut out

---

[61] Ibid, 143. See also Haight, *American Aid*, 64–65; Dallek, *Franklin D. Roosevelt*,
173–74.

[62] On January 18, for example, he instructed Johnson to bring General Arnold to see
him, telling the assistant secretary that he was "not satisfied with the limit of 170,000,000
provided for airplanes themselves. This item should be increased and the other items reduced." Watson, *Chief of Staff*, 143; Haight, *American Aid*, 65; William Frye, *Marshall,
Citizen Soldier* (New York, Bobbs-Merrill, 1947), 254–55; Langer and Gleason, *Challenge*, 48; and *PL*, 2:854.

[63] Press conference, Jan. 4, 1939, *PPA*, 8:21; "Message of President Roosevelt to Congress, January 12, 1939," *Peace and War*, 451–54.

[64] "Morgenthau Diary," 172:12–15; Haight, *American Aid*, 70–71, and "Roosevelt as
Friend," 93. Fairly complete accounts of this aspect of the military's challenge can be found
in Haight, *American Aid*, 69–94, and "Roosevelt as Friend," 92–94; Blum, *Morgenthau
Diaries*, 2:64–70; Dallek, *Franklin D. Roosevelt*, 174–75; and Cole, *Roosevelt*, 302–3.

for him because, as the French soon discovered, no American planes met their standards. This led them to focus on three experimental planes not yet in production: the Curtiss P-40 fighter, the Martin 167 bomber, and the Douglas DB-7 bomber. Unfortunately, the air corps was bitterly opposed to foreign inspection or release of any of these planes.[65] Morgenthau did his best for the French, first convincing Roosevelt that they ought to be allowed to purchase the planes in question, telling him, "If your theory [is] that England and France are our first line of defence, then . . . let's either give them the good stuff or tell them to go home, but don't give some stuff which the minute it goes up in the air it will be shot down. No sense in selling them that which we know is out of date."[66]

As a result of this conversation, Roosevelt signed an order allowing the French to inspect and purchase American planes. He also insisted on secrecy and specified that the French orders not interfere with new American orders in the spring.[67] Again, the problem was the War Department, General Arnold in particular. In a conference with the Treasury on December 22, Arnold, while backing down on the P-40, refused on grounds of military secrecy to budge on the Douglas bomber.[68] Morgenthau, however, kept pushing, telling his staff on December 28: "The President of the United States says that we consider the Maginot line our first line of defense and for that reason he wants these people to have this thing. Those are my orders." Finally, on December 29 Secretary of War Woodring capitulated, agreeing that the French could see all the planes.[69]

Even this did not settle the question, however, because General Arnold still refused to let the French near the Douglas bomber. There matters remained until Bullitt returned to Washington on January 9, learned of Monnet's plight, and told the president. Roosevelt "expressed his astonishment that his intentions had been incompletely followed," and called Woodring, Craig, and Marshall to the White House on January 10. According to Marshall's account, Roosevelt told them that "the only check to a world war, which would be understood by Germany, would be the

---

[65] Haight, *American Aid*, 72–75.

[66] Blum, *Morgenthau Diaries*, 2:65.

[67] Morgenthau told the French that this was the president's desire. Ickes, however, reports a conversation between Welles, Woodring, Morgenthau, and the president after the Cabinet meeting of December 21 about the French proposal in which, "It was agreed that a plan should be worked out as a result of which France would be able to get these planes, even if this meant a postponement of our own buying program." Ickes, *Diary*, 2:531–32. "Morgenthau Diary," 172:12–16, 19, 24; Blum, *Morgenthau Diaries*, 2:65–66; Haight, *American Aid*, 75–77.

[68] Haight, *American Aid*, 77–81; Blum, *Morgenthau Diaries*, 2:66.

[69] "Morgenthau Diary," 172:71, 158:180–83; Blum, *Morgenthau Diaries*, 2:68; Haight, *American Aid*, 80–84.

creation of a great [French] air force and a powerful force in this country."[70]

Roosevelt also called a meeting on January 16 to make his wishes plain to his top civilian advisers, including Woodring, Johnson, and Edison. Morgenthau and Bullitt were also present. The president opened the meeting by stating "that he desired that every effort be made to give [the French] all available planes, equipment and motors to assist in building up their air forces." Bullitt then explained their need for the Douglas bomber, and Woodring objected on grounds of secrecy. Following a general discussion of "different types of planes and their availability," Johnson "categorically asked the President if he desired that the Douglas Light Bomber be released to the French Government, and . . . was informed that the President meant exactly that." According to the Treasury Department memorandum of the meeting, "The President made it perfectly plain throughout the discussion this morning that it was his wish and desire that every effort be made to expedite the procurement of any types of plane desired by the French Government."[71]

After the meeting, Morgenthau asked Roosevelt to put his order to release the plane in writing, and drafted letters to that effect to the secretaries of war, navy, and the treasury. These apparently did the trick, because on January 19 General Arnold gave orders for the French to inspect and fly the Douglas bomber.[72] Thus, the military's second challenge to Roosevelt's policies, unlike its first, ended in victory for the President. What is of greatest interest in both cases, however, is not the outcome of the struggle, but Roosevelt's behavior during it, which confirms his determination both to shape a rearmament program around building airplanes and to ensure that a good number of those planes would go to the democracies. Similarly, Roosevelt's response to the next challenge shows that his commitment went beyond a willingness to do battle within his own administration to acceptance of the need to fight isolationist sentiment, even at the risk of the public controversy he devoutly wished to avoid.

In late January 1939, Roosevelt was forced to defend his plan to both Congress and the public, something he neither expected nor desired to do. While he had agreed with Morgenthau at the end of December that it

[70] Ibid., 88–89.

[71] "Morgenthau Diary," 173:39–40; Blum, *Morgenthau Diaries*, 2:70; Haight, *American Aid*, 91–92.

[72] Perhaps because the language of the letters was unusually strong (according to Haight, they contained the phrase "you are directed" and implied that the secretaries had a "choice between compliance and resignation"), Roosevelt did not sign them until Bullitt interceded. Ibid., 92.

would be appropriate to end the secrecy surrounding the sale of planes to the French, Roosevelt never meant to expose the connection between rearmament and aiding the democracies.[73] On the contrary, he stressed rearmament partly as a way to mask his intention to help Britain and France, and his attempts to inform the public of his reaction to the Munich crisis were framed as general warnings about the potential threat from the dictators that included little or nothing about aiding the allies as a means of combating it.[74]

This strategy became unworkable on January 23, 1939, when a Douglas bomber crashed in California with an official of the French Air Ministry aboard. As a consequence, the American people discovered that foreigners were being given access to American planes and perhaps military secrets as well.[75] This revelation caused an outcry from congressional isolationists, who were upset both because they suspected a "secret alliance" between the United States and France and because they believed that French access to aviation secrets had been granted over the objections of the American military.[76] General Arnold encouraged this perception when he testified before the Senate Military Affairs Committee on January 25 that he had permitted the French to inspect and fly the Douglas bomber only "at the direction of the Treasury Department." As a result, "Feelings within the committee crescendoed. A full investigation was called for, and the major officials who had taken part in the French negotiations were ordered to appear within two days."[77]

Roosevelt was thus forced to defend his policy of aiding the democracies with planes. This he did, albeit reluctantly and at times with less than total candor, apparently motivated by his perception of the security interests at stake. For example, he told the Cabinet on January 27 that he had "private advices" that Hitler would make his next move in the west rather than the east, and expressed the view, in Ickes's words, that "if Hitler breaks loose, . . . and if he attains his objective, this country is

---

[73] As Ickes noted, "Heretofore, the Treasury has been working with the French Mission in confidence, but it was decided at Cabinet meeting [Dec. 28, 1938] that the negotiations should be brought into the open." *Diary* 2:542. Unfortunately, this had not yet been done by January 23 when matters were taken out of the hands of the administration by the events described below. See also Blum, *Morgenthau Diaries*, 2:68, 80; "Morgenthau Diary," 172:65–71; and Haight, *American Aid*, 81, 84–85.

[74] See, for example, Roosevelt's State of the Union Message, Jan. 4, 1939, *PPA*, 2:1–12.

[75] Langer and Gleason, *Challenge*, 48. For the circumstances surrounding the crash, see Haight, *American Aid*, 94–95, and "Roosevelt as Friend," 94–95. For a discussion of the political repercussions of the crash, see Eliot Janeway, *The Struggle for Survival* (New Haven: Yale University Press, 1951), 32–39.

[76] Langer and Gleason, *Challenge*, 49; Watson, *Chief of Staff*, 133; Haight, *American Aid*, 94–95.

[77] Ibid., 95. See also Blum, *Morgenthau Diaries* 2:71–72.

going to suffer tremendously."[78] At lunch with Ickes the following day, Roosevelt pursued these themes, emphasizing the urgency of stopping Hitler in Europe:

> He developed the theory that our first line of defense is really the small countries of Europe that have not yet been overwhelmed by the Nazis. He seriously thinks that if Hitler extends his power over these small countries and then uses the economic weapon that will be his, he will be striking a serious blow at us without ever a thought of trying to land a soldier on our shores. There is no doubt that the President is seriously concerned about the situation.

However concerned he may have been, Roosevelt was still firmly opposed sharing his fears with the American people. Responding to Ickes's assertion that it was "vitally important to educate our own people on the issues involved in this situation," Roosevelt said "it would be absolutely impossible for him or for me to go on the air and talk to the world as we were talking. The people simply would not believe him."[79] Indeed, in his first press conference after the French plane crash, he justified the sale of planes to France in terms of its potential for advancing the American rearmament program, saying nothing whatever about the advantages of aiding the democracies—an answer that was both disingenuous and misleading.[80]

Roosevelt's unwillingness to disclose the real reason for his desire to sell airplanes to the French did not mean that he was less determined to do so. In his press conference, apart from attempting to justify the sales, he defended the role played by the Treasury. Moreover, he told Morgenthau that in testifying at the Senate Military Committee's hearings he could say that he had acted on the president's authority. Later in the day,

---

[78] Roosevelt also expressed his disillusionment with the policies available to deal with the problem, doubting the relevance of economic measures such as the reciprocal trade agreements to "an emergency such as this" and voicing regret at the way the embargo had worked in the Spanish Civil War. Ickes, *Diary*, 2:568–69.

[79] Ibid., 571–72.

[80] Responding to a direct question about whether the government had "taken any steps to assist or facilitate France in buying planes in this country," Roosevelt said:

> As you put the question, no. The actual fact is a very simple one. . . . For our own program in the future it is very desirable that we facilitate the getting of new orders to start the airplane plants going. . . . The French Government did want planes and we told them there was no reason why they should not place orders for planes—in fact, it would be an excellent thing for them to do."

"Press Conference in the White House, January 27, 1939, 10:56 A.M.," Schewe VIII, 8: no. 1562. See also Langer and Gleason, *Challenge*, 49; Watson, *Chief of Staff*, 133; Blum, *Morgenthau Diaries* 2:73; Haight, *American Aid*, 96–97. The argument that foreign plane orders would increase American productive capacity had been used earlier in an attempt to get the military's acquiescence. Ibid., 79, 91.

Roosevelt instructed the secretary to continue assisting the French. According to Morgenthau, "the President said to proceed as before . . . to go right ahead with the French . . . and let them buy what they want."[81]

Morgenthau testified before the Senate Military Affairs Committee on January 27, arguing that French orders would ultimately help American productive capacity and telling the committee that Arnold himself had signed the order permitting the French to inspect the Douglas bomber.[82] The Senate isolationists, however, were not mollified—in large measure because the War Department failed to support Morgenthau's account. Rather, in the course of Woodring's testimony, its grave reservations about selling planes to the French became all too clear. Ignoring Morgenthau's argument that the French orders would pay the development costs of the plane and get the plants into production at no expense to the United States, Woodring "by implication . . . confirmed [Senator] Clark's objection, and Arnold's, that the French order would interfere with the Army's purchasing." In addition, General Craig, while approving the sale of some planes, also expressed concern about releasing military secrets.[83]

Not surprisingly, the isolationists were incensed by this performance and Roosevelt was forced into further justification.[84] Determined to defuse the situation by explaining the rationale behind his policy, he called the members of the Senate Military Affairs Committee together on January 31, 1939, for a briefing on world affairs.[85] Speaking with "unusual candor and forthrightness," Roosevelt defended both the need to build airplanes and the desirability of aiding the democracies.[86] After laying out his post-Munich diagnosis of the German threat and describing Hitler's craving for world domination graphically and at length, Roosevelt analyzed American security requirements in the face of this threat and outlined the policies needed to meet them. The United States, he said,

> must try to prevent the domination of the world . . . by peaceful means. . . .
> What is the first line of defense in the United States? What is our ability not
> only to defend ourselves against attack on our own continental limits but
> also our right to treat with the rest of the world and to avoid putting up a

[81] "He put it right on me. He said, 'Tell them two things. We're doing it, first, because we believe that there are certain countries we want to help; and then, also, we're doing it to help our own production.'" "Morgenthau Diary," Jan. 27, 1939, 173:149–51; Blum, *Morgenthau Diaries*, 2:73; Haight, *American Aid*, 96–98.

[82] Ibid., 97; Blum, *Morgenthau Diaries*, 2:72–74.

[83] Ibid., 73–74; Haight, *American Aid*, 97–98.

[84] Cole, *Roosevelt*, 303. See also Cole, *Nye*, 154.

[85] Haight, *American Aid*, 98.

[86] Cole, *Roosevelt*, 304–6. The complete transcript of the meeting is in Schewe, 8: no. 1565. It can also be found in the Roosevelt Library, PPFl-P, Box 262, FDRL. See also Cole, *Nye*, 154–55; and Haight, "Roosevelt as Friend," 95–96. The following discussion uses Schewe.

very high barbed wire fence all around us? . . . On the Atlantic, our first line is the continued independent existence of a very large group of nations.

The key to maintaining the independence of the European nations was air power. Had Britain and France had more planes, "There would not have been any Munich." Thus, there were two very good reasons for the United States to sell planes to the French. The first had to do with putting unused factories to work and building up American productive capacity. The second was that

> We want France to continue as an independent nation. We don't want France to have to yield to this, that and the other thing because if France yields and England yields, there won't be any independent nation in Europe or Africa or anywhere else. Therefore, it is to our interest . . . to do what we can . . . to help the French and British maintain their independence.

In case his audience had missed the point, Roosevelt reiterated it in the strongest possible terms, even defending his policy from the charge that it might violate neutrality:

> I think it was Arthur Krock who said, "Isn't it unneutral?" Yes, it might be called that. But I will do every thing I possibly can do, as Chief of the Army and Navy and head of the Executive Department, to prevent any munitions from going to Germany or Italy or Japan. Why? Because self-protection is part of the American policy. And I will do everything I can to maintain the independence of these other nations by sending them all they can pay for on the barrelhead, to these about forty or fifty now independent nations of the world. Now, that is the foreign policy of the United States.

Roosevelt also hastened to reassure his listeners that his policy was intended to prevent, not encourage, American participation in war. In particular, he expressed his firm conviction that it would not require the use of American armed forces, telling the Senators, "you may be quite sure that about the last thing that this country should do is ever to send an army to Europe again."

Despite his attempt to present matters in the most reassuring light, then, Roosevelt was at last making an effort to explain his post-Munich policy and the rationale behind it to Congress. Clearly, however, he wished his remarks to go no further, repeatedly warning the committee to keep what took place confidential and cautioning them about the danger of frightening the American people. In particular, he feared that the country would misunderstand his statements about the need to prevent the domination of the world and his characterization of a number of independent countries as America's first line of defense.

This was, however, precisely the area in which Roosevelt's confidence was immediately violated. One of the senators who had been at the meeting told the press that the president had said that America's frontiers were on the Rhine.[87] News stories on the topic caused a furor throughout the country, and Roosevelt's primary response to the Munich crisis became not only a matter of public knowledge, but the subject of considerable controversy.[88]

Roosevelt reacted to the news leak in a way that only made matters worse. Beginning calmly enough, he asserted at a press conference on February 2 that American foreign policy had not changed in any way. It was based, as always, on the principles of no "entangling alliances," "the maintenance of world trade for everybody," sympathy for arms limitation, and "the peaceful maintenance of political economic and social independence of all nations in the world."[89] Any soothing effect this might have had, however, was destroyed when Roosevelt characterized the report that he had said America's frontiers lay on the Rhine as the "deliberate lie," of "some boob." Outraged by these remarks, some of the participants in the meeting "let it be known that the President had left no doubt in their minds that he intended to pursue a policy directed against aggressors, despite the existing neutrality laws."[90]

Notwithstanding the pain the entire episode had caused him, Roosevelt returned to the fray almost immediately, picking up the themes he had emphasized to the Military Affairs Committee and attempting not only to educate the press about them, but also, through them, to reach the public. In another press conference on February 17, for example, he was at great pains to clarify what he had actually said to the senators, stressing in particular the difference between noting the importance to "the safety of United States" of the continued independence of thirty or forty nations and stating that America's frontiers were on the Rhine.[91]

[87] Although Roosevelt did not say this, even a committee member who agreed that he had been misinterpreted reported that the senators had been thoroughly alarmed by what he did say. According to Senator Austin, "The President . . . scared the Committee members, who got the impression that if war came it would be practically inevitable that this country would be in it." Record of an interview with Senator Warren Austin, Dec. 8, 1939, Alsop papers. Cole, *Roosevelt*, 306–7.

[88] Haight, *American Aid*, 99, and "Roosevelt as Friend," 96.

[89] "Press Conference in the White House, February 3, 1939, 10:50 a.m.," Schewe, 8: no. 1574. Cole, *Roosevelt*, 308.

[90] Schewe, 8: no. 1574; Langer and Gleason, *Challenge*, 49; Cole, *Roosevelt*, 307. Roosevelt's intemperate response is consistent with the degree of annoyance he had already shown Morgenthau about the public airing of the dispute between the secretary and Woodring over the responsibility for authorizing the French inspection of the Douglas bomber. Morgenthau, Presidential Diary 1:0047–48.

[91] "Press Conference, on the Presidential Train En Route, from Washington to Florida City, Florida, February 17, 1939, 2:30 P.M.," Schewe, 8: no. 1598. These remarks were off the record.

Moreover, the pill of domestic opposition was sweetened by praise from overseas. On balance, Roosevelt was pleased with the outcome of what had first appeared to be a disaster, writing on March 3 to Ambassador Cudahy

> our policy during the past month . . . has had a definite effect on Germany and only a slightly less effect on Italy. . . . The howls and curses that have continued to come from Berlin and Rome convinces me that the general result has been good even if a few silly Senators reported the conversation in a wholly untruthful way.[92]

Roosevelt also could only have been pleased when Morgenthau telegraphed him the results of the latest Gallup poll, in which 69 percent answered yes to a question which, referring to "the issue which was raised after President Roosevelt's conference with the Senate Military Affairs Committee two weeks ago," asked if the United States should do everything short of war to help Britain and France if Germany and Italy went to war against them. Sixty-two percent also thought that if Germany and Italy defeated Britain and France, they would then start a war against the United States.[93]

Roosevelt's response to the isolationist challenge, then, once again shows the strength of his commitment to aiding the democracies. As in the earlier challenges by the military, he demonstrated his willingness to fight for that policy whenever it was threatened, even defending it to members of Congress and, indirectly, to the public. However disagreeable Roosevelt found this task, he did not back down.[94]

---

[92] "F.D.R. to John Cudahy in Dublin, March 4, 1939," *PL*, 862–63. Typical of the positive reaction Roosevelt received is Biddle's letter of March 4, 1939: "Your firmness of attitude, your armament program, and your decision to afford the French and British opportunity to purchase planes from us, have been greeted by official circles here with a genuine sense of satisfaction." Schewe, 8: no. 1623. Similar examples of praise for Roosevelt's policies at this time may be found in Bullitt to Roosevelt, Feb. 1, 1939, Bullitt, *For the President*, 307–8; Phillips to Roosevelt, Feb. 10, 1939, Schewe, 8: no. 1585; Bullitt to Hull, Feb. 13, 1939, and Bullitt to Roosevelt, Feb. 22, 1939, ibid., no.s 1591, 1603; Thomas W. Lamont and J.P. Morgan to Roosevelt, Feb. 14, 1939, ibid., no. 1593; Hull to Roosevelt, Feb. 21, 1939, summarizing a telegram from Ambassador Kennedy, ibid., no. 1602; and Pell to Roosevelt, March 15, 1939, ibid., no. 1614.

[93] "Henry Morgenthau, Jr., Secretary of the Treasury, to Roosevelt, Aboard the U.S.S. *Houston*, February 22, 1939," ibid., no. 1604.

[94] As Haight points out, a number of the president's contemporaries, including the French, were well aware of this demonstration of his commitment:

> What was perhaps of prime significance for French leaders that winter of 1938–39 was that their negotions for American planes had proved the sympathy of President Roosevelt and his closest advisers. Though in public he might feel forced to deny that England and France were the first line of defense for the United States and that the

Not only does this episode show Roosevelt's dedication to the policy of aiding the democracies, it also confirms the importance of that policy relative to rearmament. While Roosevelt took pains to reassure the members of the Senate Military Affairs Committee that a massive rearmament program was not what he desired, he was unyielding in his insistence on the need for airplanes, telling them that if Britain and France had had even four to five thousand planes, compared to the twelve to fifteen thousand of the Axis, "there would not have been any Munich."[95] Furthermore, while the policies of hemisphere defense, measures short of war, and neutrality revision received somewhat more attention after the November 14 meeting, they continued to share with rearmament a subordinate position relative to the policy of aiding the democracies.

With respect to hemisphere defense, Roosevelt told Alsop and Kintner that talks between himself, Hull, and Welles on "the North-South axis" began in November and, indeed, there was a marked increase in activity in that area then and in December. As Dallek points out, "Roosevelt's first line of defense against fascism in the Hemisphere was the continuation of the Good Neighbor Policy," which after Munich took the form of direct aid to Latin American nations and multilateral diplomacy at the Lima Conference in December.[96] Nevertheless, the principle impetus for action came not from the president but from the State Department and the military for whom hemisphere defense constituted the primary policy response to the Munich crisis. As Berle told Alsop and Kintner, "at the time of Munich, during the State Department's death watch over Europe, it was positively decided that the main emphasis in American foreign relations must be shifted from east and west to north and south. Under

---

American frontiers thus extended to the Rhine, the leaders of France knew that this belief was in fact the basis of his European policy.
Haight, "Roosevelt as Friend," 96.

[95] "Conference with the Senate Military Affairs Committee, January 31, 1939."

[96] Roosevelt Interview, Dec. 23, 1939, Alsop papers; Dallek, *Franklin D. Roosevelt*, 175. For examples of Roosevelt's willingness to help with Latin American security, see "Sumner Welles, Under Secretary of State, to Roosevelt, November 17, 1938," Schewe, 8: no. 1412; "Roosevelt to Antonio C. Gonzalez, Minister to Venezuela, December 6, 1938," ibid., no. 1457; and "Sumner Welles, Under Secretary of State, to Roosevelt, February 10, 1938," ibid., no. 1471. As Dallek notes, much of aid for the Latin American nations was the concern of the Standing Liaison Committee, which had been established in April 1938 and consisted of the under secretary of state, the army chief of staff, and the chief of naval operations. *Franklin D. Roosevelt*, 176. On planning for the Lima Conference, see Alsop and Kintner, *American White Paper*, 17; Ickes, *Diary*, 2:528; and "Welles to Roosevelt, November 11, 1938," Schewe, 8: no. 1412. On the conference itself, see Dallek, *Franklin D. Roosevelt*, 177; and Hull, *Memoirs*, 1:602.

this new orientation it was argued that the safety of the hemisphere was the first objective."[97]

Roosevelt was disposed to deal with the German threat to the hemisphere primarily at the diplomatic level, concentrating on ensuring hemispheric solidarity in the face of the threat of Axis subversion. To the extent that he was directly concerned with the military dimension of the threat, he focused not on defending against it but, in accordance with the rest of his foreign policy, on keeping it as far from the hemisphere as possible by aiding the democracies.[98] The military, on the other hand, took hemisphere defense literally, aiming at "the preparation of a more dynamic defense" that would protect the whole hemisphere."[99] Thus, while the basic military policy of the United States after Munich became hemisphere defense, America's foreign policy, as defined by Roosevelt, focused on deterring Germany by aiding the democracies. This difference in priorities led to considerable frustration and confusion in defining the nature and purpose of rearmament.[100]

With respect to measures short of war, Roosevelt did little in the weeks between the November 14 meeting and the German takeover of Czechoslovakia in March 1939. In the diplomatic arena, it was decided in December to reject a German protest over an intemperate speech by Secretary Ickes,[101] and in January a step toward waging a "psychological

[97] Berle interview, Alsop papers.

[98] According to Haglund, from 1938 to 1940 the administration's willingness to support the European democracies grew "in direct proportion to its perception of an increased threat to the security of the United States—a threat stemming mainly from the possible Axis domination of Latin America." "Marshall and the Question of Military Aid," 753. See also 747–48.

[99] This new motivation resulted in a spurt of planning and, ultimately, a new set of war plans that came to be known as the Rainbow plans. Watson, *Chief of Staff*, 88–89 and n. 8, 97–99; Dallek, *Franklin D. Roosevelt*, 176. See also Conn Fairchild, *Framework*, 3–6. For the response of the air force to the threat to the hemisphere, see Craven and Cate, *Army Air Forces*, 116–20; and Questor, *Deterrence Before Hiroshima*, 130. In November 1938 the American military also held staff talks with the Canadians, and the president met in Washington with Prime Minister King. During this meeting, "Roosevelt spoke of the danger of the Germans establishing a base in South America, and incidentally expressed the opinion that both Britain and Canada should set about producing large numbers of aircraft." Stacey, *Arms, Men and Governments*, 98; and James Eayrs, *In Defense of Canada: Appeasement and Rearmament* (Toronto: University of Toronto Press, 1965), 183–84.

[100] "Beneath American rearmament . . . lay a major question which was never finally answered until the day of Pearl Harbor. Was American rearmament a preparation for, or an alternative to, war?" Emerson, "Roosevelt as Commander-in-Chief," 187.

[101] According to Moffat, the president and Welles recognized that this might have "serious consequences, but decided that the Germans only responded to strong action and that any appearance of weakening now would be totally misconstrued." Even on the verbal level, however, Roosevelt's willingness to do battle with the Germans had definite limits.

peace offensive" in the form of a diplomatic opening to Italy was taken.[102] On the economic front, Roosevelt, Hull, and Welles decided in November to initiate some measures short of war, apparently believing that these would be acceptable domestically.[103] However, nothing of importance had been accomplished in the economic sphere by the time Hitler's troops marched into Prague.[104]

For both Roosevelt and Hull, the most important measure short of war was revision of the neutrality laws.[105] According to Roosevelt's testimony, the decision to attempt neutrality revision was made in November 1938, and Under Secretary Welles told Alsop and Kintner that the president, Hull, and he frequently discussed the subject at that time.[106] In his State of the Union message, Roosevelt emphasized the possibility that "our neutrality laws may operate unevenly and unfairly—may actually give aid to an aggressor and deny it to the victim." According to Divine, even though the president made no specific recommendations, the speech was widely interpreted as a call for revision of the neutrality legislation.[107]

It is noteworthy, then, that little or nothing was done about neutrality

---

On December 28, he told the Cabinet that Germany was still "sore" about Ickes's speech, "and he thought that for the time being we ought to be careful in what we said." Ickes, *Diary*, 2:533–34; 545. Hooker, *Moffat Papers*, 223. See also Alsop and Kintner, *American White Paper*, 25–26.

[102] Ickes, *Diary*, 2:548.

[103] Alsop and Kintner, *American White Paper*, 19. This was confirmed by Bullitt in January, who told Polish Ambassador Lukasciewicz that "In its relations with Italy and Germany, the United States has at its disposal various measures of pressure which have already been seriously examined and assessed. These means, chiefly of an economic character, are such that they can be applied without the slightest fear of internal opposition." Lukasiewicz, *Diplomat in Paris*, 169. See also Weinberg, *Foreign Policy of Hitler's Germany*, 521.

[104] In his memoirs, Hull indicates that such measures were first discussed in January and states that he was considering measures short of war, including economic steps, just before the German takeover of Czechoslovakia. According to Ickes, however, in this period Morgenthau was the one pushing for action against Germany, while the State Department was dragging its heels. Hull, *Memoirs*, 1:612–14; Ickes, *Diary*, 2:591.

[105] Rosenman, *Working with Roosevelt*, 183; "State of the Union Address, January 4, 1939," *Peace and War*, 449–50; and Hull, *Memoirs*, 1:612–14. See also Langer and Gleason, *Challenge*, 47; Dallek, *Franklin D. Roosevelt*, 179; and Burns, *Lion*, 389.

[106] Alsop and Kintner interviews with Roosevelt, Dec. 23, 1938, and Welles, which is undated but occurred some time late in 1939, Alsop papers. See also Alsop and Kintner, *American White Paper*, 18–19; Hull, *Memoirs*, 1:613; Drummond, *Passing of American Neutrality*, 87.

[107] Divine, *Reluctant Belligerent*, 56; "State of the Union Address, January 4, 1939," *Peace and War*, 449–50. According to Moffat, he and others in the State Department discussed neutrality revision with Hull on January 25, and all agreed that the law should be repealed. Hooker, *Moffat Papers*, 228.

revision at this time.[108] Even as late as March 7, Roosevelt was offering only "guarded support" for it, telling reporters that the neutrality legislation had not contributed to the cause of peace but spending considerably more time discussing the many situations in which the neutrality laws would be inapplicable because of the difficulty of defining a state of war.[109] In fact, Roosevelt was moved to act vigorously on neutrality revision only after the Germans marched into Prague one week later.

THE EXTERNAL CHALLENGE: RESPONDING TO THE THREAT OF WAR, MARCH 15–SEPTEMBER 1, 1939

On March 15, 1939, Hitler marched into Bohemia and Moravia, completing the occupation of Czechoslovakia. This latest German outrage not only marked the end of British appeasement, but also reaffirmed Roosevelt's commitment to the policy of aiding the democracies and led him finally to push for neutrality revision.[110]

Apart from universal condemnation, Hitler's brutal act elicited two main responses in the United States. For some it triggered a change of diagnosis about German aggressiveness, while for others, it merely confirmed one made in the aftermath of the Munich crisis.[111] Roosevelt belonged to the latter group. The Czech takeover told him nothing about Hitler he had not already learned during the crisis: the Führer was implacably aggressive and would, given the opportunity, threaten the security of the United States.[112] What did change for Roosevelt was his estimate

[108] Berle interview with Alsop and Kintner, Oct. 30, 1939, Alsop papers; Langer and Gleason, *Challenge*, 50; and Divine, *Reluctant Belligerent*, 56–57, *Roosevelt and World War II*, 25, and *Illusion*, 241.

[109] Dallek, *Franklin D. Roosevelt*, 182; Press Conference, March 7, 1939, *PPA*, 8:156–57.

[110] For an account of this event and the diplomatic maneuvering that followed it, see Langer and Gleason, *Challenge*, 62–75.

[111] Adolph Berle's reaction was typical of the first group, as he bemoaned "the fact that Hitler had given his word, as a part of Munich, not to violate the integrity of the Czech Republic, and now, only a few months later, the whole thing had gone by the board. How, therefore, could anybody deal with a country on that basis?" Berle Papers, Memos 1938–1944, Box 55, March 16, 1939, FDRL. "No one here has any illusions that the German Napoleonic machine will not extend itself almost indefinitely." Berle, *Navigating*, 201. Sumner Welles referred to the German invasion of Czechoslovakia as "the first unshaded instance of open thievery." Interview with Alsop and Kintner, late 1939, Alsop papers.

[112] That Hitler's behavior did not surprise Roosevelt does not mean he was unmoved by it. As Ickes observed after a Cabinet meeting on March 17, "the President seems to be getting madder and madder." Ickes, *Diary*, 2:597. See also a memo by Adolph Berle, Berle papers, Memos 1938–1944, March 16, 1939, Box 55, FDRL.

of the likelihood of war. As a consequence of the demise of the Czechoslovak state and the reaction it provoked from the democracies, he now feared major war might be inevitable.

His assessment was based both on this fresh proof that Germany's aims were unlimited and on new evidence that Britain and France were now willing to stand up to her. As the United States consul at Geneva pointed out, "The latest German move . . . has marked a turning point in the European situation and has rendered an eventual war almost inevitable. The Czech annexation . . . starkly reflects a determination to extend German expansion to such an extent that this ambition can only be checked by force."[113] Further, Chamberlain announced on March 17 that "he would not sacrifice British liberty for peace, and should an attempt be made to dominate the world by force, Britain would use all its power to resist." Thus, as the American ambassador to Belgium remarked, "Peace this summer is not now protected by a British policy of appeasement."[114] As Roosevelt himself explained the impact of the Czech takeover and the British guarantee,

> The hope that the world had last September that the German policy was limited and would continue to be limited to bringing contiguous German people into the Reich and only German people . . . has been dissipated by the events of the last few weeks. . . . Therefore, it is felt by people in every continent that where there was a limit last autumn, there is no limit today. . . . Now . . . it seems to have been made clear by England and France today that they have decided there must be a halt to the continuation of a policy seeking to dominate other nations and peoples and, therefore, by their action; [sic] it has been put squarely up to Germany that if there should be war it would come only by an invasion of some other nation by Germany.[115]

[113] Bucknell to Hull, March 18, 1939, *FRUS*, 1939, 1:53. On March 24, Roosevelt wrote to Ambassador MacVeagh, "I fear . . . that Hitler and Mussolini are still on the warpath." *PL*, 2:865.

[114] Dallek, *Franklin D. Roosevelt*, 183; Davies to Hull, March 30, 1939 (received on April 7), *FRUS*, 1939, 1:104. The British government communicated its views on German aggressiveness to the president personally on March 29, 1939. "British Government to Roosevelt, March 29, 1939," Schewe, 9: no. 1684. On March 31, the British formally guaranteed to defend the Poles in case of a German attack. Dallek, *Franklin D. Roosevelt*, 183; Langer and Gleason, *Challenge*, 74.

[115] "Press Conference, Warm Springs, March 31, 1939, 11:30 a.m.," Schewe, 9: no. 1691. The opinions of Lloyd George and Winston Churchill that war was now inevitable were transmitted to the president by Ambassador Davies on April 5. "Views Expressed to Joseph E. Davies, Ambassador to Belgium, by David Lloyd George, April 2, 1939," and "Views Expressed to Joseph E. Davies, Ambassador to Belgium, by Winston S. Churchill, April 1, 1939," ibid., no.s 1701a, 1701b.

Expectations of war following the Czech takeover were heightened by a series of new German and Italian moves triggering what came to be called the April crisis. The German occupation of Memel on March 22, German demands on Poland with respect to Danzig, and above all the Italian invasion of Albania on April 7 led many to fear that Germany and Italy would join forces to carry out their aggressive designs in Europe.[116] Roosevelt "and his associates could not help viewing the situation in the darkest colors."[117] The president even expressed his fears about the likelihood of war to the press, although not for direct attribution. Telling reporters that he had in the last two or three days talked with several people who had just returned from Europe, Lindbergh included, he observed that these "experts" had put the odds both of having a war in Europe and of having the democracies win it at fifty-fifty. Roosevelt was anything but reassured by these probabilities.[118]

As Ambassador Bullitt described the problem,

> The moral for us [of Hitler's recent moves] is that unless some nation in Europe stands up to Germany quickly, France and England may face defeat and such defeat would mean the French and British fleets in the hands of the Germans and the Italians. We should then have the Japs in the Pacific and an overwhelming fleet against us in the Atlantic.

Bullitt predicted that if war in Europe did occur, America would be drawn into it in less than a year, and concluded that it was necessary to begin immediately to build a large army.[119]

Roosevelt's assessment of the threat, though similar, led him in a very different direction. His primary response to the dictators' latest aggression was, in fact, his first serious attempt to obtain neutrality revision.[120]

[116] Dallek, *Franklin D. Roosevelt*, 184–85. In the midst of all of this activity, Roosevelt received further confirmation from the British of their determination to aid the Poles. See "Memorandum from the British Embassy, April 8, 1939," Schewe, 9: no. 1708.

[117] Langer and Gleason, *Challenge*, 79. Morgenthau's presidential Diary for April 1939 offers a number of examples of both his and Roosevelt's expectations of war. On April 16, for instance, the President asked Morgenthau if the Coast Guard was ready should there be war. Alsop and Kintner also record Roosevelt as inquiring of the secretary at this time: "Henry, are you ready for the worst? Because things look so bad you ought to be." Morgenthau, Presidential Diary, 1:0094; Alsop and Kintner, *American White Paper*, 47.

[118] "Press Conference in the White House, April 20, 1939, 9:10 P.M.," Schewe, 9: no. 1744. At this press conference, as well as those on April 8 and 15, Roosevelt made a considerable effort to educate the press, and through it the public, about the dangers of the international situation for the United States. The April 20 press conference, for example, lasted an hour and thirty-five minutes. Ibid., no.s 1710, 1721.

[119] Bullitt to Roosevelt, March 23, 1939, Bullitt, *For the President*, 333.

[120] "Divine, *Reluctant Belligerent*, 57, and *Illusion*, 241. See also Stromberg, *Collective Security*, 125. Other measures included diplomatic steps such as a renewal of the effort begun in January to drive a wedge between Hitler and Mussolini (Dallek, *Franklin D.*

In this respect, the Czech takeover represented a genuine turning point in his strategy.

Roosevelt's thoughts turned to neutrality revision almost immediately after the German invasion of Czechoslovakia, and action soon followed. On March 16, he told Senator Tom Connally, "If Germany invades a country and declares war, we'll be on the side of Hitler by invoking the act. . . . If we could get rid of the arms embargo, it wouldn't be so bad." On March 17, he also expressed his desire for revision in a press conference.[121]

Roosevelt lost no time in embarking on neutrality revision.[122] Key Pittman, chairman of the Senate Foreign Relations Committee, opened the campaign with a radio speech on March 19 and the next day introduced a bill that "provided for the repeal of the arms embargo and the placing of all trade with belligerents on a cash-and-carry basis."[123] Roosevelt himself would have preferred to push for revision of the entire Neutrality Act and tried to move Pittman in that direction. In the face of the senator's conviction that it could not be done, however, he was forced to abandon the idea.[124]

Roosevelt, 183–84; Langer and Gleason. *Challenge*, 67, 77–78; and *PL*, 2:875–76.), and one final diplomatic effort to deflect Hitler from the collision course he was on. (See below.) On the economic front, Roosevelt instituted the countervailing duties against Germany that had been considered a week earlier. Morgenthau Diary 169: 275–85; Blum, *Morgenthau Diaries*, 2:78–86; Ickes, *Diary*, 2:597; Langer and Gleason, *Challenge*, 68; Hull, *Memoirs*, 1:615.

[121] Connally, *My Name is Tom Connally*, 226; Press Conference, March 17, 1939, #530-A, *Presidential Press Conferences* 13:204–5; Divine, *Reluctant Belligerent*, 57. Roosevelt was not alone in favoring neutrality revision at this point. A Gallup poll on March 21, 1939 showed that 66 percent of the people favored repeal, as opposed to 50 percent in February. Ibid., 59; Dallek, *Franklin D. Roosevelt*, 183. Given its date, however, it cannot have influenced the President's decision to pursue neutrality revision.

[122] Some in the State Department received the impression that Roosevelt was not at first eager to proceed with neutrality revision. On the testimony of Roosevelt's own behavior, however, their interpretation must be discounted. See "Memo of a Phone Talk between Welles and Bullitt," March 15, 1939, *FRUS, 1939*, 1:41; Hooker, *Moffat Papers*, 232.

[123] Drummond, *Passing of American Neutrality*, 88–89; Divine, *Reluctant Belligerent*, 57–58; Langer and Gleason, *Challenge*, 79–80.

[124] F.D.R. to Cordell Hull and Sumner Welles, March 28, 1939, *PL*, 2:873; Langer and Gleason, *Challenge*, 80; Dallek, *Franklin D. Roosevelt*, 184. One reason Roosevelt wanted total revision was his fear that the embargo would hurt the Chinese who had been the target of Japanese aggression throughout 1938 and early 1939. In other respects, however, he was "cautious about direct opposition to Japan," fearing that stronger measures would provoke her into "bolder actions." Ibid., 193–95. In fact, it is striking how little Japan figured in his post-Munich policies. For a general discussion of the attempt to revise the neutrality legislation in the spring and summer of 1939, see Langer and Gleason, *Challenge*, 136–47; Dallek, *Franklin D. Roosevelt*, 187–92; and Divine, *Illusion*, 241–93. A more than usually sympathetic treatment of Pittman's role can be found in Glad, *Key Pittman*, chap. 22.

Hearings on the bill began in early April. With the events of the April crisis underlining its urgency, Roosevelt increased his efforts to support neutrality revision, attempting to educate the country to the dangers of the international situation and the futility of expecting neutrality legislation to protect the United States.[125] By the end of April, however, the Senate Foreign Relations Committee was out of Pittman's control and the legislation at a standstill. Although Roosevelt feared his open intervention might have a negative impact on Congress, he continued to work actively behind the scenes, lobbying various members on behalf of Pittman's bill.[126] This was in marked contrast to his behavior prior to the Czech takeover, when, despite his November decision to pursue neutrality revision, he did little or nothing.

In early May, Senator Pittman gave up, informing Hull on May 16 that "the situation in Europe . . . does not seem to induce any urgent action on neutrality legislation." Roosevelt, however, was not prepared to abandon the struggle. Committed to neutrality revision, even before Pittman withdrew Roosevelt had decided to turn to the House.[127] There he fought hard. On May 19, for example, he met with the House leadership, telling them emphatically that "every possible effort should be made to eliminate" the arms embargo. This "would actually prevent the outbreak of war in Europe, or if it did not prevent the outbreak of war, the elimination of that provision would make less likely a victory for the powers unfriendly to the United States."[128] Despite warnings from the House leadership that his proposal would be defeated, Roosevelt persisted in trying to gain outright repeal of the embargo, lobbying diligently behind the scenes and writing to Judge R. Walton Moore on June 7, 1939, "I am pushing the Neutrality matter and hope you will see as many people in the House and Senate as you can."[129] In spite of Roosevelt's best efforts, however, repeal of the embargo was defeated in the House on June 30.[130]

[125] See "Press Conference, Warm Springs, April 8, 1939, 11:45 a.m.," and "Press Conference in the White House, April 20, 1939, 9:10 p.m.," Schewe, 9: no.s 1710, 1744. Revision seemed even more pressing after Hitler's rebuff to Roosevelt's April 14 overture. Dallek, *Franklin D. Roosevelt*, 185; Langer and Gleason, *Challenge*, 79; and below.

[126] Ibid., 137; Dallek, *Franklin D. Roosevelt*, 187.

[127] Divine, *Reluctant Belligerent*, 59; Glad, *Key Pittman*, 247; Fred L. Israel, *Nevada's Key Pittman* (Lincoln, Neb.: University of Nebraska Press), 162–63; Dallek, *Franklin D. Roosevelt*, 188; and Langer and Gleason, *Challenge*, 137–38.

[128] Memo of the meeting by Carlton Savage, May 19, 1939, quoted in ibid., 138. See also Dallek, *Franklin D. Roosevelt*, 188; and Divine, *Reluctant Belligerent*, 59–60, and *Illusion*, 263.

[129] Hull, *Memoirs*, 1:642; "Roosevelt to R. Walton Moore, Counselor to the Department of State, June 7, 1939," Schewe, 9: no. 1859; Langer and Gleason, *Challenge*, 139–40; Dallek, *Franklin D. Roosevelt*, 189–90; Divine, *Reluctant Belligerent*, 60. The letter to Moore is also quoted in Israel's discussion of this episode. *Pittman*, 163–64

[130] Roosevelt's concern that this failure would increase the chances of war, as well as his

Roosevelt then turned once more to the Senate, where again he fought tenaciously. Nevertheless, on July 11 the Senate Foreign Relations Committee voted to defer consideration until the next session of Congress.[131] At this juncture, as Langer and Gleason have pointed out, "Since both Houses had now acted, . . . the President might well have dropped the matter, leaving the responsibility where it belonged." Instead, he attempted to get the full Senate to overrule the committee, calling together the Senate leadership on July 18 to persuade them to deal with neutrality revision before Congress recessed.[132]

Speaking for about an hour, Roosevelt used all the arguments at his command. According to Senator Austin, "the President was emphatic in his belief that repeal of the arms embargo would at least delay a European war, which he thought now was inevitable." Some senators, like Borah, were openly hostile; others were more sympathetic, but all insisted that what Roosevelt desired could not be done at the present session. "The Senate was not in good humor. . . . The debate was certain to be acrimonious. . . . In addition there was practically unanimous conclusion that the neutrality revision might not pass." Despite the universally negative response, however, the president and secretary of state continued to press for congressional action.

In the end, since the leadership was united in agreeing that the legislation could not be enacted, Roosevelt had no choice but to accept their verdict. Even then, however, he declared that he would continue the fight, not hesitating to threaten the senators with the only weapon left to him:

> He showed no personal anger. But he leaned back, smoked a cigarette, and indicated that he would go to the country with the issue. It was now clear . . . where the responsibility for failure to act belonged. He repeated that he had taken every step he could to avert a European war; that it was essential that he be given another shot. He had put his case before Congress and Congress had refused to give him more ammunition. The issue, therefore,

---

commitment to aiding the democracies if it did so, is reflected in his subsequent search for ways around the prohibitions of the Neutrality Act. The day after the House vote, he wrote to the attorney general inquiring about this possibility: "As you know, the V.P. takes the definite position that the President should not be bound at all by [neutrality] legislation as such legislation offends his constitutional powers. If we fail to get any Neutrality Bill, how far do you think I can go in ignoring the existing act—even though I did sign it? !" Dallek, *Franklin D. Roosevelt*, 189–90; Langer and Gleason, *Challenge*, 142; Divine, *Reluctant Belligerent*, 60–61; "Roosevelt to Frank Murphy, Attorney General, July 1, 1939," Schewe, 9: no. 1906.

[131] Dallek, *Franklin D. Roosevelt*, 190–91; Langer and Gleason, *Challenge*, 142–43; Divine, *Reluctant Belligerent*, 61–62, and *Illusion*, 226.

[132] Langer and Gleason, *Challenge*, 143; Dallek, *Franklin D. Roosevelt*, 192. For the text of the president's appeal to the Congress on this issue, see "Roosevelt to the Congress of the United States, July 14, 1939," Schewe, 9: no. 1926.

. . . was no longer in his or the hands of Congress. The country must decide, . . . and he indicated that he was the one who would make the issue.[133]

This Roosevelt proceeded to do, declaring that "the President and the Secretary of State maintained the definite position that failure by the Senate to take action now would weaken the leadership of the United States in exercising its potent influence in the cause of preserving peace among other nations in the event of a new crisis in Europe between now and January." He also made several strong statements placing the blame for preventing him from doing everything possible to avoid the outbreak of war squarely on the Senate, particularly the Senate Republicans.[134]

Many have tried to explain Roosevelt's approach to neutrality revision during the spring and summer of 1939. Some, like Divine, criticize him for not acting more vigorously because he feared "risking his prestige." Others, like Langer and Gleason, analyze his behavior in strategic terms: initially he stayed in the background because he thought direct intervention might jeopardize the legislation; when he realized it was in danger, he tried to change his tack, but it was too late. Still others, Dallek among them, emphasize Roosevelt's ceaseless activity on behalf of neutrality revision and the degree to which he was willing to fight for it.[135]

None of these, however—not even Divine who criticizes Roosevelt's "inept leadership"—suggests that after the Czech takeover the president was ever less than eager to obtain neutrality revision. If he failed, it was not for lack of desire. Not only was he willing to take risks he had previously been reluctant to hazard (vigorously lobbying a Congress that showed considerable hostility to him personally and exposing his policy to public scrutiny),[136] he did so in circumstances that at least in terms of his potential support, seemed little changed from those in which he had earlier decided to defer action. Despite a notable lack of success, he re-

[133] Interview with Senator Austin, Dec. 8, 1939, Alsop papers. In addition to Austin and Borah, other participants in this meeting were the secretary of state, Vice-President Garner, Presidential Press Secretary Early, Majority Leader Barkley, Minority Leader McNary, and Pittman. See Hull, *Memoirs*, 1:649–651; Langer and Gleason, *Challenge*, 143–45; Dallek, *Franklin D. Roosevelt*, 192; and Alsop and Kintner, *American White Paper*, 44–46.

[134] Quoted in Langer and Gleason, *Challenge*, 145. See press conferences on July 21 and August 8 and 29, 1939, Schewe, 9: no.s 1937, 2052, and *PPA* 8:428–29.

[135] Divine, *Reluctant Belligerent*, 63; Langer and Gleason, *Challenge*, 145–47; Dallek, *Franklin D. Roosevelt*, 187–92.

[136] Ibid., 190–91. That Roosevelt was willing to hold large-scale gatherings of the House and Senate leadership is particularly striking in view of his disastrous attempt to influence members of Congress in the January meeting with the Senate Military Affairs Committee. He could hardly have been unaware that such open appeals risked manipulation by unfriendly participants and exposure to public misunderstanding.

fused to give up the fight, clinging to the idea of repealing the arms embargo even after being definitively rebuffed by the Senate leadership.[137]

Why, after months of inactivity, did Roosevelt suddenly decide to pursue neutrality revision so vigorously? And why did he choose to respond to the German takeover of Czechoslovakia with that policy rather than another, such as rearmament, that might have been more easily achieved? Roosevelt himself blamed Pittman for delaying the neutrality fight,[138] and others have suggested political motives.[139] However, while Pittman's shortcomings or various political obstacles might explain why Roosevelt dropped neutrality revision in November, neither can account for his decision to take it up again in April and pursue it vigorously thereafter.

The explanation for Roosevelt's lack of movement on neutrality in the fall and his burst of activity in the spring lies in his goal of aiding Britain and France. He began to devote his formidable energies to neutrality revision only when it became apparent that, without it, he would no longer be able to help the democracies. Until the Czech takeover and British guarantee to Poland increased the likelihood of war, the neutrality laws could not have prevented such aid. When war threatened, revision became a necessary condition for it. Thus, it was Roosevelt's heightened expectation of war after Hitler's march into Prague that converted his verbal commitment to neutrality revision into action. Not only does Roosevelt's desire to aid the democracies explain his campaign for repeal of the embargo, however, it also explains why he responded to the takeover of Czechoslovakia in that way instead of launching a massive campaign for rearmament.

---

[137] French President Daladier recalled that during a phone conversation about additional American planes in August 1939, Roosevelt admonished him to remember that "the majority of American opinion is isolationist. Do not forget the American Senate has embargoed all the arms that you have ordered in the United States. But you can count on it, that I will overcome this opposition and raise the embargo." Quoted in Haight, *American Aid*, 136.

[138]
> The reason was Senator Pittman. Pittman kept coming down and saying "not now, not now, let's wait a couple of weeks." He would report everything was coming on fine, but nothing happened. Pittman was undoubtedly for the revision, but his political judgment was at fault. . . . In April, I decided to put the matter in Hull's hands, and both he and I began to see leading Senators, to try and speed up revision.

Roosevelt interview, Dec. 23, 1939, Alsop papers.

[139] Dallek emphasizes the animosity of a number of congressmen because of Roosevelt's purge attempts the previous fall, a feeling that was exacerbated by the conflict following the Douglas crash. Dallek, *Challenge*, 179–81. See also Divine, *Reluctant Belligerent*, 56–57; and interview with H.F., March 8, 1939, Alsop papers. The intitials H.F. undoubtedly stand for Herbert Feis.

Eliot Janeway asserts that Roosevelt blundered in forcing a confrontation with Congress over neutrality because the real issue was productive power, and because consensus on that would have been as easy to get as agreement on neutrality revision was not.[140] (On the one hand, there was considerable support in Congress for augmenting America's defenses; on the other, there was confusion about why neutrality revision should be preferable.)[141] Janeway also argues that Roosevelt failed to embrace preparedness because he feared the political consequences.[142] The evidence shows, however, that what drove Roosevelt's behavior was not politics but, again, an overriding concern with aid to the democracies. That rearmament was primarily a means to this end explains both his reluctance to launch a preparedness campaign and the nature of the effort he did undertake, which in every particular was shaped by his larger purpose. Because Roosevelt intended rearmament primarily to aid Britain and France, he was not interested in a massive program, however easy it might have been to obtain.

This interpretation is supported by Roosevelt's behavior right up to America's entry into World War II.[143] For one thing, he consistently favored the democracies whenever their needs conflicted with the military's concept of the requirements of American defense.[144] For another, during the period before September 1939 when aid to Britain and France was focused primarily on deterrence, he not only felt no need to push for a massive rearmament effort, but also seemed unconcerned that he had so little to give. For Roosevelt, the real deterrent threat was the *ultimate*

[140] "To insist on repealing the arms embargo at a time when the economy was producing no arms for any purpose was to reach for the shadow and not the substance." Janeway, *Struggle*, 108.

[141] Ibid., 108–10. See, for example, Senator Austin's account of his own response at the July 18 meeting to Roosevelt's argument that he needed neutrality revision as ammunition against the dictators: "Austin said that he thought the President had overlooked one shot remaining in his gun. Congress has just passed a two billion dollar national defense bill. . . . In voting the national defense program, Austin said he believed that Congress had given the President a new sanction which could be used effectively." Interview with Senator Austin, Dec. 8, 1939, Alsop Papers. On the disposition of Congress to give Roosevelt what he requested for national defense, see Langer and Gleason, *Challenge*, 130–31, Cole, *Roosevelt*, 267–73; Jonas, *Isolationism*, 129–34.

[142] Janeway, *Struggle*, 104–8, 111.

[143] And, some would argue, beyond it. See Leighton, "Arsenal."

[144] This is seen not only in Roosevelt's actions during the 1939 controversy over selling planes to the French, but also in his behavior after the beginning of World War II. For example, Ickes reported that at a cabinet meeting on December 8, 1939, "Jim Farley asked the President whether, if England or France wanted airplanes and we wanted them at the same time, we would insist upon deliveries to us. The President said that it was a matter of confidential information, but that, up to a certain number at any rate, we would let England and France have first call." Despite the fact that this policy caused a crisis in the War Department, Roosevelt held firm. Ickes, *Diary*, 3:84–85. See also Langer and Gleason, *Challenge*, 288–91.

availability of American productive power.[145] This, he hoped, would be sufficient to give Hitler pause during the months before the weapons themselves could be built.

Thus, even after war began in September 1939, Roosevelt failed to launch an extensive rearmament campaign of the sort advocated by Janeway, taking that step only in the spring of 1940 when for the first time it seemed that the Allies could actually lose the war. As soon as the blitzkrieg convinced him that massive arms aid would be required for the democracies to prevail, Roosevelt moved to activate American productive power.[146] Rearmament for its own sake was never the point for Roosevelt. He did not commit to an all-out effort until it became apparent not only that deterrence had failed but also that without massive aid the democracies might fail as well.

ANALYSIS

Why did Roosevelt choose aid to Britain and France as his principal response to the security threat he perceived after Munich and adhere to it so tenaciously in the face of considerable opposition? As Janeway's criticism shows, it was hardly the obvious choice, and one can easily imagine his doing otherwise.

After Munich, there were two schools of thought about the American posture toward developments in Europe. Interventionists, including Morgenthau and former Secretary of State Stimson, advocated support for Britain and France well beyond what Roosevelt thought prudent, arguing that the best course was "to expound the situation to the country and to explain in detail that the one hopeful method of stopping Hitler was to make clear to him that in case of further aggression all the resources of the United States would be at the disposal of his oppo-

---

[145] In Greenfield's words, Roosevelt's aim during the entire period from Munich to Pearl Harbor was

> to find an alternative to war rather than to prepare the nation to fight a war. This was his declared purpose in giving all-out aid short of war to Britain, China, and the U.S.S.R., at the expense of our own military preparations. What he wanted, and quickly, was not primarily rearmanent, but a demonstration of his determination to mobilize and use America's enormous war potential in the hope that this might save Great Britain, deter Japan, and make war unnecessary.

Greenfield, *American Strategy*, 54. See also Divine, *Illusion*, 230–31; and Reynolds, *Creation*, 42–43.

[146] Kittredge, "United States," 13. See also Langer and Gleason, *Challenge*, 469–80. Janeway recognizes that the beginning of the war did not provide Roosevelt with a sufficient stimulus for rearmament, but he attributes this to weakness and evasiveness rather than genuine conviction about the requirements of American security. *Struggle*, 111. See also, Langer and Gleason, *Challenge*, 269–70; and Farley, *Jim Farley's Story*, 209.

nents."[147] Isolationists, on the other hand, espoused withdrawal to a fortress America.[148] Had Roosevelt adopted either solution, we would have no need to seek a decision-making explanation for his behaviors. An interventionist policy accords with the imperatives of the international system and an isolationist policy is easily explained in terms of domestic political constraints.

Theories focusing on the structure of the international system predict that in the face of a potential security threat, the United States would join Hitler's opponents to deter further aggression and/or balance internally with a substantial effort to increase her own power. Roosevelt's policy of aiding the democracies did not directly involve either sort of balancing. For one thing, he never considered the kind of unequivocal demonstration of America's interest in Europe that might have deterred Hitler. At minimum that would have meant assuring Britain and France access to American resources in the event of war,[149] which in turn would have required vigorous efforts to make the commitment credible by educating the public to its necessity, dealing forthrightly with isolationist fears and launching a serious and early campaign for neutrality revision. Roosevelt did none of this.

[147] Langer and Gleason, *Challenge*, 49. Stimson, in a letter to the New York *Times* on March 6, 1939, called for "a direct military understanding among the United States, Great Britain, and France, for use in the event of war." Ibid. See also Stimson and Bundy, *On Active Service*, 314.

[148] Even after the onset of World War II, when contemplating the possibility of a Russo-German victory in Europe, Berle mused: "Well, I thought this poses a pretty question. Should we enter the war to relieve the now besieged countries of England and France . . . ? Or do we at once commence to treble our fleet, fortify our coast cities, and build an impregnable Atlantic line?" Berle, *Navigating*, 254. Blum's sense of the administration line up in the fall of 1938 is that

> Within the Cabinet, only Harold Ickes shared Morgenthau's sense of crisis. Secretary of War Harry Woodring, an isolationist, had little stomach for plans to expand the Army and the Air Corps, and Secretary of the Navy Charles Edison had no more spunk. Cordell Hull, the Secretary of State, remained, as he had long been, uneasy about ventures that might provoke the Axis countries, for, though Hull detested fascism, he tended to believe that peace was conditional on the self-restraint of Germany, Italy, and Japan.

Blum, *Morgenthau Diaries*, 2:44.

[149] As French Premier Chautemps observed to Bullitt

> the only effective intervention of the United States in world affairs would be if the President should be able to state that the United States would take arms against an aggressor or at least would cut off status of exports to an aggressor and send supplies to any nation or nations attacked. . . . Such a statement . . . would be sufficient to stop the aggressor states and therefore would end the risk of the United States being involved in war.

Bullitt to Hull, Jan. 4, 1938, *FRUS*, 1938, 1:2. This was not the first time that Chautemps had expressed these views. See Bullitt to Welles, Nov. 10, 1937, *FRUS*, 1937, 4:173.

Moreover, although the promise of aid when he had little to give might have been a stratagem to get the democracies to balance Hitler while America built up its own strength, there is little in Roosevelt's behavior to sustain such an interpretation.[150] After Munich, he moved steadily to involve the United States with Britain and France, willingly becoming more entangled than a policy of "ruthless caution" required.[151] He even treated the possibility of eventually being drawn into a European war with considerable equanimity.[152] Failing to take full advantage of America's geographical isolation, Roosevelt offered the democracies fairly substantial help when the threat to the United States was still remote.[153] Nor, in aiding them was he buying time in order to acquire an impressive deterrent himself. If he did not attempt to balance externally, he also declined to do so by substantially increasing American capabilities.[154] In fact, he did not engage in serious balancing of any sort until the spring of 1940, nearly two years after he first diagnosed the threat. Although he

---

[150] Indeed, he has been roundly criticized by Bruce Russett for *not* pursuing such a policy during World War II, staying out but providing the Allies with all aid short of war, or "fighting to the last ally." *No Clear and Present Danger* (New York: Harper and Row, 1972), 69.

[151] Barry Posen explains the behavior of Britain, France, and the Soviet Union in the 1930s in terms of this strategy. "Competing Images of the Soviet Union," *World Politics* 39 (1987): 584. See also Posen, *Sources of Military Doctrine*, 155, 177; and Alan Alexandroff and Richard Rosecrance, "Deterrence in 1939," *World Politics* 29 (1977):408.

[152] See, for example, his letter to Ambassador Phillips on September 15, 1938.

[153] An example of this is his neutrality-patrol scheme. According to King George VI, during their second meeting at Hyde Park in June 1939, Roosevelt was " 'terribly keen' " on it: "If he saw a U Boat he would sink her at once & wait for the consequences." The idea "is that U.S.A. should relieve us of these responsibilities." Sir John Wheeler-Bennett, *King George VI* (New York: St. Martin's Press, 1958), 390–92. See also Leutze, *Bargaining for Supremacy*, 43–44; and Morgenthau's account on April 20, 1939:

> He says that he is going to have a patrol from Newfoundland down to South America and if some submarines are laying there and try to interrupt an American flag and our Navy sinks them, it's just too bad. What are they going to do? In other words, he is going to play the game the way they are doing it now. If we fire and sink an Italian or German, well, it was just as he said, we will say the way the Japs do, "So sorry." "Never happen again." Tomorrow we sink two.

Morgenthau Diary 180:316–39. See also Blum, *Morgenthau Diaries*, 2:91. For MacKenzie King's account of the meeting between Roosevelt and George VI, see Stacey, *Arms, Men and Governments*, 98. See also, Hall *North American Supply*, 43; Lash, *Roosevelt and Churchill*, 64–65; Conn and Fairchild, *Framework*, 22–25. In March 1939, just after the Czech takeover, Roosevelt had authorized the resumption of naval staff talks with the British; these were held in June. Leutze, *Bargaining*, 34–39.

[154] This might have been his best course: "In a multipolar system, . . . status quo states in a more favorable position may pay more attention to their own military capabilities and less to coalition building, because they perceive themselves as better able to go it alone, at least for a time." Posen, *Sources of Military Doctrine*, 65.

shared the interventionists' goal of deterring Germany, Roosevelt did not adopt their policies.

Similarly, while he subscribed to the isolationists' aim of keeping out of war, Roosevelt did not accept their prescription of withdrawal and building American strength as insurance, even though such a policy would unquestionably have enjoyed considerable popular and congressional support.[155] Rather, despite the political difficulties facing other elements of his program, he consistently pushed against the domestic constraint, particularly when aid for the democracies was at stake.[156] Indeed, while some have argued that anxiety about his political position greatly influenced his post-Munich policies,[157] Roosevelt himself did not seem particularly worried, expressing little concern after setbacks in the 1938 primaries[158] and maintaining this equanimity in the face of serious Democratic losses in the election itself.[159]

Of course, despite his confidence about his personal standing and the public's ultimate acceptance of his foreign policy, Roosevelt was far from complacent about short-run domestic support—witness the fear he expressed to the Senate Military Affairs Committee about "scaring the American people" and his very different public presentation of the policies he announced to his adminstration on November 14.[160] What is

[155] As early as 1935 the American Legion coupled its isolationist prescription with "insistence on adequate defense to assure the impossibility of invasion and the unlikelihood of attack." Jonas, *Isolationism*, 123.

[156] Cole describes Roosevelt's performance in his meeting with the Senate Military Affairs Committee as "boldly frank. . . . He had described in alarming terms the seriousness of the Axis challenge. He had explained the policies he intended to follow in the face of that foreign menace. . . . It was a concerned group of Senators that left the President that Tuesday afternoon." *Roosevelt*, 306.

[157] Langer and Gleason, *Challenge*, 39.

[158] According to a reporter who interviewed him at the time, "The failure of his appeals for New Deal candidates in the primaries does not worry him, nor will he be greatly cast down if the coming elections result in further setbacks. He is pretty confident that if he were speaking for himself, on a test of his leadership in national issues, the story would be different. His sensitiveness to the feeling of the majority is so acute that he is probably right." Anne O'Hare McCormick, "As He Sees Himself," *New York Times Magazine*, Oct. 16, 1938.

[159] In the first post-election Cabinet meeting, "the election was not referred to until the end of the session when the President remarked that he did not think it had done us any damage." Ickes, *Diary*, 2:501; Cole, *Roosevelt*, 294–95. Roosevelt's calm may have been reinforced by Jim Farley's survey of hundreds of state and local Democratic leaders showing that local, state, and personal conditions had often been decisive in the voting, and that few saw the outcome as a reaction to him personally. Roosevelt read many of these letters in late November and early December. Cole, Ibid., 295. According to Farley the President "persisted in viewing the adverse results of the 1938 election as due in every case to local conditions." Farley, *Jim Farley's Story*, 154.

[160] Even after the beginning of the war in Europe, Roosevelt was by no means confident he had the support to obtain neutrality revision, asking the governor general of Canada to postpone a visit until the neutrality fight was over on the grounds that he was "almost literally walking on eggs." Dallek, *Franklin D. Roosevelt*, 202–3.

embarrassing for a domestic-politics explanation, however, is that he continued to push for those policies *despite* concern about the political fallout.[161] Domestic pressures may have produced circumspection, even secrecy; they did not cause Roosevelt to abandon his chosen policy.

Explanations of Roosevelt's post-Munich behavior focusing exclusively on either international or domestic constraints cannot be accepted merely on the grounds that he wanted to balance German power but was prevented from doing so by domestic forces. In order to be credited, these explanations must account for the course he actually did take, and that they cannot do. In adopting the policy of aiding the allies, Roosevelt made an idiosyncratic choice that seemed to please no one, isolationist or interventionist.[162]

RECOGNIZING THE VALUE CONFLICT

Roosevelt's policies can only be explained in terms of his own understanding of the problem he faced in the aftermath of Munich, an understanding based on a deep concern with both the domestic and the international-policy environments. Aiding the democracies was a response to neither international nor domestic imperatives alone but to Roosevelt's perception of the growing conflict between them.

Before Munich, he had consistently monitored the public's reaction to the international situation, as well as to his own attempts to deal with it. During the crisis itself, while recognizing the impossibility of immediate overt commitment to the democracies, he remained optimistic about the long-term direction of public sentiment, writing Phillips at the height of the crisis that "If a war starts now the situation here will be very different from 1914. . . . Today . . . ninety per cent of our people are definitely anti-German and anti-Italian in sentiment."[163]

[161] Roosevelt's willingness to push against the constraints of public opinion is all the more striking in view of the fact that he tended to exaggerate them. Langer and Gleason, *Challenge*, 49

[162] The theory of bureaucratic politics, expecting policies cobbled together to accommodate various bureaucratic and political interests, is not embarrassed by a decision that satisfies the full range of concerns of neither those driven by international imperatives nor those representing various domestic pressures. However, it too fails to explain the policies that emerged in the aftermath of Munich. Roosevelt alone was the architect of those policies and the policy outcomes do not mirror the balance of bureaucratic forces, but rather reflect the sort of subjective adjustment of values that can be explained only at the decision-making level of analysis. For more discussion of this point, see Farnham, "Value Conflict," 633–35.

[163] *PL*, 2:810–11. Roosevelt's sense of public opinion was fairly accurate. The answer to the July 27, 1938 Gallup poll question, "If England and France have a war with Germany and Italy, which would you support?" was: England and France, 65 percent; Germany and Italy, 3 percent; Neither 32 percent. *The Gallup Poll: Public Opinion 1935–*

While some have seen Roosevelt's postcrisis attempts to deal with the threat of German aggression as constrained by the knowledge that the American people "lacked the will" to act decisively,[164] his understanding of the domestic climate was considerably more nuanced.[165] Thus, his insistence at the November 14 meeting that he "must begin to lay the matter before the country" showed a measure of confidence in the possibility of educating the public.[166] Although he stressed the need for secrecy when instructing the Senate Military Affairs Committee about the seriousness of the international threat "because the country would not understand it in those terms,"[167] he also suggested that if the task were done properly, it would eventually be possible to bring people to understand the situation.[168]

1971 (New York: Random House, 1972), 1:112. While it is not known if Roosevelt saw this poll, according to Judge Rosenman he had "great respect" for public-opinion polls. Cited in Barron, *Leadership in Crisis,* 53 n. 46. In fact, beginning in the spring of 1940, Roosevelt received "a regular flow of polling information" from Princeton professor Hadley Cantril, particularly with respect to the trends in public attitudes about the war in Europe. Charles Roll, Jr., and Albert H. Cantril, *Polls: Their Use and Misuse in Politics* (New York: Basic Books, 1972), 10–11; and Hadley Cantril, *The Human Dimension* (New Brunswick, N.J.: Rutgers University Press, 1967), 35–51. I am indebted to Richard Sobel for calling this to my attention. Other relevant polls of the period may be found in "American Institute of Public Opinion—Surveys, 1938–1939," *Public Opinion Quarterly* 3 (1939):589; Jonas, *Isolationism,* 211–12; and Jacob, "Influences of World Events," 53–63.

[164] Alsop and Kintner, *American White Paper,* 15–16.

[165] For example, on October 21, 1938, he asked Arthur Murray to tell Chamberlain "that whereas a year or two ago, only ten per cent of the people of America realised that if a Germany-Italy-Japan alliance succeeded in obtaining a dominating position their next step would be South America, at least forty per cent now realised that fact. One of his difficulties, of course, was that the last of the democracies to be really hit would be the United States." Elibank, "Franklin Roosevelt," 364–65.

[166] Oliphant "Meeting," 341.

[167] See also Roosevelt's remarks to Ickes in late January 1939, and Hull's response to British warnings about Hitler, "that at the present moment reasons of internal politics made it necessary for the President to proceed with great caution." Mallet to Halifax, Jan. 1, 1939, *DBFP*, Series 3, 4:27. After the furor caused by the claim that Roosevelt had said "our frontiers are on the Rhine," when asked why anyone would attribute to him a phrase that he denied using, he answered, "Very simple. It is the kind of term that could scare the American people, politically, and out of which they could make political capital." "Press Conference, on the Presidential Train En Route from Washington to Florida City, Florida, February 17, 1939, 2:30 p.m.," Schewe, 7: no. 1598.

[168] Bullitt's report to Polish Ambassador Lukasiewicz on returning to Paris in February 1939 captures these two aspects of Roosevelt's diagnosis of the domestic situation in the aftermath of the Munich crisis:

A foreign policy of the United States as an endeavor of direct participation in the development of affairs in Europe does not and could not exist, since it would not be endorsed by public opinion, which has not changed its isolationist attitude in this respect. On the other hand, there is a noticeable increase in the interest of the Ameri-

Despite his optimism about the trend of public opinion, however, Roosevelt's domestic diagnosis confronted him with a serious policy dilemma. The security of the United States would be jeopardized by Hitler's domination of Europe, which must therefore be prevented, but America's determination to stay out of war meant that anything ostensibly leading to that outcome must be avoided. This dilemma is reflected in Under Secretary Welles's account of his discussions with Roosevelt after the Munich crisis, during which

> Two main considerations were agreed on as governing all American policy. 1) The best policy is the one which will be most likely to keep us from direct involvement. 2) But this cannot be a policy of complete isolation, for if we refuse to use our influence in the world we shall reach a stage where our foreign interests will be the playthings of other nations.[169]

Others who were aware of this value conflict believed that it could not be transcended. As Raymond Moley observed, "The promise implicit in all Roosevelt's moves—the promise in which he assuredly believes with all his heart—is that we can prevent or shorten war by active intervention in European affairs and still keep out of war ourselves. Unfortunately, it is a promise that no living human being can guarantee."[170] Roosevelt, however, was determined to avoid the sacrifice of value that either intervention or withdrawal entailed, choosing instead the policy of aiding the democracies as a way of stopping Hitler without going to war. It would promote deterrence by convincing the Führer that America would aid Britain and France in the event of war. If deterrence failed nonetheless, it would provide the democracies with the means to prevail over Germany without directly involving the United States.[171]

---

can people in the European situation, to the extent that even domestic events move into the background and lose the attention they normally enjoy.

Lukasiewicz, *Diplomat in Paris*, 168.

[169] Interview with Sumner Welles, n.d., Alsop Papers. See also Alsop and Kintner, *American White Paper*, 15–16. This view is supported by other contemporary testimony, such as Navy Secretary Edison's description of Roosevelt's state of mind in the aftermath of Munich. Expecting that war in Europe could come at any time, "All sorts of precautions were taken to get the Navy ready without alarming the people. . . . But anything like a general effort of preparation was feared as needlessly exciting." Edison interview, n.d., Alsop papers. Both of these interviews were for *American White Paper* and probably took place in December 1939.

[170] Raymond Moley, *After Seven Years* (New York: Harper and Brothers, 1939), 384.

[171] Roosevelt's reasoning is captured in a key member of the administration's analysis of Bullitt's views, which mirrored the president's:

> He regards American isolation from European affairs as utterly impossible. He considers American involvement in foreign conflict as to be avoided at all costs. Therefore, his objective is now and always has been *to prevent* a war by giving the Eu-

How are we to explain Roosevelt's definition of the problem confronting him after Munich? Of the decision-making theories discussed earlier, only the analytical and political approaches expect value conflicts to be readily recognized, and the political approach alone specifically predicts that, along with assessing the international situation, decision-makers will try to evaluate the domestic environment. However, while analytical approaches assume that value conflicts are discovered during evaluation when values are first compared,[172] Roosevelt recognized the conflict between staying out of war and stopping Hitler well before evaluating his alternatives.

This accords with the predictions of the political approach, which expects the acceptability constraint to encourage decision-makers to seek out information about values and search actively for potential conflicts before they ever begin to assess the alternatives. It is the need to act, rather than the consideration of particular policies, that leads them initially to discover value conflicts.[173] Thus, the perception that Hitler's domination of Europe would threaten American security caused Roosevelt to define the security value as "stop Hitler," converting a vague worry into a concrete problem requiring action and triggering a review of the domestic situation that disclosed a potential conflict with the value of peace.

Resolving the Value Conflict

Neither motivational nor intuitive approaches to decision-making would have predicted aid to the democracies as a solution to that value conflict. Holding that decision-makers find value conflicts too painful or too difficult to resolve, both expect a choice that is easily arrived at or psychologically comforting, one favored on a single dimension with the other

---

ropean democracies such American support that the aggressor machines will not dare to attack. The support he desires to give is not in the matter of an alliance or anything else entailing any risk to the United States. It is merely such support as the democracies will derive from our making of [*sic*] material and industrial resources freely available to them. . . . It is, of course, the goal of the President's policy also.

Memorandum of an interview with H. F., March 8, 1939, Alsop papers. For a similar interpretation of Bullitt's views, see Stromberg, *Collective Security*, 137; and Lukasiewicz, *Diplomat in Paris*, 168–70. Cole agrees with Bullitt's analysis and emphasizes in particular the degree to which it was influenced by Roosevelt's diagnosis of the mood of the country. *Roosevelt*, 298.

[172] See appendix A.

[173] At some level, of course, the decision-maker may already be aware of one or more alternatives in the sense that various ways of acting may come to mind virtually simultaneously with problem diagnosis.

values pulled into line, and thoroughly bolstered.[174] For both, the prime candidate after Munich would have been rearmament, presented as not only a safeguard to American security but also a deterrent to Hitler and thus a means of avoiding American involvement. As Janeway points out, this would also have been relatively easy to achieve. Nevertheless, rather than adopting the intellectually and emotionally least-demanding course, Roosevelt chose a more complicated policy that caused him considerable pain and trouble to defend.

Aiding the democracies was not, however, a choice the analytical approach would necessarily have foreseen. As we have noted, instead of trading off, Roosevelt sought a transcendent solution that served both values and satisfied the acceptability constraint. Since aid to the democracies, unlike overt commitment, did not conflict directly with the value of peace, it would be at least minimally acceptable even to Congress.[175] For this reason, one might consider it the optimal solution for a decision-maker with Roosevelt's value structure. The problem, however, is that it was not uniquely so. Janeway, for example, argues that the optimal choice was rearming for national and hemisphere defense while retaining the option of aiding the allies once the arms had been built. Because that policy addressed the security issue and was highly acceptable as well, it too would fall within Roosevelt's set of feasible alternatives. Thus, since the analytical approach cannot identify a uniquely optimal solution, it could not have predicted Roosevelt's choice.[176]

A political approach to decision-making, by contrast, predicts Roosevelt's choice because aid to the democracies, unlike rearmament, has one feature that makes it uniquely attractive to a political decision-maker: its ability to serve as the nucleus of a long-term political strategy to increase the acceptability of greater American engagement in international affairs.

---

[174] Ambassador Kennedy's behavior after Munich fits the predictions of the motivational approach. "While regretfully acknowledging the Nazi threat, . . . [he] strove manfully to fit it in with his preconceptions," coming up with three quite different solutions between Munich and the beginning of World War II.

> In this search for a rational justification of his deepest convictions there was one point of consistency: all three conceptions permitted the United States to stay out of war. Each argument in effect demonstrated that American interests either would not be affected by what was occurring in Europe, or could be maintained successfully without resort to violence.

Kaufmann, "Two Ambassadors," 666.

[175] Roosevelt's awareness of this comes through clearly in his presentation to the Senate Military Affairs Committee, where he offered a "vigorous defense of American airplane sales abroad as an easy method of improving American national defense." Interview with Senator Austin, Dec. 8, 1939, Alsop papers.

[176] For a discussion of the problem of indeterminacy, see Jon Elster, *Solomonic Judgments* (Paris: Cambridge University Press, 1989), 7–17.

Rearmament, though more acceptable in the short run, could not help Roosevelt with his domestic problem if Hitler remained undeterred because it would not prepare the American people for the possibility that they might ultimately have to go much further to protect their security. Roosevelt chose aid to the democracies because it allowed him to initiate a long-range strategy directed at the domestic side of the value conflict. Meeting present security requirements without "scaring" the American people, it gained time to educate them to the ultimate reality of their situation. Indeed, it was the mirror image of his domestic diagnosis.

This is also why Roosevelt went to some lengths to defend that policy but refused to push for measures that many believed might have served security better. Because aiding the democracies alone offered the possibility of transcending the value conflict in the present and over the long haul, it, unlike other policies, was worth fighting for. Consequently, Roosevelt assessed all other moves in terms of their impact on its political chances—witness his treatment of the Senate isolationists. He pressed them on measures that furthered aid to the democracies but not those entailing greater American involvement, which might alienate them and jeopardize the chances of the one policy he believed would work.[177]

That aid to the democracies was the cornerstone of a long-term strategy for enhancing acceptability also explains Roosevelt's timing. His rule of thumb was to do only what needed doing at any one moment. In the aftermath of the Munich crisis, that meant deterring Hitler from further aggression in Europe by selling planes to the democracies. When it became necessary to do more, as when the British guarantee to Poland made war likely, Roosevelt increased his efforts and pushed for neutrality revision.

This approach to timing grew out of Roosevelt's understanding that success in satisfying the security value depended upon his ability to construct a political coalition behind it. Balancing domestic and international pressures, steering a course between isolationist and interventionist demands, he moved steadily to build support for action in the international arena, doing only what was absolutely essential to deal with the external threat so that he could continue to nourish the domestic foreign-policy consensus on which future action depended. Unlike the isolationists, the lesson Roosevelt drew from the World War I was not about the United States being drawn into other people's wars, but about what was necessary to get effective action in the American political system.

---

[177] Hence Roosevelt's sensitivity to exposing a lack of consensus within his Administration. What he minded most about the French plane controversy was not that it aroused the interest of Congress but that it exposed the divisions within the administration. Similarly, Roosevelt was annoyed with Morgenthau primarily because his fight with Woodring became public. Blum, *Morgenthau Diaries*, 2:76–77.

A similar logic informed his education campaign. Believing that domestic opinion was moving in the direction of aiding the democracies, Roosevelt wished to do nothing to retard the process. Thus, he was unwilling to educate the public about the need to stop Hitler at any cost precisely because that might jeopardize the one policy he believed would let him avoid that step.[178] But when it was a question of protecting aid to the democracies, Roosevelt made quite strenuous efforts to persuade the American people, Congress, and the press of its value, seizing every opportunity to explain it and present it in a favorable light.[179]

In conducting his education campaign, Roosevelt used many tactics, including such diplomatic moves as his April 14, 1939, appeal to the dictators.[180] At times these could be quite subtle. For example, Eleanor Roosevelt has written that his invitation to the King and Queen of England in the spring of 1939 was motivated by the belief that "we might

---

[178]
The President and his advisers . . . clearly hoped that, in the long run, Britain and France would be able to defeat their opponents, especially if they could draw on the United States for material aid. The immediate need, then, seemed less for a reversal of the established attitude than for a modification of it in the sense of converting it to a stronger American initiative in the effort to prevent war and to win approval of a policy of aiding the European democracies in preparation for hostilities. This Mr. Roosevelt apparently hoped to accomplish without provoking too much public controversy, avoidance of which seemed to him at the time to be absolutely essential.

Langer and Gleason, *Challenge*, 39.

[179] On Roosevelt's attempts to educate Congress, see Senator Austin's account of the president's three meetings with the senators. Interview with Senator Austin, Dec. 8, 1939, Alsop Papers. On similar efforts directed at the press, see his press conferences of February 17, April 15, and April 20, 1939. Schewe, 8: no. 1598, 9: no.s 1721, 1744; and Bennett, *Search for Security*, 159–61. Roosevelt was not above manipulating the press into informing the public about some of the dangers he feared without directly involving himself. On February 18, for example, he told reporters, "I want to get something across, only don't put it that way. In other words, it is a thing that I cannot put as direct stuff, but it is background." He then proceeded to give them not only the information he wanted them to convey, but instructions about how to write the story. "The Five Hundred and Twenty-sixth Press Conference (Excerpts); at a CCC Camp in Florida. February 18, 1939," *PPA*, 8:140.

[180] In his Pan American Day Address and a public appeal to the dictators the following day, Roosevelt invited the dictators to give assurances that they would not attack thirty-one specific nations for at least ten years, an overture that elicited only an openly contemptuous response from Hitler. Berle, *Navigating*, 211, 213–14; Hull, *Memoirs*, 1:620–21; Ickes, *Diary*, 2:619–20, 626; Alsop and Kintner, *American White Paper*, 35–37; Langer and Gleason, *Challenge*, 83–90; Dallek, *Franklin D. Roosevelt*, 186–87. According to Welles, Roosevelt intended as much to build a record against the dictators as to rid "the world of the terrible fear of aggression. As Roosevelt himself observed to MacKenzie King on April 16, 1939, "If we are turned down the issue becomes clearer and public opinion in your country and mine will be helped." Welles interview, late 1939, Alsop Papers; *PL*, 1939, 879. See also Reynolds, *Creation*, 43.

all soon be engaged in a life-and-death struggle, in which Great Britain would be our first line of defense, [and] he hoped that their visit would create a bond of friendship between the peoples of the two countries."[181]

Clearly, Roosevelt's desire to educate the country to the realities of the international situation was tempered with caution, particularly as to timing.[182] Far from withdrawing in the face of domestic challenges, however, after Munich he behaved much as he had in the aftermath of the Quarantine Speech, giving the appearance of pulling back while actually holding to his course.[183] While he was not "deterred from pursuing increasingly internationalist policies in the face of Axis challenges from abroad, . . . the furor at home made him more cautious (and even devious) in his tactics for dealing with isolationists, with Congress, and with the American public."[184]

[181] Eleanor Roosevelt, *This I Remember* (New York: Harper and Brothers, 1949), 200; also cited in Barron, *Leadership*, 44. Roosevelt's approach to educating the public is nicely illustrated by the care with which he approached his speech at the beginning of the war in September 1939. As Alsop and Kintner recorded his subsequent account of his strategy:

> The President, after the outbreak of war, wanted to wait at least two weeks before calling Congress into session. He wanted the significance of the conflict, the forces at work, and the line-up of democracy versus dictatorship to see [sic] in. At the out break, there was nothing but talk of 'For God's Sake Keep Us Out' or 'Let's Not Talk About it at all, it is not our concern.' The President wanted time for the people to get the implications. He also wanted time to get some reaction from the country.

Notes of an interview with Roosevelt on February 9, 1940, Alsop papers. On Roosevelt's general attitude toward educating the public, see Schlesinger, *Age of Roosevelt*, 2:558.

[182] Representative Bloom somewhat inelegantly likened Roosevelt's strategy to accustoming an individual to strong drink by giving him small doses. *The Autobiography of Sol Bloom* (New York: G. P. Putnam's Sons, 1948), 246. See also Hull, *Memoirs*, 1:545. Mallet summarized Roosevelt's views for the British Foreign Office on January 27:

> The President and the Secretary of State [are] . . . anxious to do what they can to help but are obsessed by the risk of going too far ahead of public opinion and thus losing control of Congress. . . . President Roosevelt evidently feels he must exercise greatest care not to give a handle to the isolationists and he presumably feels he has in his speech of January 4th said as much as he safely can for the present.

Quoted in Cole, *Roosevelt*, 311–12.

[183] Note Cantril's observation about Roosevelt's use of public-opinion polls:

> Roosevelt regarded the reports sent him the way a general would regard information turned in by his intelligence services as he planned the strategy of a campaign. As far as I am aware, Roosevelt never altered his goals because public opinion appeared against him or was uninformed. Rather he utilitzed such information to try to bring the public around more quickly or more effectively to the course of action he felt was best for the country.

Cantril, *Human Dimension*, 41–42. See also Richard W. Steele, *Propaganda in an Open Society* (Westport, Conn.: Greenwood Press, 1985), 6.

[184] Cole, *Roosevelt*, 309.

This deviousness shows the less attractive side of Roosevelt's attempts to influence public opinion. At times concern with acceptability led him to mask his chosen policy. Thus, he neglected to mention it to Farley or Alsop and Kintner, emphasizing instead rearmament, hemisphere defense, and neutrality revision. While aid to the democracies was his response to his diagnosis of external threat, attempting to present it in ways that were unthreatening was his response to the domestic constraint.

Thus Roosevelt chose to aid the democracies because it was the one policy that would work both substantively and politically, in the long run as well as the short. Since it was at least minimally acceptable, it could transcend the value conflict in the present by allowing him to do what was needed immediately to serve the security value (bolster the democracies, begin to build planes). This bought him time to do what was required to continue to transcend it in the future (foster consensus, increase aid to the democracies if necessary, and educate the public, relying on the passage of time to create more favorable conditions for action should additional steps be required). As part of a sequencing strategy,[185] aid to the democracies served as the core of a long-range effort to resolve the value conflict not only by spacing out the satisfaction of the security value but also by expanding the domain of domestic acceptability.

Information Processing

In a remarkably short time, Roosevelt developed a coherent, hierarchically arranged group of policies to deal with the value conflict he perceived after Munich. The speed of the decision process was due to a relatively rapid screening of the alternatives made possible both by his familiarity with them and the fact that he apparently weighed them against only two values.

Ranging from the least to the most involving, the options available as a result of prior consideration were: isolation, doing nothing, disarmament, diplomatic steps and measures short of war, rearmament, hemisphere defense, neutrality revision, aid to the democracies, blockade/quarantine, overt commitment to Britain and France, and armed intervention. In evaluating these, Roosevelt seems not to have compared them directly, but rather to have measured them against the values of both security and peace (the quality of acceptability being strongly associated with the latter), treating each as a constraint and searching for a transcendent solution to the conflict between them. Such a process would have quickly eliminated the six alternatives that required trading off one

[185] See appendix B.

of those values. Applying the acceptability constraint ruled out armed intervention (and deterrent threats implying it), overt commitment, and blockade.[186] Doing nothing, isolation, and disarmament were eliminated by Roosevelt's diagnosis of the external threat.[187] What remained was aid to the democracies and the package of options he represented to Alsop and Kintner and Farley as his chosen policy: rearmament, hemisphere defense, and measures short of war, with neutrality revision as a symbol of intent.

Aiding the democracies with planes emerged from this initial screening as the clear favorite, commanding the lion's share of Roosevelt's attention between the crisis and the November 14 conference. Its prominence appears to have been an outgrowth of his evaluation of both the source of Germany's success during the crisis and the type of threat she would pose in the future. The cause of the problem was also the solution: since Hitler had prevailed at Munich due to Germany's predominance in the air, the way to stop him was to strengthen the democracies' air forces. This dovetailed neatly with the structure of the value conflict itself. On the one hand, airforce capability was the main component of the German threat to America; on the other, aiding the democracies with planes provided the means of solving the security problem without getting the country into war.[188]

That policy also provides a striking illustration of the impact of prior experience on evaluation. In May 1938, Roosevelt refused to allow the democracies to purchase planes under contract to the armed services, writing Bullitt that to do so "would contravene a wise policy of long

[186] Roosevelt told the November 14 meeting that "sending a large army abroad was . . . politically out of the question" and, as Gaddis's reference to his "fundamental aversion to the use of American manpower to bring about major geopolitical shifts in world affairs" suggests, he may have objected to this policy on ideological grounds as well. Gaddis, *Strategies of Containment* (Oxford: Oxford University Press, 1982), 7–8. See also Roosevelt's remarks to the Senate Military Affairs Committee in January 1939. Other sorts of overt commitment were not seriously considered after the crisis. Regarding a blockade, Roosevelt replied with a flat negative to the president of Mexico's suggestion to establish "a boycott against the aggressor countries," probably on the grounds of acceptability, just as he had in 1937 made domestic acceptability an absolute condition of employing a quarantine or blockade.

[187] Roosevelt's postcrisis diagnosis had not only confirmed his belief that Germany possessed the capability to threaten the United States, but led him to expect that Hitler would eventually use it. Since neither inaction nor isolation would prevent this, the diagnosis itself ruled them out. It seems likely that it also eliminated disarmament. Roosevelt's pious expression of hope to Chamberlain on October 5 about the possibility of establishing a new world order and his somewhat ambiguous reference to disarmament in an October 11 letter to King are belied by his permission for French pilots to test-fly American planes on October 4 and his October 11 call for an increase in the defense budget.

[188] Alsop and Kintner, *American White Paper*, 18.

standing. . . . On general principles, I do not believe that we should permit the diversion to other governments of planes manufactured under contract for this Government *unless the interests of our national defense are directly involved.*[189] When Munich led him to believe that aiding the democracies was indeed directly related to national defense, he reversed himself and approved the measure.[190] Since he had already evaluated it against just such a contingency ("unless the interests of our national defense are directly involved"), when that situation arose, further assessment was unnecessary.

In adopting this course, Roosevelt did not altogether eliminate the remaining group of policies. Rather, he blended them with his chosen policy, emphasizing the qualities of each that transcended any potential conflict between meeting the external threat and staying out of war.[191] Because rearmament and hemisphere defense were even more acceptable to a wide segment of the American public than aiding the democracies, they could provide cover for it.[192] Thus, as the political approach to decision-making predicts, the desire to enhance acceptability led Roosevelt to use design as well as search to arrive at a policy.

That these options had antecedents in the development of Roosevelt's foreign policy prior to the crisis accounts for the speed with which he was able to design his final policy package. Some were an integral part of his belief system; others became familiar as he evaluated them as solutions to current problems or anticipated future contingencies. His experience with rearmament was of the first variety;[193] his experience with neu-

---

[189] "William C. Bullitt, Ambassador to France, to Roosevelt, May 12, 1938," Schewe, 6:1086; "Roosevelt to William C. Bullitt, Ambassador to France, June 5, 1938," ibid., no. 1138.

[190] On October 4 he approved trial flights by French pilots of planes under construction for the navy. In December he also authorized a French effort to purchase these planes, as well as others still in the experimental stage.

[191] On blending, see appendix A.

[192] As Langer and Gleason note, "While the temper of the country and the attitude of Congress dictated caution with respect to the affairs of Europe, the President could reckon on a large measure of support, even from the isolationists, for a program of national and hemisphere defense." *Challenge*, 39–40. See also Divine, *Illusion*, 230–31; Pogue, *Marshall*, 1:322; Watson, *Chief of Staff*, 96, 132–33; Alsop and Kintner, *American White Paper*, 17; Cole, *Roosevelt*, 297–98, 357–61; and Kittredge, "United States Defense Policies," chap. 5, 39. That this was at least initially part of Roosevelt's reason for including them is suggested strongly by both his failure to mention his actual policy at his October 14 press conference, emphasizing American defense needs instead, and his lack of candor about his true purpose at the Hyde Park and the November 14 meetings.

[193] The notion of rearmament as the primary pillar of American defense violated a strongly held tenet of Roosevelt's basic philosophy: "Roosevelt was an early and firm believer in the 'arsenal of democracy' concept—the idea that the United States could most effectively contribute toward the maintenance of international order by expending technology but not manpower." Gaddis, *Strategies*, 6.

trality revision, the second; and his familiarity with hemisphere defense, of both, as was his experience with aiding the democracies.[194] The latter, in fact, was an integral part of his attitude toward rearmament as the arsenal of democracy and a measure he had frequently considered before the Munich crisis.[195]

As to the quality of Roosevelt's evaluation, although aid to the democracies emerged as a dominant alternative early in the process, there is no evidence that Roosevelt engaged in confirmation processing. Rather, he was open to new evidence, accepting some challenges to his chosen policy (compromising with the military about the ratio of planes to support systems, for example) and attempting to work around others. As Morgenthau remarked after the November 14 meeting, "in the month or so he has been talking about 'this thing,' the President has been getting more and more practical about it."[196]

On the other hand, Roosevelt does not seem to have given much thought to the costs of aiding the democracies, particularly in the event of failure. However, in view of his beliefs that stronger measures were politically unacceptable and that Hitler would ultimately threaten the United States, it may not have been unreasonable for him to adopt the strongest policy available without inquiring too closely into the risks of failure. While one can criticize Roosevelt on the grounds that his desire to act led him to make fateful decisions without adequate reflection, the political decision-maker's drive for action may also have distinct advantages, as Kaufmann points out in contrasting Roosevelt's behavior to Ambassador Kennedy's:

> the situation [after Munich] was almost out of hand from the standpoint of making rational and calculated decisions. There were so many imponderables to evaluate and equate. . . . Such are the problems which, despite the daydreams of experts, make politicians necessary. . . . Where alternatives cannot be carefully weighed for relative merit, the statesman can do worse

[194] Kittredge points out that "United States policy after 1919 became increasingly identified with programs for hemisphere defense," and during the late 1930s Roosevelt himself had become concerned about the military implications of developments in the hemisphere. While he told his Cabinet in February 1937 that "from the point of view of distance, the Britishers had always thought of Italy as we have of Brazil, but Italy's airfleet had altered that situation," by April 1938, he had come to see a Nazi-controlled Brazil as similar threat. Kittredge, "United States Defense Policies," chap. 6, 29. Ickes, *Diary*, 2:84.

[195] In February 1938, Roosevelt expressed the hope to Monnet "that the threat to ship American arms to the European democracies would make the Fascist dictators pause before launching a war." Haight, *American Aid*, 7, and "Roosevelt as Friend," 90. The topic of helping the democracies construct aircraft plants in Canada had arisen even before the crisis. See above.

[196] Presidential Diary, 1:0055.

than to define broadly the interests of his country and act boldly for their protection. That at least gives him a share in the government of events. The alternative of withdrawal involves surrendering the shape of the unknown future to other and perhaps unfriendly hands.[197]

[197] Kaufmann, "Two Ambassadors," 665.

Implications for History and Theory

MANY HAVE ARGUED THAT President Roosevelt lacked a coherent foreign policy before Pearl Harbor and merely drifted in the wake of domestic political pressures. Others have claimed that he was well aware of more effective options, but avoided them owing to his fear of political repercussions.[1] An examination of the decision-making process has shown, however, that in the wake of the Munich crisis Roosevelt concluded that Hitler's implacable aggressiveness, if left unchallenged, would eventually threaten American security, and he quickly settled on the policy of aiding Britain and France with planes, adhering to it tenaciously in the face of all opposition. Far from being immobilized by domestic politics, Roosevelt deliberately chose a course that would allow him to circumvent his isolationist opposition while attempting to transform it through a gradual process of education.

Roosevelt's approach was rooted in the political decision-maker's understanding of choice as part of an ongoing political process, combined with a disposition to keep options open until the proper course of action can emerge. As one of his closest associates described the rationale behind this strategy,

> The important thing to understand is you are never sure of how anything is going to work out when you begin. . . . Everything is the next cake of ice. . . . Do you remember Eliza in *Uncle Tom's Cabin* trying to get across the frozen, iceloaded Ohio River to freedom? Certainly Eliza had in mind freedom on the other side of the Ohio, a free state. But what she was thinking of immediately was the next cake of ice. . . . You know a fellow who is sitting up there has to balance what you can get done with what you've got. . . . The next cake of ice.[2]

[1] Burns accuses Roosevelt of lack of leadership for failing to mobilize the American people behind a more interventionist policy, seeing him as "the captive of political forces" and labeling his behavior "almost a caricature of cautiousness." *Lion*, 398.

[2] "Interview with Tommy Corcoran," *The Roosevelt Presidency: Four Intimate Perspectives of FDR*, ed. Kenneth W. Thompson (Lanham, Md: University Press of America, 1982), 34–35. See also Schlesinger's description of Roosevelt's favorite comparison of himself as a quarterback in a football game: "He could not say what the play after next was going to be until the next play was completed. 'If the play makes ten yards,' he told a press conference in April 1933, 'the succeeding play will be different from what it would have been if they had been thrown for a loss.'" *Age of Roosevelt*, 2:193.

The problem, of course, is that such a strategy may lead to actions that are ambiguous, triggering charges of drift and inconsistency. Its adherents may, like Roosevelt, be accused of sacrificing important national goals when they are in fact trying to protect their foreign policy from being destroyed before they can create a climate in which it has a chance to succeed. Their course is steady, but their path circuitous.[3] After Munich, Roosevelt did have clear long-term goals, but his method of pursuing them was often obscure to both contemporaries and historians.

Even if Roosevelt had a coherent policy, however, it could still have been the wrong one. Why, if he "was aware of the dangers inherent in the European situation," did he not "state them publicly and use his tremendous influence and prestige to induce a change in American opinion?"[4] James MacGregor Burns argues that although Roosevelt was right in believing that the "the best way to keep America out of war would be to keep war out of the world," he made a critical error by failing to convert the nation to a policy of all aid short of war in 1939.[5]

We must be careful, however, not to rely excessively on hindsight. At the very least we should distinguish what might have been done in 1940 and 1941 from what was possible earlier. In 1939, even repealing the arms embargo might not have prevented war. Not only was it politically impossible for Roosevelt to deliver the kind of threat that could have deterred Hitler but, given that he had few arms to offer, such a threat might well not have been credible.[6]

One can, of course, still argue that the policy of aiding the democracies remained in place long after more forceful American participation had become necessary. Roosevelt's policies in 1940 and 1941 are beyond the scope of this study. However, we can at least point to considerable evidence that more forthright steps might easily have failed to gain public support. Stephen Craft argues that "Americans were not in favor of deterring aggression in far off lands before late 1940, but only in preventing attack against U.S. possessions,"[7] a view many of Roosevelt's

---

[3] "Roosevelt's maneuvers in foreign affairs and politics were sometimes like those of a yachtsman who, unable to sail directly toward his destination, tacks against an unfavorable wind. At times there were minor inconsistencies when the hand at the tiller seemed unsure, but his major shifts back and forth in order to arrive at a long-range destination, especially in foreign policy, were by no means accidental." Freidel, *Franklin D. Roosevelt*, 4:454.

[4] Langer and Gleason, *Challenge*, 38–39.

[5] Burns, *Lion*, 400. See also 398–404.

[6] "At some stage an aggressor may well come to believe that the point at which he would suffer severe sanctions is so far removed and so uncertain that it does not serve as a realistic deterrent. Short-term strengths would then determine the outcome." Alexandroff and Rosecrance, "Deterrence in 1939," 422. See also Dallek, *Franklin D. Roosevelt*, 192.

[7] Stephen G. Craft, "Deterring Aggression Abroad or at Home: A Rejoinder to 'FDR's Day of Infamy,'" *SHAFR Newsletter* 24 (March 1993): 25.

contemporaries shared.[8] Moreover, the closeness of the House vote to extend the Selective Service Act suggests that even as late as August 1941 measures implying direct participation in war might have been unacceptable.[9]

Beyond this, many think that Roosevelt's policies were actually well suited to the situation he faced. Hofstadter points out that his strategy for educating the public tapped into the "deep fissure . . . in the American public mind" between the fear of facing Germany alone should Hitler prevail in Europe and a desperate wish to stay out of war, while Cole maintains that "aid-short-of-war" was "the near-perfect formula for providing the maximum assistance against the Axis that public opinion and Congress would permit."[10] Others like Leighton go even further, arguing that in laying the foundation for the United States as the "arsenal of democracy," Roosevelt's policy of aid short of war was as successful strategically as it was politically.[11]

No matter how one assesses Roosevelt's decisions in the aftermath of the Munich crisis, discovering the rationale behind them can provide considerable insight into American policy in the years before World War II. Identifying aid to Britain and France as the solution to a value conflict between stopping Hitler and staying out of war illuminates a number of steps on the road to Pearl Harbor: what Roosevelt did not do, as well as what he did. Much as he had in the wake of the Munich crisis, he took action when it was clearly a matter of protecting aid to the allies. If he was uncertain about this, as in the spring of 1941 when he "shied away" from escorting conveys, Roosevelt declined to act.[12] Thus, policies such

---

[8] Thus, Congressman Sol Bloom contended that even as late as 1940 it would have been "mortal folly," to have announced that the United States was certain to be drawn into war, because that outcome was not absolutely certain, because such a statement might have provoked a German or Japanese attack, and because "it would have been politically fatal on the domestic front," guaranteeing defeat in the 1940 elections. *Autobiography*, 245. See also the testimony of Franklin D. Roosevelt, Jr., in Thompson, *Roosevelt Presidency*, 60.

[9] William L. Langer and Everett S. Gleason, *The Undeclared War, 1940–1941* (New York: Harper and Bros., 1953), 570–74.

[10] Richard Hofstadter, "Franklin D. Roosevelt: The Patrician as Opportunist," in Leuchtenberg, *Roosevelt*, 127; Cole, *Roosevelt*, 298.

[11] Leighton, "American Arsenal," 222–24. According to Doris Kearns Goodwin, this mastery extended through World War II: "Roosevelt's success in mobilizing the nation to [an] extraordinary level of collective performance rested on his uncanny sensitivity to his followers, his ability to appraise public feeling and to lead the people one step at a time." *No Ordinary Time* (New York: Simon and Schuster, 1995), 608.

[12] "Opinion was educable, as it had been in the past, but Roosevelt undoubtedly believed that the benefits of intervention did not now justify the risks, domestic and external. As Roosevelt told Stark during a similar dilemma in 1940, 'When I don't know how to move, I stay put.'" Heinrichs, *Threshold*, 46.

as "all possible material support" for the allies in June 1940, the Destroyer Bases deal, Lend Lease (which Roosevelt publicly justified in terms of aiding the allies so the United States would not be forced to fight herself),[13] and, ultimately, escorting convoys, were not just ad hoc responses to a deteriorating international situation, but part of a wider framework for dealing sequentially with a value conflict that persisted until Pearl Harbor. Seen in this light, such steps were not new initiatives but implementing measures for a decision made shortly after Munich. Far from trying to get the country into the war through the "back door,"[14] Roosevelt was attempting to keep America out by keeping the Allies in.

The success of a political approach in explaining Roosevelt's decision-making during the Munich period also has a number of implications for our thinking about how people make decisions. For one thing, it shows how the political context affects both decision-making processes and, through them, outcomes. For another, it tells us that a very important class of decisions involving serious value conflict is often treated politically. Failure to understand this has often led to puzzlement and charges of bias. In particular, as Neustadt points out, political decision-makers have been severely criticized for their unwillingness to make value trade-offs. A political approach to decision-making explains this reluctance as a manifestation of their desire for transcendent solutions. They do not habitually ignore value complexity; they merely handle it differently.

Similarly, a political approach allows us to understand why decision-makers become more attached to certain policies than often seems reasonable. As in the case of aid to the democracies, an option that resolves a value conflict may well be preferred to one more effective in terms of substance. Moreover, even if a transcendent solution to a conflict between domestic and international values begins to unravel on the international dimension, it may be retained in an effort to buy time to educate the public to the new reality, especially if recognizing a potential trade-off could trigger political controversy that might block action altogether, or even force the choice of the wrong value.[15]

Less obvious, perhaps, is the notion that political decision-makers experience choice as an ongoing process and that this strongly influences

---

[13] Dallek, *Franklin D. Roosevelt,* 228–29, 244, 256.

[14] See Charles C. Tansill, *Back Door to War: The Roosevelt Foreign Policy, 1933–1941* (Chicago: Regnery, 1952).

[15] Roosevelt "conceived of foreign policy not as a fixed program but as a process. . . . He would do today only what was necessary and and fully intended, lest he have to do tomorrow something necessary but not intended." Eric Larrabee, *Commander in Chief* (New York: Harper and Row, 1987), 61.

their behavior. Because issues tend to recur in a political context, they may well have been dealt with previously, which gives some policy options a significant history.[16] Thus, failure to take account of prior experience may lead to the conclusion that a decision process has been marked by attenuated search, failure to consider a respectable range of alternatives, or cursory evaluation when in fact search and evaluation may already have been performed repeatedly in the past. Of course, a readily available stock of prescreened options could encourage overconfidence about their relevance to the present situation or the decision-maker's understanding of their ramifications, but when time is short, as in a crisis, having a bank account of partially evaluated options on which to draw may be quite useful.

Finally, Roosevelt's behavior confirms the hypothesis that political decision-makers experiment with different policy options as a way of acquiring information and reducing uncertainty. In particular, his experiments in the years between 1936 and 1938 suggest that, under uncertainty, action may be an integral part of the evaluation process, certainly to determine acceptability, but also to see what works substantively.

A POLITICAL APPROACH AND FOREIGN-POLICY ANALYSIS

A political approach to decision-making brings a perspective to the analysis of foreign policy that is missing from theories focusing exclusively on either the international system or domestic politics. Structural realism, for example, often fails to explain foreign-policy decisions adequately, not only because of the generality of its predictions,[17] but also because it ignores domestic constraints. In Roosevelt's situation, realist theories predict balancing. Because they are unable to take account of his domestic problem, however, they can explain neither why he did not balance seriously for almost two years, nor what he did instead.

The two-level game, in which decision-makers are expected to bargain between domestic and international forces, has been suggested as a remedy for such deficiencies.[18] While two-level games acknowledge the "Janus-faced" quality of foreign policy, however, they tell us little about

[16] As James Voss has pointed out, "In considering how an alternative policy is selected, it is important to acknowledge that choosing an alternative to an existing policy is not an isolated event. Changing a policy takes place within the context of a policy making process and that process itself is embedded in a historical context." "Finding Another Policy."

[17] George, *Bridging the Gap*, 112–13.

[18] For an account of two-level games and nested games, see respectively Robert D. Putnam, "Diplomacy and Domestic Politics: The Logic of Two-Level Games," *International Organization* 42 (1988): 427–60; and George Tsebelis, *Nested Games* (Berkeley and Los Angeles: University of California Press, 1990).

how the domestic constraint will be handled.[19] Moreover, when there is more than one equilibrium, two-level games face the problem of indeterminacy.[20] Since Roosevelt had more than one good solution available, for example, a two-level game could not have predicted his choice.

The political approach to decision-making, by contrast, could do so because it not only incorporates domestic factors into the analysis but also tells us how they are likely to be applied, and how that may influence the outcome. In particular, it suggests that political decision-makers react differently to international and domestic constraints and that the weight they assign to domestic factors will strongly affect their treatment of the international problem. Thus, in analyzing foreign-policy decision-making, we cannot assume a level playing field on which all the attributes of alternatives are freely traded off in pursuit of an optimal policy. Rather, the unavoidability of the acceptability constraint creates an implicit hierarchy among the values. Furthermore, the political approach shows how these preferences affect evaluation. Most importantly, because acceptability is an unavoidable constraint, it is likely to be applied to the alternatives first and with a noncompensatory strategy.

The political approach also makes unexpected predictions for resolving conflict between domestic and international interests, such as the choice of policies that may be less satisfactory in cost-benefit terms but better able to deal with the conflict without violating the acceptability constraint. Recognizing that a political decision-maker usually cannot ignore acceptability but will choose an alternative that is acceptable or can be made so, the political approach would have predicted both Roosevelt's refusal to sacrifice either major value and his choice of a policy around which he could build an education campaign and develop a consensus. Because the political approach explains how a good deal of the political and psychological juggling is done, therefore, it is better able to predict how domestic political considerations will affect a decision. At minimum, it suggests that except in cases of extreme threat to national security, the domestic constraint will not be easily traded off against international interests.[21]

On the other hand, incorporating domestic factors into the analysis

---

[19] Huntington, *Common Defense*, 2. The theory of two-level games ignores process, suggesting a very complicated formula for bargaining between domestic and international concerns with computational demands that may be beyond most people, yet gives no idea of how it should be done.

[20] James Johnson, "Is Talk Really Cheap?" *American Political Science Review*," 87 (1993): 79.

[21] Even then, it may not be a matter of ignoring political constraints because the recognition that security is obviously and imminently threatened may itself expand the domain of acceptability.

does not mean that foreign-policy decision-making is driven by domestic politics. A political approach does not imply that awareness of such factors alone will allow us to predict outcomes. Rather, it emphasizes the role of the decision-maker in reconciling competing values. Captive to neither international pressures nor domestic forces, political decision-makers take both into account through a process of balancing (not bargaining as in two-level games) with the goal of obtaining as much of both as possible. This is the impulse behind their quest for transcendent solutions, which at its best leads not just to marginal adjustments but to the design of new options and even the expansion of the domain of acceptability. Thus, as well as pushing against the domestic constraint, Roosevelt tried to change it, ultimately leading policy in a different direction than a domestic-politics perspective would have predicted. He used his decisions to transform the domestic environment into a place where they could succeed and, from the outset, his awareness of the need to do so shaped his choices.

A decision-making theory focusing on the impact of the political context thus offers the possibility of a richer understanding of foreign-policy outcomes than either two-level games or theories of domestic politics.[22] Because it explains more phenomena relating to the political process of foreign-policy development, it encourages a more nuanced account of the impact of domestic politics on foreign policy. Illuminating the decision processes of political decision-makers, it shows how domestic political constraints are transformed into policy through the subjective adjustment of competing values, providing, in other words, insight into how the values of the society become the preferences of the state (or, to use another vocabulary, how the state's utility function is formed).[23]

THE POLITICAL APPROACH TO DECISION-MAKING AND DECISION-MAKING THEORY

The distinction between a political approach and the three traditional approaches to decision-making does not lie merely in the strong influence of political considerations on a decision-maker's objectives. Rather, the

[22] Of course, pitting the political approach to decision-making against domestic-politics or international-systems explanations does not exclude the possibility of a multilevel explanation. As Alexander George notes, "Alternative candidate theories may not be mutually exclusive but sometimes act in a complementary way to arrive at a richer, more comprehensive explanation" (Personal communication). See also Larson, *Origins*, 324–42; and Philip E. Tetlock, "Methodological Themes and Variations," in *Behavior, Society and Nuclear War*, ed. Tetlock et al. (New York: Oxford University Press, 1989), 1:340, 365–66.

[23] As Bryan Jones has noted, "politicians are a critical key to aggregation." *Reconsidering Decision-making*, 229.

political approach provides a competing explanation. First of all, the political decision-maker offers a contrast to the intuitive approach's "cognitive miser" who is merely "muddling through." Owing to the need to reconcile conflicting interests within the framework of a decision, information processing in the political approach frequently involves considerable cognitive effort. Handling value conflicts by bargaining after a decision may require more political work, but resolving them beforehand entails more cognitive work.[24] In light of the mix of analytical and intuitive processes described earlier, however, it is perhaps most useful to view information processing in the political approach to decision-making as a "hybrid."[25] The processes that dominate may be a matter of an individual's "coping style," but any combination that allows the decision-maker to satisfy the acceptability constraint is compatible with a political approach.[26] As with the other approaches, what is most important is the *syndrome of behavior* shaped by the concern driving the decision process.[27]

Political decision-makers also have at least two traits that distinguish them from the anxiety-ridden defensive avoider of the motivational

[24] Hilsman describes "the work of making a decision" as "a form of research in which the decision-maker or problem-solver brings both a question and a concept to a body of data. He does not passively receive the data he wants, but seeks it out specifically." Hilsman, *Strategic Intelligence*, 164. This conclusion is supported not only by the observations of numerous political analysts but also by psychological theories about what motivates cognitive effort. James MacGregor Burns and Grace Tully describe the myriad of considerations, political and otherwise, that Roosevelt habitually pondered. *Lion*, 284–86; *FDR*, 86–87. See also Hermann, "Ingredients," 183–84; and Bardach, who shows the enormous effort that goes into the design of a proposal, *Skill Factor*, chap. 9. See appendix A.

[25] Tetlock, "Accountability," 324–25. For the notion that analytical and intuitive processes form a "continuum," see Kenneth R. Hammond, "A Theoretically Based Review of Theory and Research in Judgment and Decision-Making," Center for Research on Judgment and Policy, Institute of Cognitive Science, University of Colorado, Boulder, Colorado, Report No. 260 (Feb. 1986), 14–15, 24–25, 29. See also Stein and Tanter, *Rational Decision-Making*, 64, and Bardach's discussion of how the political decision-maker designs and seeks support for a proposal. *Skill Factor*, chap. 9, esp. 188–89. Observers of actual political decision-makers have also noted a combination of analytical and intuitive processes. See, for example, Frances Perkins's description of Roosevelt's cognitive style, cited in Larrabee, *Commander in Chief*, 35–36.

[26] George, "Adaptation to Stress," 189. On the relationship between personal style and the complexity of decision processes, see Abelson and Levi, "Decision-Making," 273.

[27] Because some processes such as satisficing and bolstering appear in more than one decision-making approach, none of them can be defined solely in terms of a particular process. Rather, each is distinguished by certain unique combinations of processes, and is best thought of as a *syndrome of behavior* in which a dominant concern influences what processes are employed and how they combine to form unique constellations of behavior. For a standard definition of "syndrome," see *A Comprehensive Dictionary of Psychological and Medical Terms*, ed. Horace B. English and Ava C. English (New York: David McKay, 1958), 540.

model: a disposition to act, combined with confidence in their ability to be effective, and an enjoyment of decision-making itself.[28] The desire to act is so characteristic that if its presence does not always imply that a decision will be approached politically, its absence usually signals that it will not be. Far from being stressful, the prospect of acting is exhilarating and a source of positive motivation for political decision-makers.[29] Thus, upon being offered the British prime ministership in 1940 Winston Churchill, according to King George VI, "was full of fire and determination" to take up its burdens. While Chamberlain and Halifax were "relieved" to relinquish power, Churchill "was conscious of a profound sense of relief" that he now possessed it: "At last I had the authority to give directions over the whole scene."[30]

Such positive feelings may also help political decision-makers to shoulder the extra cognitive burdens of satisfying the acceptability constraint. A study of bargaining and negotiation found that "for cognitive as well as social reasons" the ability to arrive at integrative solutions was greatly enhanced by the presence of positive affect.[31] Thus, the appetite for politics that so often marks political decision-makers may make it easier for them to achieve the transcendent solutions that allow them to resolve value conflicts.

Granted that concern with acceptability can overcome both the intuitive decision-maker's proclivity for cognitive shortcuts and the motivated decision-maker's reluctance to act at all, it may still be argued that political decision-makers are only analytical decision-makers with some-

[28] According to his secretary, Roosevelt felt "that he had been given a 'grand opportunity' to do something about the problems that beset the nation." She also speaks of his "*will* to assume primary responsibility for events, and a *will* to make decisions regarding them. . . . I heard the Boss say again and again . . . , 'All right, send it over to me. My shoulders are broad. I can carry the load.'" Tully, *FDR*, 65–66.

[29] What is stressful is a lack of activity. Again, Roosevelt's behavior offers an example: "Back in mid-1939 Henry Morgenthau . . . had noted that the president was bored. But a few months later, with the outbreak of the war, Morgenthau sensed a quickening of the spirit in his friend, who remarked to him, 'I like it when something is happening every minute.'" Lash, *Roosevelt and Churchill*, 114.

[30] Chamberlain told Halifax " 'that now that the war was becoming intense he could not but feel relieved that the final responsibility was off him.' . . . Halifax shrank from responsibility even more than Chamberlain. He had been so disturbed at the prospect of becoming prime minister that he had felt sick to his stomach. . . ." Quoted in ibid., 111. Compare this response to the cares of office with Roosevelt's advice to Rexford Tugwell, "You will have to learn . . . that public life takes a lot of sweat; but it doesn't need to get you down. You won't always be right, but you must not *suffer* from being wrong." *In Search of Roosevelt*, 305.

[31] Carnevale and Isen, "Influence of Positive Affect," 3. James David Barber has noted a correlation between positive affect, an activist temperament, and many of the characteristics found in the political approach to decision-making. *The Presidential Character*, 3d ed. (Englewood Cliffs, N.J.: Prentice-Hall, 1972).

what specialized concerns. Even Diesing admits that, provided the differences between political and other kinds of rationality are "recognized and preserved," all types, including political rationality, can ultimately be seen as "special variants of technical or economic rationality." He remains convinced nonetheless that "the unique characteristics of social, legal, and political reasoning can[not] be brought out by deriving or reducing them to economic reasoning; quite the contrary, they are brought out most clearly by contrast with economic reasoning."[32] Indeed, according to the standard of political rationality proposed by Diesing and others, dealing with an issue solely according to the requirements of technical rationality jeopardizes the attainment of any sort of utility.[33] Hence, Bardach distinguishes "the skillful political virtuoso" from "the merely rational entrepreneur, whose rationality may not save him from disaster."[34]

Those who argue that process profoundly affects choice also point to clear differences in the behavior of analytic and political decision-makers; many of the processes used by the latter violate the requirements of the analytical model.[35] Moreover, the political approach explains a

[32] For example, a military analyst is concerned with finding the "best" weapons mix to accomplish a given mission, while an assistant secretary of defense, constrained by the requirements of acceptability, must first ask if the "best" policy is feasible in a political context. The question, "How do I solve the problem?" becomes "How do I get effective action at all?" Diesing, *Reason in Society*, 2–3. See also George, *Bridging the Gap*, 2–21; Neustadt, "Presidents, Politics, and Analysis," 28.

[33] See David Mares's account of President Echevarria's economic policies in Mexico from 1970 to 1976. "Explaining the Choice of Development Strategies: Suggestions from Mexico, 1970–1982," *International Organization* 39 (1985): 667–97.

[34] Bardach, *Skill Factor*, 261. Such virtuosity may be seen in Roosevelt's justification for overruling the technically persuasive arguments of his economists and insisting that the Social Security program be financed by a payroll tax: "I guess you're right on the economics, but those taxes were never a problem of economics. They are politics all the way through. We put those payroll contributions there so as to give the contributors a legal, moral, and political right to collect their pensions and their unemployment benefits. With those taxes in there, no damn politician can ever scrap my social security program." Schlesinger, *Age of Roosevelt*, 2:308–9. Roosevelt's feelings about technicians can be seen in his remarks after his meeting with the English economist John Maynard Keynes, "I saw your friend Keynes. He left a whole rigmarole of figures. He must be a mathematician rather than a political economist." Cited in Fred Greenstein, "The Virtuosic Leadership of Franklin Delano Roosevelt," unpubl. ms. 21.

[35] Simon, "Invariants," 8–11. This line of argument will not satisfy those who insist that whatever processes decision-makers use, the outcomes license the assumption that they behave "as if" they were rational. Milton Friedman, "The Methodology of Positive Rationality," *Essays in Positive Economics*, ed. Milton Friedman (Chicago: University of Chicago Press, 1957), 3–43. See also Bruce Bueno de Mesquita, *The War Trap* (New Haven: Yale University Press, 1981), 29; Bruce Bueno de Mesquita and David Lalman, *War and Reason* (New Haven: Yale University Press, 1992). For a critique of this assumption from within the rational-choice tradition, see Tsebelis, *Nested Games*, 31–38.

great deal of behavior that model simply fails to address. In particular, theories of rational choice are silent about goal-setting,[36] which, as Hilsman points out, lies at the heart of political choice.[37] By contrast, the political approach provides considerable insight into political decision-makers' preference structures, bringing us closer to predicting their choices.[38] In identifying acceptability as an unavoidable concern it supplies a fundamental value that can profoundly affect decision outcomes, and tells us a good deal about how that value is likely to be applied—which, at the very least, mitigates the problem of indeterminacy.

What distinguishes a political approach to decision-making from an analytical one, however, is not merely its scope, but its essentially different perspective on decisions involving a clash of important values. Some analysts argue that rational-choice theory can explain the impact of the political context on decision-making by viewing acceptability as a constraint that defines a "feasible set" within which optimizing then takes place. But this formulation overlooks the fact that optimizing is not a political decision-maker's primary focus when handling that constraint —and not merely because a narrow concern with acceptability deflects his or her attention from the best solution. While the acceptability constraint may be thought of as narrowing the feasible set, its impact on decision-making is far more pervasive, strongly affecting the entire course of the decision process and often leading to outcomes that, although rational in some sense, are quite different from those produced by economic rationality.[39]

In fact, the acceptability constraint pushes decision-makers toward a politics of incorporation, often making it seem that the whole thrust of decision-making is toward blurring differences and weaving together seemingly incompatible interests.[40] The entire process centers on finding

[36] Diesing, *Reason in Society*, 3, 11–12. See also Bernard C. Cohen, "Military Policy Analysis and the Art of the Possible: A Review," *Journal of Conflict Resolution* 6 (1962): 156–57; and Heineman et al., *World of the Policy Analyst*, 71.

[37] "Is the problem of making policy in a highly diversified mass society really one of relating the different steps in making a decision to a single set of goals or is it precisely one of choosing goals—of choosing goals not in the abstract but in the convoluted context of ongoing events, with inadequate information, incomplete knowledge and understanding, and insufficient power . . . ? . . . It is here that the essence of policy-making seems to lie, in a process that is in its deepest sense political." *To Move a Nation*, 12–13.

[38] As Robert Jervis notes, "Before SEU [Subjective Expected Utility] can tell us much, . . . we have to tell it a great deal." Robert Jervis, "Rational Deterrence: Theory and Evidence," *World Politics* 41 (1989): 184. See also Robert Jervis, "Realism, Game Theory and Cooperation," *World Politics* 40 (1988): 317–49.

[39] In other words, decisions reflecting what Simon has termed "rationality without optimization." "Invariants," 8.

[40] Hilsman describes British parliamentary and American congressional systems as working to "find compromises that blur the alternatives rather than sharpen them." *To Move a Nation*, 541–42.

strategies for adjusting, balancing, and reconciling competing interests and values instead of trading them off. Rather than maximizing utility within a single decision, it involves building up political capital[41] and maximizing inclusiveness to promote effectiveness throughout the entire political context.[42]

This impulse can be seen in Roosevelt's approach to trade policy during the 1932 campaign. Faced with advisers whose views ranged from economic nationalism and protectionism to free trade and reciprocity, he stunned Raymond Moley by asking him to "weave" them together. Whether or not one shares Moley's dismay, Roosevelt's behavior suggests that the logic of inclusiveness operates in foreign as well as domestic policy, often leading to outcomes quite different from those associated with a straightforward attempt to optimize. Foreign policies, too, are likely to reflect the fact that political decision-making is not primarily about sacrificing values in order to achieve the most efficient solution, but about reconciling them to reach the most inclusive, and therefore the most acceptable, one. As Schlesinger describes Roosevelt's approach,

> He evidently felt that clear-cut administrative decisions would work only if they expressed equally clear-cut realities of administrative competence and vigor. . . . And the actualities of administrative power were to be discovered . . . by apprehending through intuition a vast constellation of political forces. His complex administrative sensibility, infinitely subtle and sensitive, was forever weighing questions of personal force, of political timing, of congressional concern, of partisan benefit, of public interest. Situations had to be permitted to develop, to crystallize, to clarify; the competing forces had to vindicate themselves in the actual pull and tug of conflict; public opinion had to face the question, consider it, pronounce upon it—only then, at the long, frazzled end, would the President's intuitions consolidate and precipitate a result.[43]

Many of the essential features of a political approach to decision-making are to be found here: an overriding concern with effective action

---

[41] This notion was suggested by Robert Shapiro.

[42] As Neustadt describes it, "A President who knows what power is and wants it has to face irreconcilables whenever he considers his own stakes in acts of choice. The sources of his influence are such that one may suffer from whatever serves another. . . . The essence of his expertise is an awareness that these are irreconcilable and that they must be reconciled. Viability in policy calls for the same awareness." Neustadt, *Presidential Power* (1980), 141. Elsewhere Neustadt explicitly contrasts the impulse to deal with incompatible objectives by trying to reconcile them to economic thinking whose "essence is a conscious and deliberate choice of preferences . . . in the interest of an optimal result from the choicemaker's standpoint." "Presidents, Politics, and Analysis," 4.

[43] Quoted in Neustadt, *Presidential Power* (1980), 116. In a similar vein, see Betty Glad, "Multidisciplinary Studies and the Relationship of Scientific Research to Public Policymaking," *Political Psychology* 9 (1988): 531.

associated with disdain for mere efficiency; sensitivity to acceptability manifested in a search for transcendent solutions; the effort to balance acceptability and substance; a willingness to experiment joined to flexibility about means; and faith in the logic of events coupled with a sense of politics as an ongoing process. Together these traits suggest that the differences between analytical and political decision-making do not reflect merely a focus on different values, but a different logic altogether.

A REPERTORY OF DECISION-MAKING APPROACHES

Unlike those who claim that their theories explain all decision-making behavior, I do not suggest that everyone operating in political settings treats decisions politically.[44] One has only to think of the many high offices in all branches of government filled by technicians who have little regard for political considerations.[45] Some are unaware of the acceptability constraint, while others point with pride to their freedom from political calculation,[46] but all join former President Jimmy Carter in asking "why not the best?"[47]

The failure of psychological and analytical theories to take account of the political context, then, does not prevent them from explaining some decision-making in the political arena. The political approach is their competitor, not their replacement.[48] In fact, the decision-making ap-

[44] See, for example, Janis and Mann, *Decision-Making*, 80.

[45] David Stockman's discussion of the decision-making process for the first Reagan budget provides a striking illustration of this. "Th[e] essential political feasibility question [of congressional support for huge cuts] was never asked. Our team had no serious legislative experience or wisdom. Most of them had no comprehension of the numbers, and I didn't really care. Mowing down the political resistance was the whole purpose of the Reagan Revolution." *Triumph*, 128. See also Neustadt, "Presidents, Politics, and Analysis," 5–23. I am indebted to Robert Jervis for this example.

[46] Thus, Governor Kirk Fordice of Mississippi defended his confrontational style, maintaining "I'm no politician, just an analytical businessman." *New York Times*, Oct. 2, 1992.

[47] David Winter, paper presented to the annual meeting of the International Society of Political Psychology, July 6, 1992. Carter "acted as if he felt that by taking the correct position he could count on public and congressional support." Quandt, *Camp David*, 10. Betty Glad also paints a picture of Carter's "mechanical approach to problem solving," which included discussing issues during the presidential campaign of 1976 "not on the basis of their importance, but in their alphabetical order." *Jimmy Carter* (New York: W. W. Norton, 1986), 483. See also Neustadt, "Presidents, Politics, and Analysis," 4.

[48] As Abelson and Levi observe,

if the accumulated evidence massively disposed toward one or another clear conclusion—that humans are (when tooled up) strict rationalists, or bounded by limited mental resources, or rife with natural misapprehensions, or vulnerable to self-defeating motives, or rational in a manner not previously anticipated by theorists—

proaches are best thought of collectively as a repertory of behaviors.[49] What such a strategy sacrifices in parsimony, it makes up for in realism. Moreover, it supplies the basis of a contingent theory of decision-making by providing a structure within which we can pit these theories against one another to explain particular cases.

The challenge, therefore, is to identify the variables influencing the use of one rather than another approach,[50] a task that should be high on the list of any research program exploring the potential of the political approach, especially given the scant attention it receives in traditional theories of decision-making. Furthermore, while at this stage we are far from being able to specify the full range of such variables, Roosevelt's behavior during the Munich period suggests some interesting possibilities. His use of a political approach when others who faced the same problem did not, coupled with evidence that he did so consistently throughout his presidency, suggests the relevance of a personality variable. On the other hand, our analysis shows that situational variables may sometimes override personality factors. It is intriguing that over the course of nearly four years the only time another approach explained Roosevelt's behavior better than the political approach was during the Munich crisis itself. This suggests that the conditions of short time and high threat to important values usually associated with crisis may affect even the most political of decision-makers, though in Roosevelt's case they did not do so as Janis and Mann predict.

Although a complete account of the repertory of decision-making ap-

---

then we would certainly want to endorse that conclusion. It seems to us clear, however, that there is a bit of truth in each position and that no definitive resolution of the argument is likely.

"Decision Making," 235.

[49] Margaret Hermann offers a similar solution for studying political leadership, suggesting that we "consider leadership as an umbrella concept, containing under it a number of different types of variables that combine to determine the nature of leadership at any point in time." "Ingredients," 168. This also raises the possibility that under the umbrella of social context there are a number of subcontexts in each of which decision-making is approached somewhat differently. This is basically Diesing's approach to describing the different varieties of rationality.

[50] As Tetlock and McGuire suggest,

From a contingency theory perspective, . . . the appropriate question is not "What kind of machine is the human information processor?" but rather "What kinds of machines do people become when confronted with particular types of environments?" . . . The major objective . . . should not be to arrive at a global characterization of the information processor, but rather to identify the personality and situational boundary conditions for the applicability of different characterizations of the information processor.

Tetlock and McGuire, "Cognitive Perspectives," 41–42.

proaches ultimately requires us to construct a variety of hypotheses that can be tested in case studies drawing on the extensive "data base" of the historical archive, even at its present level of development, the political approach offers a useful perspective.[51] If it does not apply to all decision-makers, it does provide considerable insight into how an important class of decisions are often made. Moreover, recognizing that the constraints political decision-makers labor under arise from the nature of the political context itself and not merely "politics as usual" may help us achieve the kind of sophisticated understanding of their needs which is surely a prerequisite for providing effective advice.

THE POLITICAL DECISION-MAKER

Looking at decision-making in terms of the political context highlights the special skill involved in making political decisions. Not everyone who deals with political matters exercises this skill. However, while it is possible to make decisions without considering the imperatives of the political context, it is puzzling that this is so often spoken of as desirable. Since few would approve of making legal or economic decisions without regard to the special requirements of those fields, it is odd that many consider it a virtue to treat political decisions that way.

If anything defines political decision-makers, it is a reluctance to sacrifice values. At their best they often have agendas of accommodation extending far beyond what can be encompassed by a single decision.[52] What lies behind this logic of inclusiveness is an intuitive understanding of people's deep attachment to their values, an awareness that in the political context not everything "has its price." Hilsman has observed that "most men find it easier to go against their own pecuniary interests than they do to do against a deep conviction on policy." Since "The stakes are high and the issues fundamental," "it is not surprising that

---

[51] John Lewis Gaddis, "Expanding the Data Base: Historians, Political Scientists, and the Enrichment of Security Studies," *International Security* 12 (1987): 15.

[52] As Schlesinger describes the impulse to reconcile the conflicting interests that can divide a society: "Roosevelt freely indulged in contradictions which drove logical men to despondency. . . . Each ideological system, as he must have felt, described certain aspects of American reality, each missed out on certain features, and effectiveness might therefore most probably lie not in taking one or the other but in combining and applying both to meet the needs of a particular situation. . . . Roosevelt transcended systems for the sake of a more complex vision of America." *Age of Roosevelt*, 2:193. For the notion that in a transcendent solution ideological differences are not dissolved but preserved within some basic unity, see Diesing, *Reason in Society*, 204.

passions run strong and full."[53] This suggests that although the utility model may be appropriate for choosing among means that have no intrinsic value, it is often inadequate for choosing among the ends that deeply engage people's emotions.[54]

What is needed to reconcile such differences may in fact be the special logic of political decision-makers. When successful in weaving together the diverse goals of society, they provide a real alternative not only to political combat, but to other kinds as well, and to that extent their drive for transcendent solutions performs a critical social function. Some values cannot be traded off, or even seriously compromised, without risking political upheaval, and some value conflicts cannot be resolved without inflicting grievous injury on not only individuals but whole societies—witness the many failed attempts to deal with the resurgence of passionate attachments to ethnic and national identity in the post-Soviet world of the 1990s.[55]

Although there are times when trade-offs among deeply held values are both inescapable and morally acceptable, the political decision-maker's reluctance to make them lightly has a normative as well as a political dimension. While the temporizing maneuvers of politicians are often unbearably irritating, when it is a question of sacrificing the basic values of other human beings, it may not be altogether disgraceful "to resist trade-offs, to dispute them or deny them, to press incompatible objectives until the last moment—if not past it." In such circumstances, there are worse fates than to be governed by a political leader like Roosevelt, whose deepest instincts told him "that if a large number of people wanted something very badly, it was important that they be given some measure of satisfaction."[56]

[53] Hilsman, *To Move a Nation*, 10. That is, people's preferences are not always Archimedean ("a loss of some units of one commodity can always be compensated by a gain of some units of another commodity or, to put it another way, *everything has its price*." Quoted in Elster, *Ulysses*, 126).

[54] DeRivera, *Psychological Dimension*, 113–14. See also Alexander George, "Limits of Rationality." George has also emphasized the unfortunate consequences of allowing "irreducible national interests," to be put into trade-off relationships. *Presidential Decisionmaking*, 224–25.

[55] "When serious conflicts arise over basic values, it is doubtful that either suppression or compromise is effective in producing new integration as is the expansion of interests to rearrange and recenter value priorities." Williams, "The Concept of Values," 286.

[56] Neustadt, "Presidents, Politics, and Analysis," 3–4; Hofstadter, "Roosevelt," 99.

Traditional Approaches to Decision-Making

THE ANALYTICAL APPROACH TO DECISION-MAKING

Analytical approaches to decision-making can be divided into three broad categories according to the rigor of the analysis: formal or synoptic rationality; limited analysis, in which decision-makers attempt to follow the prescriptions of formal analysis to some degree and remain committed to value maximization;[1] and bounded rationality, in which efforts to be analytical are limited by the decision-maker's intellectual shortcomings. Because it is generally agreed that the requirements of formal rationality are too stringent for most decision-makers, only the last two approaches are discussed here.[2]

While analytical theories of decision-making do not specifically treat problem diagnosis, normally analytic decision-makers "carefully monitor change in their environment" and are "receptive to new evidence." They search through all relevant options; while decision-makers need not identify all possible alternatives, they should find the most important ones and seek out information about their consequences. During revision, they must decide what evidence is pertinent, generate subjective probabilities about the likelihood of each outcome, and be sensitive to new information.[3]

Although analytical theories do not deal with the formulation and ranking of values, decision-makers are assumed to be aware of at least

[1] *Models of Man*, ed. Herbert A. Simon (New York: John Wiley, 1957), 198. See also Stein and Tanter, *Rational Decision-Making*, 13–16; Sidney Verba, "Assumptions of Rationality and Non-Rationality in Models of the International System," *World Politics* 14 (1961): 110–13; Kirkpatrick, "Psychological Views of Decision-Making," 47–48; and Snyder and Diesing, *Conflict Among Nations*, 407 n. 3. For an account of the limited analytical approach to decision-making, see Stein and Tanter, *Rational Decision-Making*, 27–32; and Janice Stein, "International Cooperation and Loss Avoidance: Framing the Problem," *International Journal* 47 (1992): 232–33, and "Can Decision-Makers Be Rational and Should They Be? Evaluating the Quality of Decisions," in *Studies in Crisis Behavior*, ed. Michael Brecher (New Brunswick, N.J.: Transaction Books, 1978), 319.

[2] Simon, *Administrative Behavior*, 81–83.

[3] Stein and Tanter, *Rational Decision-Making*, 11, 27–29. See also Stein, "Can Decision-Makers Be Rational," 324.

their most important preferences.[4] Because complete value integration is too demanding, however, it has been replaced with limited value integration.[5] While limitedly analytical decision-makers cannot order their preferences independently of considering the alternatives, they recognize value conflicts as they weigh the attributes of various alternatives against one another and make trade-offs.[6] Boundedly rational decision-makers, on the other hand, find it difficult or impossible to compare "the value of two different goods," and this may inhibit their ability to recognize value conflicts.[7]

Decision-makers handle value conflict in the limited analytical approach by comparing all known alternatives to a fixed standard of value and trading off, using a compensatory decision strategy.[8] This produces a hierarchically arranged set of alternatives based on the decision-maker's preferences. If the evaluation has been done properly and the requisite trade-offs made, all value conflicts that were recognized will be resolved. In choosing, these decision-makers follow an optimizing decision rule instructing them to select the best alternative by comparing costs and

[4] Diesing, *Reason in Society*, 12.

[5] Snyder and Diesing, *Conflict Among Nations*, 407 n. 22; Steinbruner, *Cybernetic Theory*, 31. See also Stein and Tanter, *Rational Decision-Making*, 30. The analytical assumption that people's values, attitudes, and beliefs are organized into hierarchical structures finds some support in the psychological literature. See Milton Rokeach, "A Theory of Organization and Change within Value-Attitude Systems," *Journal of Social Issues* 24 (1968): 17–18; Tetlock, "Value Pluralism," 820–21, "Cognitive Style and Political Belief Systems," 365–75, "Cognitive Style and Political Ideology," *Journal of Personality and Social Psychology* 45 (1983): 118–28; and Philip E. Tetlock, Kristen A. Hannum, and Patrick M. Micheletti, "Stability and Change in the Complexity of Senatorial Debate," *Journal of Personality and Social Psychology* 46 (1984): 979–90.

[6] Verba, "Assumptions," 110. See also Abelson and Levy, "Decision Making," 275–76, and George, *Presidential Decisionmaking*, 26.

[7] Snyder and Diesing, *Conflict Among Nations*, 342. See also Charles W. Churchman, Russell L. Ackoff, and E. Leonard Arnoff, *Introduction to Operations Research* (New York: John Wiley and Sons, 1957), 136; James G. March and Herbert Simon, *Organizations* (New York: John Wiley and Sons, 1957), 141; Verba, "Assumptions," 110. Some analysts believe that the absence of clear value preferences is a virtue. March, for example, holds that ambiguity about values is a strength because it reflects an appropriately modest assessment of people's capacity to be clear about their preferences in the face of imperfect knowledge about both themselves and what the environment has to offer. March, "Bounded Rationality," 587–608.

[8] For evidence that some decision-makers can and do employ compensatory strategies, although perhaps not exclusively, see Ola Svenson, "Cognitive Processes in Judging Cumulative Risk over Different Periods of Time," *Organizational Behavior and Human Performance* 33 (1984): 22–41; and Mintzberg et al., "Structure of Unstructured Decisions," 246–75. Stein and Tanter offer the case of Israeli decision-making in the 1967 war as evidence of the use of compensatory strategies. *Rational Decision-Making*, 312–13, 332–33.

benefits.[9] Thus, the outcome will be optimal in terms of their most important values and all value conflicts will be resolved. For this reason, the limited analytic approach is considered normative for dealing with such conflict.[10]

There is no single model of evaluation in bounded rationality, but a likely scenario is a two-stage process using mixed strategies.[11] Thus, boundedly rational decision-makers may begin an evaluation with a non-compensatory strategy such as satisficing (testing the alternatives against constraints in a sequential evaluation).[12] While they consider values separately and need not make trade-offs, they will not choose a clearly inferior solution. Like optimizers, they are seeking the "best" alternative; the difference lies in how "the best is identified."[13] Once they have reduced the alternatives to a manageable number, they may switch to a more demanding compensatory strategy.[14] This produces a set of alternatives arranged hierarchically according to the decision-maker's preferences. However, all the alternatives may not be represented because some

[9] Ibid., 29–31.

[10] Hilsman discusses the requirements of this approach as they appear in the strategic-geopolitical model of foreign policy decision-making. *Politics of Policymaking*, 44–46.

[11] This discussion combines the sophisticated version of Simon's bounded rationality model with insights from more recent work in contingency theory. Payne, "Task Complexity," 384–85; see also Hillel J. Einhorn, "Use of Nonlinear, Noncompensatory Models as a Function of Task and Amount of Information," *Organizational Behavior and Human Performance* 6 (1971): 1–27; Lee Roy Beach and Terence R. Mitchell, "A Contingency Model for the Selection of Decision Strategies," *Academy of Management Review* 3 (1978): 439–49; and Abelson and Levi, "Decision Making," 264–66.

[12] Sidney S. Siegal, "Level of Aspiration and Decision-Making," World Politics 64 (1957): 260; and March and Simon, *Organizations*, 146. For other noncompensatory strategies, see C. Whan Park, "A Seven-Point Scale and a Decision-Maker's Simplifying Choice Strategy: An Operationalized Satisficing-Plus Model," *Organizational Behavior and Human Performance* 21 (1978): 252.

[13] Snyder and Diesing, *Conflict Among Nations*, 407 n. 33. Thus, boundedly rational satisficers consider a relatively large number of values and alternatives and are willing to search past the first acceptable alternative. Simon, *Administrative Behavior*, 89; see also George, *Presidential Decisionmaking*, 40; Anderson, "Justifications and Precedents," 739 n. 1; Herbert A. Simon, "Rationality as Process and as Product of Thought," *American Economic Review* 68 (1978): 10, and "A Behavioral Model of Rational Choice," *Quarterly Journal of Economics* 69 (1955): 99–118. For evidence that decision-makers actually do behave in this fashion, see Corbin, "Decisions That Might Not Get Made," 58. Klein has shown that even satisficers attend to utility when making nontrivial decisions. Klein, "Utility," 4; see also 17–20.

[14] Research on the strategies employed in the second stage of such an evaluation is sparse and its findings sometimes controversial. Abelson and Levi, "Decision Making," 266–67. See also Stein and Tanter, *Rational Decision-Making*, 311–12. Snyder and Diesing also suggest the possibility of combining bounded rationality and maximizing strategies, *Conflict Among Nations*, 345–48.

were eliminated or overlooked in the first stage.[15] Nevertheless, within these limits, value conflicts will be recognized and resolved by trading off.[16] The outcome of the choice stage is optimal only in terms of the values and alternatives considered during evaluation, but it will yield considerable satisfaction for key values, reflecting the highest quality attainable within the constraints. Thus, while bounded rationality cannot claim the perfection of the limited analytical approach, it does not fall short by much.[17]

THE INTUITIVE APPROACH TO DECISION-MAKING

The same cannot be said of the intuitive approach, which is dominated by the need to minimize cognitive strain. In this approach, the boundaries rather than the rationality are emphasized: while the limits in bounded rationality come from "the impracticality of spending the time and effort to make truly optimal judgements," intuitive shortcomings are caused by a "genuine failure to appreciate normatively appropriate strategies."[18] Thus, unlike boundedly rational decision-makers, intuitive decision-makers do not make great efforts to overcome their limitations.

The intuitive approach is the least coherent of the theories of decision-making.[19] Because it lacks a "dominant research paradigm," the use of unrelated, and sometimes contradictory, theories to explain political behavior is all too common. Nevertheless, the field offers at least two organizing concepts: the importance of "structural and procedural" regularities in human thinking[20] and the tendency toward economy in human mental operations—the information processor as "cognitive miser."[21]

[15] Indeed, if Payne is correct, the preferentially arranged "hierarchy" will consist of only two alternatives because the decision-maker has analyzed only two. Payne, "Task Complexity," 371, 384.

[16] Shapira, "Making Trade-offs," 337–38, 343, 349–50.

[17] Because of its noncompensatory first stage, however, bounded rationality is considered utility enhancing rather than utility maximizing. Klein, "Utility," 4.

[18] Abelson and Levi, "Decision Making," 233. See also James G. March, "Bounded Rationality, Ambiguity, and the Engineering of Choice," *Bell Journal of Economic Management Science* 9 (1978): 590–91; Klein, "Utility," 2; Simon, *Administrative Behavior*, xxiv; and Kirkpatrick, "Psychological Views of Decision-Making," 51.

[19] As Steinbruner describes this field, it is "intensely researched, but loosely ordered, . . . rich in promising leads, unintegrated experimental results, partial theories, and a great many unresolved arguments." *Cybernetic Theory*, 91. See also Gordon F. Pitz and Natalie J. Sachs, "Judgment and Decision," *Annual Review of Psychology* 35 (1984): 146, 141; and Stein and Tanter, *Rational Decision-Making*, 39.

[20] Steinbruner, *Cybernetic Theory*, 91.

[21] Abelson and Levi, "Decision Making," 233. Even within the field of cognitive psychology, however, there is controversy about just how poor human beings are as thinkers.

The hallmark of an intuitive approach is the use of nonlogical cognitive processes that satisfy the need for simplicity, consistency, or both. In theories focusing on simplicity, decision-making behavior is shaped largely by the need for ease of calculation,[22] while theories based on consistency emphasize the role of beliefs and expectations and a tendency to restore consistency that has been disrupted.[23]

Although there is some disagreement about how widespread or careful attempts at diagnosis are likely to be, intuitive theories expect decision-makers to be less subject to bias at the beginning of the decision process. Moreover, they tend to agree that whatever diagnosis is made will not only influence later stages of decision-making, but also be difficult to change.[24] While diagnosis may begin with an active search for information and explanations, according to the principle of simplicity it will probably end prematurely with the discovery of the first "adequate" interpretation of the situation, adequacy often being defined according to the principle of consistency as conforming to preexisting beliefs. As a consequence, intuitive decision-makers are likely to define new situations in terms of their belief structures (schemas, scripts, etc.)[25] or by analogy

---

See, for example, Richard E. Nisbett, David H. Krantz, Christopher Jepson, and Ziva Kunda, "The Use of Statistical Heuristics in Everyday Inductive Reasoning," *Psychological Review* 90 (1983): 339–63; Ebbe B. Ebbesen and Vladimir J. Konceni, "On the External Validity of Decision-Making Research: What Do We Know About Decisions in the Real World?" in Wallsten, *Cognitive Processes*, 21–45; and E. Tory Higgins and John A. Bargh, "Social Cognition and Social Perception," *Annual Review of Psychology* 38 (1987): 414. For a more pessimistic view of human cognitive functioning, see Richard E. Nisbett and Lee Ross, *Human Inference: Strategies and Shortcomings of Social Judgment* (Englewood Cliffs, N.J.: Prentice-Hall, 1980), and the work of Amos Tversky and Daniel Kahneman, especially the defense of their theories against more optimistic views, "Extensional versus Intuitive Reasoning: The Conjunction Fallacy in Probability Judgment," *Psychological Review* 90 (1983): 293–315.

[22] Susan T. Fiske and Shelley E. Taylor, *Social Cognition* (Menlo Park, Calif.: Addison-Wesley, 1984), 12.

[23] As George puts it, the mind cannot "function without seeking to make beliefs consistent with each other and incoming information consistent with existing beliefs." *Presidential Decisionmaking*, 19; Melvin Manis, "Cognitive Social Psychology and Attitude Change," *American Behavioral Scientist* 21 (1978): 675. While few psychologists still believe that behavior is driven primarily by consistency needs, there is general agreement that people tend to prefer consistency and that preexisting beliefs may exert a disproportionate impact on information processing.

[24] Stein and Tanter, *Rational Decision-Making*, 40–41. The following account draws heavily on Stein and Tanter.

[25] Schemas, of which scripts are a subclass, are cognitive structures in which knowledge is stored. They provide a way of simplifying and organizing reality that is readily available, likely to be invoked early, and often leads to premature cognitive closure. Hazel Markus and R. B. Zajonc, "The Cognitive Perspective in Social Psychology," in Lindzey and Aronson, *Handbook of Social Psychology* 1:158; Fiske and Taylor, *Social Cognition*, chap. 6; Jennifer Crocker, Susan T. Fiske, and Shelley E. Taylor, "Schematic Bases of Belief

to their own experience or the "lessons of history,"[26] and to give undue weight to particularly vivid or dramatic information.[27] Thus, the intuitive approach predicts premature cognitive closure based on perceptual satisficing.[28]

Tendencies toward simplicity and consistency can also constrain search, although, again, the degree of distortion is disputed. In general, search is seen to extend only to options consistent with the decision-maker's belief system, previous practices, or present policies—probably because these are readily available. A search's extent and duration may also be influenced by the need to simplify, leading to premature cognitive closure, which means that the decision-maker's understanding of alternative courses of action will probably be incomplete.[29] The impact of the search process on later decision-making is similar to that of diagnosis: once made, a decision about the range of possible options will not be easily altered.

There is disagreement about the direction and source of error during

---

Change," in *Attitudinal Judgment*, ed. Richard J. Eiser (New York: Springer-Verlag, 1984), 197–226; Robert Abelson, "Script Processing in Attitude Formation and Decision Making," in *Cognition and Social Behavior*, ed. John S. Carroll and John W. Payne (Hillsdale, N. J.: Erlbaum, 1976), 33–45, and "Psychological Status of the Script Concept," *American Psychologist* 36 (1981): 715–29; Roger C. Shank and Robert P. Abelson, *Scripts, Plans, Goals, and Understanding: An Inquiry into Human Knowledge Structures* (Hillsdale, N.J.: Erlbaum, 1977); and Payne, "Contingent Decision Behavior," 382–402.

[26] For example, "What was believed to have caused the last war will be considered likely to cause the next one." Jervis, *Perception and Misperception*, 143–46, 187–91, 266–71. See also Ernest May, *"Lessons" of the Past: The Uses and Misuses of History in American Foreign Policy* (New York: Oxford University Press, 1972); Richard Neustadt and Ernest R. May, *Thinking in Time: The Uses of History for Decision-Makers* (New York: Free Press, 1986); and Yuen Foong Khong, *Analogies at War* (Princeton: Princeton University Press, 1992).

[27] Stein and Tanter, *Rational Decision-Making*, 41. For evidence of a number of attributional biases that could lead the decision-maker to misinterpret the behavior of others, as well as to misunderstand how they interpreted his own behavior, see Lee Ross, "The Intuitive Psychologist and His Shortcomings: Distortions in the Attribution Process," pp. 174–220 in *Advances in Experimental Social Psychology*, vol. 10, ed. Leonard L. Berkowitz (New York: Academic Press, 1977); John H. Harvey and Gifford Weary, "Current Issues in Attribution Theory and Research," *Annual Review of Psychology* 35 (1984): 427–59; *Attribution: Perceiving the Causes of Behavior*, ed. Edward E. Jones et al. (Morristown, N.J.: General Learning Press, 1972); Harold H. Kelley and John L. Michela, "Attribution Theory and Research," *Annual Review of Psychology* 31 (1980): 457–501; and Nisbett and Ross, *Human Inference*, chap. 3. On vividness, see Shelley E. Taylor and Suzanne C. Thompson, "Stalking the Elusive 'Vividness Effect,'" *Psychological Review* 89 (1982): 155–81.

[28] Stein and Tanter, *Rational Decision-Making*, 39–41.

[29] Stein and Tanter point out that in the national-security area readily available options that may limit search are those compatible with strategic concepts and doctrine. Ibid., 40–41, 66–67.

revision. On the one hand, biased assimilation of new information to preexisting beliefs could result in conservatism. In this view, there is a double standard for assessing the worth of consistent and inconsistent information. But some argue that using judgmental heuristics may cause revision to be too radical.[30] One factor influencing the rate and extent of revision may be the way information is presented. For example, there is likely to be greater openness to information received early than that arriving after initial impressions have hardened. Moreover, the rate at which it comes in may also have an effect, as information arriving in small doses is easier to ignore or explain away than that arriving in massive amounts, in which case revision is expected to be sharp rather than gradual. Stein and Tanter argue that radical revision is more likely further along in the decision process.

Most intuitive theories hold that people do not have stable, hierarchically arranged value systems and may know little about their values. Rather, their values change and develop according to the situation.[31] As Simon puts it, "The consequences that the organism experiences may change the pay-off function—it doesn't know how well it likes cheese until it has eaten cheese," a point also appreciated outside of the laboratory.[32] According to the founder of a British magazine, for example, "You can't go out into the street and try to find out what people want, because they don't know until they get it."[33]

The general implication of intuitive theories is that tendencies toward consistency and simplicity inhibit the recognition of value conflicts. For example, people's expectations that their values are consistent may make

[30] Ibid., 42–44; Nisbett and Ross, *Human Inference*, 41; Jervis *Perception and Misperception*, 308–10.

[31] Research has shown that preferences change not only according to the way the alternatives are described (see below), but also according to how they are elicited. Amos Tversky, Shmuel Sattath, and Paul Slovic, "Contingent Weighting in Judgment and Choice," *Psychological Review* 95 (1988): 371–84. See also Nancy Kanwisher, "Cognitive Heuristics and American Security Policy," *Journal of Conflict Resolution* 33 (1989): 666–70.

[32] March and Simon, *Organizations*, 141; Simon, "Behavioral Model," 255. This concept is also related to Cohen and Axelrod's idea that decision-makers' preferences change as a function of experience. "Coping with Complexity," 40; See also Abelson and Levi, "Decision Making," 275; Baruch Fischhoff, "Strategic Policy Preferences: A Behavioral Decision Theory," *Journal of Social Issues* 39 (1983): 145; and Tjalling C. Koopmans, "On Flexibility of Future Preference," in *Human Judgments and Optimality*, ed. Maynard W. Shelly II and Glenn L. Bryan (New York: John Wiley and Sons, 1964), 246.

[33] *New York Times*, Feb. 27, 1992. Even more extreme is the notion recently developed in behavioral decision theory that people do not merely discover but actually construct their preferences during evaluation and choice. Payne et al., "Behavioral Decision Research," 89. This, of course, flies in the face of the rational choice precept that preferences are exogenous to the decision-making process. See March, "Bounded Rationality," 600–601.

it difficult to recognize situations where they conflict.[34] Moreover, intuitive decision-makers may miss value conflicts because they evaluate a relatively small number of alternatives[35] on the basis of only a few values and employ judgmental heuristics such as those based on salience and/or availability to generate alternatives and values in the first place.[36] Decision-makers are also unlikely to recognize value conflicts if they use strategies in which values are considered separately.[37]

Several practices characterizing intuitive evaluation make value-conflict resolution problematic.[38] First of all, decision-makers may fail to apply all their values to the alternatives and/or apply them separately.[39] They may also look at too few options to permit the discovery of one that genuinely addresses the value conflict.[40] Moreover, intuitive decision strategies are likely to involve the sequential testing of alternatives against only one or two values.[41]

[34] See, for example, Tetlock, "Value Pluralism," 820, and "Cognitive Style and Political Belief Systems." Experimental support for this position may be found in Akiva Liberman and Shelly Chaiken, "Value Conflict and Thought-Induced Attitude Change," *Journal of Experimental Social Psychology* 27 (1991): 203–16. See also Robert Jervis, "*Perception and Misperception*: An Updating of the Analysis," paper presented at the fifth annual meeting of the International Society of Political Psychology (Washington, D.C., June 24–27, 1982), *Perception and Misperception*, 128, 137, and "Cognitive Bias," 4; and George, *Presidential Decisionmaking*, 33.

[35] William Hyland, the former editor of *Foreign Affairs*, noted that most State Department papers present only three alternatives: (1) veer radically to the left, (2) veer radically to the right, (3) stay on course. Remarks to the Society for Historians of American Foreign Relations, June 20, 1992.

[36] Tversky and Kahneman, "Availability," 207. See also Kelley and Michela, "Attribution Theory and Research," 466. On salience, see Shelley E. Taylor et al., "The Generalizability of Salience Effects," *Journal of Personality and Social Psychology* 37 (1979): 357–68; Fiske and Taylor, *Social Cognition*, 270–72; Manis, "Cognitive Social Psychology and Attitude Change," 685; Amos Tversky and Daniel Kahneman, "Judgment Under Uncertainty," in *Utility, Probability, and Human Decision Making*, ed. Dirk Wendt and Charles Vlek (Dordrecht: D. Reidel, 1975), 151–52; Nisbett and Ross, *Human Inference*, 48, 52.

[37] Stein and Tanter, *Rational Decision-Making*, 44–45.

[38] Intuitive decision processes cannot be divided easily into separate stages of evaluation and choice. All intuitive decision strategies function as aids to both in a more or less continuous process. Ibid., 45–47.

[39] Tetlock and McGuire, "Cognitive Perspectives," 35; Paul Slovic, "Choice Between Equally Valued Alternatives," *Journal of Experimental Psychology: Human Perception and Performance* 1 (1975): 280–87.

[40] Abelson and Levi, "Decision Making," 268–69. Hammond, "A Theoretically Based Review," 5–6, 17–18.

[41] Thus, they are noncompensatory. Abelson and Levi, "Decision Making," 259–60; Pitz and Sachs, "Judgment and Decision," 140, 152; Paul Slovic, Baruch Fischoff, and Sarah Lichtenstein, "Behavioral Decision Theory," *Annual Review of Psychology* 28 (1977): 8; Tversky, "Elimination by Aspects," 297–98; Beach and Mitchell, "A Contingency Model," 443.

Intuitive decision-makers are also likely to search for dominant solutions.[42] Because such solutions are likely to be scarce, however, they may end up with spurious dominance, as they choose on the basis of one value, pulling the others into line and avoiding value trade-offs.[43] In seeking a dominant alternative, intuitive decision-makers may go through a two-stage evaluation process as in bounded rationality, first weeding out unsatisfactory alternatives, probably on the basis of a single important value, subtly altering some by blending and eliminating others until a favorite emerges.[44] They then either perform a more intensive comparison of those remaining or, more likely, engage in "confirmation processing," which transforms a favored alternative into a dominant one.[45] Because of their diligence with respect to one alternative, moreover, they may think the evaluation more comprehensive than it actually was. Thus, avoiding value conflict is reinforced by the tendency of decision-makers to be overconfident about the validity of their judgments.[46]

Uncertainty and Risk

The problems arising from value complexity are frequently compounded by uncertainty and risk.[47] Uncertainty can affect the treatment of value conflict in a number of ways. For example, because of insufficient or

[42] "The decision-making process may actually involve trying out alternative problem definitions and decision rules until one succeeds in identifying a 'dominating option,' one that is arguably better than all competitors." Fischhoff, "Strategic Policy Preferences," 153. Dominance detection is also a feature of the editing phase of prospect theory. Abelson and Levy, "Decision Making," 250.

[43] Jervis et al., *Psychology and Deterrence*, 31. See also Payne, Bettman, and Johnson, "Behavioral Decision Research," 92–93.

[44] "Blending is apparent when more 'extreme' options are subtly changed to narrow the range of alternatives into the domain of the acceptable. . . . Elimination is observed when some options are dropped while others are retained for elaboration." Alexander, "Design," 397–98, 402. See also Mintzberg et al., "Structure of Unstructured Decisions," 252, 256–59; and Abelson and Levi, "Decision Making," 275.

[45] That is, having arrived at a preferred option, decision-makers process it much more thoroughly than any of the other alternatives in order to resolve any problems connected with it and show "unequivocally" that it "dominates other strong candidates." Ibid., 275–76. This may be combined with bolstering, or exaggerating an alternative's advantages, minimizing its disadvantages, and doing the reverse for its competitors. Stein and Tanter, *Rational Decision-making*, 45. See also Tetlock, "Value Pluralism," 820; and Mintzberg et al., "Structure of Unstructured Decisions," 258.

[46] Asher Koriat, Sarah Lichtenstein, and Baruch Fischhoff, "Reasons for Confidence," *Journal of Experimental Psychology: Human Learning and Memory* 6 (1980): 107–18.

[47] In risky decisions, decision-makers lack complete information about the outcomes of the various alternatives but can assign probabilities. In uncertain decisions, they lack even the information to do that, confronting a situation in which "the outcome probabilities are unknown and in practice unknowable." Abelson and Levi, "Decision Making," 232.

ambiguous information and the difficulty of estimating probabilities, a decision-maker may not know how key values will be affected by particular alternatives.[48] The real issue, however, is whether "the interaction between expectations and preferences" results in irrationality and bias.[49] On the one hand, the notion that people may well refuse to decide at all unless they achieve a certain level of understanding of both values and probabilities[50] suggests that attempts to reduce uncertainty may produce greater cognitve effort, leading to a greater understanding of complexity.[51] On the other hand, there is evidence that uncertainty may keep a decision-maker from recognizing the existence of value conflict.[52]

Prospect theory in particular is based on a recognition of the interactive nature of perceptions of probabilities and value. For example, attitudes toward risk are likely to be affected by the manner in which the value side of the equation is presented.[53] Moreover, if decision problems are subject to framing effects, decision-makers may evaluate alternatives according to considerations that are not relevant to either the values at stake in the decision or their own true preferences. As a consequence, they may well fail to recognize and resolve value conflicts embedded in the decision.

THE MOTIVATIONAL APPROACH TO DECISION-MAKING

Motives likely to affect decision-making behavior arise from personal or situational factors, originating in the ego needs of the decision-maker or the stress of decision-making itself. When motivated bias is cited, value extension is frequently what is meant. This refers to the intrusion into the decision process of motives that have no logical connection to the decision but are somehow aroused by it.[54] While this affects decision out-

---

[48] See ibid., 275.

[49] Stein and Tanter, *Rational Decision Making*, 45–46.

[50] Corbin, "Decisions That Might Not Get Made," 62. Abelson and Levi agree. "Decision Making," p. 275.

[51] Corbin, "Decisions That Might Not Get Made," 51–52.

[52] "Perception of value trade-offs can be muted . . . when the impact of the policy chosen upon the values in question will not be felt immediately and when the longer-term consequences of the policy cannot be reliably predicted." George, *Presidential Decisionmaking*, 34; see also Steinbruner, *Cybernetic Theory*, 108.

[53] Daniel Kahneman and Amos Tversky, "Prospect Theory," 263. Prospect theory is examined at length in *Avoiding Losses/Taking Risks: Prospect Theory and International Conflict*, ed. Barbara Farnham (Ann Arbor: University of Michigan Press, 1994).

[54] Steinbruner, *Cybernetic Theory*, 145. See also George, *Presidential Decisionmaking*, 26–27; and Jervis, "Deterrence and Perception," 15–16.

comes, it does not entail any particular decision-making process. For example, self-interested motives can be treated as additional values and satisfied through rational calculation, as they are by Machiavelli.[55]

The motivational approach to decision-making, on the other hand, reflects the sustained and systematic impact of a specific kind of emotion resulting in a distinctive pattern of behavior. It has received its fullest exposition in Janis and Mann's decisional-conflict model, which is based on the notion that the motivating force behind decision-making behavior is not the interests or personality structure of the decision-maker but the nature of decision-making itself, particularly the fact of having to choose at all.[56]

Because decision-making produces conflict, it engenders stress.[57] The degree of stress is related directly to the number and importance of the values that may have to be sacrificed as a consequence of the decision, and most analysts agree that the magnitude of stress strongly influences behavior.[58] When stress is nonexistent or very low, the decision-maker is not sufficiently motivated to act; a moderate amount of stress increases decision-making efficiency and results in "vigilant information processing";[59] when stress is severe, decision-makers will engage in

[55] Numerous attempts to analyze nonlogical motives related to the decision-maker's personality structure have failed to result in a comprehensive theory of decision-making. See Kirkpatrick, "Psychological Views of Decision-Making," 76. Recent attempts to focus on personality types include the work of James David Barber (e.g., *Presidential Character*), and David Winter, "Measuring Personality at a Distance," *Perspectives in Personality*, ed. A. J. Stewart, J. M. Healey, Jr., and D. J. Ozer (London: Jessica Kingsley Publishers, 1991), 3:B: 58–89. For a broader perspective on personality and politics see Fred I. Greenstein, *Personality and Politics* (Princeton: Princeton University Press, 1987), and *A Source Book for the Study of Personality and Politics*, ed. Fred I. Greenstein and Michael Lerner (Chicago: Markham, 1971).

[56] The following account relies primarily on the work of Janis and Mann, as well as that of George and Holsti.

[57] "A 'stressful' event is any change in the environment that typically induces a high degree of unpleasant emotion (such as anxiety, guilt, or shame) and affects normal patterns of information processing." Janis and Mann, *Decision-Making*, 46, 50. See also Richard Lazarus, *Psychological Stress and the Coping Process* (New York: McGraw-Hill, 1966), 58.

[58] Janis and Mann, *Decision-Making*, 50. George also emphasizes the role of value conflict in his account of decisional conflict. However, he sees cognitive strain brought on by uncertainty as an additional source of stress. George, *Presidential Decisionmaking*, 18, 25, 27, and "Adaptation to Stress," 181; Holsti and George, "Effects of Stress," 262–64. See also Richard S. Lazarus and Susan Folkman, *Stress, Appraisal, and Coping* (New York: Springer, 1984), 92.

[59] Janis and Mann, *Decision-Making*, 51, 54–57, 72–74, 172–74. Although Janis and Mann avoid the term rationality, the characteristics of vigilant information processing strongly suggest the limited analytical approach to decision-making.

defensive avoidance or hypervigilance, both of which affect information processing at all stages of decision-making and can result in cognitive rigidity, avoidance or distortion of information, and attenuated search.[60]

Like the analytical approach, the motivational approach is silent about both the origins of a decision-maker's values and whether or not they are organized into hierarchical systems. It does predict that defensive decision-makers will try to avoid recognizing value conflict. Expecting serious loss from any course of action, such decision-makers try to escape from fear-arousing warnings in order to alleviate acute distress.[61]

Having given up hope of dealing satisfactorily with a value conflict, decision-makers try to escape the pain of this recognition by adopting a posture of defensive avoidance, which is at the heart of the motivational approach to decision-making. This attempt to protect themselves dominates the rest of the evaluation. Thus, decision-making is far removed from analytic standards of efficiency. Evaluation and choice, in particular, are "greatly attenuated," and decision-makers who are defensive are likely to apply "primitive" all-or-nothing criteria to the assessment of policy options.[62]

Such decision-makers handle conflicting values in a variety of ways, all of which reflect the fact that what is being dealt with is not the value conflict itself but the stress it has produced. Since defensive decision-makers are seeking psychological rather than logical solutions to their problems, the outcome of a motivational approach is almost by definition a failure to resolve value conflict. Should defensive decision-makers be brought to the point of having to deal with such conflicts, however, their solution will be "spurious and illusory."[63] While giving the appearance of resolving the value conflict, such decision-makers will continue to avoid it, either by bolstering the least objectionable alternative, or through

---

[60] Ibid., 50–51, 76; Holsti and George, "Effects of Stress," 279–80, 284. In Holsti and George's concise formulation, "relations between cognitive performance and stress can be described as an 'inverted U.' Low to moderate stress may facilitate better performance; but high stress degrades it." Holsti and George, "Effects of Stress," 278.

[61] Janis and Mann, Decision-Making, 18, 57, 73–74, 173–74. What causes a decision-maker to lose hope, however, is unclear. Jack Snyder, The Ideology of the Offensive: Military Decision Making and the Disasters of 1914 (Ithaca, N.Y.: Cornell University Press, 1984), 410. But see Eric J. Johnson and Amos Tversky, "Affect, Generalization, and the Perception of Risk," Journal of Personality and Social Psychology 45 (1983): 20, 30; and Lazarus and Folkman, Stress, Appraisal, and Coping, 26–27, 32, 35, 52.

[62] Janis and Mann, Decision-Making, 58, 76, 87, 109, 172, 196, 205; Holsti and George, "Effects of Stress," 281, 303; George, Presidential Decisionmaking, 32–33, 35–36.

[63] Ibid., 29–30.

spurious transcendence (the policy-maker attempts to resolve the problem in ways that may be "psychologically comforting" but "analytically defective").[64]

Probably the most important form of defensive avoidance is bolstering.[65] Making the task of choosing easier, it occurs when decision-makers are unable either to procrastinate or to make another person responsible. Instead, they find themselves "increasingly persuaded that a single policy will permit all values to be satisfied."[66] This is particularly likely when decision-makers believe that no new information will become available, since it makes choice psychologically possible.[67]

All behavior in the motivational approach to decision-making is shaped by the inherently stressful nature of choosing.[68] Awareness of the costs of choosing any of the alternatives may lead to a period of "*anticipatory regret,*" which can act as a brake on commitment,[69] or even to a

[64] Ibid. See also DeRivera, *Psychological Dimension*, 79. Spurious transcendence can also be a function of intuitive bias.

[65] George, *Presidential Decisionmaking*, 38, 58, 82–85. A 1986 New York *Times* account of President Reagan's insistence on aid for the Nicaraguan rebels strongly suggests bolstering. As some officials put it, Reagan's

> deep conviction that Nicaragua is emerging as a second Cuba and poses a danger for Latin America and even the United States . . . is so strong that he is reluctant to accept at face value reports that the object of his $100 million aid proposal, the Nicaraguan rebel force, is in disarray. He responds to these reports by saying that the aid proposal . . . can reverse the situation. . . . "A lot of people are leery of this," said one White House official, . . . But the official added that White House aides "are not about to stick up their heads to the President and say 'Don't do it,' because the fact is, he wants to do it."

New York Times, Mar. 7, 1986. As this example also shows, if the decision-makers are sufficiently powerful, bolstering may not only distort their evaluation of an alternative in the first place but may also, by discouraging the expression of advisers' reservations, reinforce it.

[66] Holsti and George, "Effects of Stress," 281. This phenomenon has also been discussed by Jervis, *Psychology and Deterrence*, 31–32. A particularly interesting variety of bolstering in the form of overrating the probability of success is "seeing the necessary as possible." Snyder, *Ideology of the Offensive*, 18, 186. As Jervis and Lebow have both noted, domestic politics frequently provides the motivation for this. Jervis, "*Perception and Misperception:* An Updating"; Lebow, *Between Peace and War*, 272. For other bolstering tactics, see Janis and Mann, *Decision-Making*, 91–93; and George, *Presidential Decisionmaking*, 39.

[67] Janis and Mann, *Decision-Making*, 89. Like evasion, this tactic can also be a consequence of intuitive bias.

[68] "To choose one alternative necessitates that the other alternatives and their unique attractive aspects must be forgone. . . . As the point of commitment approaches, the decision-maker becomes increasingly aware of costs the decision may entail." Abelson and Levi, "Decision Making," 276. See also Einhorn and Hogarth, "Behavioral Decision Theory," 74.

[69] Abelson and Levi, "Decision Making," 276.

refusal to choose at all.[70] Some analysts, however, believe that the stress generated by the need to decide can lead to hasty and ill-considered choices, owing to the desire to remove the source of stress.[71] Either way, value conflicts will be avoided.[72]

[70] In fact, if the implicit decision rule of the motivational approach to decision-making is "Choose that which provides the greatest psychological comfort," "no choice" could well turn out to be the best fit. Corbin, "Decisions that Might Not Get Made," 49; see also Einhorn and Hogarth, "Behavioral Decision Theory," 74.

[71] Holsti cites Richard Nixon in this connection: "On the basis of the 'six crises' he experienced up to the 1960 election, Richard Nixon observed: 'Decisive action relieves the tension which builds up in a crisis. When the situation requires that an individual restrain himself from acting decisively over a long period, this can be the most wearing of all crises,'" Ole Holsti, "Proclivities for Tunnel Vision and Misperception," Paper presented at the ninth annual scientific meeting of the International Society of Political Psychology, Amsterdam, June 1986.

[72] Holsti and George, "Effects of Stress," 293. See also Stein and Tanter, *Rational Decision-Making*, 60.

Analyzing the Calculus of Political Feasibility: The Nature of the Acceptability Constraint

WHO NEEDS TO BE CONSIDERED

Determining who must find a decision acceptable in order to achieve effective action can be quite demanding,[1] particularly as "there is no reliable method of predicting who will come into the political arena."[2] As a general rule, people whose acceptance is important to a political decision-maker fall into three broad categories: those involved in making and carrying out the decision, those at whom the decision is directed, and individuals and groups whose continued support is necessary in order to be effective in the political context generally.[3]

First of all, effective action depends on acceptability to those within the decision-making structure needed to form a majority coalition to execute a decision.[4] The participation of a given group or individual will vary

---

[1] Witness the range of support Hilsman deems necessary in foreign-policy decisions:

> Within the government and outside it . . . there are different constituencies with a stake in the outcome. The State Department may have jurisdiction over the general problem, for example, while the Pentagon must implement one aspect of it and the Agency for International Development another. Even if the President's prestige and position are not involved, his approval may be a legal or a political necessity. This may be true of Congress, also. If so the outside constituencies are likely to be drawn in—interest groups, newspapermen, academic commentators, and the still wider constituency of the particular "attentive public."

To Move a Nation, 561; see also 542–43. In addition to these, Neustadt cites heads of state and local governments, the heads of private-sector groups, such as major corporations and unions, and the chiefs of foreign governments. *Presidential Politics*, (1980), 177–79.

[2] Meltsner, "Political Feasibility," 861.

[3] There are other ways of approaching the question of whom to consider when making a decision in the political context. Bardach suggests that decision-makers look at "political weightiness," which is assessed in terms of numbers, intensity of feeling, special competence, "high functional indispensibility," and "prerogative, the legal or customary right to be consulted on certain policy matters." *Skill Factor*, 208–11. Hermann suggests that accountability is also a factor. "Ingredients," 170.

[4] "That portion of the decision-making group that can carry out a strategy without the help of the remaining group members, if necessary against their active opposition." Snyder

according to a number of factors, among them the type of decision[5] and the amount of time available for dealing with it.[6] Second, as the attempts at desegregation in the United States and agricultural collectivization in the Soviet Union show, effective action is difficult to obtain in the face of stubborn resistance from the objects of the policy.[7] This takes on an added dimension in foreign-policy decisions when those directly affected are in the international as well as the domestic arena. Finally, political decision-makers must consider those whose support is needed to preserve and extend their capacity for effective action generally.[8] Thus, Neustadt stresses the need for decision-makers, when contemplating a move in the short run, to ask, "two longer-range questions: Will I be better able to get more of what I may then want next week, next month, next year? Will I be worse off later, and with whom, if I do X now, rather than Y? These are commonplaces of a politician's day. . . . They are not the same as asking . . . What does it take to get X done today."

Congressman Joe Martin's explanation of his foreign-policy decisions before World War II shows that executives are not alone in considering the impact of their decisions on the wider political context. While denying that he put political concerns above the nation's welfare, the former leader of the House Republicans acknowledged that he "also had to

---

and Diesing, *Conflict Among Nations*, 350. Dror's notion of the "required coalition" is somewhat broader and resembles George's in including Congress and the public. Dror, *Ventures*, 87, 85; George, *Presidential Decisionmaking*, 1. See also Diesing, *Reason in Society*, 171.

[5] Huntington, *Common Defense*, 5–6; see also, 123, 131–32, 174–75.

[6] Thus, crisis policy is "peculiarly the province of the Executive, since both time and secrecy limit the number of participants." On the other hand, Congress may take a more active role in program policy, which requires "implementation extending over time— foreign aid, the building of such alliance structures as NATO." Regarding anticipatory policy, which deals with possible reactions to "foreseen future contingencies" (containment or massive retaliation, for example), the circle of those directly concerned is likely to be even wider, including, as well as the executive branch and Congress, the press, academics, and "men of affairs." Hilsman, "Foreign Policy Consensus," 376–77.

[7] Thomas Risse-Kappen's study of the impact of public opinion on foreign policy shows that, at least in liberal democracies, decision-makers are aware of this. They "do not decide against an overwhelming public consensus. In most cases, mass public opinion set broad and unspecified limits to the foreign policy choices." "Public Opinion, Domestic Structure, and Foreign Policy in Liberal Democracies," *World Politics* 43 (1991): 510. See also Charles W. Ostrum, Jr., and Brian L. Job, "The President and the Political Use of Force," *American Political Science Review* 80 (1986): 541–66.

[8] Cultivating wider support also has a more direct political purpose. As Fred Greenstein has pointed out, one of Neustadt's basic insights is that an important pillar of the president's influence with those he needs to act effectively on is "their perception that he has the support of the public." "Political Style and Political Leadership," in *Clinton Presidency*, ed. Renshon, 144.

think of the political effect of these events on the fortunes of the Republican Party and to act with that thought in mind."[9]

Even more broadly speaking, political decision-makers need to attend to a decision's implications for the political society itself.[10] Moreover, they often have an ongoing concern with the health of the decision structure independent of particular decisions,[11] as well as an interest in cultivating good relations with other groups and individuals on whose support effective action depends.[12]

WHAT TO CONSIDER

The most basic cues about what is acceptable in a particular area are embodied in the beliefs and values shared by the participants in the decision process. These determine what decision-makers may properly consider, revealing "the general content and order of the universe" in which the decision-making process occurs.[13] As Anderson has observed, conformity with common beliefs and values, including "organizational goals, shared images, and standards of conduct and deliberation," can confer the legitimacy that makes it possible for a policy to succeed.[14] Not only does legitimacy enhance decision-makers' ability to justify their policies, but, as George has shown, it may also help them to gain a "more basic, durable acceptance of and support for long-range policies."[15] Furthermore, acceptability is affected by procedural as well as substantive

[9] Neustadt, *Presidential Power* (1990), xv–xvi; see also Diesing, *Reason in Society*, 171–72; Martin, *My First Fifty Years*, 89.

[10] Such considerations include not only issues with constitutional implications, but also decisions initiating "large-scale long-term changes which are likely to alter the whole organization or society considerably." Diesing, *Reason in Society*, 321. The Voting Rights Act of 1965 is a case in point.

[11] Ibid., 201–8. See also Snyder and Diesing, *Conflict Among Nations*, 354–55.

[12] Two recent presidencies illustrate the critical importance of these wider concerns. Because of lack of attention to his political base, Jimmy Carter's effectiveness was reduced to the point that "he was unable to pursue the Camp David Accords with full vigor." Similarly, President Bush's failure to attend to his relationship with Congress led, in the words of Budget Director Richard Darman, "to a ritual of confrontation," with the result that, according to the New York *Times*, Bush had "a harder time getting his way on legislation than any other President elected since World War II." Quandt, *Camp David*, 336; *New York Times*, Aug. 9, 1992.

[13] Diesing, *Reason in Society*, 171. As Hermann notes, these beliefs and values can differ not only from society to society but over time as well. "Ingredients," 172.

[14] Anderson, "Justifications and Precedents," 744–45.

[15] Personal communication, and George, "Domestic Constraints," 234–36. See also Alexander L. George, *Managing U.S.–Soviet Rivalry* (Boulder, Colo.: Westview Press, 1983), 25–28.

legitimacy. How things are done may often be as important as what is done,[16] something often overlooked by analytic problem solvers.

Precedents and justifications are another important source of acceptability, conferring "legitimacy on advocacy" and providing "bargaining advantages" by shifting "the burden of proof to opponents"[17] (thus, the importance of paying attention to history, especially recent history). Previous decisions indicate what is acceptable in terms of the political constraints they create, as well as what can be justified in terms of tradition.[18]

Decision-makers also need to be attuned to "institutional constraints,"[19] what Hermann calls "the general tenor of the times,"[20] and other pending decisions, as some otherwise desirable alternatives may become unacceptable if they significantly reduce support for other important decisions.[21] Finally, it is important to consider the impact of a deci-

[16] "Acceptability is influenced by whether a decision-maker has—or is believed to have—followed expected and legitimate procedures." Personal communication from Robert Jervis. George also notes that one reason a president consults advisers in foreign policy and national security is "to gain greater *political legitimacy* in the eyes of Congress and the public for his policies and decisions." *Presidential Decisionmaking*, 81. In discussing the distinction between procedural and distributive justice, Barner-Barry points out that if people consider that the proper procedures were followed, they are likely to "assume that the substantive outcome is just." Carol Barner-Barry and Robert Rosenwein, *Psychological Perspectives on Politics* (Englewood Cliffs, N.J.: Prentice-Hall, 1985), 273. For experimental confirmation that considerations of fairness play an important part in judgment, see Daniel Kahneman, Jack L. Knetsch, and Richard Thaler, "Fairness and the Assumptions of Economics," *Journal of Business* 59 (1986): 285–300.

[17] Anderson, "Justifications and Precedents," 740–41, 746–47.

[18] "All decisions have to be made in an actual context of actions and commitments resulting from previous decisions." Diesing, *Reason in Society*, 172. See also Majone, "Political Feasibility," 270; and Anderson, "Justifications and Precedents," 741. The impact of past decisions on present acceptability may be normative as well as political. A long history of supporting agricultural commodities, for example, may be difficult to ignore, not just because of the interests involved, but also because such support has come to be viewed as a norm.

[19] "Institutional constraints can affect policies also by limiting the range of the acceptable means of collective action. Not all social technologies that could theoretically be applied to a policy problem are necessarily compatible with the given institutional framework, and with generally accepted beliefs and values." Majone, "Political Feasibility," 270–71. Similarly, Neustadt advises the decision-maker to consult "the histories of issues, institutions, and individuals." Neustadt, *Presidential Power* (1990), 305.

[20] Different measures may be more or less acceptable depending on whether "the period [is] one of relatively little change, turmoil, or crisis or one of rapid change, much turbulence, and many crises." "Ingredients," 172–73. The scarcity or abundance of resources may also have an impact.

[21] Halperin, *Bureaucratic Politics*, 79. See also George, *Bridging the Gap*, 25. In 1993, for example, Secretary of Labor Robert Reich was forced to delay a recommendation for an increase in the minimun wage after being warned by the White House that "such a move . . . could antagonize business leaders at a time when President Clinton needs them for his

sion on the decision-maker's own political position. In fact, Neustadt suggests that attention to power concerns can be a means of testing and improving the viability of policy:

> The very breadth and sweep of [a president's] constituencies and of their calls upon him, along with the uncertainty of their response, will make him keen to see and weigh what Arthur Schlesinger has called "the balance of administrative power." This is a balance of political, managerial, psychological, and personal feasibilities. And because the President's own frame of reference is at once so all-encompassing and so political, what he sees as a balance for himself is likely to be close to what is viable in terms of public policy. What he sees in terms of power *gives him clues in terms of policy* to help him search beneath the surfaces of issues.

Neustadt also suggests that because of the complexities involved in making substantive judgments, decisions based on a search for viability may be more satisfactory than those emerging from the consideration of substance alone.[22] This sort of calculation is not without pitfalls, however. For example, Nelson points out that

> the four twentieth-century presidents who have won the largest reelection victories . . . instantly breached the bounds of permissible political action in a way that brought down the public's wrath. . . . The common feature of each of these self-inflicted wounds seems to have been the reelected president's errant conclusion that the voters had handed him a blanket authority to rule during the second term as he saw fit.[23]

---

health care and trade proposals." *New York Times*, Oct. 30, 1993. Roosevelt's lukewarm support of the antilynching bill in 1938 was probably a product of similar considerations. Sidney M. Miklis, "FDR and the Transcendence of Partisan Politics," *Political Science Quarterly* 100 (1985): 491; Thompson, *Roosevelt Presidency*, 1982, 48.

[22] "Substantive appraisals have become so tricky that the specialists in every sphere dispute among themselves. In consequence the viability of policy may be the only ground on which a substantive decision can be reached." Neustadt, *Presidential Power* (1960), 135–36. See also 109. Meltsner advocates a similar course for the policy analyst. "Political Feasibility," 864.

[23] The four cases are Roosevelt's court-packing in 1937, Lyndon Johnson's unilateral escalation of the Vietnam War in 1965, Richard Nixon's Watergate cover-up in 1972–1973, and Ronald Reagan's Iran-Contra fiasco in 1985–1986. Michael Nelson, "The President and the Court: Reinterpreting the Court Episode of 1937," *Political Science Quarterly* 103 (1988): 293. See also Quandt, *Camp David*, 13. As a consequence of the Johnson and Nixon experiences, Neustadt himself acknowledged the danger in using power alone as a clue to policy and recommended that the decision-maker also reverse the process. *Presidential Power* (1990), 214–15.

small war to prelude big one

Police action, real war

The Traditional Political Strategies

TRANSCENDENCE

Transcendence is the quintessential political strategy. It is most often achieved by showing that conflicting elements are actually compatible.[1] Thus, a decision-maker might broaden the context of the decision so that differences are overridden by a higher principle, long-range objective, or larger goal.[2] A decision-maker can also transcend value conflict by finding an alternative that actually serves both values. In resolving the Cuban missile crisis, for example, a policy was modified to serve two values that appeared to be in a trade-off relationship (dealing with the security threat posed by Soviet missiles in Cuba and avoiding the risk of war involved in military action to remove them). The need to trade off was averted with the transcendent solution of blockade, ultimatum, and assurances about the removal of Jupiter missiles from Turkey.[3]

A third way of transcending value conflict is more political but less satisfactory because it may leave some issues unresolved. The decision-maker widens the scope of the decision horizontally, adding to the values and interests at stake to dilute or submerge the incompatible ones. For example, a tax bill might be broadened so that the losers in one area

[1] As George describes it, "the inventive executive may indeed come up with a creative, novel option that genuinely resolves the apparent value conflict, demonstrating that the values in question were really congruent." *Presidential Decisionmaking*, 30.

[2] Jacobsen and Hofhansel give an example of this strategy, "Where zero-sum disputes arise in the regulatory or redistributive issue arenas, a president can (attempt to) shift the matter out of those vulnerable realms onto the higher plane of 'power politics,' where the reasons of the State are least challengeable." John Kurt Jacobsen and Claus Hofhansel, "Safeguards and Profits: Civilian Nuclear Exports, Neo-Marxism, and the Statist Approach," *International Studies Quarterly* 28 (1984): 198.

[3] As this example shows, a transcendent solution need not be perfect. When proposing the blockade and ultimatum Secretary of Defense Robert McNamara remarked, "this alternative doesn't seem to be a very acceptable one, but wait until you work on the others." Marc Trachtenberg, "The Influence of Nuclear Weapons in the Cuban Missile Crisis," *International Security* 10 (1985): 145, 149; "White House Tapes and Minutes of the Cuban Missile Crisis," Introduction to Documents, ibid., 155, 166, 165; and "Documentation, ExCom Meetings, October 1962," ibid., 171–73, 182, 192–93.

K War would bring more to mil[?]

receive enough sweeteners in other areas that they feel able to approve the entire package.[4]

Because the motivation to seek transcendent solutions is great, incentives for bias may also be considerable, leading to a resolution of value conflict that is "unrealistic, spurious and illusory."[5] The political problem is solved but the substantive one remains. One form of spurious transcendence mirrors the genuinely transcendent strategy of reconciling conflicting values by relating them to a higher goal: the decision-maker pursues competing values separately, denying that they conflict and justifying this with the higher goal of political necessity.[6] Thus, pursuing values separately can be a political strategy as well as a manifestation of cognitive limitations.

Spurious transcendence can also be a corruption of the genuinely transcendent strategy of reconciling apparently incompatible values in which the biased decision-maker formulates a policy that purports to serve all values and interests but does not. (Many have interpreted Johnson's Vietnam policy in terms of this light.)[7] Finally, a biased decision-maker can manipulate an alternative to give it the appearance of transcendence by employing the counterpart of the strategy of adding value. Instead of adding inducements to an alternative until it provides genuine utility for those whose interests are threatened, the biased decision-maker merely broadens a consensus in order to overwhelm the opposition.[8]

CALCULATED PROCRASTINATION

If a transcendent solution cannot be found and time constraints are not pressing, political decision-makers may resort to the time-honored tactic of procrastination.[9] In its rational form procrastination is "calculated";

[4] "One hallmark of successful policy makers is knowing what features to include in policy proposals in order to build supportive coalitions or to reduce resistance." May, "Politics and Policy Analysis," 112–13.

[5] George, *Presidential Decisionmaking*, 30–31.

[6] See Thomas L. Hughes, "Relativity in Foreign Policy," *Foreign Affairs* 45 (1967): 673.

[7] I. M. Destler, Leslie H. Gelb, and Anthony Lake, *Our Own Worst Enemy* (New York: Simon and Schuster, 1984), 55–56. This motivation may also have been behind President Reagan's actions in Central America, where "the domestic politics of the issue required both containment of leftists in Central America and no military intervention or loss of American life." Ibid., 81. The policies behind the Iran-Contra fiasco also look very much like a case of spurious transcendence.

[8] Jacobsen and Hofhansel, "Safeguards and Profits," 198. See also Hilsman, "Foreign Policy Consensus," 371.

[9] George distinguishes between procrastination as a strategy and as a tactic. In the first case, decision-makers habitually use procrastination as a means of dealing with uncertainty. Like President Coolidge they "conclude that the best strategy of leadership is to do as little as possible, hoping that the problems that seem to require their attention will go away or

the decision-maker "sees to it that active search, appraisal, and contingency planning continue," using the time "to reduce the uncertainty that plagues the decision he will have to make."[10]

Both New York City Mayor Robert Wagner and New York Governor Mario Cuomo used this tactic in this way. Rather than offering a cost-cutting measure to a legislature ill disposed to "accept unpopular proposals," Cuomo procrastinated until, in the words of the assembly speaker, a fiscal crisis offered him "a better chance to fight for these changes" by allowing him "to ask the ultimate question: 'What is your alternative?'" Wagner engaged in creative procrastination as a matter of "philosophy," appointing commissions to deal with problems that delay alone might solve and ruling from the center once consensus formed around him.[11]

Although procrastination is often a rational tool, it can also be biased, as when a decision-maker fails to act solely because it is politically disadvantageous. In such cases, deferring a decision until the time is more propitious can shade into inaction in order to avoid losing support.[12]

SEQUENCING

If a transcendent solution is unavailable and there is no way of modifying an alternative to make it so, the decision-maker could attempt to deal

---

find some other solution." This may be rational, but it also risks allowing crises to develop that could otherwise be avoided with timely action. When procrastination is used as a tactic, it is adopted only when a particular situation warrants it. *Presidential Decisionmaking*, 35–36.

[10] Ibid., 36. See also Neustadt's description of one form of presidential thinking: "*Don't trade off early, stand your ground, wait, delay, emulate Micawber, and only bring yourself to contemplate a compromise when you are down the road so far that you can see the whites of history's eyes . . . or when you're running out of luck.*" Neustadt, "Presidents, Politics, and Analysis," 21.

[11] *New York Times*, Feb. 14, 21, 1991. Neustadt observes that calculated procrastination can also help a decision-maker keep a decision in his own hands, pointing to Roosevelt's mastery at this. Leuchtenberg agrees: "The President's 'procrastination' was his own way both of arriving at a sense of national consensus and of reaching a decision by observing a trial by combat among rival theories." As Hughes describes the governing principle behind Roosevelt's use of this tactic, "he had in mind the practical necessity of keeping options open, or the appearance of doing so, so as not to foreclose the possibility of changing course, so as not to create disappointments prematurely, and so as to maintain ambiguities on minor matters as a means of holding or creating a consensus on major ones." *Presidential Power* (1980), 116; Leuchtenberg, *Franklin D. Roosevelt*, 238–39; Hughes, "Relativity," 673.

[12] George, *Presidential Decisionmaking*, 29, 36; Huntington describes several politically biased tactics for procrastinating, such as "avoiding controversial issues, delaying decisions on them, and referring them to other bodies for resolution." *Common Defense*, 162, italics omitted. See also Janis and Mann, *Decision-Making*, 205–6; and Hughes, "Relativity," 676.

with a decision "strategically" by sequencing. Realizing that not all interests and values at stake in a decision can be served, the decision-maker "tries to determine what has to be decided now and what can be left for decision later."[13] He or she does so, however, by acknowledging conflicting values and taking substance as well as acceptability into account. Political decision-makers may prefer sequencing to compromise because it avoids sacrificing values by spacing out their satisfaction over a period of time.

A sequencing strategy is justified by the recognition that the environment may change and that buying time may allow better information and analysis to be brought to bear on the problem. As Hilsman notes, there are sound political reasons for proceeding sequentially: "Because of the political process of consensus building by which policy is made, the acquiescence of a key constituency might be given for what could be regarded as a tentative, reversible experiment when it would be withheld for a grand leap."[14]

Sequencing brings an incremental approach to decision-making "into a framework of sophisticated policy planning" that can operate in consequential as well as trivial decisions.[15] Deliberate incrementalism should be distinguished from that which is the result of cognitive limitations. Simple satisficing is thought to lead to incrementalism primarily because a satisficing solution is likely to be unstable. Since the best solution is not sought, and therefore presumably not attained, the problem is not definitively solved. Not only are there values that remain unsatisfied, but there may be better alternatives that were not considered. The satisficing process is thus likely to be repeated over and over. Moreover, the decision-maker has no expectation that it will be otherwise. As Lindblom puts it, because decision-makers who practice incrementalism "expect to achieve goods only partially, they would expect to repeat endlessly the sequence just described."[16]

While rational sequencing involves a degree of deliberation and planning that is far removed from "muddling through," its biased form very

---

[13] George, *Presidential Decisionmaking*, 30, 41.

[14] Hilsman, *To Move a Nation*, 548. See also George, *Presidential Decisionmaking*, 40–41.

[15] George, "Adaptation to Stress," 185. David Braybrooke and Charles Lindblom, *A Strategy of Decision: Policy Evaluation as a Social Process* (New York: Free Press, 1963), 75. See also Lindblom, "Science," 74–88.

[16] Lindblom, "Science," 80. Aaron Wildavsky has suggested that the traditional practice of incrementalism should be regarded as "one of the intuitively grounded heuristics frequently relied upon by political decision-makers." Cited in Charles A. Powell, James W. Dyson, and Helen E. Purkitt, "Opening the 'Black Box': Cognitive Processing and Situational Complexity in Foreign Policy Decision Making," Paper presented at the ninth annual meeting of the International Society of Political Psychology, Amsterdam, June 1986.

much resembles the primitive incrementalism George calls "sloppy" and "myopic." When an incremental strategy is driven by political bias, rather than changing a highly acceptable policy that no longer serves the values at stake in the decision, decision-makers will tinker with it. Instead of performing surgery, they apply Band-Aids and sacrifice utility to acceptability.[17]

COMPROMISE

Should a transcendent solution be unavailable and procrastination or sequencing impossible, political decision-makers may consider a compromise in which they attempt to serve as many important values as possible but bow to the reality that some will have to be sacrificed in order to serve others.[18] Compromise is as close as political decision-makers willingly come to value trade-offs. Accepting the fact that some value conflict is unavoidable, they balance acceptability and utility, adopting the minimum standard that the decision be "at least tolerable to the loser."[19]

The need to enhance acceptability provides the rationale for Diesing's statement that "compromise is almost always a rational procedure, even when the compromise is between a good and a bad proposal."[20] Nevertheless, there are times when compromise is irrational even in a political context, as when major values are sacrificed *solely* to reach an agreement.[21] This type of compromise is a product of "consensus politics," in which the decision-maker decides "what to do on the basis of what enough people want and will support rather than attempt to master the cognitive complexity of the problem by means of analysis."[22] In one form, biased decision-makers play out in their own minds the political competition among the relevant interests, assigning the greatest weight to the ones they believe have the power to win. In another form, the decision-maker merely mediates between competing interests. This, according to Wallace Thies, was President Johnson's response in 1966 to the critics of his Vietnam policy. Faced with conflicting pressures, he

[17] For a discussion of other problems associated with the strategy of incrementalism, see George, *Presidential Decisionmaking*, 41.

[18] Ibid., 31. See also Hilsman, "Foreign Policy Consensus," 365–66.

[19] Diesing, *Reason in Society*, 210.

[20] Ibid., 204.

[21] George, *Presidential Decisionmaking*, 30. John Lewis Gaddis has distinguished between tactical compromises in the service of a larger purpose and those made simply to get agreement. Remarks on Roosevelt's use of compromise, Society of Historians of American Foreign Relations, annual meeting, June 18, 1992.

[22] George, *Presidential Decisionmaking*, 42. Huntington identifies this practice as part of the strategic legislative process. *Common Defense*, 164.

"played the role of 'brakeman,' pulling the switch against both the advocates of 'decisive escalation' and the advocates of 'disengagement.' The key was to stake out the middle ground."[23] President Carter's inability to choose between the competing approaches toward the Soviet Union of Secretary of State Cyrus Vance and National Security Adviser Zbigniew Brzezinski also had all the earmarks of biased compromise.[24]

Evidence that biased compromise can occur at the international level with equally unfortunate results is provided by Neustadt's discussion of the planning for the Israeli, French, and British attack on Egypt in 1956. In that case, a series of three-way compromises on the military plan necessary to make it acceptable to all the parties, "proved fatal" to the cover story on which the success of the operation depended.[25]

MINIMAL DECISIONS

If neither sequencing nor compromise is possible, political decision-makers may cope with their failure to satisfy all the values with a minimal decision. Possibly on the theory that what has not been decided has less chance of offending interested parties, the decision-maker opts to decide as little as possible. Schilling analyzes this strategy in his discussion of the H-bomb decision in which President Truman's choice process bore "all the aspects of a conscious search for that course of action which would close off the least number of future alternatives, one which would avoid the most choice." Unlike decision-makers who sequence, those who make minimal decisions do not schedule the satisfaction of other values in the future. Rather, they elect to decide only "what needs to be decided *now*," thus, avoiding a bruising battle and buying time.[26] Such

---

[23] Thies also points out that Johnson's inability to execute a strategy of graduated pressure that depended on a carefully controlled air war was a direct result of his need for consensus. "To the extent that the President sought to keep everyone 'on board,' he was unable to turn the bombing up or down in accordance with the goal of 'negotiating' by word and deed in an optimal fashion." Wallace J. Thies, *When Governments Collide* (Berkeley and Los Angeles: University of California Press, 1980), 352–55, 373.

[24] "[Carter's] ambivalence was nicely illustrated when, in a speech to the Naval Academy . . . , he 'stapled together' Vance and Brzezinski drafts in a hybrid formulation that raised confusion and criticism to new heights." Destler et al., *Our Own Worst Enemy*, 220.

[25] Richard E. Neustadt, *Alliance Politics* (New York: Columbia University Press, 1970), 22.

[26] As Schilling explains the rationale behind this strategy, in the American political system,

The distribution of power and responsibility among government elites is normally so dispersed that a rather wide-spread agreement among them is necessary if any given policy is to be adopted and later implemented. . . . There are many occasions when

decisions are rational as long as they do not result in the avoidance of essential choices and are adopted in the well-founded expectation of changed circumstances or new opportunities. "The strain toward agreement" that characterizes the American political process, however, can also result in minimal decisions that are thoroughly biased. In such cases, the need for consensus leads the decision-maker to avoid value conflict by formulating policies based on the lowest common denominator, sacrificing substance to gain acceptability.

The need for acceptability can also lead decision-makers to avoid making necessary choices altogether—in Schilling's phrase, to "decide without choosing." Moreover, if the issues that have not been dealt with recur, this strategy may well turn into incrementalism of the "sloppy, myopic" variety with unfortunate consequences for policy. Thus, "as the same issues come around for the second, third, and nth time, they do so in a context slightly altered by the previous minimal choices to which they have been subjected." Because choice has been fragmented, some choices may be accidentally foreclosed, while others may be made almost inadvertently, which raises the possibility that through a series of minor "tactical" decisions the government might some day find itself occupying a new "strategic" position without ever having actually chosen it.[27]

---

the necessary amount of cooperation can be achieved only by the device of avoiding disagreement, that is, by postponing the consideration of issues over which long and determined conflicts are certain to be waged.

Warner R. Schilling, "The H-Bomb Decision: How to Decide without Actually Choosing," *Political Science Quarterly* 76 (March 1961): 36–40. See also "The Politics of National Defense: Fiscal 1950," in *Strategy, Politics, and Defense Budgets*, ed. Warner R. Schilling, Paul T. Hammond, and Glenn H. Snyder (New York: Columbia University Press, 1962), 1–266.

[27] Schilling, "H-Bomb," 43–44.

Bibliography

Manuscripts and Archives

British Public Record Office, London, England

PRIME MINISTER'S PAPERS

PREM 3   USA

RECORDS OF THE WAR CABINET

CAB 21   General Files on War Committee

Department of the Army, Washington, D.C.

OFFICE OF THE CHIEF OF MILITARY HISTORY

Harry L. Hopkins Papers, Books 1–5, 6–9.

National Archives, Washington, D.C.

DIPLOMATIC BRANCH

RG 59   General Records of the Department of State Decimal File

RG 353   Records of the Standing Liaison Committee

MODERN MILITARY HISTORY BRANCH

RG 107   Records of the Office of the Secretary of War
         Correspondence of Secretary of War Stimson

RG 165   Army Chief of Staff, Secretariat
         General and Special Staffs
         Office of the Chief of Staff

RG 218   Records of the Joint Chiefs of Staff
         Davis, Vernon E., "History of the Joint Chiefs of Staff in World War II" Vols. 1–2.
         Kittredge, Captain Tracy. "United States Defense Policies and Global Strategy."

RG 334   Records of Interservice Agencies

NAVY AND OLD ARMY BRANCH

RG 218

Office of Naval History, Washington, D.C.

NAVAL HISTORICAL MONOGRAPH OFFICE

Kittredge, Captain Tracy. "United States–British Naval Cooperation, 1939–1945."

Franklin D. Roosevelt Library, Hyde Park, N.Y.

Adolf A. Berle, Jr., papers
Harry L. Hopkins papers
Henry Morgenthau, Jr., papers
Frances Perkins papers
Franklin D. Roosevelt papers
  President's Personal File
  President's Secretary's File
  Map Room File
  Official File
Samuel I. Rosenman papers
Harold D. Smith papers

Library of Congress, Washington, D.C.

Joseph and Stewart Alsop papers
Henry H. Arnold papers
Thomas Connally papers
Joseph E. Davies papers
Norman H. Davis papers
James A. Farley papers
Herbert Feis papers
Louis Fischer papers
Harold Ickes papers
Frank Knox papers
William D. Leahy papers
Breckinridge Long papers

Yale University, New Haven, Connecticut

Henry L. Stimson diary
Henry L. Stimson papers

Public Documents

Documentary Background of World War II 1931 to 1941. James W. Gantenbein, ed. New York: Columbia University Press, 1948.

Documents on British Foreign Policy, 1919–1939. Rohan Butler and Sir E. L. Woodward, ed. 3d series, Vols. 1–7. London: His Majesty's Stationery Office, 1951.

F.D.R: His Personal Letters. Vol. 3, ed. Elliot Roosevelt. New York: Duell, Sloan, and Pearce, 1950.

Franklin D. Roosevelt and Foreign Affairs. Vols. 1–3, ed. Edgar B. Nixon. Cambridge, Mass.: The Belknap Press of Harvard University Press, 1969.

Franklin D. Roosevelt and Foreign Affairs, January 1937–August 1939. Donald B. Schewe, ed. New York: Garland Publishing, 1979.

Roosevelt, Franklin D. *Complete Presidential Press Conferences of Franklin D. Roosevelt.* New York: Da Capo Press, 1972.

———. *Public Papers and Addresses*. Vols. 5–8. New York: Macmillan, 1938–1941.

United States Department of State. *Foreign Relations of the United States: Diplomatic Papers*. Annual volumes: 1937, vol. 4; 1938, vol. 1; 1939, vol. 1. Washington, D.C.: U.S. Government Printing Office.

———. *Peace and War: United States Foreign Policy, 1931–1941*. Washington, D.C.: United States Government Printing Office, 1943.

United States Congress. *Hearings before the Joint Committee on the Investigation of the Pearl Harbor Attack*. 79th Congress. Washington, D.C.: United States Government Printing Office, 1946.

———. *Report of the Joint Committee on the Investigation of the Pearl Harbor Attack*. 79th Congress, Second Session. Washington, D.C.: United States Government Printing Office, 1946.

Official Histories

Butler, J.R.M. *Grand Strategy*. Vol. 2: *September 1939–June 1941*. London: Her Majesty's Stationery Office, 1957.

Conn, Stetson, and Byron Fairchild. *The Framework of Hemisphere Defense*. Washington, D.C.: Office of the Chief of Military History, Department of the Army, 1960.

Craven, Wesley Frank, and James L. Cate, eds. *The Army Air Forces in World War II*. Chicago: University of Chicago Press, 1948–1955.

Eayrs, James. *In Defense of Canada: Appeasement and Rearmament*. Toronto: University of Toronto Press, 1965.

Hall, H. Duncan. *North American Supply*. London: Her Majesty's Stationery Office, 1955.

Matloff, Maurice, and Edwin M. Snell. *Strategic Planning for Coalition Warfare, 1941–1942*. Washington, D.C.: Department of the Army, 1953.

Stacey, C. P., *Arms, Men and Governments: The War Policies of Canada, 1939–1945*. Ottawa: Ministry of National Defense, 1970.

Watson, Mark. *The United States Army in World War II, the War Department, Chief of Staff: Prewar Plans and Preparations*. Washington, D.C.: United States Printing Office, 1950.

Woodward, Sir Llewellyn. *British Foreign Policy in the Second World War*. London: Her Majesty's Stationery Office, 1962.

Books

Adler, Selig. *The Isolationist Impulse: Its Twentieth-Century Reaction*. New York: Abelard-Schuman, 1961.

———. *The Uncertain Giant*. London: Collier Books, 1965.

Allison, Graham T. *Essence of Decision: Explaining the Cuban Missile Crisis*. Boston: Little, Brown, 1971.

Alsop, Joseph, and Robert Kintner. *American White Paper*. New York: Simon and Schuster, 1940.

Altschuler, Alan A. *The Politics of the Federal Bureaucracy*. New York: Dodd, Mead, 1968.

Arnold, H. H. *Global Mission*. New York: Harper and Brothers, 1949.

Ashby, W. Ross. *Design for a Brain*. 2d ed. New York: John Wiley and Sons, 1960.

_____. *An Introduction to Cybernetics*. New York: John Wiley and Sons, 1957.

Barber, James David. *The Presidential Character*. 3d ed. Englewood Cliffs, N.J.: Prentice-Hall, 1972.

Bardach, Eugene. *The Skill Factor in Politics*. Berkeley and Los Angeles: University of California Press, 1972.

Barner-Barry, Carol, and Robert Rosenwein. *Psychological Perspectives on Politics*: Englewood Cliffs, N.J.: Prentice-Hall, 1985.

Barron, Gloria J. *Leadership in Crisis: FDR and the Path to Intervention*. Port Washington, N.Y.: Kennikat Press, 1973.

Baruch, Bernard. *The Public Years*. New York: Holt, Rinehart, and Winston, 1960.

Beard, Charles A. *American Foreign Policy in the Making, 1932–1940*. New Haven: Yale University Press, 1946.

_____. *President Roosevelt and the Coming of the War, 1941*. New Haven: Yale University Press, 1948.

Beardsley, Philip L. *Redefining Rigor: Ideology and Statistics in Political Inquiry*. Beverly Hills: Sage, 1980.

Benes, Edward. *Memoirs of Dr. Edward Benes*. Boston: Houghton Mifflin, 1954.

Bennett, Edward M. *Franklin D. Roosevelt and the Search for Security: American-Soviet Relations, 1933–1939*. Wilmington, Del.: Scholarly Resources, 1985.

_____. *Franklin D. Roosevelt and the Search for Victory: American-Soviet Relations, 1939–1945*. Wilmington, Del.: Scholarly Resources, 1990.

Ben-Zvi, Abraham. *The Illusion of Deterrence: The Roosevelt Presidency and the Origins of the Pacific War*. Boulder, Colo.: Westview Press, 1987.

Berle, Beatrice, ed. *Navigating the Rapids, 1918–1971: From the Papers of Adolph A. Berle*. New York: Harcourt Brace Jovanovich, 1973.

Beschloss, Michael R. *Kennedy and Roosevelt*. New York: W. W. Norton, 1980.

Bialer, Uri. *The Shadow of the Bomber: The Fear of Attack and British Politics, 1932–1939*. London: Royal Historical Society, 1980.

Bloom, Sol. *The Autobiography of Sol Bloom*. New York: G. P. Putnam's Sons, 1948.

Blum, John Morton, ed. *From the Morgenthau Diaries: Years of Crisis, 1928–1938*. Vol. 1. Boston: Houghton Mifflin, 1959.

_____. *From the Morgenthau Diaries: Years of Urgency, 1938–1941*. Vol. 7. Boston: Houghton Mifflin, 1965.

Bobrow, Davis B., Steve Chan, and John A. Kringen. *Understanding Foreign Policy Decisions: The Chinese Case*. New York: Free Press, 1979.

Borg, Dorothy. *The United States and the Far East Crisis of 1933–39*. Cambridge, Mass.: Harvard University Press, 1964.

Borg, Dorothy, and Shumpei Okamoto, eds. *Pearl Harbor as History: Japanese-*

American Relations, 1931–1941. New York: Columbia University Press, 1973.

Braybrooke, David, and Charles Lindblom. *A Strategy of Decision: Policy Evaluation as a Social Process.* New York: Free Press, 1963.

Brim, Orville G., Jr., David C. Glass, David E. Lavin, and Norman Goodman. *Personality and Decision Processes.* Stanford, Calif.: Stanford University Press, 1962.

Bueno de Mesquita, Bruce. *The War Trap.* New Haven: Yale University Press, 1981.

Bueno de Mesquita, Bruce, and David Lalman. *War and Reason.* New Haven: Yale University Press, 1992.

Bullitt, Orville H., ed. *For the President: Personal and Secret, Correspondence between Franklin D. Roosevelt and William C. Bullitt.* Boston: Houghton Mifflin, 1972.

Burns, James MacGregor. *Roosevelt: The Lion and the Fox.* New York: Harcourt, Brace, 1956.

Butler, James R. M. *Lord Lothian.* London: Macmillan, 1960.

Butow, Robert J. *Tojo and the Coming of the War.* Stanford, Calif.: Stanford University Press, 1961.

Cadogan, Alexander. *The Diaries of Alexander Cadogan, 1938–1945.* Ed. David Dilks. London: Cassell, 1971.

Cantril, Hadley. *The Human Dimension.* New Brunswick, N.J.: Rutgers University Press, 1967.

––––––. *Invasion from Mars.* Princeton: Princeton Unversity Press, 1940.

Chadwin, Mark. *The Hawks of World War II.* Chapel Hill, N.C.: University of North Carolina Press, 1968.

Churchman, Charles W., Russell L. Ackoff, and E. Leonard Arnoff. *Introduction to Operations Research.* New York: John Wiley, 1957.

Cohen, Raymond. *International Politics, the Rules of the Game.* New York: Longman, 1981.

––––––. *Threat Perception in International Crisis.* Madison, Wisc.: University of Wisconsin Press, 1979.

Coit, Margaret. *Mr. Baruch.* Boston: Houghton Mifflin, 1957.

Cole, Wayne S. *America First: The Battle Against Intervention.* Madison, Wisc.: University of Wisconsin Press, 1953.

––––––. *Charles A. Lindbergh and the Battle Against American Intervention in World War II.* New York: Harcourt Brace Jovanovich, 1970.

––––––. *Roosevelt and the Isolationists, 1932–45.* Lincoln, Neb.: University of Nebraska Press, 1983.

––––––. *Senator Gerald P. Nye and American Foreign Policy.* Minneapolis: University of Minnesota Press, 1962.

Connally, Tom. *My Name is Tom Connally.* New York: Thomas Y. Crowell, 1954.

Crabb, Cecil V., and Kevin V. Mulcahy. *Presidents and Foreign Policy Making.* Baton Rouge, La.: Louisiana State University Press, 1986.

Dallek, Robert. *Democrat and Diplomat.* New York: Oxford University Press, 1968.

_____. *Franklin D. Roosevelt and American Foreign Policy, 1932–1945.* New York: Oxford University Press, 1979.

Davies, Joseph E. *Mission to Moscow.* New York: Simon and Schuster, 1941.

Davis, Forrest. *The Atlantic System.* New York: Reynal and Hitchcock, 1941.

Davis, Kenneth S. *FDR.* Vols. 1–3. New York: Random House, 1971, 1986.

DeRivera, Joseph. *The Psychological Dimension of Foreign Policy.* Columbus, Ohio: Charles E. Merrill, 1968.

Destler, I. M., Leslie H. Gelb, and Anthony Lake. *Our Own Worst Enemy.* New York: Simon and Schuster, 1984.

Diesing, Paul. *Reason in Society.* Urbana, Ill.: University of Illinois Press, 1962.

Divine, Robert A., ed. *Causes and Consequences of World War II.* Chicago: Quadrangle Books, 1969.

_____. *The Illusion of Neutrality.* Chicago: The University of Chicago Press, 1962.

_____. *The Reluctant Belligerent.* New York: John Wiley and Sons, 1965.

_____. *Roosevelt and World War II.* Baltimore: Johns Hopkins University Press, 1969.

Dodd, William E., and Martha Dodd, eds. *Ambassador Dodd's Diary, 1933–1938.* New York: Harcourt Brace, 1941.

Dror, Yehezkel. *Ventures in Policy Sciences.* New York: American Elsevier, 1971.

Drummond, Donald F. *The Passing of American Neutrality, 1937–1941.* Ann Arbor: University of Michigan Press, 1955.

Eden, Anthony. *Facing the Dictators.* Boston: Houghton Mifflin, 1962.

Elster, Jon, ed. *Rational Choice.* New York: New York University Press, 1986.

_____. *Solomonic Judgments.* Paris: Cambridge University Press, 1989.

_____. *Ulysses and the Sirens.* New York: Cambridge University Press, 1984.

English, Horace B., and Ava C. English, eds. *A Comprehensive Dictionary of Psychological and Medical Terms.* New York: David McKay, 1958.

Etheridge, Lloyd S. *A World of Men: The Private Sources of American Foreign Policy.* Cambridge, Mass.: M.I.T. Press, 1978.

Farley, James. *Jim Farley's Story.* New York: McGraw-Hill, 1948.

Farnham, Barbara, ed. *Avoiding Losses/Taking Risks: Prospect Theory and International Conflict.* Ann Arbor: University of Michigan Press, 1994.

Ferrell, Robert H. *American Diplomacy.* New York: W. W. Norton, 1975.

Festinger, Leon. *Conflict, Decision, and Dissonance.* Stanford, Calif.: Stanford University Press, 1964.

_____. *A Theory of Cognitive Dissonance.* Evanston, Ill.: Row, Peterson, 1957.

Fiske, Susan T., and Shelley E. Taylor. *Social Cognition.* Menlo Park, Calif.: Addison-Wesley, 1984.

Freidel, Frank. *Franklin D. Roosevelt.* Vols. 1–4. Boston: Little, Brown, 1952–1973.

Friedlander, Saul. *Prelude to Downfall: Hitler and the United States, 1939–1941.* New York: Alfred A. Knopf, 1967.

Frye, Alton. *Nazi Gemany and the American Hemisphere, 1933–1941.* New Haven: Yale University Press, 1967.

Frye, William, *Marshall, Citizen Soldier.* New York: Bobbs-Merrill, 1947.

Gaddis, John Lewis. *Russia, the Soviet Union, and the United States: An Interpretive History.* New York: John Wiley and Sons, 1978.

_____. *Strategies of Containment.* Oxford: Oxford University Press, 1982.

The Gallup Poll: Public Opinion 1935–1971. Vol 1, 1935–1948. New York: Random House, 1972.

George, Alexander. *Bridging the Gap: Theory and Practice in Foreign Policy.* Washington, D.C.: United States Institute of Peace, 1993.

_____. *Presidential Decisionmaking in Foreign Policy: The Effective Use of Information and Advice.* Boulder, Colo.: Westview Press, 1980.

George, Alexander, David K. Hall, and William E. Simmons. *The Limits of Coercive Diplomacy.* Boston: Little, Brown, 1971.

Gilbert, Martin. *Winston S. Churchill.* Vols. 1–6. Boston: Houghton Mifflin, 1983.

Glad, Betty. *Jimmy Carter.* New York: W. W. Norton, 1986.

_____. *Key Pittman: The Tragedy of a Senate Insider.* New York: Columbia University Press, 1986.

Goodwin, Doris Kearns. *No Ordinary Time.* New York: Simon and Schuster, 1995.

Graebner, Norman A. *America as a World Power.* Wilmington, Del.: Scholarly Resources, 1984.

_____. *Foundations of American Foreign Policy: A Realist Appraisal from Franklin to McKinley.* Wilmington, Del.: Scholarly Resources, 1985.

Greenfield, Kent Roberts. *American Strategy in World War II: A Reconsideration.* Baltimore: Johns Hopkins University Press, 1963.

Greenstein, Fred I. *Personality and Politics.* Princeton: Princeton University Press, 1987.

Greenstein, Fred I., and Michael Lerner, eds. *A Source Book for the Study of Personality and Politics.* Chicago: Markham, 1971.

Greer, Thomas H. *What Roosevelt Thought.* East Lansing, Mich.: Michigan State University Press, 1958.

Guilford, J. P. *Cognitive Psychology with a Frame of Reference.* San Diego, Calif.: Edits, 1979.

Gulick, Luther. *Administrative Reflections from World War II.* Birmingham, Ala.: University of Alabama Press, 1948.

Gunther, John. *Roosevelt in Retrospect.* New York: Harper and Brothers, 1950.

Haight, John McVickar, Jr. *American Aid to France, 1938–1940.* New York: Atheneum, 1970.

Halperin, Morton H. *Bureaucratic Politics and Foreign Policy.* Washington, D.C.: Brookings Institution, 1974.

Harriman, W. Averell, and Elie Abel. *Special Envoy to Churchill and Stalin, 1941–1946.* New York: Random House, 1975.

Heineman, Robert A., William T. Bluhm, Steven A. Peterson, and Edward N. Kearny. *The World of the Policy Analyst: Rationality, Values, and Politics.* Chatham, N.J.: Chatham House, 1990.

Heinrichs, Waldo. *Threshold of War: Franklin D. Roosevelt and American Entry into World War II.* New York: Oxford University Press, 1988.

Heradsveit, Daniel. *The Arab-Israeli Conflict: Psychological Obstacles to Peace.* Oslo: Universitesforlaget, 1979.

Hermann, Charles F., ed. *International Crisis.* New York: Free Press, 1972.

Herzstein, Robert E. *Roosevelt and Hitler.* New York: Paragon House, 1989.

Higgins, E. Tory, and Richard M. Sorrentino, eds. *Handbook of Motivation and Cognition.* Vols. 1–2. New York: Guilford Press, 1986, 1990.

Hilsman, Roger. *The Politics of Policymaking in Defense and Foreign Affairs.* Englewood Cliffs, N.J.: Prentice-Hall, 1987.

_____. *Strategic Intelligence and National Decisions.* Glencoe, Ill.: Free Press, 1956.

_____. *To Move a Nation.* Garden City, N.Y.: Doubleday, 1967.

Hodgson, Godfrey. *The Colonel: The Life and Wars of Henry Stimson, 1867–1950.* New York: Alfred A. Knopf, 1990.

Holsti, Ole R. *Crisis, Escalation, War.* Montreal: McGill-Queens University Press, 1972.

Hooker, Nancy H. ed. *The Moffat Papers: Selections from the Diplomatic Papers of Jay Pierrepont Moffat, 1919–1943.* Cambridge, Mass.: Harvard University Press, 1956.

Hopple, Gerald W. *Political Psychology and Biopolitics.* Boulder, Colo.: Westview Press, 1980.

Huckfeldt, Robert, and John Sprague. *Citizens, Politics, and Social Communication: Information and Influence in an Election Campaign.* Cambridge: Cambridge University Press, 1995.

Hughes, John Emmet, ed. *The Living Presidency.* New York: Coward McCann, 1972.

Hull, Cordell. *The Memoirs of Cordell Hull.* Vol. 1. New York: Macmillan, 1948.

Huntington, Samuel P. *The Common Defense: Strategic Programs in National Politics.* New York: Columbia University Press, 1961.

Ickes, Harold. *The Secret Diary of Harold Ickes.* Vol. 2. New York: Simon and Schuster, 1954.

Ikle, Fred Charles. *How Nations Negotiate.* New York: Harper and Row, 1964.

Iriye, Akira. *Across the Pacific: An Inner History of American-Asian Relations.* New York: Harcourt, Brace, and World, 1967.

Israel, Fred L. *Nevada's Key Pittman.* Lincoln, Neb.: University of Nebraska Press, 1963.

Israel, Fred L., ed. *The War Diary of Breckinridge Long.* Lincoln, Neb.: University of Nebraska Press, 1966.

Janeway, Eliot. *The Struggle for Survival.* New Haven: Yale University Press, 1951.

Janis, Irving L. *Crucial Decisions.* New York: Free Press, 1989.

_____. *Groupthink.* 2d ed. Boston: Houghton Mifflin, 1982.

Janis, Irving, and Leon Mann. *Decision-Making.* New York: Free Press, 1977.

Jervis, Robert. *The Illogic of American Nuclear Strategy.* Ithaca, N.Y.: Cornell University Press, 1984.

_____. *Perception and Misperception in International Politics.* Princeton: Princeton University Press, 1976.

Jervis, Robert, Richard Ned Lebow, and Janice Gross Stein, eds. *Psychology and Deterrence*. Baltimore: Johns Hopkins University Press, 1985.

Johnson, Walter. *The Battle Against Isolation*. Chicago: University of Chicago Press, 1944.

Johnson, Walter, ed. *Selected Letters of William Allen White, 1899–1943*. New York: Henry Holt, 1947.

Jonas, Manfred. *Isolationism in America*. Ithaca, N. Y.: Cornell University Press, 1966.

Jones, Bryan D. *Reconceiving Decision-making in Democratic Politics: Attention, Choice, and Public Policy*. Chicago: University of Chicago Press, 1994.

Jones, Edward E. et al., ed. *Attribution: Perceiving the Causes of Behavior*. Morristown, N.J.: General Learning Press, 1972.

Jones, Kenneth Paul, ed. *U.S. Diplomats in Europe, 1919–1941*. Santa Barbara, Calif.: ABC-Clio, 1983.

Kanawada, Leo V. *Franklin D. Roosevelt's Diplomacy and American Catholics, Italians, and Jews*. Ann Arbor: University of Michigan Press, 1982.

Katz, Daniel, and Robert L. Kahn. *The Social Psychology of Organizations*. New York: John Wiley and Sons, 1966.

Keeney, Ralph L., and Howard Raiffa. *Decision with Multiple Objectives: Preferences and Value Tradeoffs*. New York: John Wiley and Sons, 1976.

Keohane, Robert O., ed. *Neorealism and Its Critics*. New York: Columbia University Press, 1986.

Khong, Yuen Foong. *Analogies at War*. Princeton: Princeton University Press, 1992.

Kilpatrick, Carroll, ed. *Roosevelt and Daniels: A Friendship in Politics*, Chapel Hill, N.C.: University of North Carolina Press, 1952.

Kimball, Warren F. *The Juggler: Franklin Delano Roosevelt as Wartime Statesman*, Princeton: Princeton University Press, 1991.

Kimball, Warren F., ed. *Churchill and Roosevelt: Complete Correspondence*. Vol. 1, *Alliance Emerging, October 1933–November 1942*. Princeton: Princeton University Press, 1984.

Kinsella, William E. *Leadership in Isolation: F.D.R. and the Origins of the Second World War*. Boston: G. K. Hall, 1978.

Koskoff, David E. *Joseph P. Kennedy: A Life and Times*. Englewood Cliffs, N.J.: Prentice-Hall, 1974.

Langer, William L., and Everett S. Gleason. *The Challenge to Isolation, 1937–1940*. New York: Harper and Brothers, 1952.

———. *The Undeclared War, 1940–1941*. New York: Harper and Brothers, 1953.

Larrabee, Eric. *Commander in Chief*. New York: Harper and Row, 1987.

Larson, Deborah W. *Origins of Containment*. Princeton: Princeton University Press, 1985.

Lash, Joseph P. *Roosevelt and Churchill, 1939–1941: The Partnership That Saved the West*. New York: W. W. Norton, 1976.

Lasswell, Harold D. *A Pre-View of Policy Sciences*. New York: American Elsevier, 1971.

Lasswell, Harold D., and Abraham Kaplan. *Power and Society.* New Haven: Yale University Press, 1950.

Lazarus, Richard S. *Psychological Stress and the Coping Process.* New York: McGraw-Hill, 1966.

Lazarus, Richard S., and Susan Folkman. *Stress, Appraisal, and Coping.* New York: Springer, 1984.

Leahy, William D. *I Was There.* New York: McGraw-Hill, 1950.

Lebow, Richard Ned. *Between Peace and War.* Baltimore: Johns Hopkins University Press, 1981.

Lebow, Richard N., and Janice G. Stein. *We All Lost the Cold War.* Princeton: Princeton University Press, 1994.

Leuchtenberg, William. *Franklin Roosevelt and the New Deal.* New York: Harper and Row, 1963.

Leuchtenberg, William, ed. *Franklin D. Roosevelt: A Profile.* New York: Hill and Wang, 1967.

Leutze, James R. *Bargaining for Supremacy: Anglo-American Naval Collaboration, 1937–1941.* Chapel Hill, N.C.: University of North Carolina Press, 1977.

Lindbergh, Charles A. *Wartime Journals of Charles A. Lindbergh.* New York: Harcourt Brace Jovanovich, 1970.

Loewenheim, Francis L., Harold D. Langley, and Manfred Jonas, eds. *Roosevelt and Churchill: Their Secret Wartime Correspondence.* New York: Saturday Review Press, 1975.

Lukasiewicz, Juliusz. *Diplomat in Paris, 1936–1939.* Ed. Waclaw Jedrzejewicz. New York: Columbia University Press, 1970.

MacDonald, Callum A. *The United States, Britain and Appeasement, 1936–1939.* London: Macmillan, 1981.

Machiavelli, Niccolo. *The Prince.* New York: Viking Penguin, 1961.

March, James G., and Herbert Simon. *Organizations.* New York: John Wiley and Sons, 1958.

Marks, Frederick W. *Wind Over Sand: The Diplomacy of Franklin D. Roosevelt.* Athens, Ga.:, University of Georgia Press, 1988.

Martin, Joe. *My First Fifty Years in Politics.* New York: McGraw-Hill, 1960.

May, Ernest. *"Lessons" of the Past: The Uses and Misuses of History in American Foreign Policy.* New York: Oxford University Press, 1972.

Meltsner, Arnold J. *Rules for Rulers: The Politics of Advice.* Philadelphia: Temple University Press, 1990.

Moley, Raymond. *After Seven Years.* New York: Harper and Brothers, 1939.

Morgan, Patrick M. *Deterrence: A Conceptual Analysis.* Beverly Hills: Sage Library of Social Science, 1977.

Murray, Arthur. *At Close Quarters.* London: John Murray, 1946.

Murray, Williamson. *The Change in the European Balance of Power, 1938–1939.* Princeton: Princeton University Press, 1984.

Nagel, Ernest. *The Structure of Science.* Indianapolis: Hackett, 1979.

Neustadt, Richard E. *Alliance Politics.* New York: Columbia University Press, 1970.

———. *Presidential Power.* New York: John Wiley and Sons, 1960, Revised editions, New York: Columbia University Press, 1980, 1990.

Neustadt, Richard E., and Ernest R. May. *Thinking in Time: The Uses of History for Decision-Makers.* New York: Free Press, 1986.

Newell, Allen, and Herbert A. Simon. *Human Problem Solving.* Englewood Cliffs, N.J.: Prentice-Hall, 1972.

Nisbett, Richard E., and Lee Ross. *Human Inference: Strategies and Shortcomings of Social Judgment.* Englewood Cliffs, N.J.: Prentice-Hall, 1980.

Offner, Arnold A. *America and the Origins of World War II.* Boston: Houghton Mifflin, 1971.

———. *American Appeasement: United States Foreign Policy and Germany, 1933–1938.* New York: W. W. Norton, 1969.

———. *The Origins of World War II.* New York: Praeger, 1975.

Payne, James L., et al. *Motivations of Politicians.* Chicago: Nelson-Hall, 1984.

Perkins, Frances. *The Roosevelt I Knew.* New York, Viking Press, 1946.

Phillips, William. *Ventures in Diplomacy.* Boston: Beacon Press, 1952.

Pickersgill, J. W. *The Mackenzie King Record.* Vol. 1, *1939–1944.* Toronto: University of Chicago and Unversity of Toronto Presses, 1960.

Pogue, Forrest. *George C. Marshall.* Vols. 1–3. New York: Viking, 1963–1973.

Posen, Barry R. *Sources of Military Doctrine.* Ithaca, N.Y.: Cornell University Press, 1984.

Pratt, Julius W. *Cordell Hull, 1933–44.* Vols. 12–13 of *American Secretaries of State and Their Diplomacy,* ed. Samuel Flagg Bemis. New York: Cooper Square Publishers, 1964.

Quandt, William B. *Camp David: Peacemaking and Politics.* Washington, D.C.: Brookings Institution, 1986.

Questor, George. *Deterrence Before Hiroshima.* New York: John Wiley and Sons, 1966.

Rauch, Basil. *Roosevelt: From Munich to Pearl Harbor.* New York: Creative Age Press, 1950.

Raymond, Jack. *Power at the Pentagon.* New York: Harper and Row, 1964.

Reynolds, David. *The Creation of the Anglo-American Alliance, 1937–1941.* Chapel Hill, N.C.: University of North Carolina Press, 1982.

Rieselbach, Leroy N. *The Roots of Isolationism.* New York: Bobbs-Merrill, 1966.

Rokeach, Milton. *Beliefs, Attitudes, and Values: A Theory of Organization and Change.* San Francisco: Jossey-Bass, 1968.

———. *The Nature of Human Values.* New York: Free Press, 1973.

Roll, Charles, Jr., and Albert H. Cantril. *Polls: Their Use and Misuse in Politics.* New York: Basic Books, 1972.

Roosevelt, Eleanor. *Autobiography.* New York: Harper and Brothers, 1961.

———. *This I Remember.* New York: Harper and Brothers, 1949.

Roosevelt, Elliot. *As He Saw It.* New York: Duell, Sloan and Pearce, 1946.

Roosevelt, James. *Affectionately FDR.* New York: Harcourt, Brace, 1959.

Rosenman, Samuel. *Working with Roosevelt.* New York: Harper and Brothers, 1952.

Rosenman, Samuel, and Dorothy Rosenman. *Presidential Style*. New York: Harper and Row, 1976.

Ross, Walter S. *The Last Hero: Charles A. Lindbergh*. New York: Harper and Row, 1968.

Russett, Bruce. *Grasping the Democratic Peace*. Princeton: Princeton University Press, 1993.

Russett, Bruce M. *No Clear and Present Danger*. New York: Harper and Row, 1972.

Ryan, Halford. *Franklin D. Roosevelt's Rhetorical Presidency*. New York: Greenwood Press, 1988.

Schank, Roger C., and Robert P. Abelson. *Scripts Plans, Goals, and Understanding*. Hillsdale, N.J.: Erlbaum, 1977.

Schlesinger, Arthur M., Jr. *The Age of Roosevelt*. Vols. 1–3. Boston: Houghton-Mifflin, 1957–1960.

Schmitz, David F., and Richard D. Challener. *Appeasement in Europe*. Westport, Conn.: Greenwood Press, 1990.

Sherwood, Robert. *Roosevelt and Hopkins*. New York: Harper and Brothers, 1948.

Simon, Herbert A. *Administrative Behavior*. New York: Macmillan, 1957.

Skowronek, Stephen. *The Politics Presidents Make: Leadership from John Adams to George Bush*. Cambridge, Mass.: Harvard University Press, 1993.

Smith, M. Brewster. *Social Psychology and Human Values*. Chicago: Aldine, 1969.

Snyder, Glen H., and Paul Diesing. *Conflict Among Nations*. Princeton: Princeton University Press, 1977.

Snyder, Jack. *The Ideology of the Offensive: Military Decision Making and the Disasters of 1914*. Ithaca, N.Y.: Cornell University Press, 1984.

Steele, Richard W. *Propaganda in an Open Society*. Westport, Conn.: Greenwood Press, 1985.

Stein, Janice G., and Raymond Tanter. *Rational Decision-Making: Israel's Security Choices*. Columbus, Ohio: Ohio State University Press, 1980.

Steinbruner, John D. *Cybernetic Theory of Decision*. Princeton: Princeton University Press, 1974.

Stimson, Henry L., and McGeorge Bundy. *On Active Service in Peace and War*. New York: Harper and Brothers, 1948.

Stinchombe, Arthur. *Constructing Social Theories*. New York: Harcourt, Brace, and World, 1968.

Stockman, David. *The Triumph of Politics*. New York: Harper and Row, 1986.

Stromberg, Roland N. *Collective Security and American Foreign Policy: From the League of Nations to NATO*. New York: Frederick A. Praeger, 1963.

Tansill, Charles C. *Back Door to War: The Roosevelt Foreign Policy, 1933–1941*. Chicago: Regnery, 1952.

Taylor, A.J.P. *Origins of the Second World War*. New York: Atheneum, 1962.

Taylor, Telford. *Munich*. New York: Doubleday, 1979.

Thies, Wallace J. *When Governments Collide*. Berkeley and Los Angeles: University of California Press, 1980.

Thompson, Kenneth W., ed. *The Roosevelt Presidency: Four Intimate Perspectives of FDR*. Lanham, Md.: University Press of America, 1982.

Touval, Saadia. *Domestic Dynamics of Change from Confrontation to Accomodation Policies*. Princeton: Princeton University Press, 1973

Trachtenberg, Marc. *History and Strategy*. Princeton: Princeton University Press, 1991.

Tsebelis, George. *Nested Games*. Berkeley and Los Angeles: University of California Press, 1990.

Tugwell, Rexford. *The Art of Politics, as Practiced by Three Great Americans*. Garden City, N.Y.: Doubleday, 1958.

_____. *The Democratic Roosevelt*. Garden City, N.Y.: Doubleday, 1957.

_____. *In Search of Roosevelt*. Cambridge, Mass.: Harvard Unversity Press, 1972.

Tully, Grace G. *FDR, My Boss*. New York: Charles Scribner's Sons, 1949.

Van Minnen, Cornelius A., and John F. Sears, eds. *FDR and His Contemporaries*. New York: St. Martin's Press, 1992.

Vertzberger, Yaacov Y. I. *The World in Their Minds*. Stanford, Calif.: Stanford University Press, 1990.

Wallsten, Thomas S., ed. *Cognitive Processes in Choice and Decision Behavior*. Hillsdale, N.J.: Lawrence Erlbaum Associates, 1980.

Waltz, Kenneth. *Theory of International Politics*. Reading, Mass.: Addison-Wesley, 1979.

Ward, Geoffrey C. *Before the Trumpet, Young Franklin Roosevelt: 1882–1905*. New York: Harper and Row, 1986.

_____. *A First-Class Temperment: The Emergence of Franklin Roosevelt*. New York: Harper and Row, 1989.

Ward, Geoffrey C., ed. *Closest Companion*. New York: Houghton Mifflin, 1995.

Watt, Donald C. *How War Came*. New York: Pantheon, 1989.

Weinberg, Gerhard L. *The Foreign Policy of Hitler's Germany: Starting the War, 1937–1939*. Chicago: University of Chicago Press, 1980.

Welles, Sumner. *Seven Decisions That Shaped the World*. New York: Harper and Brothers, 1951.

_____. *The Time for Decision*. New York: Harper and Brothers, 1944.

Whalen, Richard. *The Founding Father*. New York: New American Library, 1964.

Wheeler-Bennett, Sir John. *King George VI*. New York: St Martin's Press, 1958.

Wilson, Hugh R., Jr. *A Career Diplomat*. New York, Vantage Press. 1960.

_____. *A Diplomat Between Wars*. New York: Longmans, Green, 1941.

Wiltz, John. *From Isolation to War, 1931–1941*, New York: Thomas Y. Crowell, 1968.

Articles

Abel, Theodore. "The Element of Decision in the Pattern of War." *American Sociological Review* 6 (1941): 853–59.

Abelson, Robert P. "Modes of Resolution of Belief Dilemmas." *Journal of Conflict Resolution* 3 (1959): 343–52.

––––––. "Psychological Status of the Script Concept." *American Psychologist* 36 (1981): 715–29.

––––––. "Script Processing in Attitude Formation and Decision Making." In *Cognition and Social Behavior*, ed. John S. Carroll and John W. Payne, 33–45. Hillsdale, N.J.: Lawrence Erlbaum Associates, 1976.

Abelson, Robert P., Donald R. Kinder, Mark T. Peters, and Susan T. Fiske. "Affective and Semantic Components in Political Person Perception." *Journal of Personality and Social Psychology* 42 (1982): 619–30.

Abelson, Robert P., and Ariel Levi. "Decision Making and Decision Theory." In *Handbook of Social Psychology*, vol. 1, ed. Gardner Lindzey and Elliot Aronson. 231–310. New York: Random House, 1985.

Alexander, Ernest R. "Design of Alternatives in Organizational Contents." *Administrative Science Quarterly* 24 (1979): 382–404.

Alexandroff, Alan, and Richard Rosecrance. "Deterence in 1939." *World Politics* 29 (1977): 404–24.

Almond, Gabriel A., and Stephen J. Genco. "Clouds, Clocks, and Politics." *World Politics* 29 (1977): 489–522.

"American Institute of Public Opinion Surveys, 1938–1939." *Public Opinion Quarterly* 3 (1939): 581–607.

Anderson, Paul A. "Justifications and Precedents as Constraints in Foreign Policy Decision-Making." *American Journal of Political Science* 25 (1982): 738–61.

Art, Robert J. "Bureaucratic Politics and American Foreign Policy: A Critique." *Policy Sciences* 4 (1973): 467–90.

Axelrod, Robert. "Argumentation in Foreign Policy Settings: Britain in 1918, Munich in 1938, and Japan in 1940." *Journal of Conflict Resolution* 21 (1977): 727–56.

Bazerman, Max H. "Negotiator Judgement." *American Behavioral Scientist* 27 (1983): 211–28.

Beach, Lee Roy, and Terence R. Mitchell. "A Contingency Model for the Selection of Decision Strategies." *Academy of Management Review* 3 (1978): 439–49.

Beals, Carlton. "Totalitarian Inroads in Latin America." *Foreign Affairs* 17 (1938): 78–89.

Beck, Robert J. "Munich's Lessons Reconsidered." *International Security* 14 (1989): 161–91.

Bem, Daryl J. "Self-Perception Theory." In *Advances in Experimental Social Psychology*, vol. 6, ed. Leonard Berkowitz, 1–62. New York: Academic Press, 1972.

Bennett, W. Lance. "Perception and Cognition: An Information Processing Framework for Politics." In *Handbook of Political Behavior*, vol. 1, ed. S. L. Long, 69–175. New York: Plenum, 1981.

Ben-Zvi, Abraham. "Warning, Decision, and Action: A Response," *International Studies Quarterly* 21 (1977): 553–59.

Bidwell, Percy W. "Latin America, Germany and the Hull Program" *Foreign Affairs* 17 (1939): 374–90.

Billings, Robert S., and Mary Lou Schoolman. "Administrator's Estimates of the Probability Outcomes of School Desegregation." *Organizational Behavior and Human Performance* 26 (1980): 97–114.

Borg, Dorothy. "Notes on Roosevelt's Quarantine Speech." *Political Science Quarterly* 72 (1957): 405–33.

Bourgin, Simon. "Public Relations of Naval Expansion." *Public Opinion Quarterly* 3 (1939): 113–17.

Braden, Marsha, and Elaine Walster. "The Effect of Anticipated Dissonance on Pre-decision Behavior." In *Conflict, Decision, and Dissonance*, ed. Leon Festinger et al. Stanford, Calif.: Stanford University Press, 1964.

Cantril, Hadley. "America Faces the War: A Study in Public Opinion." *Public Opinion Quarterly* 4 (1940): 387–407.

Cantril, Hadley, Donald Rugg, and Frederick Williams. "America Faces the War: Shifts in Opinion," *Public Opinion Quarterly* 4 (1940): 651–56.

Carnevale, Peter J. D., and Alice M. Isen. "The Influence of Positive Affect and Visual Access on the Discovery of Integrative Solutions in Bilateral Negotiation." *Organizational Behavior and Human Decision Processes* 37 (1986): 1–13.

Carroll, John S. "Analyzing Decision Behavior: The Magician's Audience." In Wallsten, *Cognitive Processes*, 69–76.

Chaiken, Shelly, and Mark Baldwin. "Affective-Cognitive Consistency and the Effect of Salient Behavioral Information on the Self-Perception of Attitudes." *Journal of Personality and Social Psychology* 41 (1981): 1–12.

Chambers, Clarke. "FDR: Pragmatic-Idealist." In Leuchtenberg, *Franklin D. Roosevelt.*

Christensen-Szalanski, Jay J. J. "Problem-Solving Strategies: A Selection Mechanism, Some Implications, and Some Data." *Organizational Behavior and Human Performance* 22 (1978): 307–23.

Cohen, Benjamin V. "The Presidency as I See it." In Hughes, *The Living Presidency.*

Cohen, Bernard C. "Military Policy Analysis and the Art of the Possible: A Review." *Journal of Conflict Resolution* 6 (1962): 154–59.

Cohen, Michael D., and Robert Axelrod, "Coping with Complexity: The Adaptive Value of Changing Utility." *American Economic Review* 74 (1984): 30–42.

Cole, Wayne S. "American Entry into World War II: A Historiographical Appraisal." *Mississippi Valley Historical Review* 42 (1957): 595–617.

Conn, Stetson. "Changing Concepts of National Defense in the United States, 1937–1941." *Military Affairs* 28 (1964): 1–7.

Corbin, Ruth M. "Decisions That Might Not Get Made." In Wallsten, *Cognitive Processes,* 47–67.

Craft, Stephen G. "Deterring Aggression Abroad or at Home: A Rejoinder to 'FDR's Day of Infamy,'" *SHAFR Newsletter* 24 (March 1993): 22–28.

Crocker, Jennifer, Susan T. Fiske, and Shelley E. Taylor. "Schematic Bases of Belief Change." In *Attitudinal Judgment*, ed. Richard J. Eiser, 197–226. New York: Springer-Verlag, 1984.

Cvetkovich, George. "Cognitive Accommodation, Language, and Social Responsibility." *Social Psychology* 42 (1978): 149–55.

Dallek, Robert. "Beyond Tradition: The Diplomatic Careers of William E. Dodd and George S. Messersmith, 1933–1938." *South Atlantic Quarterly* 66 (1967): 233–44.

Davis, Mark A., and Philip Bobko. "Contextual Effects on Escalation Processes in Public Sector Decision Making." *Organizational Behavior and Human Decision Processes* 37 (1986): 121–38.

Destler, I. M. "National Security Advice to U.S. Presidents." *World Politics* 29 (1977): 143–76.

Dinerstein, Herbert. "The Impact of Air Power on the International Scene, 1933–1940." *Military Affairs* 19 (Summer 1955): 65–71.

Divine, Robert. "Diplomatic Historians and World War II." In Divine, *Causes and Consequences*, 3–30.

Ebbesen, Ebbe B., and Vladimir J. Konceni. "On the External Validity of Decision-Making Research: What Do We Know About Decisions in the Real World?" In Wallsten, *Cognitive Processes*, 21–45.

Eckstein, Harry. "Case Study and Theory in Political Science." In *Handbook of Politial Science*, vol. 7, ed. Fred I. Greenstein and Nelson W. Polsby, 79–137. Reading, Mass.: Addison-Wesley, 1975.

Edwards, Ward. "Dynamic Decision Theory and Probabilistic Information Processing." *Human Factors* 4 (1961): 59–73.

Einhorn, Hillel J. "The Use of Nonlinear, Noncompensatory Models in Decision Making." *Psychological Bulletin* 73 (1970): 221–30.

———. "Use of Nonlinear, Noncompensatory Models as a Function of Task and Amount of Information." *Organizational Behavior and Human Performance* 6 (1971): 1–27.

Einhorn, Hillel J., and Robin M. Hogarth. "Behavioral Decision Theory: Processes of Judgement and Choice." *Annual Review of Psychology* 32 (1981): 53–88.

Einhorn, Hillel J., Don N. Kleinmuntz, and Benjamin Kleinmuntz. "Linear Regression and Process-Tracing Models of Judgement." *Psychological Review* 86 (1979): 465–85.

Elibank, Viscount. "Franklin Roosevelt, Friend of Britain." *Contemporary Review* 187 (1955): 362–68.

Emerson, William R. "F.D.R. (1941–1945)." In *The Ultimate Decision: The President as Commander-in-Chief*, ed. Ernest R. May, 181–207. New York: Braziller, 1960.

———. "Franklin Roosevelt as Commander-in-Chief in World War II." *Military Affairs* 22 (1958): 181–207.

Farnham, Barbara. "Political Cognition and Decision-making." *Political Psychology* 11 (March 1990): 83–111.

Fazio, Russell H., Mark P. Zanna, and Joel Cooper. "Dissonance and Self-Perception: An Integrative View of Each Theory's Proper Domain of Application." *Journal of Experimental Social Psychology* 13 (1977): 464–79.

Fensterwald, Bernard J. "The Anatomy of American 'Isolationism' and 'Expansionism,' Part I," *Journal of Conflict Resolution* 2 (1958): 111–39.

Ferrell, Robert H. "Pearl Harbor and the Revisionists." *The Historian* 17 (1955): 215–33.

Fischhoff, Baruch. "Strategic Policy Preferences: A Behavioral Decision Theory." *Journal of Social Issues* 39 (1983): 133–60.

Fortas, Abe. "The Presidency as I Have Seen It." In Hughes, *The Living Presidency*.

Friedman, Milton. "The Methodology of Positive Rationality." In *Essays in Positive Economics*, ed. Milton Friedman, 3–43. Chicago: University of Chicago Press, 1957.

Gaddis, John Lewis. "Expanding the Data Base: Historians, Political Scientists, and the Enrichment of Security Studies. *International Security* 12 (1987): 3–21.

Gallup, George, and Claude Robinson. "American Institute of Public Opinion—Surveys, 1935–38." *Public Opinion Quarterly* 3 (1938): 373–98.

Gellman, Irwin F. "The New Deal's Use of Naziism in Latin America." In *Perspectives in Latin American Diplomacy: Essays on Europe, Latin America, China, and the Cold War*, ed. Jules Davis, 178–207. New York: Arno Press, 1976.

George, Alexander L. "Adaptation to Stress in Political Decision Making: The Individual, Small Group, and Organizational Contexts." In *Coping and Adaptation*, ed. George V. Coelho, Daniel A. Hamburg, and John E. Adams, 176–245. New York: Basic Books, 1974.

———. "Case Studies and Theory Development: The Method of Structured Focussed Comparison." In *Diplomacy: New Approaches*, ed. Paul Gordon Lauren, 43–68. New York: Free Press, 1979.

———. "The Causal Nexus Between Cognitive Beliefs and Decision-Making Behavior: The 'Operational Code' Belief System." In *Psychological Models in International Politics*, ed. Lawrence S. Falkowski, 95–124. Boulder, Colo.: Westview Press, 1979.

———. "Domestic Constraints on Regime Change in U. S. Foreign Policy." In *Change in the International System*, ed. Ole R. Hosti, Randolph Siverson, and Alexander L. George, 233–62. Boulder, Colo.: Westview Press, 1980.

———. "The Operational Code." *International Studies Quarterly* 13 (1969): 190–222.

Geva, Nehemia, and Alex Mintz. "The Experimental Analyses of Conflict Processes Project: Preliminary Findings." *International Studies Notes* 18 (Spring 1993): 15–29.

Glad, Betty. "Multidisciplinary Studies and the Relationship of Scientific Research to Public Policymaking." *Political Psychology* 9 (1988): 527–37.

Greenstein, Fred I. "Political Style and Political Leadership." in *The Clinton Presidency*, ed. Stanley A. Renshon, 137–47. Boulder, Colo.: Westview Press, 1995.

Grether, David M. "Recent Psychological Studies of Behavior under Uncertainty." *American Economic Review* 68 (1978): 70–74.

Haight, John McVickar, Jr. "France and the Aftermath of Roosevelt's 'Quarantine' Speech." *World Politics* 14, (1962): 282–306.

———. "France, the United States, and the Munich Crisis." *Journal of Modern History* 32 (1960): 340–58.

———. "Franklin D. Roosevelt and a Naval Quarantine of Japan." *Pacific Historical Review* 40 (1971): 203–20.

————. "Roosevelt and the Aftermath of His Quarantine Speech." *Review of Politics* 24 (1962): 233–59.

————. "Roosevelt as Friend of France." In Divine, *Causes and Consequences*, 87–97.

Harrison, Richard A. "The United States and Great Britain: Presidential Diplomacy and Alternatives to Appeasement in the 1930s." In Schmitz and Challener, *Appeasement in Europe*, 103–43.

Harvey, John H., and Gifford Weary. "Current Issues in Attribution Theory and Research." *Annual Review of Psychology* 35 (1984): 427–59.

Heinrichs, Waldo H., Jr. "The Role of the Navy." In Borg and Okamoto, *Pearl Harbor as History*, 197–223.

Henson, Edward L., Jr. "Britain, America, and the Month of Munich." *International Relations* 2 (1962): 291–301.

Hermann, Charles F. "Threat, Time, and Surprise: A Simulation of International Crisis." In Hermann, *International Crisis*.

Hermann, Margaret G. "Ingredients of Leadership." In *Political Psychology*, ed. Margaret G. Hermann, 167–92. San Francisco: Jossey-Bass, 1986.

————. "Prologue: What Is Political Psychology?" in ibid., 1–10.

Higgins, E. Tory, and John A. Bargh. "Social Cognition and Social Perception." *Annual Review of Psychology* 38 (1987): 369–425.

Hilsman, Roger. "The Foreign Policy Consensus: An Interim Report." *Journal of Conflict Resolution* 3 (1959): 361–82.

Hoffman, Martin L. "Affect, Cognition, and Motivation." In *Handbook of Motivation and Cognition*, ed. Richard M. Sorrentino and E. Tory Higgins. New York: Guilford Press, 1986.

Hofstadter, Richard. "Franklin D. Roosevelt: The Patrician as Opportunist." In Leuchtenberg, *Franklin D. Roosevelt*, 96–134.

Holsti, Ole R. "The Belief System and National Images: A Case Study." *Journal of Conflict Resolution* 6 (1962): 244–252.

————. "Cognitive Dynamics and Images of the Enemy." *Journal of International Affairs* 21 (1967): 16–39.

————. "Crisis, Stress and Decision-Making." *International Social Science Journal* 23 (1971): 53–67.

————. "Foreign Policy Formation Viewed Cognitively." In *The Structure of Decision*, ed. Robert Axelrod, 18–54. Princeton: Princeton University Press, 1976.

————. "Public Opinion and Foreign Policy: Challenges to the Almond-Lippman Consensus." *International Studies Quarterly* 36 (1992): 439–66.

Holsti, Ole R., and Alexander George. "Effects of Stress on the Performance of Foreign Policy-Makers." In *Political Science Annual*, vol. 6, ed. Cornelius Cotter, 255–319. Indianapolis: Bobbs-Merrill, 1975.

Homer, Pamela M. "A Structural Equation Test of the Value-Attitude-Behavior Hierarchy." *Journal of Personality and Social Psychology* 54 (1988): 638–46.

Hurwitz, Jon, Mark Peffley, and Mitchell Seligson. "Foreign Policy Belief Systems in Comparative Perspective: The United States and Costa Rica." *International Studies Quarterly* 37 (1993): 245–70.

Jacob, Philip E. "Influence of World Events on U.S. 'Neutrality' Opinion." *Public Opinion Quarterly* 4 (1940): 48–65.

Jacobsen, John Kurt, and Claus Hofhansel. "Safeguards and Profits: Civilian Nuclear Exports, Neo-Marxism, and the Statist Approach." *International Studies Quarterly* 28 (1984): 195–218.

Janis, Irving. "Decisional Conflicts, a Theoretical Analysis." *Journal of Conflict Resolution* 3 (March 1959): 6–27.

Jervis, Robert. "Cognition and Political Behavior." In *Political Cognition*, ed. Richard R. Lau and David O. Sears, 319–36. Lawrence Erlbaum Associates: Hillsdale, N.J., 1986.

_____. "Deterrence and Perception." *International Security* 7 (1982): 3–30.

_____. "Domino Beliefs and Strategic Behavior." In *Dominoes and Bandwagons*, ed. Robert Jervis and Jack Snyder. New York: Oxford University Press, 1991.

_____. "Foreign Policy Motivation: A General Theory and a Case Study, by Richard Cottam," *Political Science Quarterly* 93 (1978): 327–28.

_____. "Intelligence and Foreign Policy: A Review Essay." *International Security* 11 (1986): 141–61.

_____. "Perceiving and Coping with Threat." In Jervis et al., *Psychology and Deterrence.*

_____. "Political Decision-Making: Recent Contributions." *Political Psychology* 2 (Summer 1980): 86–101.

_____. "The Political Implications of Loss Aversion." *Political Psychology* 13 (June 1992): 187–204.

_____. "Rational Deterrence: Theory and Evidence." *World Politics* 41 (1989): 183–207.

_____. "Realism, Game Theory and Cooperation." *World Politics* 40 (1988): 317–49.

_____. "Representativeness in Policy Judgments." *Political Psychology* 7 (1986): 483–505.

Johnson, Eric J., and Amos Tversky. "Affect, Generalization, and the Perception of Risk." *Journal of Personality and Social Psychology* 45 (1983): 20–31.

Johnson, James. "Is Talk Really Cheap?" *American Political Science Review* 87 (1993): 74–86.

Kahn, David. "United States Views of Germany and Japan in 1941." In *Knowing One's Enemies: Intelligence Assessment Before the Two World Wars*, ed. Ernest R. May, 476–501. Princeton: Princeton University Press, 1984.

Kahneman, Daniel, "Reference Points, Anchors, Norms, and Mixed Feelings," *Organizational Behavior and Human Decision Processes*, 51 (1992): 296–312.

Kahneman, Daniel, and Amos Tversky. "Choices, Values, and Frames." *American Psychologist* 39 (1984): 341–50.

_____. "Prospect Theory: An Analysis of Decision Under Risk," *Econometrica* 47 (1979): 263–92.

_____. "The Psychology of Preferences." *Scientific American* 246 (1982): 160–73.

_____. "Subjective Probability: A Judgment of Representativeness," *Cognitive Psychology* 3 (1972): 430–54.

Kanwisher, Nancy. "Cognitive Heuristics and American Security Policy." *Journal of Conflict Resolution* 33 (1989): 652–75.

Kaufmann, William W. "Two American Ambassadors: Bullitt and Kennedy." In *The Diplomats, 1919–1939*, ed. Gordon A. Craig and Felix Gilbert, 2:649–81. New York: Atheneum, 1963.

Kaysen, Carl. "Is War Obsolete?" *International Security* 14 (Spring 1990): 42–64.

Kelley, Harold H., and John L. Michela. "Attribution Theory and Research." *Annual Review of Psychology* 31 (1980): 457–501.

Kelman, Herbert C. "Social-Psychological Approaches to the Study of International Relations." In *International Behavior*, ed. Herbert C. Kelman, 594–670. New York: Holt, Rinehart, and Winston, 1965.

Kelman, Herbert C., and Reuben Baron. "Determinants of Modes of Resolving Inconsistency." In *Theories of Cognitive Consistency*, ed. Robert P. Abelson et al., 670–83. Chicago: Rand McNally, 1968.

Kirkpatrick, Samuel A. "Psychological Views of Decision-Making." In *Political Science Annual*, vol. 6, ed. Cornelius Cotter, 39–112. Indianapolis, Bobbs-Merrill, 1975.

Kissinger, Henry. "Reflections on Power and Diplomacy." In *Dimensions of Diplomacy*, ed. E.A.J. Johnson, 17–39. Baltimore: Johns Hopkins University Press, 1964.

Klein, Noreen M. "Utility and Decision Strategies, a Second Look at the Decision Maker." *Organizational Behavior and Human Performance* 31 (1983): 1–25.

Koopmans, Tjalling C. "On Flexibility of Future Preference." In *Human Judgments and Optimality*, ed. Maynard W. Shelly II and Glenn L. Bryan. New York: John Wiley and Sons, 1964.

Koriat, Asher, Sarah Lichtenstein, and Baruch Fischoff. "Reasons for Confidence." *Journal of Experimental Psychology: Human Learning and Memory* 6 (1980): 107–18.

Krasner, Stephen D. "Toward Understanding in International Relations." *International Studies Quarterly* 29 (1985): 137–44.

Lau, Richard R., and David O. Sears. "Social Cognition and Political Cognition." In *Political Cognition*, ed. Richard R. Lau and David O. Sears, 347–66. Hillsdale, N.J.: Lawrence Erlbaum Associates, 1986.

Lazarus, Richard S. "Thoughts on the Relations Between Emotion and Cognition." *American Psychologist* 37 (1982): 1019–24.

Leighton, Richard M. "The American Arsenal Policy in World War II: A Retrospective View." In *Some Pathways in Twentieth Century History*, ed. Daniel R. Beaver, 221–52. Detroit: Wayne State University Press, 1969.

Leuchtenberg, William E. "Franklin D. Roosevelt: The First Modern President." In *Leadership in the Modern Presidency*, ed. Fred I. Greenstein, 7–40. Cambridge, Mass.: Harvard University Press, 1988.

Levi, Ariel, and Philip E. Tetlock. "A Cognitive Analysis of Japan's 1941 Decision for War." *Journal of Conflict Resolution* 24 (1980): 195–211.

Levin, Irwin P., Richard D. Johnson, Craig P. Russo, and Patricia J. Deldin. "Framing Effects in Judgment Tasks with Varying Amounts of Information." *Organizational Behavior and Human Decision Processes* 36 (1985): 262–77.

Liberman, Akiva, and Shelly Chaiken. "Value Conflict and Thought-Induced Attitude Change." *Journal of Experimental Social Psychology* 27 (1991): 203–16.

Lindblom, Charles E. "The Science of 'Muddling Through,'" *Public Administration Review* 19 (1959): 74–88.

Lockhart, Charles. "The Varying Fortunes of Incremental Commitment: An Inquiry into the Cuban and Southeast Asian Cases." *International Studies Quarterly* 19 (March 1975): 44–66.

Loewenheim, Francis L. "An Illusion That Shaped History: New Light on the History and Historiography of American Peace Efforts Before Munich." In *Some Pathways in Twentieth Century History*, ed. Daniel R. Beaver, 177–219. Detroit: Wayne State University Press, 1969.

———. "The Untold Story of FDR and Munich—and Its Cover-up." *Houston Chronicle*, Oct. 1, 1978.

Machiavelli, Niccolo, "The Prince," and "The Discourses on Livy." In *The Portable Machiavelli*, ed. Peter Bandanella and Mark Musa, 177–417. New York: Penguin Books, 1979.

Majone, Grandomenico. "On the Notion of Political Feasibility." *European Journal of Political Research* 3 (1975): 259–74.

Manis, Melvin. "Cognitive Social Psychology and Attitude Change." *American Behavioral Scientist* 21 (1978): 675–90.

March, James G. "Bounded Rationality, Ambiguity, and the Engineering of Choice." *Bell Journal of Economic Management Science* 9 (1978): 587–608.

Marcus, George E. "The Structure of Emotional Response: 1984 Presidential Candidates." *American Political Science Review* 82 (1982): 737–61.

Mares, David R. "Explaining the Choice of Development Strategies: Suggestions from Mexico, 1970–1982." *International Organization* 39 (1985): 667–97.

Markus, Hazel, and R. B. Zajonc. "The Cognitive Perspective in Social Psychology." In *Handbook of Social Psychology*, 3d ed., vol. 1, ed. Gardner Lindzey and Elliot Aronson, 137–230. New York: Random House, 1985.

Marx, Frederick W. "FDR's Day of Infamy: Fifty Years Later." *SHAFR Newsletter* 23 (Sept. 1992): 41.

May, Peter J. "Politics and Policy Analysis." *Political Science Quarterly* 101 (1986): 109–25.

McClellan, David. "The 'Operational Code' Approach to the Study of Political Leaders: Dean Acheson's Philosophical and Instrumental Beliefs." *Canadian Journal of Political Science* 4 (1971): 52–75.

McCormick, Anne O'Hare. "As He Sees Himself." *New York Times Magazine*, Oct. 16, 1938, 1.

Meddin, Jay. "Attitudes, Values and Related Concepts: A System of Classification." *Social Science Quarterly* 55 (1975): 889–900.

Meltsner, Arnold J. "Political Feasibility and Policy Analysis." *Public Administration Review* 32 (November/December 1972): 859–67.

Miklis, Sidney M. "FDR and the Transcendence of Partisan Politics." *Political Science Quarterly* 100 (1985): 479–504.

Milburn, Thomas, and Robert S. Billings. "Decision-Making Perspectives from

Psychology: Dealing with Risk and Uncertainty." *American Behavioral Scientist* 20 (Sept.–Oct. 1976): 111–26.

Mintz, Alex. "The Decision to Attack Iraq: A Non-compensatory Theory of Decision-making." *Journal of Conflict Resolution* 37 (1993): 595–618.

Mintzberg, Henry, Duru Raisinghani, and Andre Theoret. "The Structure of Unstructured Decisions." *Administrative Science Quarterly* 21 (1976): 246–75.

Moley, Raymond. "History's Bone of Contention." In Leuchtenberg, *Franklin D. Roosevelt*, 149–64.

Montgomery, Henry, and Ola Svenson. "On Decision Rules and Information Processing Strategies for Choices Among Multiattribute Alternatives." *Scandinavian Journal of Psychology* 33 (1976): 283–91.

Moss, Kenneth. "George Messersmith and Nazi Germany." In Jones, *U.S. Diplomats in Europe*, 113–26.

Nelson, Michael. "The President and the Court: Reinterpreting the Court Episode of 1937." *Political Science Quarterly* 103 (1988): 267–93.

Neustadt, Richard E. "Presidents, Politics, and Analysis." Brewster C. Denney Lecture Series, Institute of Public Management, Graduate School of Public Affairs, University of Washington (May 13, 1986): 3–35.

Nisbett, Richard E., David H. Krantz, Christopher Jepson, and Ziva Kunda. "The Use of Statistical Heuristics in Everyday Inductive Reasoning." *Psychological Review* 90 (1983): 339–63.

Offner, Arnold A. "Misperception and Reality: Roosevelt, Hitler, and the Search for a New Order in Europe." *Diplomatic History* 15 (Fall 1991): 607–29.

O'Reilly, Charles A. "The Use of Information in Organizational Decision-making." In *Research in Organizational Behavior*, vol. 5, ed. Barry M. Staw and L. L. Cummings. Greenwich, Conn.: JAI Press, 1983.

Ostrum, Charles W., Jr., and Brian L. Job. "The President and the Political Use of Force." *American Political Science Review* 80 (1986): 541–66.

Park, C. Whan. "A Conflict Resolution Choice Model." *Journal of Consumer Research* 5 (1978): 124–37.

————. "A Seven-Point Scale and a Decision-Maker's Simplifying Choice Strategy: An Operationalized Satisficing-Plus Model." *Organizational Behavior and Human Performance* 21 (1978): 252–71.

Payne, John W. "Contingent Decision Behavior." *Psychological Bulletin* 92 (1982): 382–402.

————. "Task Complexity and Contingent Processing in Decision Making: An Information Search and Protocol Analysis." *Organizational Behavior and Human Performance* 16 (1976): 366–87.

Payne, John W. James R. Bettman, and Eric J. Johnson. "Behavioral Decision Research: A Constructive Processing Perspective." *Annual Review of Psychology* 48 (1992): 87–131.

Pelz, Stephan. "Changing International Systems, the World Balance of Power, and the United States, 1776–1976." *Diplomatic History* 15 (Winter 1991): 47–81.

Perkins, Dexter. "Was Roosevelt Wrong?" *Virginia Quarterly Review* 30 (1954): 355–72.

Pitz, Gordon F., and Natalie J. Sachs. "Judgment and Decision." *Annual Review of Psychology* 35 (1984): 139–63.

Price-Williams, D. R. "Cognition." In *A Dictionary of the Social Sciences*, ed. Julius Gould and William Kolb, 99. New York: Free Press, 1964.

Putnam, Robert D. "Diplomacy and Domestic Politics: The Logic of Two-Level Games." *International Organization* 42 (1988): 427–60.

Quattrone, George A., and Amos Tversky. "Causal versus Diagnostic Contingencies: On Self-Deception and on the Voter's Illusion." *Journal of Personality and Social Psychology* 46 (1984): 237–48.

————. "Contrasting Rational and Psychological Analyses of Political Choice." *American Political Science Review* 82 (1988): 719–36.

Reagan, Michael. "The Helium Controversy." In *American Civil-Military Decisions*, ed. Harold Stein, 43–57. Birmingham, Ala.: University of Alabama Press, 1963.

Renshon, Stanley A. "Character, Judgment, and Political Leadership." In *The Clinton Presidency*, ed. Stanley A. Renshon, 57–87. Boulder, Colo.: Westview Press, 1995.

Richardson, J. L. "New Perspectives on Appeasement: Some Implications for International Relations." *World Politics* 40 (1988): 289–316.

Risse-Kappen, Thomas. "Public Opinion, Domestic Structure, and Foreign Policy in Liberal Democracies." *World Politics* 43 (1991): 479–512.

Robinson, James A. "Decision-Making: Political Aspects." In *International Encyclopedia of the Social Sciences*, ed. David Sills. New York: Macmillan and Free Press, 1968.

Rokeach, Milton. "Attitudes: The Nature of Attitudes." In ibid., 449–58.

————. "Change and Stability in American Value Systems, 1968–1971." In *Understanding Human Values*, ed. Milton Rokeach, 129–47. New York: Free Press, 1979.

————. "Some Unresolved Issues in Theories of Beliefs, Attitudes, and Values." *Nebraska Symposium on Motivation, 1979: Beliefs, Attitudes and Values*, ed. Monte M. Page, 261–304. Lincoln, Neb.: University of Nebraska Press, 1980.

————. "A Theory of Organization and Change within Value-Attitude Systems." *Journal of Social Issues* 24 (1968): 13–33.

Rokeach, Milton and Joel W. Grube. "Can Values Be Arbitrarily Manipulated?" In Rokeach, *Understanding Human Values*, 241–56.

Rosenman, Samuel I. "The Presidency as I Have Seen It." In Hughes, *The Living Presidency*.

Ross, Lee. "The Intuitive Psychologist and His Shortcomings: Distortions in the Attribution Process." In Leonard L. Berkowitz, ed., *Advances in Experimental Social Psychology*, 10:174–280. New York: Academic Press, 1977.

Schilling, Warner R. "The H-Bomb Decision: How to Decide without Actually Choosing." *Political Science Quarterly* 76 (March 1961): 24–46.

————. "The Politics of National Defense: Fiscal 1950." In *Strategy, Politics, and Defense Budgets*, ed. Warner R. Schilling, Paul T. Hammond, and Glenn H. Snyder, 1–266. New York: Columbia University Press, 1962.

Schlesinger, Arther M., Jr. "Franklin D. Roosevelt's Internationalism." In Van Minnen and Sears, *FDR and His Contemporaries*, 3–16.

Schwarz, Norbert, "Feelings as Information." In Higgins and Sorrentino, *Handbook of Motivation and Cognition*, 2:527–61.

Scott, William A. "Rationality and Non-rationality of International Attitudes." *Journal of Conflict Resolution* 2 (1958): 8–16.

Searing, Donald D. "Measuring Politicians' Values: Administration and Assessment of a Ranking Technique in the British House of Commons." *American Political Science Review* 72 (March 1978): 65–79.

Shapira, Zur. "Making Trade-offs Between Job Attributes." *Organizational Behavior and Human Performance* 28 (1981): 331–55.

Shepard, Roger N. "On Subjectively Optimum Selection Among Multi-attribute Alternatives." In *Human Judgments and Optimality*, ed. Maynard W. Shelly II and Glenn L. Bryan. New York: John Wiley and Sons, 1964.

Shugan, Steven M. "The Cost of Thinking." *Journal of Consumer Research* 7 (Sept. 1980): 99–111.

Siegal, Sidney S. "Level of Aspiration and Decision-Making." *World Politics* 64 (1957): 253–62.

Simon, Herbert A. "A Behavioral Model of Rational Choice." *Quarterly Journal of Economics* 69 (1955): 99–118.

———. "Invariants of Human Behavior." *Annual Review of Psychology* 41 (1990): 1–19.

———. "Rationality and Administrative Decision Making." In *Models of Man*, ed. Herbert A. Simon, 196–206. New York: John Wiley and Sons, 1957.

———. "Rationality as Process and as Product of Thought." *American Economic Review* 68 (1978): 1–16.

Singer, J. David. "The Level of Analysis Problem in International Relations." *World Politics* 14 (Oct. 1961): 77–92.

Slovic, Paul. "Choice Between Equally Valued Alternatives." *Journal of Experimental Psychology: Human Perception and Performance* 1 (1975): 280–87.

Slovic, Paul, Baruch Fischoff, and Sarah Lichtenstein. "Behavioral Decision Theory." *Annual Review of Psychology* 28 (1977): 1–39.

Stein, Janice Gross. "Building Politics into Psychology: The Misperception of Threat." *Political Psychology* 9 (1988): 245–71.

———. "Can Decision-Makers Be Rational and Should They Be? Evaluating the Quality of Decisions." In *Studies in Crisis Behavior*, ed. Michael Brecher, 316–39. New Brunswick, N.J.: Transaction Books, 1978.

———. "International Cooperation and Loss Avoidance: Framing the Problem." *International Journal* 47 (1992): 202–34.

Svenson, Ola. "Cognitive Processes in Judging Cumulative Risk over Different Periods of Time." *Organizational Behavior and Human Performance* 33 (1984): 22–41.

Taylor, Shelley E., and Suzanne C. Thompson. "Stalking the Elusive 'Vividness Effect.'" *Psychological Review* 89 (1982) 155–81.

Taylor, Shelley E., et al., "The Generalizability of Salience Effects." *Journal of Personality and Social Psychology* 37 (1979): 357–68.

Philip E. Tetlock. "Accountability and the Perseverance of First Impressions." *Social Psychology Quarterly* 46 (1983): 285–92.

_____. "Accountability: The Neglected Social Context of Judgment and Choice." *Research in Organizational Behavior* 7 (1985): 295–332.

_____. "Cognitive Style and Political Belief Systems in the British House of Commons." *Journal of Personality and Social Psychology* 46 (1984): 365–75.

_____. "Cognitive Style and Political Ideology." *Journal of Personality and and Social Psychology* 45 (1983): 118–28.

_____. "Policy-Makers' Images of International Conflict." *Journal of Social Issues* 39 (1983): 67–86.

_____. "Pre- to Postelection Shifts in Presidential Rhetoric: Impression or Cognitive Adjustment?" *Journal of Personality and Social Psychology* 41 (1981): 207–12.

_____. "A Value Pluralism Model of Ideological Reasoning." *Journal of Personality and Social Psychology* 50 (1986): 819–27.

Tetlock, Philip E., Kristen A. Hannum, and Patrick M. Micheletti. "Stability and Change in the Complexity of Senatorial Debate." *Journal of Personality and Social Psychology* 46 (1984): 979–90.

Thompson, John A. "The Exaggeration of American Vulnerablity: The Anatomy of a Tradition," *Diplomatic History* 16 (Winter 1992): 23–43.

Tiller, Mikel G., and Russell H. Fazio. "Relation Between Attitudes and Later Behavior Following Dissonance-Produced Attitude Change." *Personality and Social Psychology Bulletin* 8 (1982): 280–85.

Trachtenberg, Marc. "The Influence of Nuclear Weapons in the Cuban Missile Crisis." *International Security* 10 (1985): 137–203.

Tugwell, Rexford. "The Compromising Roosevelt." In Leuchtenberg, *Franklin D. Roosevelt*, 165–93.

_____. "The Experimental Roosevelt," in ibid., 60–95.

Tversky, Amos. "Elimination by Aspects." *Psychological Review* 79 (1972): 281–99.

_____. "Intransitivity of Preferences." *Psychological Review* 76 (1969): 31–48.

Tversky, Amos, and Daniel Kahneman. "Availability: A Heuristic for Judging Frequency and Probability." *Cognitive Psychology* 5 (1973): 207–32.

_____. "Extensional versus Intuitive Reasoning: The Conjunction Fallacy in Probability Judgment." *Psychological Review* 90 (1983): 293–315.

_____. "The Framing of Decisions and the Psychology of Choice." *Science* 211 (1981): 453–58.

_____. "Judgment Under Uncertainty." In *Utility, Probability, and Human Decision Making*, ed. Dirk Wendt and Charles Vlek, 141–62. Dordrecht: D. Reidel Publishing Co., 1975.

_____. "Rational Choice and the Framing of Decisions." *Journal of Business* 59 (Oct. 1986): S251-78.

Tversky, Amos, Shmuel Sattath, and Paul Slovic. "Contingent Weighting in Judgment and Choice." *Psychological Review* 95 (1988): 371–84.

Verba, Sidney. "Assumptions of Rationality and Non-Rationality in Models of the International System." *World Politics* 14 (1961): 93–117.

Vieth, Jane K. "Joseph P. Kennedy and British Appeasement." In Jones, *U.S. Diplomats in Europe*, 165–82.

Waller, William S., and Terence R. Mitchell. "The Effects of Context on the Selection of Decision Strategies for the Cost Variance Investigation Problem." *Organizational Behavior and Human Performance* 33 (1984): 397–413.

Weinberg, Gerhard L. "Munich after Fifty Years." *Foreign Affairs* 67 (Fall 1988): 165–78.

Weinberger, Joel, and David C. McClelland. "Cognitive versus Traditional Motivational Models." In Higgins and Sorrentino, *Handbook of Motivation and Cognition*, 2:562–97.

Williams, Robin, Jr. "The Concept of Values." In *International Encyclopedia of the Social Sciences*, ed. David Sills, 283–87. New York: Macmillan and Free Press, 1968.

Winter, David. "Measuring Personality at a Distance." In *Perspectives in Personality*, ed. A. J. Stewart, J. M. Henley, Jr., and D. J. Ozer, 3:B:58–89. London: Jessica Kingsley Publishers, 1991.

Wolfers, Arnold. "The Actors in International Politics." In *Discord and Collaboration*, ed. Arnold Wolfers, 3–24. Baltimore: Johns Hopkins University Press, 1962.

Wright, Gordon. "Ambassador Bullitt and the Fall of France." *World Politics* 10 (Oct. 1957): 63–90.

Zajonc, Robert B. "Feeling and Thinking: Preferences Need No Inferences." *American Psychologist* 35 (1980): 151–75.

Other Unpublished Material

Bennett, Edward M. "Love and Hate: FDR and Anglo-American Relations in the 1930s." Paper presented at the Society of Historians of American Foreign Relations, June 1992.

Farnham, Barbara. "Value Conflict and Political Decision-Making: Roosevelt and the Munich Crisis." Ph.D. diss., Columbia University, 1991.

George, Alexander L. "Case Studies and Theory Development." Paper presented to the second annual Symposium on Information Processing in Organizations, Carnegie-Mellon University, Pittsburgh, October 15–16, 1982.

——. "Limits of Rationality in Designing Public Policy and Developing Policy-relevant Theory: A Discussion Paper." Dartmouth College, Hanover, N.H., n.d.

Greenstein, Fred. "The Virtuosic Leadership of Franklin Delano Roosevelt." unpubl. ms.

Hammond, Kenneth R. "A Theoretically Based Review of Theory and Research in Judgment and Decision-Making." Center for Research on Judgment and Policy, Institute of Cognitive Science, University of Colorado, Boulder, Colo., Report No. 260, Feb. 1986.

Hermann, Margaret G., Charles F. Hermann, and Joe D. Hagan. "How Decision Units Shape Foreign Policy." Paper delivered at the 1991 annual meeting of the International Society of Political Psychology, Helsinki, Finland, 1991.

Holsti, Ole R. "Proclivities for Tunnel Vision and Misperception." Paper presented at the ninth annual meeting of the International Society of Political Psychology, Amsterdam, June 1986.

Jervis, Robert. "*Perception and Misperception*: An Updating of the Analysis." Paper presented at the fifth annual meeting of the International Society of Political Psychology, Washington, D.C., June 24–27, 1982.

———. "The Political Implications of Loss Aversion." unpubl. ms., 1989.

Marcus, George E., W. Russell Neuman, Michael MacKuen, and John L. Sullivan. "Dynamic Models of Emotional Response: The Multiple Roles of Affect in Politics." Paper delivered to the annual meeting of the International Society of Political Psychology, Cambridge, Mass., July 1993.

Powell, Charles A., James W. Dyson, and Helen E. Purkitt. "Opening the 'Black Box': Cognitive Processing and Situational Complexity in Foreign Policy Decision Making." Paper presented at the annual meeting of the International Society of Political Psychology, Amsterdam, June 1986.

Rood, Harold. "Strategy out of Silence: American Military Policy and Preparations for War, 1919–1940." Ph.D. diss., University of California, Berkeley, 1961.

Simon, Herbert A. "Human Nature in Politics: The Dialogue of Psychology with Political Science." Madison Lecture, American Political Science Association Convention, Washington, D.C., August 31, 1984.

Stein, Janice Gross. "Deterrence and Reassurance." Committee on the Contribution of the Behavioral Sciences to the Prevention of Nuclear War, National Research Council, June 1987.

———. "International Cooperation and Loss Avoidance: Framing the Problem," draft, Oct. 1991.

Sylvan, Donald A., James F. Voss, and Keith Ronczka. "Foreign Policy Creativity: Conceptualizations and Consequences of Decision Rules and Stress." Paper presented at the fifteenth annual meeting of the International Society of Political Psychology, San Francisco, July 4–8, 1992.

Tetlock, Philip E., and Charles McGuire, Jr. "Cognitive Perspectives on Foreign Policy." Unpublished version of a chapter in *Political Behavior Annual*, ed. S. Long.

Trachtenberg, Marc. "Strategic Thought in America, 1952–1966." Paper presented at the University of Pennsylvania, April 23, 1985.

Voss, James F. "Finding Another Policy: Problem Representation and Problem Solution." Paper presented at the annual meeting of the International Society of Political Psychology, Washington, D.C., July 10, 1990.

Index

About the Author

BARBARA REARDEN FARNHAM is a Research Associate at the Institute of War and Peace Studies.